KU-161-252

Sexualities, Work and Organizations

Sexuality is arguably the most under-researched of all diversity areas in work organizations, with minority sexuality being one of the most difficult areas to research. There is a comparative paucity of well-researched qualitative data in this area and the lack of information has made it difficult for researchers, students and consultants alike to consider the organizational impact of minority sexuality. This book brings together and relates stories of minority sexual identity from six organizations drawn from three different industry sectors: the Emergency Services, the Civil Service and the Banking sector.

Real-life stories by lesbians, gay men, bisexuals or transsexuals in organizations can be very difficult to record, but in this book, sexual minorities freely recount stories of their own workplace experiences. Three main themes emerge from the data: silence, disclosure and response. Issues of voice and silence are particularly pertinent for those who are not part of the dominant heterosexual discourse; issues of disclosure are highly important for sexual minorities for whom coming out is a major defining moment; and, highly unusually, in this book we get an insight into how people respond to sexual minorities, as other employees' reactions to stories are related too. This book makes a significant contribution to our understanding of the discursive construction of identity in the workplace, as experienced by sexual minorities and provides a snapshot of minority working lives at the beginning of the twenty-first century.

This is an extremely well-written, highly innovative, timely and engaging book which will have a broad and long-standing appeal within the academic community and beyond. As well as human resources management, the book will also be of interest to scholars in other areas such as sociology, and general business and management.

James Ward is a Visiting Research Fellow at Kingston Business School, Surrey and Managing Consultant for the PA Consulting Group in London, specializing in organization design and development. His research interests include identity in the workplace, minority sexuality and storytelling. He gained his PhD, which looked at the construction of minority sexual identity in work organizations, from Tanaka Business School at Imperial College, University of London.

LIVERPOOL JMU LIBRARY

3 1111 01389 9396

Routledge studies in employment and work relations in context
Edited by Tony Elger and Peter Fairbrother

The aim of the employment and work relations in context series is to address questions relating to the evolving patterns and politics of work, employment, management and industrial relations. There is a concern to trace out the ways in which wider policy-making, especially by national governments and transnational corporations, impinges upon specific workplaces, occupations, labour markets, localities and regions. This invites attention to developments at an international level, marking out patterns of globalization, state policy and practices in the context of globalization and the impact of these processes on labour. A particular feature of the series is the consideration of forms of worker and citizen organization and mobilization. The studies address major analytical and policy issues through case study and comparative research.

Sexualities, Work and Organizations

Stories by gay men and women in the workplace at the beginning of the twenty-first century

James Ward

Routledge
Taylor & Francis Group

LONDON AND NEW YORK

First published 2008
by Routledge
2 Park Square, Milton Park, Abingdon, Oxon OX14 4RN

Simultaneously published in the USA and Canada
by Routledge
711 Third Avenue, New York, NY 10017

Routledge is an imprint of the Taylor & Francis Group, an informa business

First issued in paperback 2012

© 2008 James Ward

Typeset in Times by Wearset Ltd, Boldon, Tyne and Wear

All rights reserved. No part of this book may be reprinted or reproduced or
utilized in any form or by any electronic, mechanical, or other means, now
known or hereafter invented, including photocopying and recording, or in
any information storage or retrieval system, without permission in writing
from the publishers.

British Library Cataloguing in Publication Data
A catalogue record for this book is available from the British Library

Library of Congress Cataloging in Publication Data
A catalog record for this book has been requested

ISBN13: 978-0-415-54216-6 (pbk)
ISBN13: 978-0-415-39699-8 (hbk)
ISBN13: 978-0-203-93924-6 (ebk)

To my partner Ray, who has constantly supported me and encouraged me to write

Contents

Acknowledgements

I would like to acknowledge the contribution from individual lesbians, gay men, bisexual men and women, and transsexuals who gave their time, openly telling stories of their work experiences; without them this book would not have been possible. Although their stories are as they told them, all their names have been changed.

I would also like to thank the publishers of *Human Relations*, *Sociological Review*, *Culture and Organization* and *Gender, Work and Organization* for their kind permission to use copyright material.

Finally, but most importantly, my tutor and friend, Professor Diana Winstanley, coached me and critiqued my writing over a number of years and helped to shape the final outcome; she sadly died in 2006 and so did not live to see the book in print, but she made a huge contribution to both the book and my own personal development.

Introduction

Over the past few years in the United Kingdom, homosexuality has made the headlines time and time again. From the age of consent issue, to the sexual offences bill, from potential schism in the Anglican Church to Civil Partnerships, there has been no end of references in the media to minority sexuality. The world of work is no exception; in 2003, the Employment Equality (Sexual Orientation) Regulations provided legal protection at work for sexual minorities for the first time. Not only is this is a huge step forward for gay men and women, but there has also been significant interest amongst employers and researchers alike in the experiences of sexual minorities in work organizations.

And yet, minority sexuality is arguably the most difficult and under-researched of all diversity areas in work organizations, resulting in a comparative paucity of well-researched qualitative data. That is not to say that studies have not been carried out into the work experiences of sexual minorities, but the focus of this research has been on the individual rather than on the organization they work for, leading to little homogeneity of jobs and careers in the literature. This situation has arisen mainly because of the difficulty in getting hold of people willing to take part in research projects; previously, relatively few people were out in the workplace, and those that were did not want to draw unwelcome attention to themselves at a time when there was no legal protection in the workplace, meaning that they could have lost their job on the whim of their employer with no legal recourse. Generally, in previous research studies, volunteers were recruited through gay organizations and by advertising in the gay press. An example of this type of research was reported in *Gay Life in Corporate America* by Woods and Lucas (1993); they interviewed some ninety people, most of them from different professional backgrounds, contacted through gay organizations and 'snowballing', where one interviewee put them in contact with another through personal introduction.

Now, at the beginning of the twenty-first century, due to societal changes and different public attitudes towards homosexuality, it is possible to recruit gay research respondents from specific organizations. This book therefore approaches the area from a different perspective to previous studies, bringing together and relating stories of minority sexual identity from six organizations drawn from three different industry sectors: the Emergency Services, the Civil

Service and the Banking sector. However, whilst collecting stories from gay individuals about their workplace experiences is difficult enough, a much greater challenge is recording any kind of comment that other people make about sexual minorities at work. With the aim of addressing this challenge, this book describes the method that I used, a novel, double-level storytelling process, described as follows: sexual minorities recounted stories of their own workplace experiences, and then I retold these stories in organizational focus groups, thus creating further discourse through the retelling of these stories. I have grouped the data from the stories and the focus groups under three main themes: Coming Out, Silent Lives and Working Out. Although sexuality is talked about, issues of voice and silence are particularly pertinent for those who are not part of the dominant heterosexual discourse. Disclosure of minority sexual identity presents the individual with a range of choices. Some choose to stay silent; others find their sexuality accidentally discovered, some are open about their minority sexuality when they start in a new workplace. Others decide at some stage to 'come out' to colleagues and friends. The act of disclosure or lack of it, and the response it engenders, has widespread repercussions for one's identity in the workplace. The book aims to contribute to our understanding of the workplace discursive construction of minority sexual identity, as well as contributing to our understanding of silence, disclosure and difference in organizations.

1 The power of stories

In the introduction, I suggested that sexuality, particularly minority sexuality, is arguably the most under-researched of all diversity areas in work organizations. This is the case, I believe, for a variety of different reasons: until very recently there was a lack of access to research subjects, as gay men and women were unwilling to come out at work because of their fear of unfair treatment, discrimination and victimization; gay people in the workplace have also been unwilling to talk to researchers because of the danger of inadvertent disclosure; whatever the assurances by the researcher that anonymity will be maintained there are nevertheless cases of people whose identity was accidentally revealed, which is enough to make gay people very nervous of taking part in research projects. Work organizations were also reluctant to take part in this sort of research. No matter how well-intentioned the organization's diversity programme, or how equality-focused the HR manager, lesbian and gay employees always came near the bottom of the diversity hierarchy. Perhaps they thought that sexuality belonged to the private domain of the individual; perhaps they were embarrassed to say the words lesbian or gay. Whatever the reason for this lacuna, most will agree that the diversity agenda in many organizations has, in the past, generally been focused on gender and race.

And yet, at the beginning of the twenty-first century, this situation is changing as evidenced in part by the change in the legislative climate. Previously, there was no legal protection for sexual minorities in the workplace in the United Kingdom, but in 2003 the Employment Equality Regulations (Sexual Orientation) were passed into law, making discrimination at work on the grounds of sexual orientation illegal for the first time. Aside from the legislative imperative to change, companies have also witnessed the growing number of self-organizing gay groups and lesbian and gay networks within organizations, where people are not only prepared to be out at work, but also work together in these networks to help reduce the isolation that many gay people at work feel. As it becomes more of an issue in the workplace, managers are more interested to know what the issues are so that they can improve recruitment and retention in their organization. And, as it becomes more of an issue for managers, so academics and researchers, both in the organization theory and general sociology fields want to know more about the dynamics. So how can an organization or its diversity manager or human resources manager find out what it is like for sexual minorities in the workplace? And how should an organizational researcher carry out research into this area?

This book describes the output of one particular approach, which is to listen to and study the stories of ordinary lesbians and gay men working in organizations. I used this approach in carrying out my PhD research between 2000 and 2004, during which I collected literally hundreds of stories from lesbians, gay men, bisexuals and transsexuals about their experiences in the workplace, both positive and negative. I had several reasons for adopting this approach. First, I believe that inside every person there is a story waiting to get out, although it is true to say that some people are naturally better storytellers than others. Then there is the idea that a person's story, or personal collection of stories, go to make up their identity; by studying these self-narratives it is possible to have an insight into their development, and therefore the development of minority sexual identity in the workplace. Finally, stories are becoming an increasingly important lens through which researchers are studying organizations, and the reality of organizational life.

Everyone has a story to tell. MacIntyre (1981: 201) has described human beings as being 'in actions and practice, as well as ... fictions, essentially a storytelling animal'. This idea is developed further by Dan McAdams (1997) who states, 'We are all tellers of tales'. We enjoy telling stories about our everyday experiences, what happened at work that day, or what we did at the weekend when we arrive in the office on Monday morning. As MacIntyre suggests, we enjoy telling fictional stories as well as telling stories of what has actually happened to us, and to relive experiences in some way. Sometimes fiction serves as pure entertainment for the listener; sometimes it is an embellishment to a factual story. Sometimes the facts of the story might change, not because there is a deliberate intent to deceive on the part of the storyteller, but because there is a genuine need to rationalize the events *post factum*. Should we be worried that we cannot believe everything about a story that we are told? Clearly it depends on a number of factors. First, there is the purpose of the story; if the purpose is merely to entertain, we do not mind suspending our disbelief, in the hope that we are going to be amused or even horrified. If the purpose of the story is to inform, we hope that the basis for the story is true, even if the details have been altered somewhat for dramatic effect, the so-called poetic licence. The telling of a story sets up a contract between storyteller and listener; poetic licence is part of that contract, but if the story is one of personal experience, particularly quite negative experiences, as is the case with many lesbians and gay men at work, credibility also has to be a major part of that contract.

Some of us will experience quite complex and confusing experiences in the workplace, which we struggle to make sense of, even after some considerable time. By telling stories of our experiences, we seek to provide these confusing experiences with a sense of coherence by arranging these episodes of our lives into stories. In other words, we use stories in the workplace as a way of making sense of our experience. Brown (2003: 97) refers to stories and narratives as 'processes for sensemaking'; stories, as they are the preferred sense-making currency of human relationships, have become an important symbolic form, through which meanings in organizations are constructed and shared. Stories are one type of communication that contributes to sense-making in organizations; dialogues that processually constitute organizations also contribute to ongoing processes of narrative construction and refinement. And then the stories that are authored through dialogues are another symbolic means by which meaning is variously negotiated, shared and contested.

People do not just tell stories: they tell stories to 'enact' an account of themselves and their community. It has been recognized in the literature that the notion of identities as types of self-constructing narratives is a rich, and yet relatively unexplored area. Individual identity narratives are not solely private concerns, but are instead 'intensely governed' by, for example, social conventions, community scrutiny and legal norms. Identity can be conceptualized, therefore, as a rather complex outcome of a variety of different processes and one way that identity can be expressed, understood, and in turn created, is by the telling, listening and reacting to stories. Ricoeur (1991: 77) has described identity as 'the durable character of an individual', which is constructed by narrative. McAdams' thesis is that we make ourselves and our identity through the stories and myths that we create and tell about ourselves (McAdams, 1997). Sims (2003: 1197) describes this same phenomenon by suggesting that we lead storied lives, continually producing storied versions of what is happening and what has happened in our lives. Kitzinger (1987: 90) also reminds us that studying identity 'accounts' is a useful way of studying subjectivity, since 'a lesbian identity is a woman's subjective experience of the intrasubjective account of her own lesbianism'. She goes on to assert that since the researcher has no direct access to the subjectivity of the individual, it is necessary to rely on what individuals are able and willing to say about it: 'An account of lesbian identity is the story (or one of the stories) a woman tells about her subjective experience of her lesbianism' (Kitzinger, 1987: 90).

So, what is a story?

David Boje (1991a: 9) suggests that the process of collective storytelling occurs as a multitude of tellers relate bits of storylines and in aggregate the full tale is collectively created, told, revised and maintained. He defines a story quite simply as: 'An exchange between two or more persons during which a past or anticipated experience was being referenced, recounted, interpreted or challenged' (Boje, 1991a: 8).

Another definition of a story, following the Aristotlean tradition, is that stories have a beginning, middle and an end, and are held together by a plot. However, Boje's definition allows for other narrative devices that convey meaning, such as clichés, platitudes and labels. Gabriel (2000: 2) has expressed concern at, 'the increasing tendency to view every sign, every snippet of conversation, every image and every cliché as either being a story or telling a story'.

Indeed, many organizational stories, reported by researchers, amount to little more than 'slogans' virtually drained of meaning. One of the reasons for this, suggested by Gabriel is that members of organizations are neither storytellers nor story-listeners, only information handlers. The reality is probably somewhere in between; it is true that employees are officially information-handlers, but unofficially, and more by accident than design, they can also be good storytellers.

The importance of plot has been discussed by many researchers, with some such as Boje (1991b) dismissing it, and others arguing that events need a plot to bring them into a meaningful whole. The importance of plot goes back to Aristotle where the difference was made between a simple story, relying on chronology, and a story with plot which arranges events according to a sense of causality. The stories which are described in this book all have a plot to a greater or lesser extent, and the plot does describe events which are causative, that is to say contain an event which causes something else to happen. A plot makes a story much more powerful in putting its message across, and because without plot, a story relies on pure chronology, which would mean a lack of the richness required to explore this topic. In other words, plot is an important sense-making device. As the sociologist Weick put it:

> the requirements necessary to produce a good narrative provide a plausible frame for sensemaking. Stories posit a history for an outcome. They gather strands of experience into a plot that produces that outcome. The plot follows either the sequence beginning-middle-end or the sequence situation-transformation-situation. But sequence is the source of sense.
>
> (Weick, 1995: 128)

Storytelling in organizational research

In recent years, there has been a growing interest in organization studies, which focuses on the link between storytelling and organization. Although storytelling is an ancient medium for communication, it is also becoming an increasingly important lens through which researchers are studying organizations. It has a rich history in other areas of academic life with serious studies having been undertaken about myth, narrative and storytelling in different theoretical traditions and disciplines. It has become popular in the field of organizational studies as it is recognized as being useful for expressing employee organizational experience, confirming shared meaning of organizational members, but most importantly amending and altering organizational reality. It is therefore not just about recounting experience, it is also a means of creating the discourse which constitutes organizational reality.

Storytelling is a relatively recent addition to the area of organization studies, though, only really becoming a legitimate topic for organizational researchers in the 1990s, but it is one which has grown in importance as researchers explore their power to communicate the character of the organization in stories which are essentially part of the fabric and life of organizations. Indeed, Boje (1995) has referred to organizations as storytelling systems. People process information and manage the collective memory of the organization through storytelling, though of course stories are not the only means by which meaning is mediated in organizations, as referred to above.

Stories give an insight to the narrative production of identity

Czarniawska (1997) suggests that identity may be appropriately conceptualized as a narrative process where the individual and the people around them are continually involved in producing the narrative: 'A continuous process of narration where both the narrator and the audience are involved in formulating, editing, applauding and refusing various elements of the ever-produced narrative' (Czarniawska, 1997 in Humphreys and Brown, 2002: 423).

Czarniawska's view of identity as narrative is not dissimilar to Giddens' idea of biography, but she develops the idea by introducing an audience, and the audience's role in developing the biography. Whereas Giddens posits the notion of reflexivity, Czarniawska suggests that others are involved; in this way, the identity of individuals is at stake in their interactions with others, notably in terms of how they choose to present themselves to others in order to manage both their perceptions of self and others' impressions of them. The idea that subjectivity can be developed and expressed as a narrative process was important for the development of my methodology in this project. The narrative process can also be conceptualized as something which is constantly performed; everything an individual does is in relation to their own narrative, which creates and sustains their identity.

Stories give a voice to the previously marginalized

This project aims, then, to bring together the narrative study of minority sexualities and the use of storytelling in organization studies. Indeed, it might be suggested that one of the types of distinctively new stories about lesbian and gay people is the type of stories about sexual minorities as employees in organizations. Stories which are specifically about homosexuals have been largely absent from the organizational literature, even though stories about homosexuals per se come from a long tradition, which has changed over the years, as described by Plummer:

> In Renaissance England, it was partially the story of a world of drunken and sexual excess – surrounded by werewolves, anti-Christs and witches. In the early western twentieth century, it was partially a story told by 'sexperts': of pathologies, conditions, continuums, disorders and disease, side by side with the creation of a distinct homosexual identity and the elements of a diverse homosexual culture with a unique sensibility. There are many signs – not to mention academic treatises – that suggest the past century has witnessed the creation of distinctively new stories around homosexualities.
>
> (Plummer, 1995: 81–82)

Research looking at organizational stories is an excellent vehicle for addressing the dynamics of power, dominant groups and lesser-heard voices in organizations. It is important to recognize that the power in this type of research lies with the storyteller, as they have the power to decide what sort of stories they will tell and which ones they will withhold, although Czarniawska's notion (1998: 42) is perhaps a little extreme when she suggests that the interviewers are interview victims more so than the interviewees. Clearly, an organization will have a plurality of stories, voices and realities, as well as a multiplicity of ways to interpret stories. The choice here of following the gay story in the organization privileges one voice, and privileges it over many others, although it should be remembered that it is a voice that has previously been silenced. One epistemological impact of privileging a previously silenced voice is the idea of the confessional discourse, where the researcher and the reader are expected to assume that experience recounted through confession is an authoritative source of knowledge. Yiannis Gabriel suggests that this puts a responsibility on the researcher not only to celebrate the story, but to privilege those that deserve to be privileged and silence those that deserve to be silenced. This in itself created quite a quandary for me: by carrying out this kind of storytelling research and collecting a large number of stories, I had to decide whose stories to tell.

Advantages in adopting a storytelling approach

Although Czarniawska (1998: 5) suggests that the advantage of using narrative, even with its alternative mode of knowing, remains uncertain, I identified two major advantages of using storytelling, or narrative enquiry, as a result of this research. First, there was the power to surface information about people who had previously been denied a voice. Second, telling stories about the organization was a useful medium for employees to articulate issues of sexuality at work, which otherwise they would find difficult to describe. Indeed, Wallemacq and Sims (1998: 121) suggest that some people are denied the right to make sense, because they have been unable to produce a narrative to go along with a situation. There are also other analytic advantages in locating identity in individuals' self-narratives. This approach permits the researcher to treat identity as being continuously constituted and reconstituted through discursive practices, and does not require the researcher to describe identity as a fixed, unchanging monolith. Another analytic advantage is the fact that stories are a vehicle for individuals to emplot self-conceptions and experiences, which in turn facilitate self-understanding. This enables us to place people's beliefs in a historical, biographical context regarding what they believe to be most significant about themselves.

Research involving narrative techniques affords the researcher with an opportunity to share personal experiences, the impact that the story has on the researcher, and the impact that the researcher has on the research. After all, the construction of any work always bears the mark of the person who created it. Since this book tells many stories it would be unfair, perhaps even unethical, not to tell my own. I therefore begin this book by locating myself and one of the events that led up to the research undertaking.

Ethical challenges in storytelling research

In meeting the ethical challenge of this sort of research, it is necessary to identify the perspective of the researcher, so that the limitations of the researcher's point of view are identified, whilst explaining why the researcher has analysed the stories in a particular way. As a gay man, my own identity helped to gain access to the respondents and helped build up the trust required to carry out the interviews. It is important to acknowledge this as it may explain why I analysed these stories as I did, as well as explaining the approach of developing a reflexive interaction within the research engagement.

There are other ethical challenges to carrying out this type of research, apart from deciding whose stories to tell. For example, researching the experiences of a minority which often remains silent for reasons of self-preservation, and then repeating the stories in a wider forum is an act that might be described by some as unethical. Indeed, the uncovering of people's private experiences in anthropological studies has been described by the French post-structuralist philosopher, Jacques Derrida, as an 'act of violence'. However, I believe that there is a major advantage to going this: in the same way that the organizational researcher, Barbara Czarniawska, set up a 'conversation' between various texts that otherwise not have 'spoken' to one another, my project has also given life to texts that otherwise might have remained hidden. And, by sharing these texts more widely, different texts, even opposing ones, have been forced to talk to one another. It should not be forgotten, though, that the terms on which these conversations between texts are held, are my terms, essentially those set out by the researcher, and by my carrying out the analysis, I have had the last word. The clear ethical dilemma for me, therefore, in presenting these stories in a book, is making sure that I remain faithful to the voices from the field, the voices that had previously remained silent.

Another ethical challenge is that of retelling narratives, which may not be true, a challenge which was referred to earlier in this chapter. I have talked about my research widely, and presented at a number of different conferences, and one thing that continues to fascinate people is whether the stories I was told were true. And, why not? I think this is a valid question, particularly in the field of empirical research in organizations, where stories are unique amongst discursive devices in that they have a plot, but also claim to represent reality. Poetic licence is a vital feature of the storyteller's voice, but does this mean it should not matter whether the story is true or not? The answer to this is often that the truth of the story lies not in its accurate depiction of facts but in its meaning. Since one of the aims in this research was to develop a method which could access personal experience as well as examples of discourse within the organization, this interpretation is an important one. Interestingly, the question of whether stories should be true or not was raised at two separate points during the research itself: first, during one of the focus groups, a participant identified themselves as the subject of the story, and declared it to be untrue. The discussion had to be brought to an end, partly because of the group's concern about the validity of the story. Second, purely fortuitously, and in an entirely different context, I found out that parts of a story that I had collected a year earlier were inaccurate. In the first case, the participant of the focus group was the subject of the story and had been portrayed in a poor light. Despite her claims that the story was untrue, after further investigation, it turned out that it was she who had been lying and the story turned out to be true in every detail, corroborated by credible witnesses. In the second case, the inaccuracies were embellishments, and could be defined as poetic licence, and the main plot of the story remained true and effective. My faith in the veracity of the stories was restored, but as a result I retained a healthy scepticism, recognizing that stories do not have to be true, but they do have to demonstrate verisimilitude for them to be taken seriously.

When poetic licence is taken too far it can seriously damage the legitimacy of the authority of the storyteller and, indeed, the researcher. But these two incidents do serve to illustrate Yiannis Gabriel's concerns about the hegemony of 'voice', or knowledge through personal experience. The risk in organizational research is that the voice of personal experience may be made up of illusions and self-deceptions and yet may still be accepted as the authentic source of understanding and sense-making in organizations. This risk implies a potential new direction for storytelling research in two ways: first, that researchers themselves become responsible for disentangling the voices, understanding them and privileging those that deserve to be privileged and then silencing those that deserve to be silenced; second, the researcher's task is not merely to retell the story or narrative, but to use the story as a vehicle for accessing deeper truths in the organization.

How this research came about: a reflexive note

Several years ago, I had a conversation that was to change my life. At the time I was working for a major multinational, an organization that is almost a household name, where I believed, like many other lesbian and gay people, that my sexual orientation had nothing to do with my work and that I had never been discriminated against. Sadly, it was not to continue. I was doing well; I had been working in California, made a success of it, and was then asked to go and manage a sales office in Southeast Asia. This was a challenge I felt able to meet, and a promotion I was grateful to accept. Until, that is, I found out soon afterwards that homosexuality is illegal in Singapore, where the job was to be based, and punishable by twenty-five years in prison. It took my (same-sex) partner and me less than ten minutes to decide that this was not going to be possible. I returned to work to turn down the role. I had been out at work for some time, but it transpired in the course of the conversation with my boss that he did not know. When I told him why I could not go to Singapore, I was expecting some warm words of comfort, at least an assurance that it did not matter and perhaps an indication of the next exciting role that was awaiting me. Instead, he declaimed six words that have stayed with me ever since, 'Your career is at an end.' The law changed in 2003 in the United Kingdom, making it unlawful to discriminate against people at work on the basis of their sexual orientation. This does not mean that had the law been in place a couple of years earlier this incident would not have happened. As it was, my manager was perfectly within his legal rights at that time to end my career. But laws do not make good people, they merely provide a sanction against poor behaviour, and indicate where the limits of good behaviour lie. It took me some time to face up to what had happened; part of the motivation for carrying out this research, and subsequently writing this book, was to work through this event that had happened some years earlier. In a Foucauldian sense, perhaps this book is my resistance. Writing this book is cathartic in that I, as well as all the people who took part in this research, will have narratively developed an understanding of our own experience, though for me the fear and dread of that, or something similar, happening again will never be completely expurgated. The whole process has changed me and, of course, my identity.

Methodologically, this book is important for human resource managers and line managers in organizations, as well as those students and researchers of organizational behaviour, and for individuals who belong to a minority, whatever that may be. The book will help to develop an understanding of the dynamics of minority identity in the workplace, as well as the power of storytelling as a lens for understanding organizations and the minorities who work within them. Personally, it has allowed me to bring together my interest in organizations with my own long-standing interest in language. I started my academic life as a linguist, and it has been a source of personal fulfilment to bring my interest in languages and linguistics to bear on my later interest in organizations. And, of course, there is always my love of stories…

2 Putting the stories in context

As suggested in the previous chapter, while stories are an excellent way of opening up a window on organizational dynamics as well as highlighting individual experience within those organizations, individual identity narratives are not solely private concerns, but are instead 'intensely governed' by, for example, social conventions, community scrutiny and legal norms. It is therefore interesting to understand the wider context of minority sexuality in the United Kingdom and beyond in order better to understand the stories that are told in this book about people's real life experiences in organizations. So, what are society's views and attitudes towards gay people at the beginning of the twenty-first century? Well, first, it is important to note that the very idea of gay people, that is to say that men who have sex with men, and women who have sex with women, having a different identity to those who have sex with the opposite sex is a relatively recent phenomenon, and one which is less than 150 years old. Second, the way in which that identity has been viewed by society has changed, with a very different legislative climate developing for gay people generally in the United Kingdom. Third, the impact on the workplace is that minority sexuality has a much higher profile than previously, with legislative changes also affecting the workplace, and a greater number of gay professional groups in existence.

Gay identity is a recent phenomenon

The ideas of Michel Foucault, the French post-structuralist philosopher, expounded in particular in his *History of Sexuality* published in 1976, are important to this project. He was gay himself, and was one of the most important thinkers in developing our understanding of homosexuality. He also challenged our understanding of sexuality as an essential, biological feature of our being by suggesting that sexuality was socially constructed, pointing to a remarkable proliferation of discourses about sexuality in the nineteenth century. But one of Foucault's most provocative assertions, and certainly one that acted as a catalyst for the development of Queer Theory, was that modern homosexuality is of comparatively recent origin, having grown out of a particular context in the 1870s. It was at this time that there was a historical shift in the conceptualizing of homosexuality from a behaviour to an identity, although an identity which was constructed by society at that time as a category of knowledge.

The sociologist Jeffrey Weeks, working at around the same time, in his seminal work *Coming Out: Homosexual Politics in Britain from the Nineteenth Century to the Present*, presented the idea that coming out, while usually seen as a personal process, can also, through the acceptance and public demonstration of the validity of homosexuality, be seen as an historic process. This is an interesting idea, although it does suggest that acceptance of homosexuality has gradually increased from the latter part of the nineteenth century to the present day. In actual fact, whilst it is true to say that we are living in a period of unrivalled tolerance of homosexuality in modern times, the path has not been smooth and, indeed, more akin to a rollercoaster.

Both Foucault and Weeks agree on the starting point of the mid to late nineteenth century for a discussion on homosexual identity. There is clear evidence in the later decades of the nineteenth century of the development of a new sense of identity amongst many homosexual individuals, and a crucial element in this would undoubtedly have been the new public salience of homosexuality, reinforced by the legal situation. This provocative assertion, made by Foucault and Weeks in the mid-1970s, that modern homosexuality is of comparatively recent origin, and that it is a social construction developing as a result of dominant discourses, would certainly have acted as a catalyst for a growing body of literature on sexualities since the 1970s.

There have been, of course, different 'waves' of discourses that have impacted on sexuality at different points in time, and highlighting the changes in these discourses through history is useful for considering sexual identity. But the reason for starting the discussion of homosexual identity in the mid to late nineteenth century is that these discourses, certainly as expressed by law in Western Europe from the sixteenth to the nineteenth century, were focused on sexual acts, not a particular type of person. For example, the 1533 Act of Henry VIII stipulated that 'all acts of buggery were against nature, whether between man and woman, man and beast or man and man', and the penalty for this abomination was death. It is true that there is some evidence that terms such as 'molly', to refer to an effeminate gay man, or 'sapphist', to refer to a masculine lesbian, were in usage as early as the seventeenth century, and this evidence is cited by those who would argue for an earlier conception of homosexual identity. It is also true that to be a molly at that time attracted severe penalties: in 1726, Mother Clap's Molly House in London was raided by police, resulting in Clap's death and the execution at Tyburn of all the men arrested (both the subject of a book on gay history by Rictor Norton and a play of the same name by Mark Ravenhill). Nevertheless, it can still be argued that the focus of attention, and the resulting punishment, was on the act or behaviour rather than on the person or identity. The punishment continued to be of the highest sanction from the sixteenth to the nineteenth centuries. This was true outside Britain, as well as within its borders. Between 1730 and 1811, a widespread panic in the Dutch Republic led to a spectacular series of trials for sodomy, with persecutions leading to the death penalty. Death by hanging continued to be the punishment for sodomy in Britain; the last known execution for sodomy in Britain was carried out in 1836, and in England, the penalty for conviction for sodomy was only reduced from hanging to imprisonment in 1861.

Around the same time, there was an emergence of sexual types and identities, with one of these being the homosexual. Indeed, the very word 'homosexuality' is a neologism, or an invented word, which was invented in the late 1860s, appearing for the first time in 1869 in a German pamphlet written by Karl-Maria Kertbeny. The development of a homosexual identity followed on from this, becoming indispensable as a form of perversion against which a real man or woman could be defined.

A word on Queer Theory

The study of minority sexuality has moved rapidly through a series of major transformations and changes, including the name that academics gave to the field of study. One of the first transformations was the sociological challenge to the accepted wisdom that sexuality was natural, while homosexuality was deviant. With the subsequent rise of social constructionism, the next step was to challenge the current understanding of sexual categorization. This gave rise, in the early 1980s, to the Lesbian and Gay Studies movement, a prominent political expression of a politics organized around sexual expression and a more positive analysis of minority sexual identity. Many of the academic studies at this time sought to explain the origin, social meaning and form of the modern homosexual. But, the problem was that this academic and political movement was seen to support an ethnic model of sexuality, which was broadly essentialist, and was seen to be exclusive of other identities, especially of race and gender, and the categories of lesbian and gay were seen to be disciplining forces for social categorization.

Queer Theory and Queer Studies have grown out of the more traditional lesbian and gay studies. It is a social constructionist, discursive approach to minority sexuality and, although the term 'queer' was once a term of abuse, it has come to be used differently to describe this area of study. It emerged in the late 1980s and 1990s, a postmodern academic movement, heavily influenced by post-structuralist theory and loosely tied to confrontational queer politics. It is interesting that Queer Theorists have been successful at reappropriating the term 'queer', whereas others have been less successful with other terms; for example, a term like 'nigger', where despite some recent efforts at reclamation, its use, as arch queer-theorist Judith Butler says, 'appears capable of only re-inscribing its pain' (Butler, 1993: 223).

Basically, the theory goes that sexuality is seen as a production of power and knowledge, expressed principally through discourse. Understanding minority sexuality in the workplace through stories is consistent with this view. The aim of Queer Theory was to build an identity of resistance, challenging common beliefs about gender and sexuality, from their representation in film, literature and music to their placement in the social and physical sciences. The cross-discipline approach taken by Queer Theory means that organization studies is a potentially fruitful area for studying minority sexuality. Queer Theory encourages analysis of how the creation of a reviled gay identity in Western societies has often been a method by which heterosexuality assured themselves of their superiority through the construction of minority sexuality as an inferior identity and as a reviled category of knowledge.

For those students, academics and managers in organizations who would like to read around the subject I will mention a few of the principal writers in the area. One of the first queer publications was Diana Fuss' edited work *Inside/Out*, which came to represent a central statement about Queer Theory. This was closely followed by Butler's seminal work *Gender Trouble*, which, by building on the work of linguist philosopher, J.L. Austin, suggested that gender is performative, and that gender and sexuality are historical constructions which we act out. Eve Kosofsky Sedgwick's *Epistemology of the Closet* explores contradictory conceptual models of homosexuality, that is to say how homosexuality represents the identity of a minority, but at the same time helps to constructs heterosexual identity. In a typically deconstructive move, she attempted to show the unhelpful side of binary oppositions, the prime example being that when something is 'out', it implies something else being 'closeted'. Well-known names in the area of Queer Studies also include David Halperin, who wrote a gay hagiography to Foucault, highlighting the Foucauldian basis for much of the work belonging to the queer movement and Stephen Seidman, whose edited collection of papers, *Queer Theory/Sociology* brings together the two fields of Queer Theory and sociology for the first time.

So, what does this mean for identity? Queer theorists have suggested that minority sexual identity is fluid and multiple. What is more, psychologists and sociologists have long argued that the same individual exhibits multiple identities; this idea is not new, with Mead suggesting that there is a 'parliament of selves' within each person. This is particularly pertinent for a discussion of sexuality, since many people in the West, as Jeffrey Weeks has noted, like to describe who they are by telling of their sexuality: 'I am gay/straight.' But, in reality, people do not fit into one of two fixed categories of sexuality; gay and straight. In common with other post-structuralist understandings of the exclusionary and regulatory nature of binary identity categories, Queer Theory rejects the idea of a unified homosexual identity and sees the construction of sexual identities around the hierarchically-structured, binary opposition of hetero/homosexual as inherently unstable. Heterosexuality is also problematized and is rendered as much less monolithic and unassailable than earlier. In Queer Theory, there is a shift in focus from the margins on the homosexual to a focus on the constitution of the homo/heterosexual binary. It is difficult to make generalizations about entire categories of people who organize their lives around various sexual orientations; some lead mainstream lives, others transgressive ones and the differences are often linked to variations in race and social class. The lesson from the queer theorists is that the variations are often the answer, rather than the similarities.

People can move between these different sexualities at different points in their lives. There are sexualities which define gender attraction such as gay, straight and bisexual. But even bisexuality is just one example of the fluid and multifaceted nature of sexual identity. There are other types of minority sexual identity other than gay or lesbian: asexuality, which denies attraction of either gender; and transsexuality which redefines the gender of the individual. There are also sexualities to do with sexual practice and behaviour, which cut across gender or sexual orientation such as sadomasochism and fetishism. Sexual identities are fluid and ever-changing: people who may have previously considered themselves heterosexual come out as gay, whilst gay people get married and have children, whilst others may choose an alternative sexual identity for political reasons.

However, where the queer theorists' argument starts to crumble is when you apply the postmodern view of fluid identities to organizational reality. As the organization studies academic, Joshua Gamson, aptly put it: you may want to reject the idea of a fixed identity, but those who would discriminate against you in organizations will soon give you one. And then there is the fact that, as Jeffrey Weeks described, most people do congregate at some point around labels: gay or straight. On the one hand, the idea of multiple, fluid identities is an important notion, but on the other, organizational reality is such that employees will identify with one sexual identity or another. The identity of being either lesbian, gay or bisexual is an important one for the individuals concerned, and we should therefore consider how attitudes have developed over time towards those identities.

Societal attitudes to homosexuality are constantly changing

In the late nineteenth century, just as the homosexual was constructed as an identity by society, so was a negative view of that very same identity. The homosexual was pathologized as a perverse or deviant type, at best a case of arrested development and an aberration from the heterosexual norm. And with the emergence of homosexuality as an identity, came the emergence of what Weeks terms the medical model of homosexuality, where the notions of sin and crime developed into concepts of sickness and mental illness. Homosexuality therefore developed as a congenital abnormality rather than the sinful and evil behaviour with which it had been previously associated. The scientific discourse was to rage for a long time as to whether homosexuality was acquired or congenital, and whether it was ineradicable or curable. And the medical model of homosexuality where it was conceived of as a sickness or mental illness continued until relatively recently. It was not until 1973 that the American Psychiatric Association removed homosexuality from the official manual that lists mental and emotional disorders, in response to what it has since described as new, better-designed research available at that time. Although no longer viewed as a disease, the debate over whether homosexuality is genetic or whether it is learned continues today.

And although the law, science and medicine were quite negative in the way that they had established limits for gay people, there were positive aspects of gay identity to emerge. Foucault suggested that where power is exercised, there is also resistance. A practical example of Foucault's theory is the way that gay people used other societal developments to allow themselves to develop a firmer concept of their own identity, as a response to the ways in which the law and medicine attempted to pathologize them; in other words the 'resistance' was a stronger gay identity. Urbanization and the spread of free wage labour had had an enormous impact on individuals at this time. Industrialization created cities and anonymity, whilst a more mobile workforce meant it was easier to live as a single person. The emergence of sexual orientation as a component of personal identity was closely tied to changes in the organization of economic activity. Industrialization and urbanization allowed many men and women to separate from the traditional farm-based family and from their traditional productive roles as farm labourers as well as their traditional reproductive roles as heterosexual men and women and parents. Urban wage labour markets provided the economic means for men and women to create lives apart from heterosexual marriage and to create different sexual identities.

These conditions were to allow gay and lesbian communities to develop, which was the case, for example, in Germany from 1900 to the early 1930s. Persecution of homosexuals gained renewed vigour as the Nazis came into power, and they publicly attested their aim of attempting to eradicate homosexuality. According to Stonewall (the professional lobbying group for lesbian, gay and bisexual equality in the United Kingdom), an estimated 50,000 gay men were sentenced and imprisoned, some of whom faced the death penalty. Up to 15,000 gay men were deported to concentration camps and made to wear the pink triangle symbol which identified them as homosexual men. Many of these 'Pink Triangle' detainees were subjected to horrific treatment ranging from starvation and hard labour, to medical experiments, castration and death. Lesbianism was not illegal in Germany, so lesbians did not suffer the same level of persecution as gay men. After the war, neither the Allies nor the German or Austrian states recognized gay men or lesbians as victims alongside other groups, so they were not considered eligible for compensation. Only in 2001 was the German and Swiss Bank compensation programme extended to include gay victims. Nazi laws against homosexuality remained in place in Germany until 1967.

In the United Kingdom, the penalty for homosexuality had remained imprisonment since 1861. It was a groundbreaking moment therefore when, in 1957, the Wolfenden Committee published its report recommending decriminalization of consensual homosexual behaviour between adults, although the Sexual Offences Act, which in effect decriminalized homosexual activity between consenting adults over the age of twenty-one, and in private, did not come into law until 1967. The application of this new law was patchy in different parts of the United Kingdom, however; it only came into effect in England, and male homosexuality was not decriminalized in Scotland until 1980, in Northern Ireland until 1982, and in the Isle of Man until 1992.

Nevertheless, huge strides forward have been made since decriminalization in the different countries of the United Kingdom. It is difficult to say why progress towards equality has been made so quickly in such a short space of time, although true equality is still a long way off. Andrew Sullivan, the well-known gay journalist, in an article in the *New Republic* in 2005, suggested that society started to respond more positively to gay people after having vilified them in the most terrible way at the time of the AIDS epidemic in the early 1980s. AIDS was seen by society in general in the 1980s as some kind of retribution for immoral behaviour. It could, as Sullivan suggests, have led to quarantining or the collapse of nascent gay institutions. Instead, it had the opposite effect, suggesting once again the playing out of Foucault's idea of power and resistance. In response to the appalling treatment that AIDS victims and gay people in general received at that time, there was also political lobbying and renewed political activism amongst the gay communities. This resistance was strengthened still further in response to the passing of Section 28 of the Local Government Act in 1988 by the then Conservative government of Margaret Thatcher, designed to prevent the promotion of positive images of homosexuality by local authorities. Stonewall was founded in the following year, marking a new beginning for political lobbying for gay equality in the United Kingdom.

Since then, a number of important legislative changes have been made: the government voted on the equalization of the age of consent in 1998, which came into force in 2001; in the year 2000, the government lifted its ban of gay men and lesbians in the armed forces; in 2002, equal rights were extended to same-sex couples applying for the adoption of children; in 2003, the Section 28 legislation was repealed; also in 2003, the Employment Equality (Sexual Orientation) Regulations became law; in 2004 the Civil Partnership Act was passed, giving same-sex couples the same rights as heterosexual couples and it came into law in 2005, although the government stopped short of calling it marriage.

Such changes have not only been in the legislative arena. People of my generation, the last of the baby-boomers, grew up with the portrayal of gay men as camp figures of fun; comedians such as John Inman and Larry Grayson hardly provided society with a positive image of gay men. Then in 2000, Channel 4's groundbreaking *Queer as Folk* burst onto our screens with an unapologetic portrayal of gay life in Manchester, with a lot of the action being centred around Canal Street, Manchester's gay village. During that time and since, there have been countless, positive examples of gay men and women integrated into the media mainstream, and examples include programmes with universal appeal: the runner-up in the first *Big Brother* in the year 2000 was Anna, a gay, ex-novice nun, followed in 2001 by Brian, an out gay man, and there have been programmes such as *Queer Eye for the Straight Guy*, and gay-themed comedy shows such as *Will and Grace*.

There are now openly gay legislators in the United Kingdom; in 2002, Alan Duncan became the first serving British Conservative Party MP to voluntarily come out publicly as gay, and the Labour Party has had a number of gay MPs, such as Chris Smith, the first out gay cabinet minister, Angela Eagle, Ben Bradshaw and Stephen Twigg, and others. There are mainstream entertainment figures who no longer see coming out as career suicide; for example George Michael, Ellen DeGeneres and Elton John, who took advantage of the new laws regarding homosexual partnerships in December 2005 to celebrate his Civil Partnership with David Furnish. Interestingly, the media, in referring to his marriage (*sic*), seemed to be more concerned with talking about how the lavish the celebrations were than whether or not the idea of officially sanctioned gay partnerships were to be approved of.

Minority sexual identity in the workplace

And yet, whilst the lives of famous gay people such as Little Richard, Dusty Springfield and Elton John go some way to charting the changes in the way that society views homosexuality, they do not necessarily reflect what life is like for ordinary gay men and women at the beginning of the twenty-first century. Macro-discourse at a societal level is a useful tool for historians and political scientists, but it is micro-discourse, the stories and interactions of our everyday lives, which give an insight into what life is really like for ordinary people. This book is about the world of work and work organizations, where many of us spend our lives, and sexual minorities are no different. It is important for three principal reasons; first, although legislation has been introduced which prohibits discrimination against anyone on the basis of the sexuality in the workplace, the issues that sexual minorities face at work are far from over. Second, minority sexuality at work really does matter. Third, but no less importantly, sexual orientation in the workplace is an under-researched area, and has in the past failed to attract its fair share of attention from managers and researchers alike.

Legislation is not the end of the story

Legislation is essential in bringing about change, as it is a marker by society of a minimum required standard of behaviour. But laws do not make good people, they are there to provide a sanction against poor behaviour and then only if it is reported. So, whilst the Employment Equality (Sexual Orientation) Regulations of 2003 were a welcome addition to equal opportunities legislation, the issues that lesbians and gay men face on a day-to-day basis in their working lives are far from over. We know that despite equal pay legislation introduced in the 1970s designed to deliver pay parity between men and women, there is still an imbalance in financial rewards in the world of work more than thirty years later between male and female employees. And despite a whole raft of other well-meaning legislation such as Sex Discrimination Acts 1975 and 1986, the Race Relations Act 1976, the Race Relations Amendment Act 2000, the Disability Discrimination Act 1995, and subsequent amendments, issues of managing diversity within work organizations have not gone away. Legal protection against discrimination may be a good starting point, but it is not the whole story. In extending protection against discrimination in the workplace against gay people, sexual orientation still struggles to be a recognized element of the diversity agenda within organizations, and this despite the rhetoric of some the large organizations.

Sexual orientation in the workplace is an under-researched area

When I began this research into the experiences of lesbians, gay men and bisexuals in the workplace, there was a clear perception that of all diversity categories, there remains one that continues to be under-researched by organizational researchers: minority sexuality. Indeed, it is one of the most taboo topics within contemporary organizational theory. Even though the move to business case justifications for diversity interventions has broadened definitions of diversity to include sexual orientation, the lack of any sort of imperative, legal or otherwise, until recently, for organizations to show any interest in this area has meant that references to sexual orientation in the diversity literature in the past have been at best cursory, perhaps giving a definition of diversity to include sexual orientation before returning quickly to the discussion on race or gender. Sexual orientation has also received less attention from organizational researchers in that it is, unlike most other forms of diversity, invisible, and in many cases silent, and invisible forms of diversity have been less researched in the management area than visible forms such as gender or race. Finally, this is also an opportunity for gay people, who have up to now largely been invisible in the workplace, to tell their stories; this book attempts to give them a voice, a voice which had been previously silenced. Invisibility has provided, and continues to provide, researchers with a unique set of difficulties. There is a lack of information on what the issues actually are, which people are affected and where they work, as well as how their identity is formed by the organizational culture in which they work. Indeed, despite the large amount of research in lesbian and gay studies, only a small portion of the research is evident in core sociology textbooks and research literature, let alone organization studies literature. Most theory books in sociology and organization studies continue to overlook Queer Theory, excluding sexual minorities from the larger sociological landscape. This is not a recent phenomenon; some time ago Arlene Stein and Ken Plummer (1994) made the case that gay and lesbian issues inhabit the margins of sociology. That said, it appears that the situation is starting to change, with a small number articles with a focus on minority sexuality now starting to appear in mainstream, peer-reviewed cross-discipline and organization studies journals such as *Personnel Review, Journal of Management Studies, Human Relations* and *Sociological Review*. This suggests that perhaps sexual minorities are moving from the margins to the mainstream and that there is a growing academic interest in sexuality amongst organizational and diversity researchers.

Minority sexuality in the workplace matters

During this research project, a question was raised by many people: does sexuality in the workplace matter? The view held by many people is that it does not. It is expressed in different ways: during the field work for this project, even diversity professionals made comments such as, 'that is personal to the individual', or 'the organization is not ready to take action in this area'. In addition, heterosexual employees said things such as 'I don't talk about my sexuality at work – why should they?'. Perhaps the most confusing quotations come from lesbian, gay and bisexual employees themselves, who say 'My sexuality has nothing to do with my career', a comment made many times during my research interviews. In this context then, it is unsurprising that this has been an under-researched area; organizational researchers depend on finding willing organizations as research subjects, and it is only relatively recently that organizations are starting to show an interest in this area. Despite these views, however, I would still maintain that sexuality has an enormous impact on the relations we form at work with our colleagues and customers, how well we perform, and ultimately the quality of our work, and my research bears this out.

An individual's identity and their sense of who they are has been the subject of much general research, and it has been recognized that this issue can be much more complex for a lesbian or gay man; just coming to terms with their own identity can be incredibly taxing in itself. The psychological drain of constantly managing an identity, especially as in some cases this is a front, can interfere with other aspects of development such as the career, not to mention the energy which is put into learning how to manage the oppressive consequences of homophobic attitudes and behaviour in the workplace. Often, though, the decision is taken by employees to disclose their orientation to others in the workplace, and this is one of the most important career decisions faced by gay employees. Sexual minorities may well choose to keep their sexuality out of the workplace, but in doing so they are making a decision which heterosexual colleagues do not have to make. They are also isolating themselves from a potentially very creative source of interaction. They may also choose to talk about their sexuality openly, in the same way that their heterosexual colleagues do. In either case, as they make this decision, their sexuality necessarily becomes, by definition, something to do with their career.

Not only do we spend a lot of time there, but workplaces and work organizations are also sexual places, in a number of different ways. First, organizations are segregated places, with sexual minorities congregating in certain work organizations. Second, people interact on a sexual level at work. Third, sexuality can also be expressed in the workplace in many different, sometimes even non-sexual, ways.

Organizations are segregated places, with sexual minorities congregating in certain work organizations. Previous research suggests that sexual minorities may congregate in some occupations rather than others. One reason for this may be geography; gays and lesbians are more likely to be located in urban areas than other people. One study in the United States found that 59 per cent of men in same sex couples were clustered in only twenty cities. Gay people move to urban areas, among other reasons, to find a tolerant labour market and a supportive gay community. Another reason may be the perceived tolerance of certain occupations; in 1997, Badgett and King studied the occupational choice by gays and lesbians and how closely it followed the occupational patterns of anti-gay sentiments. Their results suggest that while gay men cluster in more tolerant occupations, lesbians, who, they suggested, tend to work in more macho cultures like the police, do not.

In 1993, James Woods and Jay Lucas published their seminal work *The Corporate Closet*, which was the first in-depth study of its kind of gay life in corporate America. In it they described how people interact in a sexual way at work; the way people dress, their jokes and their interactions, even flirtations. It is interesting to note that a number of people interviewed as part of this project had met a partner, long- or short-term, at work. Clearly, actual sexual contact at work is rare, but the workplace nevertheless involves a good deal of socializing, and opportunities to meet friends, boyfriends, girlfriends, husbands, wives and partners. There are official and unofficial social events where such partners and friends are invited. Traditionally, these are occasions where sexual minorities have felt excluded, although this is increasingly becoming rare. This research has shown that, increasingly, lesbians and gay men now bring their same-sex partners to social functions and this is well received by many of their colleagues.

Sexuality is also expressed at work in non-sexual ways, since discussions at work, even innocent ones, imply sexual orientation; talk of the weekend, the family and the children reinforce the heterosexual orientation of the majority of employees, and again it is a situation from which many people, though not exclusively sexual minorities, feel excluded. The laddish or macho culture of the organizations, which took part in this research project was often raised as an issue, to be expected in the police and fire service, but less expected though still present in the Civil Service and the banks. The way this expressed itself ranged from the sort of banter heard in the station or office, to the type of after-work socializing, to an almost obsessive preoccupation by heterosexual men with certain sporting activities. On numerous occasions, sexual minorities felt excluded from conversation.

Scope of the project

In defining the scope of this project it was necessary to decide which groups or categories would be included in the study, and which would be excluded. To restrict the study to one particular category, which has been done in previous empirical research, for example gay men, in the Woods and Lucas study, or lesbians, for example a study by Boatwright, Gilbert *et al.* in 1996, was felt to be too narrow for the study of minority, that is to say non-heterosexual, sexual identity. The scope was minority sexual orientation, and therefore initially included lesbian, gay and bisexual identities. The scope was then broadened out to include transsexual identities, somewhat of an unusual inclusion perhaps, since the category is about gender identification, rather than sexual orientation; it is also covered by separate legislation, which is not discussed in the book. However, transgender individuals chose voluntarily to take part in the study, classifying themselves as belonging to a minority sexuality and, in addition, they have interesting issues of sexual orientation, which do not change when they change their gender. Through gender reassignment, a previously heterosexual man may become a lesbian, or a gay man may become a heterosexual woman, and it was felt that they had interesting insights to offer on the issues of minority sexual identity in the workplace. In addition, transsexual respondents in my research explained that, because they are a relatively small minority group, they feel that if they did not belong with the lesbian, gay and bisexual community, they would have very little representation in the workplace. Interestingly, Diana Fuss (1991) suggests that the heterosexual/homosexual binary can only secure its 'seemingly inviolable dialectical structure' only by assimilating and internalizing other sexualities such as bisexuality and transsexualism. It is interesting that the assimilation takes place within the homosexual half of the binary, leaving heterosexuality untainted by any deviation from what is 'normal'.

Those classifications which I deliberately excluded were those which were based on sexual behaviour rather than attraction or orientation, such as sadists, masochists or fetishists of any particular kind. Also excluded were paedophiles, or those who seek out intergenerational sexual relations below the legal common age of consent in the United Kingdom.

A word on terminology: a glossary of terms has been provided at the end of the book, which the reader may find useful. Terminology has been used which is aimed to be inclusive such as 'queer', previously a term of abuse, but now reclaimed, and 'sexual minorities', that is to say those who are not heterosexual. Queer Theory is referred to, as well as Lesbian and Gay Studies; the former is a more recent academic movement recognizing the impact of discourse and language as well as the fluidity and instability of identity. The latter refers more to the academic area of study in the 1970s and 1980s, which focused on the essential identity of lesbians and gay men.

The organizations

The organizations that took part in this storytelling research were willing participants in the main, but all of them requested anonymity. The study of sexual minorities in organizations is likely to be sensitive for the individuals concerned, but also for the organization, for whom public criticism may be damaging and indeed counterproductive. Nevertheless, I have tried to provide a balance for the reader between the anonymity sought by the organizations and the need to give enough information about them to make the context meaningful. I have therefore chosen not to name any one particular organization, recognizing that I will have to make reference to the type of organization, and at times the type of activity that they undertake. This is clearly frustrating; whilst in one sense this project closes a gap in the literature by carrying out research in specific organizations, it is not possible to name them. Nevertheless, all six organizations are amongst the most well-known organizations in the United Kingdom, and all of them are organizations with which many ordinary people will have had dealings in one form or another.

The six organizations represented a range of businesses, grouped into three main sectors or areas of activity and made up of: two banks, two government departments and two emergency services. The two latter groups, government departments and emergency services, are of course publicly owned, while the two banks represented the private sector. Three of the organizations have about 5,000 employees or less, which I have defined as small. The other three have more than 70,000, which I have defined as large. Using the Deal and Kennedy definitions of culture, the organizations represent two different cultures – process and tough-guy cultures. The two Civil Service organizations represent the process cultures, and the two emergency service organizations represent the tough-guy cultures, whilst the two banks have significant subcultures within them that represent both. For example, personal and financial services and consumer banking may well be described as having a process culture, whilst the more macho environment of investment banking with its trading floor fulfils the criteria of the tough-guy culture. It is useful to have a mix of different organizational characteristics, so that any comparative analysis can be more informed. At a very basic level, the research findings may show that individual variables are not enough to explain certain phenomena; for example, different findings in two large organizations may suggest that the size of the organizations does not provide adequate explanation.

Alpha Bank: a major international bank

Alpha Bank is a major American international bank and financial services firm. Alpha has an annual revenue of just over $18 billion, with its headquarters in New York, and operations in fifty countries worldwide. In 2000, the bank went through a major merger, combining one of the world's largest commercial banks, with one of the world's best-known investment banks. Both institutions had histories going back over 200 years. The bank has five main divisions, including the investment bank, treasury and security services, private banking, private equity investing and retail. Diversity management has a very high profile at the bank; it has a comprehensive diversity education programme and corporate support for employee networking groups, which have a participation of over 5,000 employees worldwide.

Beta Bank: a major United Kingdom banking group

Beta Bank is a major banking group and one of the largest financial services groups in the United Kingdom. It has seven business groups: personal financial services, business banking, a credit card division, private clients, global investors, capital markets and an African division. Beta Bank has a presence in over sixty countries, serves over twenty million customers worldwide and employs over 78,000 people. Shareholders' funds were in the region of £15 billion at the time of writing. Beta Bank has been extremely active in the area of equality and diversity; some of its wide-ranging achievements have included the appointment of diversity managers, with different managers responsible for different diversity categories, the setting up of task forces in each of the diversity category areas and a wide-ranging employee survey. Sexual orientation was included in each of these three areas of achievement. There has also been an organization-wide equality and diversity awareness training programme, including video and intranet training material, and a four-hour individual foundation module in diversity.

The Micro Department: a small government department

The Micro Department is one of the smaller United Kingdom government departments and employs about 4,000 people. It was formed in 2001 from the de-merger of one of the larger departments. It is a policy department with very little public contact outside its immediate area of expertise, although it does have a number of cross-government initiatives, working with other departments. It has a headquarters in London with regional offices in Sheffield, Runcorn and Darlington. Despite the traditional feel, the department has made significant progress in managing diversity in recent years. Employees receive equal opportunities training, there are regular workshops on various different aspects of diversity, and equal opportunities have formed the basis for specific measures included in annual performance appraisal forms. Although, in the past, the focus has been largely on the better-known areas of diversity such as race and gender, the department has nevertheless made significant progress in other areas such as sexuality. There is an employee network for lesbians and gay men, testimonials from gay employees have been used at equality conferences in the organization, and a banner carrying the department's name has been carried at London's annual Lesbian and Gay Pride march.

The Delta Department: a large government department

The Delta Department is one of the larger government departments, employing approximately 84.000 people. It is a major 'processing' department and therefore has operations as well as policy. With a head office in London and major offices in all large towns throughout the country and enquiry offices in the smallest of communities, it is a fragmented organization but with a high level of contact with the public. The Delta Department demonstrates its commitment to equality and diversity at the highest levels of the organization; its chairman has been the Diversity Champion for the Home Civil Service, and the board and senior managers are actively involved in promoting understanding of diversity as a way to deliver quality customer service, and to create a positive working environment. A panel of directors from across the department have acted as Diversity Champions to set business direction and to oversee the implementation of equality and diversity objectives. It has monitored representation at different levels of the organization on the basis of race, gender and disability and, in 2003, monitored sexual identity for the first time through the inclusion of a question on sexuality in the 2003 staff survey. Recent progress has included a diversity and equality intranet site to share good practice in both diversity and equality implementation, equality targets at national, regional and area level and a recently established consultancy team, 'Business through Diversity', to help embed diversity into all business processes.

Shire Fire Service: a semi-rural fire brigade

The Shire Fire Service is a small regional division of the United Kingdom Fire Service. With only 850 people in its employment, this was the smallest organization to take part in this project. The service is in a semi-rural location, with a number of medium-sized towns, and therefore there is a mix of whole-time and retained, or part-time, firefighters. Retained firefighters are usually employed in rural areas or those areas where the fire risk is relatively low. Nevertheless, given the density and nature of the industrial base in certain areas of the county, Shire Fire Service has a disproportionately high level of operational risk. In addition to operational firefighters, the service is made up of control staff and support staff. There are approximately 740 operational firefighters, twenty-four control staff and eighty-seven support staff. There is a total of twenty-four fire stations, with nine of them being whole-time stations. Following the Home Office Thematic Review in 1999, and subsequent equality and diversity initiatives, the Shire Fire Service is in a good position to make a real difference within the organization for minorities, having instigated a number of local initiatives: there is a full-time equal opportunities officer who takes part in a network of personnel managers and equality practitioners; the chief fire officer takes a leading role in equality issues in the United Kingdom Fire Service and played a significant part in organizing a recent national equalities convention; and finally, awareness training is scheduled to take place in the near future for various different diversity categories.

The Rural Constabulary: a rural police force

The Rural Constabulary is the largest rural police force in the United Kingdom covering the largest geographical police area in England, extending 180 miles in length. To give some impression of the scale of the area, the police headquarters of the Rural Constabulary is actually nearer to London than the furthest extremity of the force's area of responsibility. Policing a large rural population, and covering large distances, makes responding to target times for emergencies a challenge for the force. Even within a largely rural area, there are still urban communities, which make tackling crime more complex; cities present their own unique policing issues, as do the popular seaside resorts in the area. There is a seasonal influx of tourists, causing the population to rise from about one and a half million to eight million; dealing with such a large number of tourists presents its own problems, especially as the Rural Constabulary has fewer officers per members of the population than most other areas of the country. There are over 5,000 employees, including 2,000 support staff, making the Rural Constabulary one of the largest employers in the area, though still one of the smaller organizations in this project.

3   The working closet

For many years, there has been an inherent contradiction in being gay and working for an organization; whilst out gay employees are more committed to their organization, and are likely to feel more fulfilled and do a better job, there has been significant, well-documented discrimination against sexual minorities in organizations. As a result, a regular, continuing feature of lesbians' and gay men's experience in the workplace is the pervasive fear of discrimination. One of the interviewees in this project described what the atmosphere had been like when he joined the organization:

> It wasn't a subject you could easily broach with other people it was a secret. The environment was pretty hostile. It's a pretty macho environment, even in head office. Homophobia was pretty rife. Not at all a safe environment [when I joined]. I remember correspondence in the magazine about employees' sexuality and the editor put it down very quickly saying it wasn't a suitable subject for discussion.

Even though this interviewee admitted that the atmosphere at work had generally improved over the past few years, he still maintained that management of this fear means that people are either forced to remain closeted at work, separating their lives between work and leisure, or in some cases to remain closeted altogether.

In 1993, Woods and Lucas supported this idea by asserting that the 'closet' is a major metaphor for lesbian and gay people in the workplace. And it is this that distinguishes minority sexuality from other aspects of the diversity agenda; the fact that it is possible for someone's sexuality to remain hidden, or for lesbian, gay or bisexual people to stay 'in the closet', distinguishes sexual orientation from most of the other diversity categories such as race or gender, where difference from the norm is immediately visible. Clearly, this fact is both a distinguishing feature and an argument against taking minority sexuality seriously at all; some would argue that if sexual orientation can remain hidden it cannot be an issue at work at all, since it is not possible to be insulted on the basis of something that is secret or hidden. The truth is, of course, that insults, or jokes in poor taste, do not have to be directed at any one individual for them to be hurtful. If general banter is disrespectful of gay men and women it can indicate that the culture is not safe for the gay man or woman to come out. In addition, there is the negative impact of the rumour mill, where individuals are suspected of being gay; if this is true, the fear of being discovered can be heightened. Russ, now a very high-ranking police officer in the Rural Constabulary, recounts what happened when he first joined the police force. He explained that it was an organization where 'you want to be accepted by your supervisors and peers'. The problem was that it was rather a crude culture back then, and one where 'policewomen were groped and all the rest of it' and so the fact that he was someone who, in his own words, did not 'fart or grope women' was enough to suggest to his colleagues that he was gay. Indeed, his tutor constable, the officer assigned to him to show him the ropes when he joined the force, told him that 'the sergeant's trying to get you kicked out because he thinks you're a pouf'. This suspicion alone, not based on any knowledge, was enough to make the sergeant in question put in negative reports about Russ on a regular basis over a period of about a year. It was only when the sergeant was moved that this behaviour stopped.

Being in the closet, and not feeling able to tell anybody at work about one's sexual orientation can put constant pressure on an individual and have a negative effect on them and their work. One Civil Servant, who worked in the Micro Department, and who had previously had a customer-facing job, told me about the effects of constantly having to cover up his sexual identity: 'Depression; used to fly off the handle. Because I was on the counter, my first thought was – are they able to notice? Am I acting straight?'

Another Civil Servant described the effect on him of not being out at work:

> It can affect your work adversely. If you're not comfortable, it can affect your work. You're frightened, aren't you? Of what other people might say. Also you're being a dishonest person not saying where you've been or what you've been doing.

John, another Civil Servant, but this time in the Delta Department, a much bigger organization, described the reaction to his not being out at work which had much more serious emotional consequences for him:

> There was also the issue that I hadn't told anybody, not just at work, so that was another thing. I wasn't used to telling people, and I hadn't accepted it for myself. But it would have been better and easier, had there been an accepting environment at work that would have encouraged me more. It made me feel suicidal, it made me feel dreadful. I didn't want to go into work; not that that kind of attitude was going on everyday, but I knew it would crop up because being homophobic was a normal part of how people behaved. I knew it would keep coming up, and it always did, and every time it did it would cut me to ribbons, even if it wasn't directed at me personally. Many times I did try to leave the Delta Department, but the job I could do, I

was good at it, and I don't think wherever I'd gone I would have found much difference. Unless I'd gone into a gay environment, so in the end I ended up staying.

Pete, a police officer, also described the heavy emotional effect of not coming out at work:

My story is slightly different. After a period of time, about January 1998, I had my first real boyfriend. I didn't know whether or not I wanted to stay in the police force, because I didn't see my sexuality as fitting in. Eighty per cent as a result of my sexuality, I was diagnosed with depression and was off work for about eight weeks. During that period of time I was starting to resolve things in my mind. I've never had a girlfriend since then.

Brad, a firefighter, also talked about the effects of not being in the closet, although for him one of the aspects he found troubling was the idea that he might be the only gay firefighter in the service:

At the training school, as I say, I knew I was gay, but it was all, you know, kept ... kept in secret. And I led a double life for about three or four years. I never told anyone in fire service at all until probably about four years into my career. After the two year probation period, I then asked for a transfer up to my home station, and got it; and, yeah there was...

At this point in the story, Brad's voice trailed off, and he takes a deep sigh as he remembers the emotion of the situation. He picked up the narrative once again:

there was just this horrible sense of fear in yourself, that you're living this double life. And why should you be doing it, when nobody else is doing it? I always thought I was the only gay fireman in the United Kingdom, and I was told by many people or asked the question – would you be sacked if your employers found out? And at that stage I always thought that I would be; I had just assumed that it would be a no-go area, because of the militaristic overtones that were a constant presence in the fire service culture. You know that you could be reprimanded and sacked for being gay within the fire service. I always assumed that and that was just very naive on my behalf. Yeah, I was thinking about it the other day; I just wish that the day I started to feel insecure about myself being in the fire service and being gay, I wish had approached the Union officials at the time.

In 1963, the sociologist Erving Goffman published his seminal work *Stigma*, which developed an important analysis of the dynamics of non-disclosure and identity management. I believe that Goffman's approach to homosexuality now appears to be outdated, as we read his work with the societal views of today and not those of the 1960s, but his theories nevertheless have a lot to offer and his examples bring the subject of stigma to life. He refers to three types of stigma: physical deformities, blemishes of individual character and tribal stigma. He puts homosexuality into the second category, along with mental disorder, imprisonment, addiction and alcoholism. Clearly, this classification dates his work, placing it firmly in the middle of the twentieth century; now, at the beginning of the twenty-first century, this is a difficult concept to accept politically and sociologically since homosexuality is no longer classified as an illness, as addiction and alcoholism now are and, in the United Kingdom at least, being gay no longer results in imprisonment. As the diversity movement now sees sexual orientation as a diversity category, it is probably more appropriate to conceptualize minority sexual orientation in the category of tribal stigma, along with race and religion. Nevertheless, Goffman's work has some important insights to offer about the management of identity, and we should look beyond the specifics of the ways in which he refers to homosexuality, to his ideas of stigma in general. Goffman suggests that the need to manage one's identity occurs because there is a discrepancy between an individual's actual social identity and their virtual one. Where the difference is not known, or not immediately apparent, the individual has a discreditable identity, whereas when they make their difference known to others, their identity becomes discredited.

Goffman remarks that visibility is an important issue for stigmatized minorities, but should be distinguished from 'known-about-ness', (Goffman, 1963b: 65). Some diversity categories, such as race and gender, are clearly visible, whilst others are not. Sexual orientation is, generally speaking, invisible, although not the only diversity category which is; religious belief, for example, is another category which is hard to distinguish first by looking at someone. Goffman distinguishes between this idea of invisibility and the idea of known-about-ness; for example, it may not be apparent that someone at work is gay, but other people may know that they are, with the implication that they generally have prior information about that particular individual. Of course, a constant dilemma for lesbians or gay men in organizations is whether to increase the level of their known-about-ness in the organization and to reveal their sexual orientation to their colleagues or not. Indeed, much of the research in this area suggests that there is some variability in the degree of openness and disclosure at work; even if people are not out to everyone they meet, they may well have confided in one or two close colleagues. Nevertheless, there are some people who choose not to reveal their sexuality to anyone and remain hidden from view, and they do this for various different reasons: it may be the fear of harassment, or it might be for more physical reasons such as bullying or violence to property or person.

And if people do not disclose their minority sexual identity, they still have a sexual identity; they just have to manage it in a different way. This managing of one's public identity is called in Goffman's words the 'presentation of self'. In different situations and environments, and depending on whom individuals are with, people are expected to exhibit different forms of appropriate behaviour. As they finish one encounter or interaction and begin another one, they adjust their presentation of self in relation to what is demanded in that particular situation. Such a view is often thought to imply that an individual has as many selves as there are different contexts for interacting with people. On the other hand, it may mean that people take their values and ideals from the society around them, and change the way that they act and react in response to them, going on to express those same values in their performance, or presentation of self. Goffman uses a 1922 quotation by Cooley, which I will reproduce here in full, because I found it really useful in explaining why we, as human beings, present ourselves in certain ways. He talks about adopting a social, or subject, position which is different, or 'better', than the individual's self-identity, with a view to putting over to other people a professional or class identity:

> If we never tried to seem a little better than we are, how could we improve or train ourselves from the outside inward? And the same impulse to show the world a better or idealized aspect of ourselves finds an organized expression in the various profession and classes, each of which has to some extent a cant or pose, which its members assume, unconsciously for the most part, but which has the effect of a conspiracy to work upon the credulity of the rest of the world.
>
> (Cooley, 1922 in Goffman, 1969: 31)

Basically, then, the presentation of self as conceptualized by Goffman can be explained as putting on a show for other people, either where the individual is taken in by their own performance, or where they are deliberately trying to delude their audience. And deluding the audience might be in the interests of the audience, in the case of white lies, or not, where someone is telling the customer what they want to hear. These are two extremes, and reality will fall somewhere in between; the important idea here, however, is that the person which is presented to the audience is, in fact, a mask. It is the self we are striving to live up to, or the self we would like to be. The term performance refers to all the activity of an individual in front of a particular set of observers and which has some influence on those observers. This is the case whether or not we are talking about sexuality, although, of course it is particularly relevant to our discussion here of covering up minority sexuality.

Goffman described this performance as a 'front'. In the workplace, an individual may be required to present a front to be consistent with the image demanded by a particular profession. He gives the examples of surgeons or police officers to demonstrate this point; both of these professions have to carry out certain functions, perhaps not strictly necessary ones, in order for the audience to have faith that the individual actually belongs to that profession. For example, a police officer has to wear a uniform and make notes in a pocket book, whilst a surgeon has to wear a white coat. An individual's front is not always consistent, though; it is contingent on the role that the person is playing. Therefore, a person may present a different front at home, at work, or indeed in different situations in the work environment. This idea is apposite for sexual minorities, who may well separate work and home, and perform different identities, and display their front in a different way in each place. For example, during this research project, there were examples of managers who were out to their friends, but not at work, and also examples of police officers who were not out as gay at work, and not 'out' as police officers to their gay friends. Clearly, there is a risk in presenting a 'front', and the fear of being found out is an ever-present weight on the minds of gay people who are in the closet at work and, as previously mentioned, the effort that they put into maintaining this is draining and creates a vulnerability within them.

The ways that gay people express their 'front' have been described in two principal ways: covering and passing. The first of these, 'covering', is where gay men and lesbians do not signal their sexual orientation and are therefore often thought to be heterosexual. The individual simply does not disclose information. Olivier, a gay Frenchman working in London as a trader for the Alpha Bank told me:

> I'd never lied. If someone had asked me outright, I would never have said no, and I always had used gender non-specific language. I had not necessarily corrected somebody when they were wrong; I was very clear about that in myself – I wasn't going to come out, but I wasn't going to pretend I was straight. Coming out included somebody turning to me and saying, so what's your partner's name, and I answered it! And that was it!

Brad, the gay firefighter we heard from earlier explained what it was like for him in covering his minority sexuality in the fire service:

> Before I came out, it was very difficult. I don't do lies very well. I find it difficult to remember that I might have said something to one person and something else to another. I don't put up a front very well. I would just avoid talking about specific situations. If the conversation went towards the future, marriage, settling down, I would avoid it. I would lead it off into a different subject. The same if people were talking about the weekend, I would just say I went shopping. I felt very constrained, I wasn't myself and frustrated. I was working with about twenty or thirty people. There was one person who was obviously gay but wouldn't come out. His name was George and he was quite camp but tried to hide it. I knew that he was gay but he would never talk about it. I looked at him and thought I don't want to go down that road, I don't want to be like that in ten or twenty years time.

Covering is facilitated through 'institutional heterosexuality', which is a phenomenon where most people working for an organization assume that all their colleagues are heterosexual unless there is evidence to the contrary. Scott, a firefighter, had relocated from a different part of the United Kingdom, and his colleagues were very welcoming, trying to set him up with girls that they knew. One day, in an effort to be sociable, they called round to his flat, unannounced. He told me:

They always think there's a woman involved. A couple of guys came round to the flat one day, and my partner was in the flat, and – panic! What do I do now? I invited them in, and my partner was in one of the bedrooms on the computer, and he stayed in the bedroom. I pushed these guys into the living room. One guy went to the bathroom; not only did he not notice that there were two toothbrushes, he didn't notice that there were also two razors … It totally went over their heads.

Some gay people who cover may be ready to disclose their minority sexuality to their colleagues, but refrain from doing not because they fear the repercussions, but because they do not want the information to dominate every aspect of their work experience and to get in the way of their working relationships. In the following quotation from some research by Mintz and Rothblum in 1997, this lesbian university employee allowed her colleagues to believe that she was heterosexual:

> In terms of lesbian identity, the university culture was one of silence, and that was the model I followed. I found it particularly awkward not to do so because everyone at work knew me as straight and to change this perception would take what I thought to be a dramatic act.
>
> (Mintz and Rothblum, 1997: 7)

Kate, a police officer, met her partner at work, although she belonged to a different police force. She described to me what it was like not being out at work and not being able to tell her work colleagues about her relationship:

> Difficult. I had to refer to her as 'my friend'. I didn't feel able to say I was having a relationship with this woman. Because she lived away, the social activities at work never became a problem because I always went on my own, whereas occasionally I could have taken her, but that would have been too much. She wasn't out either and that would have been a problem for her as well.

Other people cover at work, because they don't see any point in coming out. Stew, a gay support officer working for the police said:

> It's always different when you have a partner basically, and as I'm on my own at the moment, it's more difficult to discuss my private life at work. My colleagues know that I've been out a number of times with someone. There are obviously things that I'm not talking about, but they must have sussed, just because of the way I am. The job that I do involves going out and meeting people and I don't want to come over as loud and brash. I want to come over as the organization demands.

The second of these two fronts is described as 'passing', where the individual, faced with potential discrimination, lies in order to be seen as heterosexual. In particular, the individual allows themselves to be seen as homosexual by one group of people, for example other homosexuals, but not by other groups, for example their work colleagues. Probably the most extreme case of passing, where people actually lie in order to be considered as heterosexual, was recounted to me by Jack, a police officer who presented a front at both work and home for many years. I met him in his home one day and, sitting at his kitchen table, he told me what it had been like not to be out to his colleagues, nor his wife:

> It was torment. I was tormenting myself, I suppose. But it wasn't like fifteen years ago I wanted to come out. I was in a different place in my life. It wasn't that I wasn't getting something I wanted. I was OK, but not as sorted as I am now.

Jack admitted that being gay had not really been an issue when he joined the police. At that stage, he had been having relationships with women and he was unsure in his own mind that he was actually gay. Now, he describes himself as having been gay all along, but at the time he says that he:

> wasn't out even to myself. Because of the whole denial thing, I was having sex with men, doing all the things you shouldn't do. I started worrying about it when there was more of a chance I was going to get recognized. That almost happened. The only people I had more than casual sex with wouldn't get my phone number and I travelled more than seventy miles away, keeping a barrier between work and anyone I was having sex with.

Jack continued to get into his car on his days off to have anonymous sex with men, and to do it so far away that he would not be recognized. And then something happened which was to change his life. Jack picks up the story again:

> My son was born. That was a very difficult time. It took a lot of sorting out. I split up with his mum before he was born. I was utterly confused. We now have a relationship that works and I see my son every week. During that time I was wandering around saying I've got to do something about this. I was still going away, driving seventy miles or more to have sex with men…

The way that Jack managed this situation with his friends and colleagues at work depended on who it was that asked, although he did not tell anyone the truth. He described the way that he interacted with other people:

> The answers they got were designed to tell them no more than I wanted to know. You become very good at it. Some I would say I'd just been away for the weekend. If you give them that dead answer they don't pry much further. Now I know who guessed. Those who did have an inkling didn't ask. I was thirty-three or thirty-four and they knew that I had a son.

Jack was perhaps unusual in that he did not confide in anyone. By his own admission, things were tough:

> I know there won't be anything tougher than getting through the three years after my son was born, and then dealing with the fact that I was gay and that I needed to do something about it. There was the point at which I said I'm coming out, but that was 12 months in the building up. I'm not one to rush into anything!

In Jack's case, a police officer who was not out at work, he preferred to put a good seventy miles between where he worked and where he had sex, for fear of being recognized by his work colleagues.

In 1989, Marny Hall, a well-known American academic and researcher on minority sexuality, wrote about a study of hers in which some lesbians brought 'dates' to office functions and even had separate house-warming parties for heterosexual colleagues and lesbian friends (Hall, 1989: 133). This is a practical example of the informing nature of the 'with' relationship that Erving Goffman refers to, which means that the social identity of those that the individual is with, informs the social identity of the individual themselves (Goffman, 1963b: 64). This was demonstrated empirically in my research as well: Charlie was a firefighter who explained that the culture of the fire service was such that he felt he had to pretend to be heterosexual, even if that meant bringing a decoy-date with him to social functions:

> The fire service is very close knit; everybody knows everybody else's business, and their very protective of you if they like you, and that extends to trying to find you a girlfriend or a wife, making sure you have a nice settled home life. So if you haven't got a girlfriend, they'll take it you can't get one, and they'll try to find one for you. That was quite often difficult. There was quite an active social life; at Christmas they'd be the dinner at [one place and then another]. It's a cruel term to use, but I'd wheel out the token women, an old school friend, and she'd come along to these events, so that she would detract from the issue and suspicion would then be removed. I felt I had to. I could pick up on the way people felt about gay people.

Russ, on joining the Rural Constabulary, decided to get himself a girlfriend to whom he eventually became engaged, to cover his tracks. He just came to the conclusion that, being in the police, he would have to conceal his orientation. As it was, he called the engagement off after six months because he 'knew it was wrong'. Shaun, also a police officer, amazingly decided to remain in the closet at work even though he lived with his partner in the same village of a few hundred people where his police station was located:

> I like [my station] very much and I didn't want to move. I was working with about ten people, two per shift. When I started, I tried to fit in. You'd drive up the road with your tutor and if he said 'look at her' I'd go 'yeah, yeah'

and you'd try to fit in. You'd test the water. I'd never go into somewhere and say I'm gay. On my first day it was the last thing on my mind. I've had a partner for nearly nine years who lives with me. It didn't bother me because I was coming home at the end of the day. I think of myself as quite a popular person, I just wanted to fit in and make sure that people liked me.

Harry, a trader working for Alpha Bank told me:

> I kept myself to myself and that was it. People did question whether I had a girlfriend and I lied quite a few times. I feel guilty about that now, but I didn't have the confidence to say that I was gay. Instead I said that I had girlfriends and stuff like that. There were only one or two people that the subject came up with, about the social life. Didn't come up that often. It was more to do with my own self-confidence and being gay; I wasn't 100 per cent comfortable with it. I wasn't out to very many people at all and I didn't want to come out to anybody else until I felt the confidence to tell. It was more to do with self-confidence and it wasn't anything specific to do with the Alpha Bank. I knew if I did with hindsight that the vast majority of people wouldn't have given a toss really.

Sexual minorities are in an almost unique position, as they can decide whether or not to come out based on the environment around them. Richard, a Civil Servant in the Micro Department, told me:

> I can't say that, I'm trying to think back, there were instances when people would say things and I was a bit of a coward and I wouldn't say anything. Occasionally those comments would make me think thank goodness I haven't told anybody. It's a very laddish culture.

And so, in his case, he listed to the banter going on around him and congratulated himself for not having come out at work. Similarly, Aaron, who started work in Beta Bank's international division, told me how he decided to remain in the closet at work:

> I then started this job in London with the international bank. It was different and when I first started there I was a little worried. I picked up fairly quickly that it wasn't the sort of place where I would come out. I didn't feel as comfortable, due to the people around me. I didn't notice any gay people there. There were more men and more older people. It was a bit of surprise, really. I wondered what it would be like and chatted to my partner about it. It's quite important to me not to lie to people and not to be dishonest, but there are different levels of avoiding the topic without lying about your sexuality.

Some of the people I talked to during this research were involved in passing at work and at home. One Civil Servant named Joe, who worked for the Delta

Department, told me that he only said he was bisexual because he was married; otherwise he considered himself to be gay. Additionally, he could not come out at work, because that would force him to come out as gay at home too, and he was not prepared to do that:

> I do say that I am bisexual, because I am happily married, although I would say it's more of a friendship than a relationship. We have two children. Being married it does put a block on you being more open and making it clear to other people. As you get older you do ask yourself whether you're living a lie. [Coming out] is not an option because of home. If I told people at work, then I would have to do something more constructive at home. It's easier not to address the problem than to try and do something about it.

In 1996, James M. Croteau, an American academic from Western Michigan University, who specializes in the scholarship of lesbian, gay and bisexual issues reviewed a number of previous quantitative studies: in two of them about 30 per cent of the lesbians interviewed did not think anyone at work knew about their sexuality. Marny Hall reminds us that even when there is no serious discrimination, the reasons why people choose not to come out at work are not surprising: anti-gay jokes; presumption of heterosexuality; and questions regarding when the person is getting married is a constant reminder of their difference, with the result that employees are constantly preoccupied with concealing this aspect of their lives. 'The process of concealment called for constant attention to every nuance of social interaction' (Hall, 1989: 129).

In my research I found that some people had some unusual information about themselves, which they did not disclose at work: for example, Will was a successful e-commerce professional who worked at Beta Bank and lived with his same-sex partner and his child. He told me:

> I was sent to work in Ashford, in Kent. But I lived in London with my partner and his daughter. I found it difficult to talk about the fact that I had childcare commitments. I was gone from the house for sixteen hours. It made the whole thing very difficult. It took me three years to tell Beta Bank that I had a child, to say that I had to work in London. They sent me to Swindon after Ashford because I still didn't feel as if I could say anything.

At other times, interviewees, such as Paula, a Civil Servant who worked for the Delta Department, recounted stories of passing at work, which suggested that other people at work may have guessed what her personal circumstances actually were, even if she denied them:

> I got into a relationship that lasted eighteen years on and off. I met her through the Civil Service, because we were both members of the Civil Service sports club. She was in the prison service, but not out at the time. She was a few years older than me and we weren't out at all, but we got a

house together and everybody must have known that we were gay. We were just friends and friends always get mortgages together, don't they! It was difficult in that I didn't have any problems with anybody at work, never encountered any prejudice or anything, and we had our own circle of friends, but it was difficult at work because you couldn't talk. What I actually got to resent in the end was that people would talk about their relationship openly, or 'God I couldn't get to sleep last night because he was snoring his head off'. I felt I couldn't do that. We pretended that we didn't sleep in the same bed, and that sort of thing, it was silly. It was quite some time before I came out at work. We were out to our friends, but I didn't come out at work until I was well into my twenties

Judith Butler, the feminist, lesbian academic, suggests in *Gender Trouble* that there is an unavoidable paradox in the 'speech act' of coming out. Sexual minorities, by remaining silent and in the closet, are invisible and lack power. Through the process of coming out, they become visible and are no longer silent, but they can still lack power because of the hegemonic relationship of what has been termed the homo–hetero binary. So therefore, coming out does not mean gaining power as such, merely changing the dynamic of the relationship. Sexual minorities may well remain the weaker partner in the homo–hetero societal relationship, but the reason is no longer silence; instead, it is the loss of control over discourse.

The next story, and the final vignette in this chapter, is about an Alpha Bank employee, a gay man, who is not out at work. Through this story we get an insight into the thought processes that an individual goes through in making the decision to become more engaged with the gay networking group, and therefore out to some people at the bank. It is extremely unusual to have access to stories of people who are not out at work, and even more so stories of where they have been outed. I was never told his name, but let us call him Phil. In this story, then, Phil has joined Alpha Bank as a graduate trainee. He was not out at work, but nevertheless wants to join the lesbian and gay network, and is persuaded by his colleague Rupert to put his name on the email circulation list of the network. He is warned that his name would be visible, but that without such visibility it would send the wrong signals around the organization about the network itself. Phil would not talk to me himself, although I asked if he would, and Rupert passed on my request, because he was so afraid of the potential repercussions, and after reading his story you can understand his reaction. Instead, Rupert told me the story as follows,

Phil was a little bit concerned about the email mailing list that we had within our group, because technically, anyone could just look up the groups name and see who the members of that group are. And we advised him before he put his name on, well, yes, technically, anyone could see who the members of the network were, if they wanted to. We could have made it a secret group, but what message does it send out to everyone else, if the members of the group themselves aren't prepared to be out? And then Phil said 'OK I'll go on the group mailing list'. Soon afterwards, he came back to his workplace one afternoon, and realized that his colleagues, and his direct manager, thought that for a bit of fun they would look up to see who was in the gay group at Alpha Bank. He was standing behind them, and they were scrolling down the list of names, and then, all of a sudden, they stumbled on Phil's name. There was an awkward silence and a long pause. Then the ribbing started and there was some dreadful language used to his face. He didn't know what to do – his direct manager was involved with the horseplay, the gestures and the joking-around. He was new to the organization and didn't feel comfortable ... ultimately he had to live with the group and didn't want to make a fuss. And so since then, he has just let it die a quiet death.

This story is a good example of the way that stories can self-deconstruct. When the incident happened it was the manager who had the power over Phil and, indeed, abused his position of power and trust; however, in the retelling of the story, he is demeaned as the sympathy of the listener is with Phil and his plight. Interestingly, although this story is told by Rupert, who is a gay man himself, and therefore someone who potentially should be able to understand the dynamics of workplace bullying, the words he actually used were 'horseplay, gestures and joking-around' – the word 'bullying' is absent from Rupert's account. Also absent is any suggestion of a formal complaint. Rupert almost makes reference to this, but stops short of actually saying this; after he said 'did not feel comfortable', his voice tailed off and he paused. Clearly making a formal complaint, or any suggestion that this might have been the course of action, would have been very serious in their organization. Instead, having thought about his words, he said that Phil did not want to 'make a fuss'. Clearly, his unwillingness to make a fuss helped to keep the incident in the private domain.

In Phil's story, agency, or the ability of the individual to control events, clearly does not belong to the individual; the example is illustrative of the Foucauldian approach to discourse theory, supported by the critical school, who reject human agency as a determining influence and decentre the human subject. Indeed, as Foucault states: 'discourse is not life; its time is not yours' (Foucault, 1991: 71). This story also illustrates what Judith Butler describes as power understood as the divine power of naming (Butler, 1997: 32), where Phil becomes gay for the first time in the eyes of his colleagues as they call him gay, and he has no power to refute the accusation. The performative act of naming him as gay is supported by the evidence of the email list, in front of everyone's eyes.

In summary, then, it is clear from these stories that not being out at work is not merely an absence of information. Every day, sexual minorities are putting effort and energy into covering and passing in order to avoid what they perceive to be the negative consequences of coming out. From these stories it is also clear that people will go to extraordinary lengths not to admit their true sexuality to

LIVERPOOL JOHN MOORES UNIVERSITY
LEARNING SERVICES

other people, and sometimes to themselves. However, most of these people, and others that I interviewed, did eventually come out to their colleagues at work. This act of disclosure is a crucially defining feature of the work experience of sexual minorities, and one that many people do not have to go through. In the next chapter, I will discuss the dynamics of coming out, and look at more stories from people who have gone through this at work.

4 Coming out at work

Coming out is an act of self-disclosure, specifically the act of disclosing previously undisclosed minority sexual identity, and one which has received much attention in the literature on sexual minorities in the workplace. It is a subject which continues to command interest and attention; in 1991, Eve Kosofsky Sedgwick asserted that: 'gay uncovering seems if anything heightened in surprise and delectability, rather than staled, by the increasingly intense atmosphere of public articulations' (Sedgwick, 1991: 67).

And yet, the issue here is not just about the disclosing of information that was previously withheld. Coming out is a process with a number of different aspects to it that have resonance for the individual. In many cases, the individual makes a choice to come out, perhaps considered over a long time, even years, choosing the time and the place as well as the person to tell. Sometimes the individual has no choice at all and is outed. In any case, coming out is a reiterated act and one characterized by the continual performance of out identity. This chapter looks at this sociological phenomenon of gay men and women coming out in the workplace through their stories.

In 1999, research by Jill Humphrey, published in the journal *Gender, Work & Organization*, looked at organizational dynamics for lesbians and gay men in public sector occupations, and her research suggested that there are three reasons why people decide to come out at work: first, the respondents felt that it was an issue of honesty and integrity at the personal level; second, they felt that there were significant benefits in building open relationships at the professional level; and finally, there were respondents who thought it was important to educate colleagues about sexual minorities.

In the 1996 piece of research led by American academic Karen Boatwright, where ten gay women in a variety of occupations were interviewed, the respondents suggested that coming out was an important experience; one of them said that she had 'captured something' that had previously been 'denied'. The coming out process was also described as a second adolescence, but because they were older, they had better coping strategies. Woods and Lucas described in their research about how gay men often speak of coming out as the final frontier, as if it were the final destination on a long, arduous journey. Coming out is indeed a process of disclosing something that has previously been hidden, but it is more than that; it is part of fashioning a lesbian or gay self that did not exist before coming out began. In other words, being gay or lesbian is not a truth that is discovered, it is a performance which is enacted.

Although much of the lesbian and gay literature has focused on the disclosure decision taken by the individual, there is less research on the response from others in the organization to sexual difference. In Humphrey's study, twenty-three lesbian and gay individuals in public sector jobs were interviewed, and some of them recounted the reactions from other people when they came out at work, including avoidance and lack of acceptance. Of course, with actual discrimination being common, and the fear of potential discrimination epidemic, it is easy to think that the response to difference is always a negative one, which is not always the case.

So, is coming out subject to a choice on the part of the individual? The question of agency, or choice, in the act of coming out is an interesting one; in Butler's account of performativity, the individual is conditioned by discourse and does not allow for agency or free will on the part of the individual. The stories in this section do, in fact, to a greater or lesser extent, help to illustrate the point that agency resides less with the individual than might be thought intuitively. In one story, the gay person is put in an invidious position where they have to come out as an act of resistance; in Butler's words: 'the injurious effects of discourse become the painful resources by which a resignifying practice is wrought' (Butler, 1993: 224).

While the decision to come out may be fraught with difficulty, the moment may be thrust upon individuals, and they can even be 'outed' by their colleagues, being put in a situation where they have no choice at all.

Discourse in the work context has two important elements to it: talk and social practice, and it is interesting to see that the act of coming out actually brings these two elements together. John Austin was a British philosopher and linguist whose work formed the basis for work by later philosophers such as Foucault and Butler. He talked about the importance of recognizing the importance of certain types or moments of speech that produce certain effects as their consequence. He made the difference between speech and social practice, on the other hand, which is an act or action which produces certain effects as its consequence. An example of social practice without any language or speech involved, in this research, would be the social practice of firefighters showering together; this encouraged a gay firefighter to remain in the closet. However, Austin brought these two concepts together and defined speech acts as moments of speech which do what they say, at the same time as saying it, a concept that was later taken up by Butler. This is well illustrated by the act of coming out as it actually brings these two elements of speech and action together.

Of course, the act of coming out itself is important, particularly to the individual. However, almost as important is the discursive response of others to the act of coming out. This response can take either the form of speech or social practice. Before coming out there is a dissonance between the self-identity, where the individual knows that they have a minority sexuality, and the social identity where the individual chooses not to reveal this to others. This reintegration is not always a positive move, because the eventual impact on social identity is so dependent on the reaction from others. In other words, coming out may increase individual self-esteem, but the reality is that reactions and context have a major impact on the individual.

Although many gay people choose not to reveal their sexual orientation at work, a study by Day and Schoenrade in 1997 found that homosexual employees who are more open about their orientation are also more likely to feel psychologically committed to their current organization as well as experiencing less conflict. They also found that this was likely to be real commitment, rather than a sense of being stuck in the organization. Nevertheless, the decision to come out is one of the most important career decisions faced by gay employees and one that many others do not have to make. During the research process, some themes have recurred and become prominent. One of these was the significance of coming out for the individual and the benefits that they accrued through this process. When asked to describe what it was like coming out, most interviewees described it 'the high point' of their careers. Jonathon, an employee of the Delta Department told me about when he came out:

> My defining moment was, I think, when I was able to come out completely. I brought my partner to the Christmas party, which to me was completely unheard of, and there were no repercussions of any sort. It gave me enough confidence to really get into my work. To the point where I was one of the best workers in the office and it got me promotion in the end.

Jonathon talked about the level of his confidence improving; this is consistent with the view that the uncovering of silence is constitutive of a positive gay identity. He was not alone in describing his 'defining moment' at work as his coming out, but it is important to remember that it does not always signal an empowering move.

Disclosing undisclosed subjectivity

The management of one's identity in the workplace, either through covering one's minority sexual identity or through passing as heterosexual, logically leads to a further possibility; that of disclosing the information to other people. And by voluntarily disclosing the information, the individual transforms themselves from someone with potentially discreditable information to manage, to someone with uneasy social situations to negotiate.

The decision to come out cannot be taken lightly, and there are a whole host of concerns to be considered. For example, there is the level of homophobia in the workplace, or even in the industry, the attitude of colleagues towards lesbians and gay men, and how they are treated. One person at Alpha Bank told me:

People that I'm right now working with, I would imagine that if I went and I asked them do you know I am gay, the answer would probably be no. The majority. And I think that's their own ignorance and lack of just assuming I'm straight, you know that heterosexism and stuff. It's not even that it's a homophobic environment or anything, I live my life, if people ask me what I did on the weekend, I tell them. It's not as if I have tried to hide it at all, it's just that they haven't raised it. I just find it interesting, because this is the longest I've gone without people knowing.

The following story comes from the fire service and it is well known that this is a hostile environment for gay men. There are also more personal considerations, such as the individual's confidence to challenge homophobia, or the way that they are going to respond to colleagues once they have come out. Andy was only recently qualified as a firefighter when I spoke to him and his memories of training school were still fresh in his mind. He did not want to tell anybody that he was gay when he was at training school. He was new to the fire service and, besides, as Andy put it himself, 'I'd only known everyone about ten weeks. I've got enough grief here just trying to get through.' Facilities in the fire service can be quite basic to say the least. At a time when many public gyms and swimming baths are offering individual changing facilities, the fire service still expects its firefighters, male and female, gay and straight, to get undressed in front of one another, and so perhaps it should have been no surprise when Andy described the male showers at the training school which were 'a bit antiquated, just one big tiled wall, with shower heads coming out, so it was very open and exposed'. And the changing room was hardly much better, 'just one big room with benches around'. Real or imagined, the way in which colleagues react to people once they have come out is a fear which has to be managed and, in Andy's case, he 'didn't really need the added grief of people all walking out of the shower'. Whether or not they would actually have done that is a moot point; the fear of them doing that clearly affected his confidence in coming out at work. Andy picks up the rest of the story:

So I thought I'd just leave it and if anyone asks, I'd tell them. We then had two weeks training in breathing apparatus, we finished that and started on the final training. At lunchtime I walked into the lockers where all the other lads were sitting and someone started whistling the theme tune from Police Academy, the one they played when they were in a gay bar called the Blue Oyster Club. I walked in, I sat down and they stopped. I thought – don't be paranoid, obviously there's a joke going on, you've walked in the middle of it, and you think it's all about you. That Friday, I was in the changing rooms, just cleaning my shoes, and this guy comes in and he's pacing up and down, and I could tell he wanted to say something and he couldn't. He kept trying to talk to me and he couldn't. It became blindingly obvious to me what he wanted to ask me, and it's a bit sad really, but I found it quite funny because he was finding it so difficult; hey, there are only a few perks you get when you come out. So eventually I turned round and said, 'What do you want to ask me?' The other chap replied, 'I can't say' so I said, 'The answer's yes.'

In order to come out a gay man or lesbian must say or do something, which will disclose that information to others; as Woods and Lucas have pointed out, silence on the subject constitutes an implicit claim to be heterosexual. And yet, even if the individual wants to come out, there may be circumstances or elements of the working environment, which might discourage them from doing so. Andy's story is an example of one such environment in the fire service where the close living conditions and communal facilities made it difficult for him as a gay man to be visible.

Andy's story also shows how social practice and physical arrangements can have an effect on identity, even though they may not be strictly part of the coming out process. The fact that firefighters showered together in his training school at that time has an impact on his readiness to come out at work. He was afraid of their reaction and as he says, he 'didn't really need the added grief of people all walking out of the shower because I was in there'. The other, presumably heterosexual, firefighters are the ones with the power in this story, even though it has not been exercised; they have the potential power to walk out of the showers and create the embarrassment. But the story also shows how power can be reversed; in the coming out scene, Andy's colleague wanted to ask about his sexual orientation but was too embarrassed to do so, stumbling over his words, wanting to ask whether Andy was gay or not and pacing up and down because he was too embarrassed to ask. And then, by saying 'the answer's yes', Andy performed the act of coming out; by saying the words, he had also performed the deed, demonstrating John Austin's point about words and deeds coming together in the 'speech act'. Judith Butler described the same phenomenon as 'performativity'. However, I believe that coming out in the fire service, which is a very hostile environment on the whole for lesbians and gay men is not only performative; it is also introduces Foucault's concept of parrhesia, where an individual admits to information and it is potentially damaging for them to do so. By coming out, the individual is knowingly putting themselves in an inferior position, even perhaps at risk. Andy's coming out in the fire service was potentially dangerous, involving a risk to himself, but also this was a statement which had the potential of hurting or angering his interlocutor, (Foucault, 2001: 17). When John Austin, Jacques Derrida and Judith Butler talk about performance, they all give the example of the priest declaiming the marriage vows as an example of the speech act bringing speech and action into one. Coming out is not the same kind of performance as the much quoted marriage vows, because the latter involves no risk and symbolizes the approbation of society and invites the participants into a range of significantly enhanced lifestyle benefits, whilst the former, the act of coming out, involves significant risk to the individual, and in the act actually exclude themselves from many of the benefits that society has to offer. Coming out can be an act of fearless speech, and whilst sexual identity may be performative, coming out is perhaps better understood as an example of parrhesia.

In any case, Andy's being in the closet, keeping his sexual identity hidden from view was for a variety of reasons; fear of harassment, bullying and physical violence. But overall, the decision not to reveal his sexuality was driven by the physical environment, that is to say the communal showers, and the perceived fear of what might happen if his colleagues were to find out that he was gay. In a less formal setting, such as a sports centre, for example, the choice might be taken not to shower to avoid potential embarrassment. Given that this is at work, however, and that the type of work means there is a regular need for showering, it is not an option to avoid taking a shower altogether. There are other aspects of the physical arrangements in fire stations which make coming out difficult; rest areas are equipped like dormitories and the beds are made with sheets and blankets. Although these are officially only rest areas, and firefighters should be clothed in order to respond in the fastest possible time, it is not uncommon for firefighters to treat them as proper dormitories and undress completely. Gay firefighters have described how they are concerned how others will react when they find out that they are gay; will they change their behaviour? Will their colleagues stop undressing to go to bed? Or will they, as gay men, be banned from the dormitory altogether? One of the focus group participants suggested that it is easier for gay white men than for other minorities because they can choose whether or not to be out at work. For example, one straight firefighter in the Shire Fire Service said:

> Gay groups have got an advantage. They have two ways of going, haven't they? You can be gay, or you can keep it to yourself. The hoo-ha with the deputy in Manchester; he was dead right. Absolutely dead right. It was easier for him to do what he wants as a gay white male, than as an Asian or a female.

This person was referring to an incident where the deputy chief fire officer in the Manchester Fire Service apparently lost his job because he allegedly said that he would rather be gay than black in the fire service.

However, this person then went on to suggest why gay people might have difficulties when they come out at work:

> The reason they have a harder time with the bigots when they do come out is that they know that there has been a secret that has been kept. Would you trust someone who had kept a secret away from you that had worked with you for ten years? And suddenly let you in on that secret? If I worked with you though and then turned round and said, oh by the way, I'm gay . . .

This then introduced an exchange of views amongst the watch, or shift, on why gay people might not be totally open at work. One person said that 'It'd be a shock', whilst another firefighter maintained that 'if you've known someone for ten years, it shouldn't affect the friendship'. The rest of the exchange went like this:

'You can't dislike someone 'cos they've kept something from you'

'I think that's a bit naïve'

'During that time you could have been asked to be my best man, god-father to my children, and then after all that time you say you're gay...'

'It's the same principle as a little white lie; and you've got to tell a lot of little white lies.'

'If you are visibly a minority group you're relationship will be maintained – they will either love you or hate you. The problem you have is if you're gay, no one knows until you want them to know. The problem comes when you make assumptions, and then you admit to not being heterosexual and some people are going to have the reaction – why didn't you tell me before?'

'Don't you think it's because it's relatively new?'

'It is, and even if you're happy with them coming out your relationship will change...'

'...Gays would make great spies because they inhabit a secret world.'

The fire service is an organization which has many signs and symbols, although, of course, it is not the only organization which has them. Examples of these symbols include: the uniform, representing the semi-disciplined service; the sirens and fire engines, representing the emergency response aspect of the service; the clearly visible fire stations, representing the high public profile that the service enjoys. These different symbols have an impact on minority sexual identity. The work environment also creates situations in which heterosexuals can show how uncomfortable they feel around homosexuals. The following extract is from a focus group made up of straight firefighters on a watch in the fire service:

'Something that's interesting for me, that takes it away from the emotional side, is the physical arrangements, the shower blocks and things. You have separate showers for males and females because there's the potential for physical relationships, so shouldn't there be similar arrangements for lesbians and gay men? It's a potential environment for mutual attraction.'

'You'd be worried about showering with him, because he'd be watching your arse. You'd feel a bit uncomfortable with it.'

'The same potential is there if you are showering males and females together, so therefore there should be some kind of sensible control measure in place that protects the privacy of the individuals. Same for the gay man; the group hasn't said that they're gay.'

'Couldn't have separate facilities for gay men through, could you, because you'd have to have separate facilities for every gay man.'

'If we have to do it, we have to do it, same with sleeping accommodation. We are one of the only services that do that. In the forces they have separate accommodation. It's about personal space isn't it?'

The comments suggest that the issue is as much about straight men feeling that they are under the gaze of gay men, as it is about temptation and mutual attraction. Because there are separate showering facilities for men and women, and that one of the reasons is to prevent mutual attraction, one respondent thought the same principle should be applied to mutual attraction between men.

Firefighters themselves recognized that the specific working environment of the fire service not only changed their behaviour, but made it more difficult for them:

It's more difficult for us in the fire service, because you are in a very closed environment – you're sleeping together in the same environment, shower, wash, cook and eat. In most working environments you sit at your desk and then you go.

Some respondents identified difficulties with addressing this issue. One problem was around how many different facilities you need. For example, should there be a third set of showers and changing rooms for gay men? Should there be individual facilities for lesbians and gay men? Or should everyone have the right to privacy when showering and changing? Another issue was around the number of people who have to get showered and changed, making individual facilities difficult to implement. However, many respondents felt that the real issue was about privacy and personal dignity at work for everyone, and that no one should have to change and shower in public if it makes them feel uncomfortable. For example, this is a short exchange that took place in the headquarters focus group at Shire Fire Service:

'I think it's more a female thing – women don't, and some men don't and I think the reality is that if you're a sexuality minority or not, do people feel comfortable getting changed in a communal changing room? The issues are that if we feel that people don't feel comfortable, then we should change the facilities for everybody.'

'If we have to do it, we have to do it; the same with sleeping accommodation. We are one of the only services that do that. In the forces they have separate accommodation. It's about personal space isn't it?'

The question that this discussion raises is: what does it matter? What are the implications? Is it just about personal dignity, or does it have further implications for the effectiveness of the fire service. Some respondents thought that there were further implications and the following quotation describes how these facilities might be a barrier to men and women joining:

It's things about propriety and personal dignity that are barriers to men, women and any sexuality joining the services like the fire service, because they know they are going to be put in an uncomfortable position, they are not going to like it, and they are not going to join. It is only those people who don't care who are going to join anyway, irrespective of their gender or sexuality.

There is often a difference between the way that firefighters behave on the fire-ground and that way they behave as a watch when they are back at the station. There is a physical sign or symbol, which represents the barrier: the fire bell. As soon as the fire bells ring, the firefighters are focused on getting to the scene of the incident. When they are responding to an incident they are focused on doing their job, and putting the fire out, if the incident is a fire. Only when the incident is over, and they receive the instruction to return to the station, do they return to the normal life of the firefighter which consists of a lot of hanging around. Why is there so much hanging around in the fire service? Well, unlike a bank's call centre, where we are quite used to being put on hold and being told that all the bank's operatives are busy, we could not have a permanently busy fire service. We would not want to ring 999 only to be told that the fire service were out on another job! So, they hang around at the fire station for an incident to occur. And it is during this time that there is a lot of opportunities for banter, ribbing and horseplay, a regular feature of life on a watch. This is particularly linked to the passive waiting for something to happen, as opposed to the active service when there is an incident or an emergency; symbols are needed to highlight the transition.

The following quotation from a firefighter in another group in a Shire Fire Service watch explains this:

People from minority groups use these policies and procedures for their own gain; they know that when they come to places like this. If the wrong thing is said, they have a big stick in the back pocket. Females, I think, one or two of them will have had a rough ride, but others have definitely taken advantage.

[...]

There's still banter on an incident.

[...]

There are two different areas of work – there's in here and then there's when the bells go down; that's when you really got to work. You don't know where you're going or what you're going to. When you get there you decide what the level of severity it is, somebody dying or injured for example, and there's never any consideration as to gender or race, not from my point of view. And I've never heard it from anybody, not in my service. And then you come back here, although you're working here you're also working together that's when the problems start, when you're on your stand down period. You would speak to your friends differently than you would to your wife, if you're married, or your mother; some men don't swear in front of their wife, but they swear in front of their friends. Especially on nights, you live, rather than work together.

[...]

I find your question an interesting one; you sometimes see on TV a fire where someone's died and you'll see a policeman or a firefighter having a laugh and a joke, and it's a shame but that's just how we deal with it.

The response to difference is therefore at variance in the two different spaces. In the fire station, which is not necessarily viewed as a workplace per se by firefighters, there is a lot of 'hanging around' as firefighters wait for an incident to happen. The response to difference in this 'space' is potentially hostile and is made up of banter and horseplay. If bullying is going to happen, this is when and where it is assumed it is going to happen. The fire bell then moves people from the casual, informal banter time to a different 'space', where the focus is on performance, where all differences are put aside and getting the job done overrides all else. The fire bell is therefore a way of regulating time and space and interaction. The experience of being gay is different in each zone. The fire bell is the link between the passive waiting which typifies much of the job of the firefighter and the active role of responding to an incident. The active 'space' is one which typifies inclusion and teamwork; there is no distinction between firefighters, as they are all focused on getting the job done. However, in the 'passive' space there are many opportunities for exclusion, which is felt particularly by sexual minorities. The passive space is a time for social activities of various sorts; playing pool, basketball and, of course, eating. In the following example, a gay firefighter tells of stories he has heard, where lesbians and gay men are excluded from eating together:

> I do know of cases where people have been totally and utterly excluded. From silly things like eating facilities – people would refuse to eat with individuals – they would order food from a Chinese restaurant or Indian and the gay man or lesbian wouldn't be asked to order anything. There would be social activities that the person wouldn't be included in; all those things lead to massive exclusion and massive psychological damage with the individual involved. You might be strong-willed enough not to let it bother you, probably have your own life when you go home anyway. But that working environment gets to you eventually.

Sharing a laugh and a joke is an important survival mechanism for those in mundane jobs and, ironically, despite the image that Hollywood films like *Backdraft* and TV programmes like *London's Burning* would portray, the job of a firefighter is mundane a lot of the time. The fire service has traditionally been a semi-disciplined service with restrictions on the freedom that firefighters have to do or say what they want; in this context, humour allows them the licence to say things that otherwise could not be said. Usually, 'respecting difference' is understood as meaning respecting minorities. However, I found that, in the fire service in particular, this can also mean respecting those who are prejudiced or homophobic. There was a widely held view amongst the firefighters in these focus groups that prejudice should be accommodated. That is not to say prejudice in the sense of discriminatory behaviour; their views were quite firm that this should be dealt with seriously. The kind of prejudice that firefighters believe should be accommodated is where a firefighter has a problem working with a gay person. An example of this view is as follows:

> The management have got a duty to keep everybody happy; if someone's got a problem with a gay person, they can go to their boss and say 'I'm not happy with this, can I transfer to another watch?' I think the manager has a duty to try and accommodate that person.

One view went so far as to suggest that when people are appointed to work on a particular station, they should be made aware if there are any out gay people there, so that the new recruit can refuse if they do not find working with gay people acceptable.

> You have to make people coming in aware that there is a gay person on the station; If someone's overtly gay, you could be putting someone in who doesn't like gays but has been put in under false pretences.

Above all, if someone holds homophobic views and refuses to work with lesbian and gay colleagues, the straight firefighters in the Shire Fire Service felt that they should not be made to feel embarrassed about holding these views: 'If he can't work with them because they're gay and it's upsetting him, he should ask for a transfer, but he shouldn't be made to feel embarrassed about it because that's his personal view.'

These views are contentious, and yet paradoxical. On the one hand, minorities are seen as needing protection from the majority's actions and reactions, and ultimately legislative solutions are seen as being a clear route to achieving this. However, even laws cannot counteract hostile feelings, only hostile acts. These views are paradoxical because they express the liberal 'problem', which is that by giving freedom for some to express their minority sexual identity, others are given less freedom to express or even hold views hostile to that particular identity. Of course, part of the problem of seeing these opinions as innately wrong is that sexual minorities are then constantly cast in the role of victim, and puts the responsibility for change on the shoulders of others. This raises the question of whether tolerance should indeed go both ways.

Choosing the time and place

The French post-structuralist philosopher, Jacques Derrida, deconstructed John Austin's approach to speech and action and the performative uses of language; Derrida maintained that to be properly performative, language must be serious and intentional. If, in the example of the wedding ceremony, one of the most well-known and most often quoted examples of performativity, the vows were said by an actor, or as a joke, the language would no longer have the same meaning or power, and would be 'void'. The same would apply to the place of the wedding ceremony; even though we are becoming more and more used to unusual places for commitment ceremonies to take place, there is something more serious and meaningful about licensed premises. In the same way, if coming out is announced without some serious intent, then the statement will be empty. Woods and Lucas also suggest that there has to be a 'frame', in terms of time and place, for coming out; without such a frame, others will see the act of coming out as puzzling. For example: 'the idea of going up to someone and bluntly stating 'I'm gay' without further elaboration will elicit laughter from a lesbian or gay audience' (Woods and Lucas, 1993: 174).

To be truly performative, the act has to have some serious intent behind it, such as a gesture of friendship, a political demand, or framing personal disclosure as a matter of integrity. The form of disclosure is crucial, as the way that people come out and reveal the information to their colleagues will influence the way in which their colleagues will relate to them. Sexual minorities cannot always freely take the decision to come out and whilst some people will have the opportunity to give careful thought to it, others will have the situation thrust upon them. Many sexual minorities will be able to assess the prevailing organizational climate before disclosing their sexual orientation. Because being lesbian, gay or bisexual is an invisible aspect of diversity, it is possible for sexual minorities to sample prevailing opinion, as if they were heterosexual, before they come out; it is a recognized phenomenon that people react differently around visible minorities, and their colleagues would not behave in the same way if they were 'out' or visible. This is the case for many serving police officers who have chosen not to disclose their minority sexual identity to their work colleagues, as they work in a corporate culture which is still, in many cases, hostile to gay men and women.

But, of course, not taking part sometimes just fuels the rumour machine. Someone who chooses not to go down the pub with the lads after work, or perhaps does not join in with the office banter about the latest Chelsea game has committed a big enough act of heresy that his colleagues will label him 'gay'. Stefan was just such a police officer, conscientious, hard-working but ultimately unwilling to enter into the banter that went on in the office and on the streets with his colleagues. Stefan told me:

> I didn't take part in the banter that goes on. It's a very macho culture, very bawdy, so you get these guys leering out of the windows of the van, making sexist comments, you know, real Neanderthal, early man type behaviour. Because I didn't take part, it just reinforced the rumour that I must be gay, not making comments about so-and-so's tits.

He was labelled gay, but it was only a rumour. No one knew for certain at that stage since he had not come out to his work colleagues. But that did not stop his colleagues starting down a path of the most appalling bullying behaviour. Stefan again:

> Then things started happening; I had some damage to my locker, some minor damage, some people put some stickers on my locker, abusive stickers. And then you know those forms where you have to present your driver's documents and driver's licence? They're self carbonating and someone had written on it with a pen top or the back end of a pencil or a pen, so the top copy appeared clean. I stopped a motorist and wrote the top copy out, tore it off and there was 'dirty faggot' written underneath. That happened a few times. And I had things through the internal despatch, things about AIDS. A couple of people had refused to work with me, on the grounds that they were Catholics, and their religion prohibited it, but they hadn't come to me about it. They went to one of the sergeants and asked for their duties to be changed because they were due to be posted in a vehicle with me. What is even more bizarre is that I happen to be a Catholic as well!

One of the issues here, apart of the serious level of homophobic bullying taking place inside the police force, is a wider issue about choosing the moment to come out; often, someone will gradually make the choice to come out and will not only choose the moment, but also the person. At other times it is not always a considered act and there is sometimes no choice involved at all. Sometimes, the act of coming out is in response to teasing, or even bullying. In Stefan's story, the teasing or bullying was of a very serious nature and was beginning to impinge, not only on his quality of work, but also on his wanting to stay in the police altogether. And so, in response to all this bullying he was left with the decision of what to do about it. He continued with his story as follows:

> It got to the point where I was trying to make a decision about whether or not to stay in the police. I made a decision to speak to my chief inspector; the options were either a full investigation, which would be like a witch hunt, or to speak to the team and tell them the rumours were true.

Stefan rejected the chief inspector's idea of a full investigation of the wrongdoing, and decided that the best course of action was to come out to the whole shift:

> The following Thursday, about three in the morning, we had a team meeting. I was first on the agenda! And the subject was all the things that had happened to me. There were about forty people there: the Inspector, four or five sergeants and about thirty PCs. Everyone had their heads hung quite low.

It is quite interesting how the hierarchy is reversed at this point in the story; the whole shift, which include the bullies, was forced to sit there with their heads bowed as they listen to their gay colleague:

> They knew what was going on. It was nerve-wracking. It was absolutely horrendous, to have to justify yourself in front of forty-five people. And you're an agenda item! Your sexual orientation is top of the agenda for a team meeting! It is quite bizarre. They were shocked to bits. So I told the team and then I went up to the canteen to wait; it was horrible, like waiting for an exam or something. Then one by one people came up, the women first, to say it was OK.

The way the story is told, it sounds as if the shift was saying that it was OK to be gay, almost as if they are giving permission for him to express his minority sexuality. Stefan does not say whether they apologized for their appalling behaviour, either for carrying out the bullying, or the bystanders allowing it to go on. The silent voice in this story is that of the bystander, the person who allowed this bullying to go on. Bullies usually carry out their terrible deeds with the full knowledge of the people around them, and they are only successful in their endeavours because no one tries to stop them.

This story of coming out also illustrates the performative nature of coming out, as it involves a performative declaration. The concept of performativity emphasizes that much of language consists of performative utterances where discourse becomes social practice, or, in other words, talk becomes action.

Stefan subsequently had further difficulties in the police, which made the type of bullying described in this story look very mild indeed. Nevertheless, he has stayed with the organization and, at the time of writing, he has been promoted to the rank of Inspector, and this demonstrates perhaps above all else the passionate feelings that some people have for the organizations they work for, which carry them through all types of adversity.

Humour in the workplace is a recognized phenomenon, and an alternative reading of this story could suggest practical jokes. Putting stickers on someone's locker or writing in a self-carbonating 'fine' book are presumably variants of practical jokes that are carried out all the time on unsuspecting new recruits. Of course, in this case, the locker stickers were abusive and the words written in the fine book were 'dirty faggot'. The dividing line between horseplay and homophobic bullying, as in this case, can be quite fine.

Interestingly, Stefan's story was reflected in reality during the research project, when it was presented to a focus group of police officers in the Rural Constabulary. It just so happened to be their team meeting at the beginning of a shift. The police officers themselves identified how ironic it was that whilst the story was about the idea of sexuality being an agenda item in a team briefing, here they were again sitting in a team briefing discussing sexuality. Generally, in police focus groups, the reaction to this story was generally one of disbelief. One focus group participant's suggestion was that the details of the story were a 'magnification' of the truth, saying that the story described 'some of the sort of petty snipes that are coming at the individual'. Indeed, this person said that 'it'd be naïve to say that those sorts of things didn't happen, but I think it's been ... I'd like to think it's a magnification'. This was not the view of all people who heard the story, however. A good number of police focus group participants actually recognized that these sorts of things went on, 'I think to the contrary, rather than being magnified, I think if the full story were told, I think there'd be a lot more; I have been aware of similar incidents.'

One, perhaps overly honest, participant in the police focus groups in the Rural Constabulary suggested that the way that sexual minorities are treated in the police has vastly improved in recent years. Now, it is only sniping and verbal abuse rather than physical attack, which used to take place years ago. He said:

> the focus has changed in the last 20 years – as an ex-serviceman we used to deal with gays in a far more physical manner than we do today. It's more sniping today than physical attack and extermination. We used to be quite brutal.

It is rather shocking that this individual has used the word 'extermination' for the way in which sexual minorities were treated in the past; they were physically attacked, presumably with the aim of getting rid of them altogether. Indeed, another focus group participant continued on the same theme and confirmed that it was grounds to be dismissed from the police force altogether. Of course, this sort of treatment was not reserved for sexual minorities; women also used to get some rough treatment as well, based solely on their gender regardless of their sexual orientation. One woman in the police focus groups, a former police officer herself, recalled an example of the initiation ceremonies that would be reserved for women in the police force:

> WPCs used to be tipped upside down to find out whether they were wearing suspenders or tights ... Not in relation to homosexuality but still. It's disappearing. You have to go back some time for people to recall incidents of that kind.

As an interesting aside, it is probably worth mentioning that this example itself is not an isolated incident; while writing this book, I was talking to a colleague who had carried out some focus groups in a totally different force on the subject of gender and women's experiences and had heard the very same story, over twenty-five years ago! And, in this case, although the majority of focus group participants had a great deal of sympathy for the suffering that Stefan had gone through, others were less sympathetic and were of the view that this sort of treatment from one's colleagues helps to harden the individual for when they have to go and deal with the public.

The focus group described the concept that bullying of gay people is a valve to let off steam; of course, just as a valve is a device to allow movement in one direction only, resistance is not welcome, and you are supposed, as a lesbian or gay police officer, sponge-like, to soak up the stress of your heterosexual colleagues. There is an assumption that when they say that this 'horseplay' is to relieve the stress from seeing terrible things that it is only the heterosexual majority who see terrible things and that the gay minority do not. Some focus group participants maintained that things are getting better in the police and the type of bullying that was described in the story could have happened ten years ago, but not now. Others were not so sure.

One former woman police officer exclaimed:

> My reaction is – what a wimp! How did he manage on the streets if he couldn't take this sort of thing from his colleagues? I'm an ex-police officer and I served for eight years in the 1980s (WPC), this is behaviour that went on, but you just laughed it off, because it's policemen's humour. We see some awful things, but there has to be a valve to let it off. I know it's not politically correct any more, but you give as good as you get and I think he's making a big fuss about nothing. Making himself into a martyr because he's labelled 'gay'. I've been a WPC – I know what it's like to be a victim, both from members of the public and fellow colleagues. You give as good as you get.

It was also suggested that it was necessary to harden people up before they went out onto the streets because police officers would be relying on each other, and this would be even more applicable in the larger, city forces; it was suggested that the size of force or constabulary has a real impact on the collective behaviour of the police officers. One police officer in a focus group in the Rural Constabulary said:

> The size has a lot to do with it. The culture of a large number of policemen – the culture that they work in produces that. You're relying on someone to protect you when the chips are down. You're relying on someone to be there, not like an office environment where there isn't an element of real danger.

Another police officer in a focus group suggested that 'If he works for the police, to a certain extent he's representing the police,' and that:

> if you go around flaunting anything that's unusual … it isn't so much the people you're working with, but the people on the street pick up things quicker than anyone else. It can become a confrontational issue with members of the public. So you have to hide whatever your views are, you have to become a policeman, you can't show any undue character when you're dealing with people on the street.

The idea that the public will 'pick things up quicker than anyone else' is a fascinating assertion to make; the police are supposed to be more observant, sharper and better able to interpret signs than the general public. What this officer is actually doing is creating a limited legitimacy for gay people in the police by warning them against being seen or noticed by the public. One of the ways in which the gay discourse is dominated is by saying that you have to 'hide' as a policeman, and cannot show any 'undue character'. Clearly it is intended to be understood that being gay means displaying 'undue character'; perhaps synonyms for undue in this context are excessive or disproportionate, and one has to assume that this police officer believes that certain sexualities are seen as excessive whereas others are not. He went on to explain that:

> Members of the public, especially after they've drunk several cans of beer on a Friday night are not so considerate. They're extreme bigots so if you show any sign of … you're asking for trouble and you'll get your colleagues in trouble. At 1 o'clock in the morning they're not so considerate…

Here he maintains that gay officers will also bring trouble down on the heads of their colleagues, 'you're asking for trouble and you'll get your colleagues in trouble'. The gay person is therefore a liability for his or her colleagues. And if trouble rains down on the head of a potentially vulnerable gay police officer, there is no suggestion of protecting them; his suggestion that they are 'asking for trouble' suggests that merely by being gay, they deserve everything they get, and they will be left to the consequences of the violence they have invited upon themselves. However, the same officer went on to say that:

> You don't want to be talking about anything at work in the canteen that may upset someone else. If you're in a group of people and someone's going to be upset by it … it's a balance isn't it. We're talking sexually, but it could be religion, it could be anything, and we were all religious, you wouldn't want one person there running down religion, because you're antagonizing aren't you? It doesn't matter whether it's sexuality or anything else, you should just keep your views to yourself or keep them moderate. If you're upsetting someone you shouldn't be saying it – it works two ways: obviously in the first scenario the homosexual was being victimized, but someone who had strong views against that could be upset if too many people were talking about it casually as if, you know, as if everyone accepted it. As a policeman you should be able to judge when you are upsetting people. You have to be able to see with members of the public whether you're upsetting them – use the same principle with your colleagues.

So, these incidents are considered to be like tests, to see whether the individual is capable of protecting you in situations of extreme danger. To that extent, it is a rather brutal working culture, where the 'pack' hunts out the weakest member and then persecutes them in order to see whether or not they survive.

A gay man or lesbian was conceptualized in this focus group in the Rural

Constabulary as someone who antagonizes others, and who gets their colleagues into trouble. The focus group also thought that sexual minorities can choose whether to express their views about their minority sexuality. Ironically, the gay person was conceptualized by these people as a persecutor, attacking colleagues who happen to hold strong views opposing homosexuality. They suggested that gay people are effectively people who need to hide, particularly in terms of the outward signs of their homosexuality.

This is to portray the bullying that goes on as mere joking, but joking with a useful purpose since it is preparation for the outside world. It is possible to see that in the case, they are making a gay person out to be weak; the language that is used includes 'victim', 'wimp', 'couldn't take this sort of thing', 'making a big fuss about nothing'. Interestingly, the main person speaking is a woman who suffered similar types of abuse when she was a WPC in the 1980s, although she only served for eight years and does not say why she stopped. Could it be that she could not take the treatment she was receiving any more? Why is she defending the continuing poor treatment of people at work? There is an element of the self-fulfilling prophecy to this text; if gay people are seen as weak and sensitive, and if they react to bullying and complain, they are seen even more as weak.

Now, the need for police officers, in particular, to hide aspects of themselves, of their personality or their identity, when they are dealing with the public is an example of the use of the body in paid work, described by Deborah Kerfoot, in 2000, as 'a physical dependency which is not fully elaborated in language'. This concept of police officers having to hide when at work is also consistent with Erving Goffman's idea of conceptualizing certain types of work as dramaturgy; the work becomes dramatized, because the individual is not only expected to describe their capability in a certain area, but also to demonstrate it through their performance in the workplace.

Kerfoot is referring to managers in their performance at work, but the idea is equally applicable to police officers. The mark of a competent police officer is their ability to identify types of bodily designations and behaviours that are valued, and then to display their body and behave in a manner that is culturally acceptable to their organization's body code. Most obviously this relates to dress and physical appearance, which relates to the use of uniform in the police and fire service, but could just as easily refer, in the case of gay men or lesbians, to overtly effeminate or masculine behaviour. In both the police and fire service, employees are concerned with proving that they are trustworthy and reliable and the need to establish trust with the individual and to show that in extremis the team could rely on that individual has already been discussed.

There is a growing sociological interest in the body in social practice, as well as an interest in the body as a means of expressing sexual identities and the fact that organizations such as the police and fire service use uniform cannot be ignored. The uniform moves the employee away from any individual expression of identity. Although the body plays an important part amongst the contemporary theorizing about the self, and outside the workplace we are freer than ever before to construct a whole range of different self-identities from a commoditized society of ideas and social interaction, inside work we are still expected to use our bodies to conform, rather than show individuality and to show outward traits of masculinity.

In one focus group discussion in the Shire Fire Service, coming out was discussed in response to the various stories on coming out in the fire service that were presented to the group. One of the participants brought up of coming out as 'flaunting' one's sexuality, once again demonstrating Fairclough's (1989) idea of dominant discourses containing dominated ones.

> 95 per cent of people in this job don't have a problem with anything … as long as it's not flaunted in front of them, literally flaunted in front of them; I'm on about the actual person. If you get a gay person that goes over the top and winds you up that way, that's when the problem starts. I could take you to quite a few people that you wouldn't know about their sexuality until they actually told you. They are the ones that people don't have a problem with. It's the people that feel they are being victimized and they go out and out to flaunt their sexuality. It's the ones that say 'I was there last night and way-hey!' (laughs). That's flaunting it. You can't deal with the problem, if you don't know where the problem is.

The same phenomenon is illustrated of putting the gay person in the role of aggressor, though expressed slightly differently as the gay person is seen as someone who 'winds you up that way'. It conceptualized here as the gay person's fault for causing the problem and aggression in the first place. Indeed the person speaking identifies the moment of coming out as the moment when the problem starts. The main speaker seems quite proud to know people that keep their sexuality to themselves, again justifying the limiting of minority dominated discourses. Another interesting aspect is that the speaker identifies that it is precisely those people that see themselves in the role of the victim that are the problem. It is suggested that flaunting is not just coming out; it is also boasting of sexual acts. Clearly, it is impossible to know whether the speaker was referring to a person who actually did boast of sexual acts, or whether this is a hypothetical situation. However, it is again putting limits on a person's freedom, and therefore an expression of the power relations that exist.

Being outed through a deliberate act

Of course, the act of coming out is not always one which is desired or intended by the individual concerned; sometimes coming out at work is forced. Someone can be outed, which, in the language of Judith Butler, is the performative naming of someone as lesbian or gay, 'where to utter is to create the effect uttered', (Butler, 1997: 32). And, this performative naming does not have to happen with the subject's knowledge; one can be named or constituted out of earshot, as was described in the story told to me by Justin who works for Beta

Bank. Justin is a call centre manager who manages a team of people answering queries from members of the public. There is quite a high turnover and so he is often taking on new members of staff. He explained that when he has new joiners he makes the effort to go over to the training room to collect them from their induction session. This gives him an opportunity to introduce himself to the new recruits. He told me:

> I would introduce myself, what my job is, what I do, what their responsibilities are, what my responsibilities are to them, what they can expect of me and what I can expect from them and so on. Normally I'm introduced by name and some basic business information about me. On this one occasion I came into the group, and there were these little sniggers, but I did my piece, introduced myself.

Justin then explained to me that there had been two gay men in the group who were partners at the time and had joined his team. He went on to explain that very soon afterwards he had an opportunity to talk to one of them:

> I had a one-to-one with one of them, and the subject of my briefing to the induction group came up, and the guy said to me you do realize that before you came into the room the lecturer said 'just so that you are all aware he is gay'. And I thought, does that have any relevance to my job? I mean would I have introduced anyone as 'this is your team-leader and he's straight?' It's a reminder that although I work in a fairly progressive area of the bank, there are still those types of people who work here who don't really get it. One of my team was particularly homophobic and as a result of this, he caused all sorts of problems. He kept making comments about 'it repulses me' and 'it makes me feel sick' and I had to manage this person; I wouldn't have had to put up with that if I hadn't been introduced as a gay man.

This story introduces Butler's idea of being named *in absentia*, and the shock that potentially results when someone is named as gay without their knowledge. In this case Justin believed that he had one identity or subject position, but as he entered the room there is a dissonance between the identity of the subject position that Justin believed he had taken up, and the actual way that the others saw him. He identifies the ridiculousness of this type of introduction himself. With a heterosexual manager, there would have been no reference to his sexuality.

This story seems to have a purpose of warning, and telling others to beware. For whatever reason, the manager running the induction believes that they have to warn the new recruits that their manager is gay, either because he is seen as predatory and therefore a danger to them potentially, or because he is afraid that they might say something and that they have to be warned not to use politically incorrect language. One member of a Beta Bank focus group said, 'Makes it sound like he's going to come onto you, sort of thing – you know – beware. Whereas, if he got to know you it would be different.' A common theme in organizational stories is that of the mistake. In this case it is the manager running the induction programme who has made the mistake, perhaps an honest one, and this story is highlighting their weakness and inconsistency. Someone else in the focus group said, 'It's making an assumption – he didn't know, did he?'

Most of the focus group participants in Beta Bank took exception to this story, suggesting that the supervisor had not been right to introduce the person as gay before they came into the room. The group also identified that there are different ways of coming out and of outing someone, and the way that this happened, or, at least, the way the story is told, it comes across in a very predatory way.

This is an example of the exchange in the Beta Bank focus group:

> 'There are different ways of coming out and of outing, but here he's seen as a predator, beware.'
>
> 'But even the opposite way, you know, he's gay so don't say anything bad to him, it's ignorant. It's up to the guy to tell them if he wants to.'
>
> 'It's like saying this is so and so – she were a purse-snatcher. You wouldn't say that would you.'
>
> 'I have mixed feelings about this though, sometimes I think they should know.'

Interestingly, in this discussion about coming out, and 'outing', a female participant then 'outs' one of the gay men in the room, Johnny (at least to me – the others may already have known that he was gay). She then goes on to out another man as well by referring to 'you two'. There is another gay man in the group but he does not come out until later in the focus group session. Interestingly, there was no selection for sexuality in setting up this focus group, instead it was a routine shift in a call centre, where there just happened to be three gay men in a group of ten people. In the discussion of the story, they end up replicating the story in front of the researcher, by suggesting 'Here's someone you might consider speaking to, and by the way he's gay'. Having said that, it is a particularly thoughtful suggestion; if you replace the gay character with say, a female character, then introducing a new woman team member to the other woman in the team on a one-to-one basis would be a pleasant way of effecting an introduction. Their discussion on the subject continued as follows:

> 'If you had someone in your team and they were struggling and they were gay, it might be appropriate to introduce them to Johnny to have a chat – one-to-one might be appropriate. You know, here's someone you might consider speaking to, and by the way he's gay, but not in front of everyone. It's completely irrelevant. If you're doing sexual orientation and you say – we're going to watch this video and then have a discussion and then say this team leader that's coming in is gay and is proud of it and wants to take questions from you, that's different isn't it.'

'You need to find out how far you can go early on. You know you two if you didn't joke about it first, then no-one else would. But because you two are open about it in the first place. If someone is really serious about it and says, "I'm gay and not a lot of people know about it", you know that you don't go "alright you queer", whereas with Johnny you could.'

'Before Johnny came I was much more of that opinion, I'd lay low, and Johnny pushed the boundaries. And it's a question of numbers, once you've got more than a certain number of people, you're no longer a minority.'

However, another one of the focus groups saw this story in quite a positive light, saying,

I believe he was acting in the best of motives, in terms of trying to warn people; it is possible to do the wrong things though from the nicest of motives. That, perhaps, is where education needs to come in; It's like a colleague of mine is very fat and her manager sometimes warns people before she comes into the room, because they don't want that 'Oh my God! She's extremely fat!' reaction.

The difference, of course, is that if someone is extremely fat it is immediately visible, and the reaction that the person is trying to avoid is a reaction to the visibility of the difference, which would be immediate. Sexuality is not immediately visible; the induction manager is perhaps trying to avoid someone saying the wrong thing, either then or in advertently at some point in the future.

Being outed through circumstance

Goffman suggested that once 'out', that is to say once people have revealed previously hidden information about themselves, they are then in the position of constantly having to manage information about themselves that is potentially discrediting. Coming out, that is to say revealing information about one's minority sexual identity is on the one hand exactly that; it is a process of revealing something that has previously been hidden. Arlene Stein suggests that it is more than that; it is also part of fashioning a lesbian or gay self that did not exist before coming out began (Stein, 2003: 132). In other words, being gay or lesbian is not a truth that is discovered, it is a performance, which is enacted over and over again.

Goffman suggests that the reaction of the audience may be worse, when they suspect that the performance is not genuine.

When the audience is known to be secretly sceptical of the reality that is being impressed upon them, we have been ready to appreciate their tendency to pounce on trifling flaws as a sign that the whole show is false; but as students of social life we have been less ready to appreciate that even sympathetic audiences can be momentarily disturbed, shocked and weakened in their faith by the discovery of a picayune discrepancy in the impressions presented to them.

(Goffman, 1969: 45)

Again, this concept is particularly apt for sexual minorities in organizations; as individuals try to conceal their sexual identity, and put on a front in the workplace, people around them react with shock when they come out.

Jez, who is a gay member of police support staff, told me the following story about the time that they were arrested for cruising (gay slang which means looking for casual sex partners in a public place, though not necessarily to have sex in public). Gay sex is only partially decriminalized in the United Kingdom and, when Jez was arrested, seeking out sexual partners in a public place was an illegal activity for gay men. Having been arrested, and working for the police, he was automatically suspended. This, of course, meant that when he returned to the workplace he had to come out to his colleagues; he also, to use Goffman's terminology, had to constantly manage information about himself, which was potentially discrediting. 'I had no choice about coming out', Jez told me. He continued:

> I got arrested. For cruising, would you believe it? It was pretty awful at the time and very embarrassing. I went through a difficult time for a couple of months, because I was suspended. I didn't have a court case or anything. Looking back, it's done me the biggest favour ever. I wouldn't have wanted to do it that way, and I wouldn't want to do it again. Even though I was a civilian, I was automatically suspended. It took a month and a half in the end. It was a bit like being in prison really. I got a warning, basically, and if I hadn't worked for the police, I wouldn't have got that. I was very fortunate in that sense. It was awful being at home. I didn't tell many people or my friends. My parents didn't know and don't know to this day. I had to report to the police station if I was going out for more than three hours, during work time. I had to go to the police welfare; I went once a week initially. I was very lucky because my boss intervened and said that if I wanted to go back I could. They were very happy to have me back. I started back within a few days of the enquiry ending. The people in the office were fine, but there were reactions from other people. Some people ignored me completely, wouldn't speak to me in the corridor, and some people didn't make any effort. My job involves dealing with police officers and my boss was concerned about the way they would react. But there were positive reactions too. There was one particular guy, older. He was CID at the time. I was on the stairs and he came up to me and shook my hand. He said it was very good that I'd come back and that I was very brave. That was very positive and helped a lot – it boosted my confidence.

This story has a quality of 'misfortune' about it. Jez was punished, even though the case did not go to court, and although Jez survives and is stronger through it 'looking back it did me the biggest favour ever', it was unfortunate that he was caught in the first place. This story is an interesting one in the context of the police because the issue of cruising has dominated discussions between the police and the lesbian and gay communities in recent years. But, just as in any organization, perhaps even more so in the police, there are both formal and informal rules, and members of the organization are expected to play by the rules. Jez's particular story transgresses the formal rules, that is to say he has broken the law, but it also transgresses the informal rules; research carried out by Marc Burke, an academic and former police officer, suggests that homosexuals are the social group most disliked by the police. Many forces organized specialized squads of officers to deal specifically with gay sexual offences in public places (Burke, 1993), although it is recognized that many forces, including this one, have now turned greater attention to the perpetrators of hate crime against gay people.

Civilians in the police do not get the same protection as police officers, who work under police regulations, and generally speaking they are treated less well than police officers at work. In this case, however, Jez was perhaps treated better than a police officer in that he was allowed to return to work, even though he was automatically suspended; as a police officer he may well have lost his job altogether. He also had to go to police welfare, an interesting term, since it demonstrates the power relations in operation in the organization. Employees have to be looked after. Since one of the functions of welfare is psychological counselling, the idea of welfare suggests that the police may sometimes medicalize sexuality. Previous research by Clair in 1998 suggests that there is in fact a tendency in the police to bureaucratize sex and desire. Jez never said whether he was happy to go back to work, only that his boss was happy to have him back; he had quite a passive approach to telling the story, putting the power firmly in the hands of his police employers, allowing them to express tolerance, or otherwise, of what he had done. Jez expressed no bitterness, only gratitude that it was not worse. His description of when he returned to work is an example of the power relations in operation in the organization; silence is used as a means of expressing power, as many of his colleagues would not speak to him, and the exception of the long-serving police officer who shook his hand was particularly poignant.

Interestingly, the term cruising needed to be explained to the police focus groups in the Rural Constabulary. Clearly, one would not expect all members of the police force, sworn and unsworn staff, to be aware of all legislation. That would be unrealistic. But given that the area of sexual offences has been subject to some over-zealous policing in the past (this was not the only story of being arrested amongst the interviewees in this project), it is ironic that almost no one in the police focus groups knew what the term meant. Once it had been explained to them, they confused the term with other forms of sexual behaviour. For example, one police officer said:

> If it's a recent incident, I think people will be OK about him being gay, but it's the fact that he was soliciting which will cause people to have mixed

feelings about his gayness or homosexuality. It's not normal for other sexualities to tout. If you want to, go to a bar like most people.

A support officer continued with another comment on Jez's story: 'He had been out looking to score that night, and it's the same – gays cruising for other gays, or someone looking for a prostitute, it's that element of sordidness that people don't like.'

Finally, a police officer rounded off the discussion with the following comment: 'It's distasteful. Part of a homosexual lifestyle is this cottaging aspect. It floats some boats and not others.' It seemed to be a common misapprehension amongst focus group participants that Jez was selling sex; they used the word tout, meaning pestering customers for business, soliciting and accosting someone for an immoral purpose. They used a word to describe him more commonly used with prostitutes who are selling sex, and then went on to liken him to someone looking for a prostitute. The third speaker, a senior operational police officer, then confuses the term with cottaging, which specifically refers to having sex in public toilets. Without going into any defence or criticism of any of these practices or behaviours, it is interesting to see how the subject position of the gay man is conflated with different sexual behaviours, some of which are considered to be reprehensible by society.

It is interesting that the first speaker said that people would be 'OK about him being gay', and therefore accepting of his minority sexual identity. But it seems that people might have mixed feelings once his being gay stops being just an identity and people are confronted with the idea of actual sexual behaviour, linking in to Norman Fairclough's ideas of power expressed by people putting limits on their tolerance of minorities. What happens is that one type of discourse is established as the dominant one in a given social domain, and, at the same time, it establishes certain ideological assumptions as commonsensical, and a certain discourse becomes a rule in the organization. Discourse, when conceptualized as a vehicle for power, can mean the 'domination of one discourse by another, in an oppositional relationship' (Fairclough, 1989: 91), and the dominated discourse is under pressure to be silenced, suppressed and eliminated. Dominant discourses can also contain oppositional discourses (Fairclough, 1989), which means that the dominant discourse credits the oppositional one with a certain limited legitimacy and protection. The minority is tolerated and accepted rather than put on an equal footing. In the case of Jez's story, the dominant discourse in the organization is that actually being gay is OK, but that is the limit. Any information, which suggests that he actually has had sex, goes beyond the limit that has been placed upon him.

Coming out publicly

Some people struggle to find the right time and place to come out, and their difficulty in finding the right frame sometimes means that they fail to come out altogether. Gay people sometimes feel that their 'secret' is not always in their control, ultimately revealing their minority sexuality in some unintended way such as their physical appearance, or the way that they dress. One lesbian who wore jeans to a clerical job suggested that she actually forced her sexuality down people's throats through the way that she dressed. Another woman inadvertently came out to her work colleagues by cutting her hair short. She described this act as an inadvertent 'tip-off', a 'mistake'.

Some try to take a minimal approach, by dropping hints or allowing others to stumble across evidence such as photographs of same-sex partners; it is quite common for stigmatized individuals to play down their presence for fear of a backlash, just as Rosabeth Moss Kanter, in her seminal 'Men and Women of the Corporation' (1977), described how women try to become socially invisible in the workplace. Brad is a very engaging firefighter who told the story of coming out to his shift, which he did almost by accident, but very publicly nevertheless. Although Brad found it traumatic at the time, even he thought it was amusing in the retelling. Central to his story is the phenomenon which is 'Mr Gay UK'. Basically this is a male beauty contest; regional heats are held around the country in gay pubs and clubs, and the final is held in one of the well-known gay clubs in London such as 'Heaven'. Brad always maintained that he had not entered the contest voluntarily, maintaining that he had been pushed onto a stage one night in a nightclub. Whether this is true, or poetic licence we will never know. Here, Brad picks up the story:

> so I got onto the stage a little bit drunk, and won the heat, it was straight into the final. And I didn't know, but they filmed it for the television. I was in Barbados for a couple of weeks and when I came back from holiday and I got a phone call from a member of my family to say that I'd been on telly. I went to work. Nothing was said on the day shifts, and then the night shift, it started to creep out you know with people making comments. Then someone pulled me to one side and said, 'Oh, by the way, we saw you on telly the other night, Mr Gay UK'.

This comic story ends with quite a sinister twist, as Brad's colleague says to him 'I think you'd better start being open to people.' Power relations are reversed within the story, with Brad coming across as confident, if a little naïve. He did after all qualify for the final of Mr Gay UK, and knows he is handsome enough not to be embarrassed by telling a story about entering a beauty contest. However, at the end of his story he is threatened by a colleague, becoming a victim, which happens in the majority of these stories. The implication of this, of course, is that he has kept something secret. Clearly, the irony of the situation is that within the gay community at large, Brad has been anything but secretive, even standing on stage and having his physical beauty judged by other gay men, putting himself under their gaze, as it were. He has only been secretive to the extent that he has not advertised his sexuality in the workplace.

It seems though that Brad is not alone. Firefighters are notoriously proud of serving the public and of being a firefighter, and yet they also seem proud of their reputation for being physically fit and good-looking, suggesting that, just as in other occupations, there may be an aesthetics of fire service work. There are also instances where firefighters have used the positive reputation that they enjoy with the public to win themselves popularity. Whilst I was carrying out this research, the chief fire officer of the Shire Fire Service told me about a similar incident where a firefighter from their service had gone on *Blind Date* (a well-known television show where men and women who have not previously met are sent on a blind date). The firefighter had a marvellous time and enjoyed great popularity with the viewing public and fellow contestants, partly, it was suggested because of this occupation; the chief fire officer on the other hand, was horrified to think that the shallow, superficial way that the television show is considered may have brought the service, which after all has a very serious purpose, into disrepute.

Brad's story adds to our understanding of the performative aspect of coming out. As previously discussed, one of the famous examples of performativity is J.L. Austin's example of the marriage ceremony. Austin maintained that much of language was made up of performative utterances. In other words, by saying something, people perform the action at the same time. In 1962, in his seminal work *How to do Things with Words*, Austin was able to demonstrate the considerable extent to which language is used performatively. He maintained that the words have to be said in the right context for it to become performative; for example, the priest declaiming the marriage vows is only performative during the wedding ceremony but not outside it.

Butler used this and developed the idea in a queer way by talking about the performativity of gender by using the example of drag. But as Butler says, herself, this example was then taken by some to be exemplary of performativity; 'even if drag is performative, not all performativity is drag' (Butler, 1993: 230). But it does have some parallels to this example of the Mr Gay UK contest. First, it is subversive: parodying heterosexual beauty contests, just as drag subverts heterosexual gender ideals. It puts the male body in the position of sexual scrutiny. Second, just as in Butler's example, the Mr Gay UK contest represents an embodying, in this case the repeated process of embodying sexuality. Third, the contest and the fact that it was broadcast on television underline the theatricality of the performative act. Butler warns that the theatricality of performativity need not be 'conflated with self-display or self-creation' (Butler, 1993: 232), although self-display is an integral part of the performative nature of the coming out act in Brad's story. Indeed, what Brad's story does do, portraying him semi-naked, on television and in a gay beauty contest is to mime and 'render hyperbolic' (Butler, 1993: 232) the discursive convention of the heterosexual firefighter that it also reverses.

Coming out is a repeated act

Coming out is a repeated act. The concentration is always on the first time a person comes out, especially for the individual concerned who will remember the first time above all others, and this suggests a single undifferentiated act. This is misleading because coming out is something, due to the constant presumption of heterosexuality, which the lesbian or gay man has to do in every new work situation. It is this repeated act, where the individual announces something to an audience that Butler in her *Gender Trouble* describes as being 'performative'. Like most of the academic concepts to do with identity, this word is made up, a neologism, coming from the word performance, but additionally introducing the concept of the act being reiterative and citational practice rather than being single and deliberate. Indeed, Butler herself suggested that being out depends to some extent on being in the closet, and being out must reproduce the closet again and again in order to be out. In the workplace, the individual is constantly being put in new situations and is constantly faced with the decision of whether to come out or not. Where news of the individual's sexual identity has gone before them to the new situation, they may already have gone through the cycle from silence to disclosure, even though the decision to go through that process was not their own, but they are still within the cycle because they have to manage the response from other people.

Rupert is a young banker, in his late twenties, working for Alpha Bank in the private client division, looking after what are termed 'high net-worth' clients, basically people with a lot of money to invest. As such, he worked in a very international atmosphere, spending quite a bit of time socializing and entertaining, both with clients and colleagues. He described this environment he worked in as being somewhere where homosexuality is 'for some people less of a problem than for others'. Rupert was a very engaging raconteur and, as he warmed to his story, he recounted how some people had different reactions to others, 'some colleagues I detected a distinct cooling off. Others couldn't be warmer; we have a great joke about it'. But then coming out is not just a one-off act, and there are constantly new situations at work. Rupert described how one night, there was a team dinner and a new colleague came along with her husband. Here he tells the story in his own words:

> there were maybe eight or nine of us. I had come out by this point, but, as she was new, she obviously didn't know about me. And again, it's not something I'm going to tell someone about automatically. And I remember her question, well, she said, 'So, I want to know about everyone's personal lives here; we know that John's married and you know Jake's engaged and erm you know Michael, well he's just split up with his girlfriend and then there's Rupert. Well we're not quite sure about Rupert...'. Of course, she meant it in the sense of, I'm not quite sure about Rupert because I don't know whether he's married or not. But immediately, two of my colleagues including my boss immediately got terribly defensive about this on my behalf and said, 'It's just being different, that's all it is', sort of leaping to my defence. In fact, they were being overly sensitive about a comment that was just totally harmless.

Of course, this story is illustrative of two aspects of coming out. One is the repeated aspect of the coming out process as already discussed. The other is the moment of surprise or shock, either for the audience, or for the individual themselves, when the act of coming out is performed as a result of either accident or deliberate force. In this story, Rupert is put in a situation where he is forced to come out, albeit by accident, but he was nevertheless laughing as he told it. It was particularly the way his colleagues actually rushed to defend him, and in quite a clumsy way.

Coming out is a process in different ways; in terms of the different stages that lead up to coming out, in terms of the performative nature of the act itself, and in terms of the performative nature of living a minority sexual identity. Andy's story illustrated the performative, illocutionary act of coming out, whilst Stefan's story showed the performative as part of convention. The discursive construction of identity *in absentia* was illustrated in Justin's story, who was named as gay in front of this new call centre team.

Summary

These stories add to our understanding of how our identity is impacted by the coming out process. Although respondents had described coming out as one of the most significant and important points in their career, very few, if any of the stories suggested that coming out was something that the individual sought out. To a greater or lesser extent all the storytellers described themselves as victims of a system that forced them into it, from Andy, the firefighter who did not want to come out because of the showers, to Stefan, the police officer who came out in an effort to stop his colleagues bullying him. This is consistent with the Foucauldian view that we are not free agents, and our actions are not as a result of free choice; instead, we are driven to act in response to external forces, as an act of resistance to existing power relations.

It is interesting to see how employees of the various organizations react to the stories. In the police, the identity created for sexual minorities by the speaker is as someone who antagonizes others, and who gets their colleagues into trouble. According to the police officers who took part in these focus groups, gay men and women can choose whether or not to express their views about their own sexuality, and by implication are at liberty to choose their sexuality. A gay person was also constructed to be someone who is put in the position of persecutor and attacks those colleagues who hold strong views on the subject. In the Beta Bank call centre, the subject position created for the gay man is one of a joking, light-hearted person who makes people laugh.

These stories have also highlighted a difference in work context; there is more interpersonal contact in the police and the fire service than in the other organizations, and it is perhaps harder for people in those organizations to carry on a masquerade of identity. The close personal relations in these organizations also mean that the costs are higher for coming out because of the dangers of potential negative reactions. In government departments and banks, there seems to be less interpersonal interaction, and less interest in the personal lives of one's work colleagues which means that, on the one hand, it is easier to be in the closet, but on the other, there is also a reduced risk associated with coming out.

Coming out means moving from silence to disclosure, but actually the issue of silence is much more complex; the discourses of, and around, sexual minorities are often silenced, but in different ways. Coming out, in terms of disclosing minority sexual identity, means leaving silence behind and it is to the subject of silence that we turn in the next section. Real life stories will again be presented which demonstrate that some organizations actively censor all mention of sexuality, whilst in others informal social practices do not allow lesbians and gay men to have a voice. This raises a number of questions: can identities be formed by language when that very language is absent? How do gay employees frame their sense of who they are, when faced with silence? What does silence look like? I will attempt to answer these questions by asserting that there are different aspects of silence: silence as it affects the individual; leaving silence behind; silence in its relation to language; and silence as a device within the organization, such as censorship or repression.

5 Silent lives

It is perhaps clichéd to talk about homosexuality these days as 'the love that dare not speak its name'. It has become somewhat of a hackneyed phrase, as the knowledge that homosexuals have had to hide from view for a very long time, unable to talk about their experiences, has entered mainstream consciousness. And yet, silence still is an issue for sexual minorities, and probably more so in the workplace than anywhere else. It can also be quite a complex issue as discourses about minority sexuality are often silenced in different ways: some organizations actively censor all mention of sexuality, whilst in others informal social practices do not allow lesbians and gay men to have a voice. Sins of commission and omission respectively.

This raises a number of questions about the way in which minority sexual identity in work organizations is understood: can identities be formed by language when that very language is absent? How do gay employees frame their sense of who they are when faced with silence? If silence is such a big issue for minorities in organizations, how does it manifest itself? And how can we study it? In this chapter, I am going to take the theme of silence and address some of its key characteristics in an organizational context, illustrated with stories from gay men and women.

Silence, I believe, is just as an important part of discourse as talk itself; its changing shape is a key component in shaping the audible discourse around it. Silence takes on a number of different shapes, forms and aspects within organizations: there is silence as it affects the individual; what happens when an individual comes out and therefore leaves silence behind; the dynamics of silence where there is an absence of language; and then there is silence, expressed as the 'blank response'. Silence can also be used as a device within organizations, such as censorship or repression. Silence also has an impact on the research process.

Why, then, is it important to look at the shape of silence at all? Why bother considering silence? Well, my contention is that you may miss an awful lot of the dynamics within organizations if you do not consider what is not said, as well as what is said. I believe that painting a picture of an organization's discourse is made much richer by considering the silence that surrounds talk, as well as the talk itself. In other words, silence can be conceptualized as a 'negative space' within discourse, a key element of discourse, but one where speech may be absent, or a significant part of the message is delivered by silent means. When language is absent, the dynamics of power and knowledge continue to play out through power relations, which continue to shape social practices and set new social practices into play.

Silence is a negative space within discourse

We can conceptualize talk within discourse as something which is 'present', and silence, as something within the same discursive field, but which is 'absent'. Jacques Derrida, the controversial French post-modernist philosopher, used the ideas of presence and absence in his work, linking the act of speech to the idea of being present with the act of writing implying absence. He maintained that writing, although a powerful medium, operates on absences. It does not need the presence of the writer or the writer's consciousness to have a powerful effect and neither does the reader need to be present to be referred to.

Silence can demonstrate similar dynamics. Silence is an example of absence, but it can still be powerful, linked as it is to the talk or the speech, which it surrounds. The shape of silence may be constructed by the discourse which exists around it; gaps in discourse, contingent on the organization, can play as powerful a role as speech itself, even becoming part of the organization's discursive practices. If you accept that silence is an integral part of discourse, constructed by the discourse that surrounds it, then it can also be assumed that silence, existing as it does in binary opposition to discourse, helps to construct discourse in return.

In order to understand the shape of silence and to be able to describe the dynamics of silence within work organizations, and to understand why we need to talk about silence at all, I have borrowed a term from the vocabulary of two-dimensional visual language in practical art: *negative space*. Positive space is the space occupied by the drawing object and negative space is the space behind the object or between two objects. In practical art, it is often the practice not only to draw the composition, but also to draw the negative spaces, which force an awareness of the composition as a whole. In the same way, it is suggested that a focus on, and deconstruction of, the negative space of silence forces an awareness of the positive space of discourse. Another brief example may help to explain this concept: when drawing, for example, a leaf, concentration on the leaf alone would lead us to draw what we know to be a leaf, rather than what we see. We know what a leaf looks like, so why bother to check that we have drawn it correctly? Because we have no preconceived notion about the shape of a space, by focusing on the negative space, which surrounds the leaf, it becomes necessary to look very carefully at what we are drawing. In the same way, when deconstructing discourse we may be tempted to understand what we know to be the meaning rather than what we hear in spoken discourse or read in written discourse, or text. By focusing on silence, or the negative space, which exists between talk, it forces us to have an awareness of the discourse as a whole, and by describing the dynamics of silence within organizations, the organizational discourse takes on new meaning.

Stories about silence by gay men and women

The issue of silence is not a new one for sexual minorities; homosexuality has been known, after all, as the 'love that dare not speak its name', and there is a burgeoning literature on silence in organization studies. But the data from my research suggests that the area is more complex than simply the silencing of talk, with silence emerging as a significant factor and being characterized in a number of different ways and guises.

I first identified silence as a key theme when I carried out my research study in the Micro Department. There can be no doubt that, compared to less positive organizations, the department was a very good place to work for sexual minorities: there was little overt discrimination; efforts were made to limit covert discrimination, such as third-party reviewing of annual appraisals; the employee network for lesbian and gay employees was very high profile; and personal accounts abounded with positive stories. The organization appeared to be a positive place for lesbians and gay men. However, a pattern of 'silence as absence' started to build up, both from the research approach, as well as emerging from the data.

After I became aware of this as an issue for gay men and women at work, I realized that this pattern of silence continued to be a feature of the research as I continued my research with the other organizations. The stories that follow come from across the different organizations that I worked with, but all have the theme of silence in common.

The silence of the closet

The following story illustrates the phenomenon of the closet and undisclosed self-identity. This is a story told by Gary, a gay man working in the Delta Department, and based in a small regional office. Gary felt that he could not come out, and the story is concerned with his creating a new identity for himself:

> I desperately wanted to be straight, and then I realized that there was no way that that was going to happen. So, I thought if I can't be straight and I don't want to be gay, then I'll just be nothing. I'll just go to work, go home, watch telly, go to bed, just do nothing and that went on for many years.

Gary then told me about the time that he saw a report on the television about a homophobic murder in Manchester: a gay man had been murdered and thrown into the canal. The news programme showed some newsreel footage taken inside a gay club, although as Gary said 'it wasn't even a Manchester club!' And, although this was about a murder, the showing of gay people enjoying themselves in a nightclub on television had a profound effect on him:

> When I saw this footage of people dancing in a club, I thought I'd like, just once in my life, to go and see that. Not to make a habit of it, but just to see

it once. And so I did, one day, and then I thought it was brilliant, it was the best night of my life, I must go again. And I did, and then by the time I went a third time, I thought I had to be openly gay. I thought I want to be like these people, I don't want to be hiding and ashamed and feeling wrong, bad and evil. I want to be happy and positive and enjoy life and find friends and find someone to love, and participate in real life.

Gary then described how he made a plan to become openly gay, in order to negotiate coming out amongst the people he had lived and worked with for a long time. Before he came out, he had been working in a small, regional office in a small town, 'unlike now, where I'm in a very large office in a city'. Gary picks up the story:

I'd worked with some of those people for twenty years, and I felt that I couldn't tell these people, I couldn't face having lied to them for all these years. Some of them knew and guessed, but it hadn't been discussed. I thought the only way I can do it is to move, change jobs, move to a new office and a new town and a new city. Move home and change my name and completely come up with a brand new life. A new identity, and that way I knew I could be openly gay, but it had to be from a fresh start. I severed all connections with my previous life.

Another couple of years went by after Gary had taken his decision to come out, during which time he started to implement the first key elements of his plan. For instance, one action he had decided on was to move away to the city:

It took a long time to organize it all, but I finally got my transfer to the Manchester office, which was more of a gay environment: there was the gay village and there was somewhere I could go. I started in the new office and I wasn't going to let it slide again, I wasn't going to go back into this cocoon again of being straight, or letting people think I was straight. I decided I must let people know as soon as possible that I was gay. Yes, I changed my name. The name I have now is not my original name. But it was part of the process that I needed to go through to become the person that I wanted to be. I didn't want any connection with the old person, because the old life was miserable and I wanted to cut that off completely.

I met Gary in Canal Street in Manchester which, in retrospect, was quite a poignant place to meet, given his story about the gay murder there. Meeting in gay bars was by no means a regular choice of meeting place for all interviewees; some people even chose their place of work. With Gary, though, it seemed an apposite choice; it was as though he was still going through the process of announcing who he was to the outside world. He came to the interview wearing various different insignia: the red AIDS ribbon and Stonewall's rainbow ribbon for gay equality are two that I remember, and I believe that he was wearing them in order to suggest to other people that he might be gay. Goffman described these sorts of badges as 'stigma symbols', signs which draw attention to a potentially debasing identity discrepancy, breaking up the overall coherent picture of someone who appears 'normal' at first sight. In this case the initial picture was a coherent one of an office worker: Gary had come straight from work, wearing a navy blazer with grey trousers. His 'gay insignia' served to interrupt the coherent whole of the anodyne office worker, created by his formal dress. It also served his purpose of ensuring that no one would again make the mistake of thinking that he was straight. The wearing of gay insignia contrasts with what Goffman called 'prestige symbols', which the heterosexual male might wear in the workplace, such as wedding rings. (Of course, since December 2005 and the Civil Partnership Act in the UK, the wearing of wedding rings is a prestige symbol open to gay men and women too.)

Gary's story is a sad one, not least because a death forms a key element: there was a murder in Canal Street before Gary became aware of the means to free himself from his oppression. And although oppression is a very strong word I think it's quite appropriate for Gary's situation. Gary was also, I believe, the victim of his own oppression. He was not in the closet because he feared persecution if he came out to his colleagues, but because he had worked with them for such a long time, had built up a working relationship with them, and therefore could not face telling them even though he suspected that some of them knew anyway. Gary described the process of his coming out as moving from what he defines as 'nothing' to what he described as 'something', that is being gay, changing his name along the way. Though shocking, and perhaps unthinkable to many of us, changing one's name is not that unusual or unknown and is one of the most common ways of changing identities; people who live under the burden of an unwanted identity often want to acquire a different personal identity to leave their previous life behind. More extreme examples of people changing their identities have involved scarring fingers to alter fingerprints and destroying birth certificates. Those people that read about Gary reacted more often than not with sadness, often to the fact that he had changed his name. One person said, 'One of the sad things in there is his wanting to change name and location, because he obviously feels guilty he's been lying to people. But why should he feel guilty? At the end of the day – it's his sexuality.' I think the story tells us a lot about how difficult Gary found it to come out and his relationships at work were part of that: he only took action after twenty years when he realized that his existence was so miserable that he could not stand it any more.

For me, the negative space in this story is made up of its silent voices; the voices of Gary's colleagues, the ones that he left behind in the small-town office and the colleagues in his present office. It would have been interesting to interview them to see whether his colleagues in the first office had known that he was gay and whether they cared anyway. What did they think of his moving away? Did they not think it was weird that he disappeared without trace? And, what of his new colleagues? How did he announce his sexuality to them when he arrived? Sometimes it is possible to explore the negative space surrounding a story, but on this occasion it was not possible. What was possible, though, was exploring the story in the focus groups: they readily identified the working environment as having an impact on an individual's silence. The Delta Department is quite fragmented in nature and, although it does have a number of very large offices, it is made up of a national network of very small offices. To work in one of the latter can be very challenging from a number of perspectives; one of the reasons given was that 'people have more set ways than in a bigger environment'. They also suggested that the fact of the matter is that 'no matter what you say, people will gossip'. They explained this by saying that smaller offices tend to be in smaller communities, with less exposure to different kinds of people. In one focus group, which took place in a small community in rural Scotland, one participant said:

> It's very difficult to get a transfer to a small office; when I put to come here I was told that I would have to wait until someone died. They have great difficulty accepting you if you're somebody else, never mind your sexuality. It's very cliquish.

Another focus group participant was not surprised by the story at all. Indeed, they described it as being 'totally expected'. They went on to explain:

> I went to work in London in the 80s an I can imagine a lot of people will have gone to work in big cities to seek the anonymity; probably if you're gay there are going to be more opportunities in big cities in clubs and places to go. It doesn't surprise me.

The silence of thinking you're on your own

Coming out means leaving silence behind in more ways than one. It is very easy to feel isolated when you belong to a minority group in the workplace, especially when it is hard to spot other people who might belong to the same minority. And because minority sexuality is such a taboo in the United Kingdom fire service sexual minorities are invisible to the heterosexual majority as well as to other lesbians and gay men. Andy, a gay firefighter told me about the moment that he found out that he was not alone in being gay in the fire service:

> I think as a gay man the high point for me was when I'd been there for under a year and I saw the Union banner at the London Lesbian and Gay Pride march; I walked up and found out that there were other gay firefighters. I really did think I was the only gay firefighter. That was the high point knowing that there were other gay people in the fire service. I don't know whether I thought I was going to be carrying the torch on my own. As far as I was concerned, I didn't know anyone else in the fire service who was gay.

The reason that Andy found out that there were other gay firefighters was that he saw other people wearing the same uniform. The fire service uniform has attracted a lot of attention in recent years and not a little controversy. Most of the debate about whether the fire service should wear a uniform or not has centred around the need for discipline in the service and the need for a physical expression of rank. The uniform is a symbol of the disciplined nature of the service, as well as being a symbol of its history and its links with the armed forces. Much of the debate about uniform has arisen as opinion is divided over whether the fire service should break this link, and therefore do away with the uniform. Within this debate, however, there has been little acknowledgement of the role that uniform in the fire service has played for sexual minorities, even though the way that people dress is intricately linked to issues of organizational culture. Uniforms can act as a mask, thereby hiding sexual orientation, with certain uniforms, such as the firefighter's, having a certain affectionate place in lesbian, gay and bisexual culture.

Silence: no talk just action

As mentioned previously, silence can also be conceptualized as an absence of language and, although there is often a response to sexual orientation in work organizations in one way or another, it is true that this response often this takes the form of silence. The response might not involve language, but instead is simply an action, though one that is just as powerful in its significance as a verbal one would have been for those that are on the receiving end. This story was one of those stories which had gained almost mythical status; everyone I talked to in Beta Bank had heard of the incident and recounted their own version. The launch of the bank's lesbian and gay network was publicized by distributing leaflets around the organization. Leaflets were put on everyone's desk. Jim, an employee in the bank's contact centre on the south coast, and who had been very active in setting up the network, told me:

> We knew that it could have been difficult for someone to be seen reading it, but we felt that the only way of advertising the launch was to put posters up, distribute leaflets and put it on the Intranet. In my (open-plan) office, someone – they weren't sure who it was – had gathered up all the leaflets and put them all on one person's desk. It wasn't an isolated incident either; in other offices, there were other gay people who came into work and found fifteen or twenty leaflets on their desk.

Jim went on to explain that Beta Bank's response was rather unsatisfying as it was left unresolved; no one knew what happened to the 'victims', nor was a perpetrator identified. Nevertheless, while carrying out the focus groups, one person admitted that he had been in a group that thought it would be a good joke to do this, although he said that the group actually decided not to move the leaflets:

> We were quite impressed that the bank had organized an event like this; there was a bit of discussion about whether we should pile them all up on

somebody's desk, to make light of it, but then the majority said – hang on that's not actually that funny.

This response was one without language and therefore a silent one, but at the same time was a most definite reaction to the placing of the leaflets. I believe that this reaction grew out of a view that I came up against in organizations time and again; it is the idea that anything about sexual orientation cannot be for heterosexuals, which is rather like the idea that Joanne Martin put forward in her 1992 work *Cultures in Organizations: Three Perspectives*, that issues of gender concern women only. In fact, in the example from Beta Bank, the lesbian and gay network had intended to distribute the leaflets to anyone in the organization who was supportive of sexual minorities, but clearly many recipients assumed that you would only be interested if you were gay yourself. It is worthy of note that the reaction happened simultaneously across the bank almost as if it were a concerted, coordinated effort, although it was not; many different people had had the same reaction to the placing of the leaflets and had responded in the same way. As a result of all this, Beta Bank chose to do nothing.

Not all was negative, however. The main object in distributing these leaflets was to raise the visibility of sexual minorities in the bank and publicize the fact that the lesbian and gay network was being launched, and to that extent it was successful because the action of distributing leaflets in the bank also created discourse about sexual minorities. Some examples were quoted during the focus groups. For example, the leaflet also offered participants at the launch access to the bank's corporate rates at local hotels; this caused comments such as: 'Somebody said that because we were offering them reduced rates to stay in a hotel, we were encouraging them to have sex. That's rubbish! I think that's insulting'. Amongst the young group of call centre operatives, the launch was seen as non-controversial: 'it's a social thing, isn't it?'. Even so, they actually had not heard about the launch themselves.

Silence: the blank response

Coming out can often be met with silence from others in organizations, which can be characterized simply as a blank response. On occasion, people in the Micro Department reacted with disinterest to the fact that their colleagues were gay, which is a recognized way of keeping minority sexuality closeted, hidden and silent. Steve was one of a number of men whom I met during the course of this research who had once been married and then come out as gay. This gave them quite a unique perspective on how people react to differently to heterosexuals and homosexuals in the workplace. Steve compared the two experiences as follows:

The reaction to my coming out was no reaction. I didn't encounter any hostility. There was gossip about it but not to my face. The big difference I noticed in the way colleagues treat me is the degree of interest they show in my life outside work. When I was married, it was a two-way process; there was mutual interest in the mundane things in life, what we did at the weekend, kids, pets, even the trip to the supermarket. That way of communicating is now closed off to me, to some extent.

Steve had moved from being married to a woman, to having a gay relationship, and felt that his second relationship was not recognized as valid by his colleagues at work in the same way that his heterosexual relationship had been.

I've noticed that I can be asking people about what they do, but as soon as I start talking about what I'm doing they shut down, because they're not prepared to hear, even though it's tedious and boring. Some people will talk about their children ad nauseum and what they did at the weekend, but then if I say what my partner and I did at the weekend, it's 'oh well back to work, got lots of emails!'. I regard the relationship I'm in now as equally valid to the one I had when I was married. This isn't the case with the people I work closely with so much, but is especially obvious with people I don't know particularly well.

Of course, we only have Steve's point of view here and every story has at least two sides to it. It may be that what he was telling them was really tedious and boring and they did not want to hear it, just because of that! Nevertheless, the lack of talk and interest in his private life made him feel different, abnormal and excluded. The way that language achieves closeness and intimacy between people through informal communication is an area which has been subject to quite a bit of research focus. It was referred to as 'phatic communion' by the anthropologist Malinowski in 1923, who described the way that we might use speech, not as a means of communication but as a means of oiling the wheels of social interaction. For example, in Britain, when we greet each other by saying 'nice morning, isn't it?', it is a means of interacting with each other rather than indicating real interest in the weather. It is also a means of defusing the potential hostility of silence in situations where speech is the usual means of communication. Steve's scenario, described above, suggests that by 'shutting down' and avoiding this social communication, the respondent's colleagues, consciously or unconsciously, are using silence as a tool of hostility. Work colleagues create social reality for gay people in the workplace, as much through the absence of what might be said, and what is left unsaid, as what is said. Of course, it is not only sexual minorities who suffer from the blank response: in 2003, David Sims discussed the issue in terms of middle managers who may suffer senior managers showing total disdain for the narrative of their lives, walking roughshod over the story they are creating. This reminds us that many different discourses are in operation in organizations and the narratives of sexual minorities represent just one genre of discourse. Many of the stories, narratives and situations that are recounted here could well happen to other groups of people in the organization.

When I discussed Steve's story with the focus groups, their reaction suggested that people may fear two things: one is the fear of offending, so it is easier to say nothing, and maintain the silence; the second is the fear of finding out too much. Gay men and lesbians are often seen as a lascivious and sexually-charged stereotype and so people hold back from asking about someone's weekend, if they know them to be gay, in case they hear about things which they would find embarrassing or offensive. In other words, they might get involved in a conversation of which the details might be unwelcome. One participant in a focus group said: 'There is a limit (to what you want to know about a gay person), but you can't control it – the only thing is to walk away.' They compared the potential embarrassment of talking to a gay man about his weekend with the embarrassment felt by work colleagues when an employee comes back to work after a death in the family, which might often be dealt with by avoidance and embarrassed silences. Another focus group participant said:

> The reason they clam up is that they assume that he is going to tell them exactly what he got up to that weekend, and they don't want to know. That would be their ignorance – he does do boring things, but because they've never met a gay person before they think he puts his pink spandex trousers on. I would assume it's something they've never encountered before and so don't know how to treat it. It's like when someone comes back to work after a death in the family – you don't know what to say to people – you don't know how to treat them. You don't want to ask if they're alright because you don't want to upset them, but you don't want to not ask if they're OK because you might think they don't care. And people in that office are thinking – if I ask him this he might think I'm prying.

The comparison the speaker makes of speaking to a gay man is with speaking to someone who has had a death in the family. On the face of it, the latter only happens once, whereas one is confronted with a colleague's sexuality on a daily basis. Another participant suggested that you might have a joke with a heterosexual about what they did at the weekend, but not with a homosexual colleague:

> We've got a girl on our section who's been going out with a bloke for a long time and they went away this weekend to a hotel, and I said when they got back – did you see any daylight – you haven't got a tan! But you wouldn't say that to a bloke who had taken his boyfriend away.

The idea that gay people have a sexuality whereas straight people do not is again demonstrated in this extract; so, for example, you can joke about a woman going away for the weekend with her boyfriend and not seeing the light of day, without it being an overly-sexualized comment. But, as the focus group participant said, you would not say that to a gay man because the context then becomes too sexual. Another participant said:

If I was a lesbian, I'd want to make people around me aware that it was OK. I remember coming back off holiday one year with a really good tan – there was nothing else to do in the resort other than get drunk and lie on the beach. We don't have a lot of ethnic minorities here, but there was this Indian girl and she came downstairs and said – God! You're browner than me! She said that, not me. I didn't say I've got a better tan than you. Then it was OK.

Many people accept that although stereotyping is not unusual between strangers, as people become more familiar with each other a friendlier relationship and better understanding gradually develop. Minorities often seek out ways of speeding this process up. It will come as no surprise that Erving Goffman has a name for the technique that people use: 'breaking through'. The Indian girl, to whom the focus group participant referred, had developed her own method of 'breaking through', by making a connection between the participant's summer tan and her own darker skin colour. Goffman makes a recommendation for people with a stigma in their dealing with 'Normals', that is to say those people who do not have a stigma, or in this case heterosexuals:

> Normals really mean no harm; when they do, it is because they don't know better. They should therefore be tactfully helped to act nicely. Slights, snubs and untactful remarks should not be answered in kind … When the stigmatized person finds that Normals have difficulty in ignoring his failing, he should try to help them and the social situation by conscious efforts to reduce tension.
>
> (Goffman, 1963b: 141)

Goffman then goes on to recount the story of a man who would always, on entering a room, whip out a packet of cigarettes and light a cigarette ostentatiously. After a short while, when he knew people would be amazed at what he could do with no hands, he would say out loud, 'at least I never have to worry about burning my fingers!' (Goffman, 1963b: 142). In the same way, responsibility is placed on the shoulders of the sexual minorities for lightening the atmosphere, joking or using banter to put the heterosexual majority at their ease.

A colleague of Steve's felt aggrieved because work social events were peppered with heterosexual couplings, which then went on to form the subjects of office gossip, but in his case did not, which he attributed to his being gay and therefore not of interest:

> There's a long tradition in the Civil Service of going off for a couple of days and staying in some hotel, and having these huge 'getting-to-know-you' sessions … And one occasion, quite a long time ago, I got off with somebody basically, very publicly – oh yeah, it was very public. I don't think it came as any great shock, maybe the incident came as a shock, but the basics of it didn't. I mean it wasn't anything I did deliberately. Since

then nobody ever said a word to me about it. It was almost like it didn't happen.

This particular event, by its unusual nature, being a homosexual and not a heterosexual coupling at an office party, was perhaps more likely to be talked about. Yet as far as the respondent was concerned, it was totally ignored by colleagues and other employees. By not being talked about, events are starved of the oxygen which would breathe life into them and give them meaning. By ignoring alternative sexualities, by refusing them the currency of social discourse the organization makes it more difficult for sexual minorities to construct an 'out' social identity, as the subject positions are not created and are therefore not there for people to take up. But importantly, what is absent in this scenario is any sort of naming, an important form of social acknowledgement. Gay people may be discriminated against at work because they fail to appear in accordance with accepted gendered norms and in this case the respondent failed to appear in accordance with accepted the heterosexual performance of coming to a social engagement with an opposite sex partner.

In the previous stories, silence was the manifestation of the refusal by the majority to engage in discussions of sexuality. But silence does not always mean the same in different contexts. Silence can also be a means of suppression by the majority, by not allowing certain things to be talked about. One comment of complaint from the focus groups was why we should be talking about lesbians and gay men at all. Heterosexuals were not singled out for special treatment so why should homosexuals be? One woman in the Micro Department said that:

> They have a right to exist in the working environment, but my sexuality is of no interest to anybody else. I don't have a website, and I don't have my picture in (the magazine). I just think they should be treated like everyone else in the department. What are we doing for single mothers?

This sort of comment was not that unusual and the issue of 'special treatment' is one which is contested across a number of diversity areas: race, gender, marital status as well as sexuality. As shown above, attempts to promote more visibility for one group can cause resentment by members of others. There is not always solidarity amongst members of the targeted group over such actions, nor support from those of other disadvantaged groups. But the alternative is the suppression and silencing of them altogether, rendering them invisible and making it harder for them to develop confidence and power through shared identity. Indeed, silencing discourse around sexual minorities is a very effective way of suppressing their identity, and those who would seek to do that might even go as far as denying that they even exist. In the Micro Department, this was most noticeable in the following story, which did the rounds of the organization:

> They have an Equal Opportunities Conference every year, and someone gave a testimony about what it was like to work in that particular office. At

one of these conferences, someone said it's not an issue in Darlington because they haven't got any (gays). That's gone down in history as the Darlington incident. The story goes round and round the department. It just showed how people there were frightened. As you move North it got more difficult for people.

This story was repeated time and again by different people during the research, first by a gay member of the department and then subsequently when it was used in the focus groups it seemed to be well-known by the people who participated. One person even said, 'This story about Darlington is trotted out at every conference'. Of course, the strength and effect that the story has in the organization starts to get lost when it is repeated so much. The following participant gave the background to the story. The comment was made at a diversity workshop by people who worked in Darlington, who maintained that there are not any gay people there. Nevertheless, as this participant notes, it is only because they do not know who they are:

> People in the Darlington workshop said that there weren't any gay people there so it wasn't an issue, but I could name at least five people on the Darlington site, except they're all in the closet – and why do you think they're all in the closet? Why do you think it takes somebody from London to facilitate a workshop of this nature in Darlington?

One focus group participant noted how worrying it was that the story was still doing the rounds:

> I was actually at the conference and heard that statement, and it's very easy to laugh and say 'how funny'. What's more worrying is that there is still that statement a year on, or two years on, and we're still smiling. It's a bit worrying that we haven't moved off there.

Another focus group participant suggested that the story was evidence of fear:

> I think it's evidence of something that's very worrying: evidence of fear. I'm a gay man and I worked in Darlington, and I wouldn't have contemplated coming out in Darlington. To be fair to London, it took me a further twenty-five years to come out in London, because I didn't think I'd get a fair hearing from colleagues in London. I was completely wrong I have to say. I encountered overwhelming support and a sense of belonging that helped me through the period. We often look on this as a north-south divide and it isn't: it's a big city thing.

Clearly the implication of the story, and of the comments in the subsequent focus groups, was that it was harder for gay people 'up North'; this participant, on the other hand, maintained that it was not an issue of North or South, but it was an issue of whether the office was located in a big city or not. I described this type of silence as suppression. It is not only the majority who can suppress stories, of course. One of the issues in using storytelling as a data-collection method is the idea that the researcher has very little power over the content of the research. In telling their story the interviewee has the power to surprise or shock, but ultimately they have the power whether to disclose something at all and they can choose not to reveal important elements of the story. However, I think this is better described as censorship, albeit censorship which is in the gift of the individual storyteller.

Silence as censorship

However, censorship does not remain at this level. Once told, stories can still struggle to be heard, not because, as we saw in the previous example, colleagues do not wish to discuss the subject, but on a more formal level the organization attempts to censor and silence. The difference between organizational censorship and unofficial suppression is that this type of censorship is an expression of official power. It is a process of which the researcher has to be aware and certainly one in which they may become involved, as censorship is an active process which may follow the act of uncovering certain types of information. The next story shows how, through legislation, the oppositional terms of heterosexual and homosexual have continued to be hierarchically constructed; the two terms are in a constant state of interdependence, as in order for heterosexuals to be prioritized and shown to be superior, the 'Other' or homosexuals have to be debased. 'Section 28' in the story refers to the common name for Section 28 of the Local Government Act 1986. This was a particularly pernicious piece of legislation, brought in by Margaret Thatcher's Conservative government, which prohibited local authorities in England and Wales, with an equivalent piece of legislation in Scotland, from 'promoting' homosexuality, and labelled gay family relationships as 'pretend'. It has since been repealed by a Labour administration. Raj's story comes from the Micro Department, a central government policy department, when the government first started talking about its repeal. I met him at a coffee shop in London; it was clear that the incident had affected him deeply, as the retelling of it was a deeply emotional experience for him:

> I was dealing with the whole area of HIV, drugs and health. There was a lot of very positive stuff that went on there. I was right in the midst of that. There were lots of strong personalities; lots of them with their own personal agendas and a propensity to go to the press and leak things. The first two or three years went very well. Lots of successes, lots of firsts. But, of course, in the midst of all of this we have the spectre of the repeal of Section 28. Things were getting increasingly difficult with the minister and his then political advisers. There were lots of unhappy, edgy ministers. I'd taken a hell of a lot of that stuff, and it all went pear-shaped at the last minute. The churches got involved, who, of course, are not slow at turning things to their

agenda; they thought it was totally inappropriate for a gay man to have such a strong say in the repeal of Section 28. I was then moved from my job and the story hit the newspapers. I was left to face a barrage of reporters on his own, with little support from the department.

As Raj gave me more detail about what happened, it transpired that he believed that the then Secretary of State and senior Civil Servants in the Micro Department had made the assumption that a gay man could not give impartial advice on an area dealing with homosexual issues. He was moved from his job to another area unconnected with gay issues, and someone from the Micro Department, someone allegedly quite senior in the department, leaked the story to the newspapers. To add insult to injury, the department gave him no support whatsoever and he was left to deal with tabloid newspaper reporters who were 'doorstepping' him at both home and work. One of the methods recommended by David Boje on the interpretation of stories in organizational storytelling research is to reinterpret the story, using a different kind of hierarchy. I think it helps point out how crazy the story is by retelling it with a woman in the role of the protagonist. They would have been dealing with women's issues, perhaps things like equal pay or improved childcare to allow women to return to work after having a baby. Something like equal pay would have been subject to legislation; indeed, over thirty years ago there was the Equal Pay Act. Once can imagine that in the mid-1970s, relations between a Civil Servant, the minister and his political advisers could have been quite difficult to manage. But it is difficult to imagine, certainly looking back with through the lens of the twenty-first century, that it should be totally inappropriate for a woman to have a say in the development of Equal Pay legislation. And it becomes almost impossible to imagine that a woman would have been moved from their job, or that their employer would have tried to humiliate them publicly by leaking the story to the tabloid newspapers.

A number of additional issues can be identified in this story when the hierarchy is replaced. First, it draws attention to the fact that Section 28 had been described as a 'spectre'; retelling the story, it would have been very strange indeed to describe the amendments to the Equal Pay Act in terms of a 'spectre'. Another element of the story that jumps out is the idea that the ministers, though obliged to push through this legislation, are not very keen at all, which was probably the case when the concept of equal pay was introduced. But, the reader is tempted to ask why the churches' involvement? What is their agenda? If this had actually been a scenario, it is likely that a different argument would have been used; instead of impartiality, advocacy would have been preferred, including women to ensure valuable access to their experience on the issue. This would lead to a very different conclusion; rather than being illegitimate, counting a woman as one of its members would have been seen as a prerequisite.

Conflating diversity issues can create problems, but the reinterpretation of this story, using a different hierarchy, and putting a woman in the role of the protagonist does demonstrate that different norms may be applied; where one working party on an issue seeks impartiality another seeks the representation, advocacy or experience of the disadvantaged group. The focus group particip- ants identified the same inconsistency of approach saying:

> The department doesn't have a problem with someone with a disability being involved with disability policy, but I think they do have a problem (with lesbians and gay men) when it comes to the press asking 'are these people fit to set policy'. And I think the department does have a problem with someone who is open about their sexuality appearing in the press.

This story was so explosive that it was subject to censorship of one kind or another on three separate occasions. The first example of silencing encountered in this research in relation to this story came in the next few seconds after the telling, as Raj asked me to switch off the tape recorder. The then Secretary of State was, allegedly, notoriously homophobic. Raj was too frightened to record examples of his homophobia, and repeating them here might be legally inadvis- able for me (it is interesting to note that even in the act of discussing this area of censorship, I felt it advisable to censor material for my own protection from liti- gation). The second instance of this story being silenced came soon afterwards, when I was asked by the organization not to use the story during the focus groups. But the story would not go quietly; it surfaced in every single one of the focus groups I carried out. The third time that this story was silenced, and actu- ally censored, was in the final report presented to the organization. Given the fact that everyone had talked about it, it would have been misleading of me not to mention it in the final report at all; I deliberated over this issue for quite some time and then finally decided to outline the story and people's reactions to it in the briefest of ways. The organization asked for it to be deleted completely before the report was submitted.

As Foucault says: 'Silence protects power.' Norman Fairclough, who has written widely on the subject of power and discourse, picks up on this point by discussing the idea that the majority tries to express power by eliminating dis- course about the minority. And, what better way to eliminate a minority dis- course, and assert the power of the dominant discourse than to remove the actual person responsible for the minority discourse?

Silence can protect

Silence can also be a mechanism of protection. The next story comes from Alpha Bank, and concerns an email that was sent around to all staff in prepara- tion for a series of focus groups that would take place to support the bank's diversity initiatives. Mark, a team leader in the bank's back office, picks up the story:

> This year, because of the merger, Alpha Bank was doing focus groups on various aspects of diversity, and they sent out this big email with all these

buttons to click on if you wanted to attend all these various forums; one for gender issues, one for race issues, then they had this narrative at the bottom where they said if you are interested in sexual orientation issues please contact this separate phone number. Now what they were trying to do was give someone with sexual orientation issues a confidential route, but what they didn't do was give gay employees a button, like they gave everyone else. There was a follow-up meeting and a focus group was created.

Every time I have told this story people have laughed. I find it transformative as a story, in that it decentres the traditional victim and unexpectedly puts the representatives of the organization in its place. Initially, sexual minorities are seen as the victims of the story because they were not given a voting button; but then the alternative, a separate phone number, is seen as so ridiculous that the story turns the victims into unwitting heroes and the Human Resources department, ironically, becomes the butt of the story, even though their initial action, was intended to be protective and they were acting from the best possible of intentions. A common theme in these stories is often a mistake, or a story of someone 'putting their foot in it'.

Because many heterosexuals believe that homosexuality should remain hidden, they prefer sexual minorities not to talk about their sexuality openly. This is often because they are often frightened of offending an individual by asking them to be open about an area of their lives that they believe should remain in the private domain. In this story, though, Alpha Bank's sexual minorities were encouraged to keep their sexuality in the private domain by not being given a focus group. Treating sexual orientation as something to be hidden and silenced keeps it in the private domain, although it is easy to think of other areas of diversity where the reaction is not to keep it private. It may be, of course, that closeted employees would appreciate the extra protection afforded by the helpline number, and not be offended by it. I have found that sexual orientation is often treated as a special case in organizations and is seen as a more sensitive, even shameful matter which therefore then has to be dealt with confidentially

Finally, silence can be viewed as self-protection and resistance. A crucial feature of Foucault's analysis is the concept of 'reverse discourse' where minorities are not only created, but also hostile discourse creates the opportunity for resistance. Silence can be used as a means of resistance in two principal ways. First, by remaining in the closet and remaining silent, sexual minorities can refuse to collaborate with the heteronormative discourses of the majority. They also control their own discourse; control is lost to an extent once silence is left behind. Identity may then become one of fragmentation and splitting into public façade and private view. This splitting can be notoriously difficult to research unless there is some leakage from the private into the public arena, for example where the interview becomes seen as a private confessional enabling some of the public façade to slip. Silence in this sense then becomes a form of passive resistance. It is much harder to do battle with something which is not tangibly present. Whereas silence in many contexts is associated with lack of power, the

LIVERPOOL JOHN MOORES UNIVERSITY
LEARNING SERVICES

withholding of knowledge which may otherwise provide others with words which can be used as 'evidence' or for 'persecution' can be empowering, and can also provide access into a world of talk that may otherwise be denied to someone. For example the silent person on their sexual orientation may overhear opinions which disclosure would send underground.

Summary

This exploration of silence through the medium of stories has shown that silence can take on multiple meanings and roles. There is the idea that undisclosed minority sexual identity is silent subjectivity; 'coming out' and taking up subject positions means leaving silence behind, which enables the adopted subject position to be more congruent with subjectivity. There can be an absence of language or an absence of a response altogether. Silencing can be used by a group as an active means of suppressing the 'Other', in this case minority sexualities. Silence can also be an example of censorship in the organization, demonstrating Foucault's view that silence can be an agent of power in its own right. In addition, silence can be used as a means of self-protection, either by not coming out and thereby refusing the heteronormative agenda, which exists in organizations or when, paradoxically, sexual minorities are in the majority, they can, themselves, use silence as a means of resistance.

6   Working out

Discrimination against lesbians and gay men in the workplace can be formal and informal, including verbal harassment, property violence and loss of credibility or acceptance. More formal types of discrimination can include decisions not to promote, to fire or not to hire, or to pay someone less on the basis of sexual orientation. Research carried out in the US by Lee Badgett in 1995 reported that gay men were on average paid 20 per cent less than their heterosexual counterparts, whereas lesbians, although paid less than heterosexual men, were paid on a par with women. In the United Kingdom, research also carried out in 1995 suggested that 36 per cent of employers would be less likely to offer a job to a gay man, and 31 per cent to a lesbian, whilst in the US, a study in 1997 suggested that 26 per cent of employers would not promote homosexuals.

Sadly, the introduction of the Employment Equality (Sexual Orientation) Regulations 2003 has not eradicated homophobic discrimination in the workplace. Not that anyone would have expected it to; more than thirty years since the introduction of the Equal Pay Act in the United Kingdom, women are still receiving substantially less financial compensation for their paid work than men. It could be argued that, to achieve legislative compliance or to achieve greater commitment from its employees, organizations should have policies and procedures in place which encourage the positive treatment of sexual minorities, or at least to prevent direct or indirect discrimination against them. UNISON, the white-collar union, achieved this through the creation of a lesbian and gay network and this sub-cultural grouping actually became part of the organizational structure in the union's commitment to self-organization. This is perhaps not so unusual now, but it was groundbreaking when it was created at the end of the 1990s. And yet, even policies are not the whole answer; coming fast on the heels of my own research was a related project looking at the workplace experience of lesbians, gay men and bisexuals carried out by Fiona Colgan and colleagues at London Metropolitan University. The project presented its key findings in June 2006, showing that there was still a wide discrepancy between employers' policies on sexual orientation, the actual practice by employers in the workplace, and the perception of how successful these were by the employees. Eighty-one per cent of the employers who took part in the survey were perceived to be 'gay-friendly', but only two-thirds of these were seen in the same light by their gay employees.

Nevertheless, what legislation does do is to focus the organizational mind as well as giving individuals a route to take action, should they be unfortunate enough to suffer discrimination in the workplace. Although the majority of cases do not get to the tribunal stage, and of those the majority are settled prior to the actual tribunal, there are still some examples: in March 2006, Peter Lewis, a gay male City executive had accused his employer, HSBC, Britain's biggest bank, of sacking him because of his sexuality. Mr Lewis, who was earning £1m a year as a trader, argued that HSBC had fired him unfairly after an incident in the gym at the firm's London headquarters. The accusation centred around Mr Lewis having looked improperly at a colleague in the changing rooms. In the first test of new anti-discrimination employment laws, he brought a legal action for £5m damages. The tribunal ruled that Lewis had not been sacked because of his sexuality, but it did find HSBC guilty on four other counts of 'unlawful discrimination on the grounds of sexual orientation' in the way his dismissal was handled.

However, the aim of this chapter is not to explore the legislative framework in any depth, but to illustrate how people react to minority sexuality in the workplace. In other words, what is it like working 'out' at the beginning of the twenty-first century? There are stories of exclusion, as one might expect, but there are also stories of inclusion. I have chosen stories which describe the way that sexual minorities have acted and interacted with rites and rituals in organizations, as well as the type of humour and banter which exists around sexual minorities.

Exclusion in the workplace

The ultimate exclusion for an employee is to be excluded altogether and sadly there have been numerous instances of lesbian and gay people losing their jobs. A study, in 1999, described the experiences of twenty-three lesbians and gay men who had been interviewed; of these, three had been discharged from the military on the grounds of homosexuality, three had been outed in the national tabloids which had resulted in their retirement from work, one lesbian had voluntarily transferred due to homophobia in the workplace, one gay man had been dismissed due to fears about AIDS, and others suspected they had not been offered jobs in the first place (Humphrey, 1999: 136). Interestingly, decades of discrimination in the armed forces were challenged in 2006, as openly gay members of the Royal Navy marched in the gay Euro Pride festival held in London. And they did so in full uniform, with the support of their organization. That is not to say that marching in uniform provides all the answers, even though it is a great step forward; those lesbians and gay men who did lose their jobs from the armed forces because of their sexuality have since received little or no compensation, even though the government has accepted that its actions were illegal.

Witch-hunts and persecution

Now, although it is hard to find parallels to the witch-hunts and persecution that went on in the armed services in civilian life, the closest examples perhaps come from civilian, uniformed services: the police and fire services. Freddie, a very senior officer in the police told me his story, which was a harrowing one of long-running discrimination. He started off by telling me that his sexuality had hardly ever been an issue. He hadn't been out at work and knew very few gay people: 'I certainly wouldn't have gone to a gay pub or buy a gay magazine if I had known where they were.'

He was promoted and moved locations to another station as an Inspector and had eighteen police constables and two sergeants reporting to him. He also had eight probationers at the police station. Freddie told me:

> I had always enjoyed working with probationers because their enthusiasm rubs off; because they're funny; because they do things wrong; and they're good for everyone to bond around. We had the best results; we were the section that everyone wanted to go on because we were lively. There was a lad who was a PC. He was totally idle, disorganized, but I also thought he didn't know what the point was, but he was a likeable, fit bloke, funny but in a funny sort of way. He was very street-wise and very good dealing with criminals. He just couldn't get his paperwork right. He'd done a year's service and I spoke to his sergeant and said he's crap at this. He said I've got so many of them I haven't got time to look at what they're doing. Anyway this lad was doing so many things wrong, he was turning up late, so he was always getting bollockings from the sergeant, and he was getting so bad we were about to take the decision whether to kick him out of the Job or not.

The 'Job' is the way that police officers usually refer to their career in the police force. Anyway, Freddie saw the potential in this still-raw recruit and looked for other ways of mentoring him. He continued:

> I put him out with a couple of PCs who were good and they said the problem is his paperwork. So, I sat him down with one of the sergeants and did an action plan, and we all signed this piece of paper in a little book – a performance contract if you like – saying that he would do work control sheets every day, and all his work was going to be monitored every day for a month. I really believed that that would bring him round.

About a month later, there was a change in personnel, and all the sergeants at the station moved around, swapping their responsibilities in the process. So, another sergeant took responsibility for the under-performing probationer. Freddie asked the new sergeant how the probationer was doing: ' "He's still crap", the sergeant replied. So I said, "He can't be – he's been on this performance contract thing for a month." '

At this point, Freddie decided to intervene and approached the probationer directly: 'I said to this lad, "Bring your work control sheets". And he said, "What work control sheets?" I replied, "The ones you're supposed to have been doing!" '

Exasperated, Freddie spoke to one of the sergeants who said he'd told him that he had ripped them up, because the probationer was doing fine. Freddie continued with the story:

> Well you never rip these things up, they're not evidential, but you keep them, they're like an audit trail. I thought this was a bit odd. And this lad was about to go up to HQ to see the ACC as a last chance before being kicked out. And I asked to speak to the ACC and said that this sergeant obviously hasn't done the things he was supposed to do. The kid's not crap he just hasn't had any help. So I suggested he write to Internal Affairs to investigate this sergeant for neglect of duty. He was prepared to let this lad get kicked out rather than admit he hadn't done his job properly. The sergeant was a bit of a piss-head, always skiving off work. He'd disillusioned me a bit because I'd trusted him. So this sergeant started a smear campaign. I begged them to move the sergeant off the section, because he was working with people who were going to have to give evidence against him. HQ refused to move him, and he was now out to destroy me. He suspected that I was gay and was going to use that as his weapon against me. At a social event he told another PC's wife that I was queer and that her husband was gay and that we were having a relationship at work. The real trouble came when the Internal Affairs department came down to interview people about the sergeant on the section who was in neglect of his duty, and the probationer and another lad became very cagey and stopped speaking to me. So, I approached the probationer and asked him,
>
> 'What's going on?' He was always honest and just broke down.
>
> 'They told me not to tell you. They were asking questions about whether you were queer or not, and what type of jokes you tell. All the questions were about you and not about the sergeant. They asked very little about him.'
>
> I checked with the other PC and it was the same. I went home and I just broke down. I just thought they're out to get me because I'm gay. I didn't know any other gay people to speak to. None of my friends knew I was gay.
>
> There were other things like we were having this weekend in Spain and some of the probationers couldn't afford it, so one of these lads came to me and said that he couldn't afford it. So I said I'd put it on my credit card and he could pay it back over three months. But Internal Affairs found out and they were trying to say that I was trying to pay for his ticket, the young lad. But he said that I'd lent him the money. I really thought my career was going to end at that stage.
>
> As it happened, the probationer and I became even friendlier. He was in trouble, and so was I, and as a result we formed this bond. I didn't come out

to him but we did used to go down the pub. At that stage I thought I've got to tell him and I felt devious if I didn't tell him, bearing in mind he'd told me all about himself. So I told him and he said, 'Bloody hell!' He kept that completely to himself.

Unfortunately, Freddie's problems did not end there. Freddie told me that there was an assistant chief constable at the time who was, allegedly, notoriously homophobic and very religious. Freddie picked up the story again:

It was about Christmas four years ago; I sent an email to myself (at the time everyone could read everyone else's messages) saying 'Dear all, just to say that following the investigation the chief constable is going to let me stay on at this station, Happy Christmas to all'. I sent that message to myself knowing that there were so many people wanting to know how I got on with the chief and would read my message to see what had happened. I didn't send it to anyone else, just to myself so that other people could go on the network and read it. Within an hour, I had a message from the homophobic ACC, saying 'your message hasn't helped, this may change things'. I spoke to my boss, the chief super, who was very supportive, who said that it was absolutely outrageous – they won't leave you alone will they? She comes back a day later and calls me in, very stern face and said, 'You aren't going to like this. They're investigating you again.' She was almost in tears and said, 'There's been an allegation made that you're living with another officer. The allegation is that you and the probationer are living as two homosexuals.' I never thought I'd come out with it but I said, 'I'm just fucked off with this. I'm going to tell you something now that I've never told a senior officer before.' But I couldn't say it, I just said, 'Yeah, *I* am. *He's* not and he knows *I* am. Big deal! Who's made the complaint?' I was in tears at this stage.

So I started to tell all my friends. A few close friends. There was a couple round the corner. There were big cuddles, tears and they said they knew anyway. About three days later I told my parents. I'm an only child and they had no idea. Devastated. My chief super sees me and she interviews my neighbour who's also a policeman to see who stays at my house. She put in writing who'd made the allegation, a female officer who'd seen the probationer and me at a party. I'd sent a card to this girl and put 'Love Freddie', and because he's lazy and hadn't bought a card he signed mine as well. She misread that. The two allegations were 'Breach of Police Regulations', because I hadn't declared who I was living with, and the other one was 'Bringing Discredit on the Police Service', which is a real biggy.

I came out to everyone. I just got people together in the office and told them. I could actually say 'I'm gay' by then. A lot of people were emotional, which made me emotional. It was good because the feedback was good, but there was no support. My boss put a report up to the chief constable saying that the allegations were false, but in the process I'd decided to come out and declare my sexuality. I thought that was an end to it. I did put a report back in to the chief constable saying I'm now out, but what's going to happen to this sergeant who made the allegation. Didn't get a reply. I said to my boss that I hadn't had a reply and she got quite shirty saying I think you should just forget it. She'd been bollocked for telling me in the first place. I thought there's not much more that can happen, now. About a year after that, a woman I knew twenty years ago in Plymouth rejoined the force and I bumped into her at HQ. She said I got married, left the job, now he's gone off with someone else and I'm on my own again so I've joined The Job to get some money. So I took her out for a meal, she said I always knew you were gay, and said,

'I can't take you out for a meal in return, because I'm broke, but come round to the house and I'll cook you something. My ex-husband has got the kids.' I go round there one Sunday evening; she cooks a nice meal, knock at the door, in come the three kids, along with the ex, and within a minute he's got his face in mine going, 'Fuck off. Are you a homosexual or what? I don't want you round my kids. All homosexuals are paedophiles.' Now he's a detective in another part of the force, so I said,

'I think we'd better forget this, you'd better leave and we'll pretend it didn't happen.'

I put in a four page report when I got back to work. My mate took it up to HQ. The deputy chief constable said he would take it seriously and he said he would assign a chief superintendent to look into it. Two years later I still haven't been interviewed about it! In the meantime, they spoke to this bloke who made all sorts of counter allegations; the force then began a dossier on me. The person who'd been assigned to investigate the incident started investigating me. I went and saw the chief and complained. He didn't know about it, but said that if a complaint had been made it had to be investigated. And I said – no one has spoken to me! So he appointed someone, and I was interviewed for trying to get a lift home in a panda car whilst coming out of a nightclub, which wasn't true, peeking at someone's girlfriend through a crack in the door, all sorts of crap. At the end of it, I had the Federation there, I was choked; I couldn't believe that I had made a serious allegation which hadn't been followed up and yet they were inter-viewing me about all this crap. They went through my personnel file, and because I hadn't been sick in sixteen years they tried to imply that even that was false. I then decided to take the force to court, and even the solicitor said that this was outrageous, because I had so much evidence against the force. When I started writing to them through a solicitor they starting inves-tigating me even more. The force had made a balls-up, but instead of admit-ting it, they tried to find more against me to try and shut me up. In the end they appointed the assistant chief constable to sort it out, because no one in the force had sorted it out. The chief then put the Integrity Unit to investi-gate my claim; I'd been moved to HQ by this time and they were telling me all sorts of things, like my email was being monitored. I'd been told by the

Federation and by a senior officer that my phone was tapped in my office. It didn't bother me because all they'd find out was the truth. In the end, there was a public declaration on our Force Orders, saying that we accept that I had been treated unfairly on several occasions. I also had a £10,000 settlement, which was sufficient to ensure they wouldn't do it again, but not so big that people would think I was doing it for the money. The money was never, ever part of the goal, but I wanted them to think that they would never do it again. The probationer got £2,500.

That was last Christmas. Ironically in January of this year, a PC rang me – apparently I was being investigated by Internal Affairs for having sent a letter to someone's wife four years ago. I of course went straight to the solicitor, and the chief went ballistic again. The force hadn't put the mechanisms in place to protect me. If I hadn't done it, the chief would have just self-destructed.

It's like Stephen Lawrence, in that although it's a bad experience, some good's come out of it. We're one of the forces that's adamant that diversity isn't just race, it's also gay issues. In other forces, they'll only address race and won't address gay issues. In some areas we've got far more gay officers than black people.

Freddie also told me how he uses this story positively by retelling it in diversity courses arranged by the police. He told me:

I get messages afterwards. I had one from one woman who said it made her think that whatever you want in life you have to keep going, you must never give in. You have hurdles but you must overcome them. I always say that you must take comfort in your friends as well. My family still don't know anything about this, but my friends did and your friends are what keep you going.

Not all stories are quite as dramatic as Freddie's, though; inclusion and exclusion is often much more subtle. Being identified as an outsider may lead to social isolation and hostility. In this research project, one lesbian in the fire service was included in the watch banter through her male colleagues betting on who would be able to sleep with her first, whilst exclusion was arrived at informally through the withdrawal of affection and excluding a gay colleague from eating with the group.

Self-exclusion

Another form of exclusion is the self-exclusion that gay people impose on themselves, and the increased division between work and home, involving a simple double-life of those at work who think they know the whole person, and those outside work who really do. In another study in 1989, one lesbian recounted, 'these guys go home and their friends are the same people they see all day. For me, coming to work means bowing out of my own world completely, and going into theirs' (Hall, 1989: 131). The lesbians in Marny Hall's study also realized that if they shared the ordinary events of their day-to-day lives, they would show that they were different from everyone else. One way to avoid this was simply to avoid heterosexual colleagues and any situation where they might have to socialize with them. There are also situations where the individual lives a 'double-double' life, moving in two circles each of which is unaware that the other exists with its own and different biography; an example of this might be the police officer who does not come out as gay in the workplace, but equally does not tell their gay friends outside work that they are in the police, because their identity might be discredited in either context.

One method of socialization is literally just to socialize with colleagues; most jobs do involve a degree of socializing, leading to countless situations which involve sexuality. Traditionally, male activities such as sporting activities are opportunities to do business and become part of the team. And, although gay men are not necessarily unwelcome in any of these settings, they may find themselves unwilling or unable to join in the sexual banter that accompanies these occasions. And for those people who wish to exclude their gay colleagues, social occasions are another opportunity to do so. However, socialization into the job and the organization can sometimes take more of a sinister overtone for sexual minorities, and it is not uncommon for them to go through some kind of initiation. Some of the stories in this chapter will touch on the types of initiation rites that people are invited to take part in when they join these organizations.

Like members of other non-dominant groups, sexual minorities cannot always predict whether they will be accepted and may find it difficult to predict the reactions of other people. On the other hand, it is sometimes easy to predict the reactions of others; it is true to say that, unlike other non-dominant groups, lesbian and gay people are not always visible and so those people who would be reticent about making racist comments in front of a black colleague may not hold back from homophobic banter purely because they perceive no sexual minorities to be present.

Much of the research carried out to date focuses on the 'gay man' or 'lesbian' as their focus in research, irrespective of where they work. A very small number of articles, however, has considered the organizational context; a few studies in the past have even looked at small organizations where sexual minorities were in the majority: Weston and Rofel published a 1997 study of conflict and trust in a lesbian car-repair workshop in the US and, more recently, in 2002, Atila Bruni and Sylvia Gherardi published an account of a research project carried out in a gay newspaper in Italy. The former was an anthropological analysis, using a case study approach, of a strike in a lesbian workshop, called Amazon. The researchers interviewed eight out of the ten women who worked there, including the two owners. The strike was about a number of issues, but largely about pay and conditions. The major difference in being out at Amazon to coming out in a straight organization was, as one mechanic put it '(that you) didn't *have* to talk about being dykes. It was pretty obvious!' (Weston and Rofel, 1997: 28). In a sense, Amazon was no different to any other small business which fosters 'multiplex' relationships between its employees, that is to say enabling employees to build up relationships which transgressed the work/home divide, but the research found that a principal effect of allowing employees to be themselves in the workplace was to integrate emotions into workplace dynamics. In particular, this manifested itself as a strong sense of trust, and a feeling that a common lesbian identity would overcome other differences. In Bruni and Gherardi's ethnographic case study of a gay newspaper in Italy, the researcher was a straight man who was asked, during his time hanging around in the offices of the newspaper, whether he had a boyfriend or whether he was single. He replied truthfully that he was single, but neglected to mention his sexuality and the fact that he was straight. What is interesting about this piece of research is that it demonstrates that the same dynamic of 'covering' one's sexuality that I discussed in the previous chapter can be as relevant to a straight man in a gay environment as it can for a gay man in a straight environment. Bruni did, in fact, come out to his client as straight at a later date.

Another piece of research to look at the issue of homosexuality in organizations was a case study carried out by Elizabeth Wilson in the year 2000. She looked at the area of inclusion and exclusion in three different organizations, considering the treatment of diversity within the framework of organizational culture. The original aim of the research was to explore how men and women progress in organizations, but this inevitably led to consideration of how other groups, including homosexuals, fared. In one of the companies, a professional services organization, it was reported that 'one would have to be very discrete if one were gay' (Wilson, 2000: 288). In another one, a media organization, it was suggested that it was 'OK to be gay' (Wilson, 2000: 293). Wilson highlighted the importance of analysing symbols in organizations; she showed that one of the characteristics of the media organization, which differentiated it, was that sexuality was not brushed under the carpet and sex was a significant 'symbol' in the organization. This would suggest that those organizations which are prepared to talk about sexuality and acknowledge the existence of sexual minorities may represent a more positive environment for them. A major symbol in some organizations and occupations, which can have an impact on sexual minorities, is the use of uniform. An often quoted advantage of uniform is that it can alleviate some of the problems of sorting through the wardrobe in the morning in deciding what to wear. More importantly, from the gay employee's point of view, it can potentially reduce an employee's visible difference. Although a large body of work exists on the importance of signs and symbols in organizations, less work has been carried out on the impact of organizational symbols on sexual minorities. This was an area that Susan Miller, a Delaware based academic, looked at in the US when she and her colleagues carried out a study into a Midwestern police department, published in 2003. The study suggested that police culture typically embraces symbols of aggressive masculinity, such as physical strength and toughness, while also adopting behaviours intended to reinforce their heterosexuality, such as dominating behaviour towards women and the ridiculing and harassment of gay people. Latterly, in 2006, a London Metropolitan University project targeted sixteen gay-friendly organizations, although the data seemed to focus more on the individual and their experience rather than the organization in which they worked.

An important part of a gay man's or lesbian's workplace experience is the language that other people use at work about sexual minorities. Even in quite accepting organizational cultures, language use can be less than welcoming. In Wilson's case study, despite the organization being relatively accepting of gay men, it was reported that in a group discussion heterosexual men still felt able to make comments such as 'enough of them about', 'nearly overrun' and 'not here – we got rid of them all' (Wilson, 2000: 293). Homophobic remarks are commonplace, and it may be no more than a joke, comment or anecdote that sets the tone. In a survey of lesbian and gay journalists reported by Woods and Lucas, 81 per cent had heard derogatory comments about gays or lesbians in general or about a specific employee (Woods and Lucas, 1993: 16). Often, sexuality is linked to the person's ability to do the job. For example one trader on Wall Street said of a colleague that it was bizarre 'that the guy's a fucking faggot and he's still trading' (Woods and Lucas, 1993: 17). However, it is not possible to mention language without mentioning the fact that whilst vilified, sexual minorities are paradoxically also largely ignored (Woods and Lucas, 1993: 5). Even in forward-thinking organizations where progressive diversity management practices have given a voice to previously silenced sexual minorities, discourse around those very same sexual minorities may be, ironically, sometimes silenced. The literature seems to be inconsistent in this area: there is a focus on derogatory language with less discussion on other important areas of discourse, such as issues of stereotyping, issues of what is said and what is silent and also examples of language of affirmation and acceptance.

Team-working and group behaviour can have a tremendous impact, both positively and negatively on the lesbian or gay individual in the workplace. Humphrey reported in her study published in 1999 that one heterosexual female assistant would not work with her lesbian manager because of group pressure from other colleagues. Also, managers in service roles may be out with colleagues internally, but may not be out to the public, as in the case of one lesbian social worker reported by Humphrey. One adolescent client found out and requested a change in carer, which leads to a change in behaviour between working with colleagues and external service provision. This situation often arises with lesbian, gay and bisexual teachers who may well be out with colleagues in the staffroom, but are not out to pupils or their parents. In the fire service there is a difference in external service provision, where firefighters take pride in giving everyone the same high standard of service, and internal working with colleagues, where there are frequent examples of sexual minorities being badly treated.

Where lesbian, gay, bisexual and transgender people have been in the minority in organizations and unwilling to be identified, it has not been easy on the whole for researchers to select specific organizations and study the dynamics of minority sexuality within them. Three recent studies, however, are an exception, having focused on single organizations: the British police (Burke, 1993); UNISON, a trades union in the United Kingdom (Colgan, 1999a); and a study of lesbian and gay police officer in a Midwestern police department in the US (Miller *et al.*, 2003). Burke's study reported the experiences of lesbian and gay police officers, largely in their own words. In 1999, Colgan's study drew on interviews with twenty-five lesbian and gay union members in order to illustrate the value of developing lesbian and gay networks. In 2003, Miller *et al.* took an interesting approach, recognizing that the police is an occupation which is gendered and sexualized and their research, involving sending anonymous questionnaires to seventeen police officers, looked at the ways in which heterosexual masculinity informed practices and social interactions within policing. These studies have attempted to give an insight into specific organizations and what it is about them that create a positive or negative environment for sexual minorities in the workplace. I think that it is interesting to note that two out of these three examples are in the police, suggesting that there may be something about the stereotypical masculinity of the police which attracts researchers' attention.

The ultimate exclusion at work is to lose your job. Generally speaking, it's very hard to prove that this is as a result of homophobia or that sexuality is in some way to blame, but that's not to say that there aren't plenty of examples where people believe that their sexuality was the reason they had to leave work. In Humphrey's study, where twenty-three lesbians and gay men were interviewed, three had been discharged from the military on the grounds of homosexuality, three had been outed in the national tabloids which had resulted in their retirement from work, one lesbian had voluntarily transferred due to homophobia in the workplace, one gay man had been dismissed due to fears about AIDS, and others suspected they had not been offered jobs in the first place. Since 2003, it has been illegal in the United Kingdom to discriminate at work on the grounds of sexual orientation; this does not mean that discrimination no longer happens. For a case to come to light it is dependent on the individual being brave enough to bring a case against their employer, as well as having enough firm evidence to back it up. Inclusion and exclusion at work isn't always as clear cut as keeping or losing your job; although a number of the interviewees in this research project had received some pretty harsh treatment, including several who had been outed or attacked by the national tabloid press, I found that inclusion and exclusion in the organizations that I studied is often much more subtle.

Excluding customers

The following story is about a customer of Beta Bank who went into a branch to open up a joint cheque account with his same-sex partner. The application was refused by the personal banker because she believed, wrongly, that it was not possible to have a joint cheque account with a same sex partner:

> I've heard stuff where people speak to a male and assume their partner is female and make assumptions. But after all, it was only a year ago that the

bank's policy stated that you had to be married to have a joint staff account. That was changed after a piece of work carried out by the Sexual Orientation Task Force. Now anyone can have a cheque account with their partner. I don't think that ever applied to our customers; even so, there was a customer who recently rang up a personal banker in a branch in the Southeast and said that he wanted to come into the branch to put his partner onto his account as a joint account holder. She said 'Fine, no problem we can do that for you.' He told the personal banker his partner's name, and she said 'is that your Father?', and he replied, 'No, no it's my partner'. And her whole attitude changed. And she said, 'Oh no, you can't do that it's got to be a family member, or a member of the opposite sex.' It's factually incorrect, but this story made me think, if we're saying things like that to our customers, what are we like to our colleagues?

Considering that it had been the bank's policy until relatively recently that staff should be married in order to qualify for a joint staff account, it is perhaps not surprising that the personal banker misunderstood the regulations. Participants in the focus groups commented that this 'Sounds very familiar'. It wasn't clear whether this was because they had heard the story before or whether they had heard of similar things happening. Interestingly, the bank's employees didn't see this unfortunate incident happening as a result of the personal banker's own views, but instead as a result of what the personal banker believed the rules to be: 'I think if the personal banker believed that that was the bank's rule they wouldn't challenge it; they're just thinking 'That's the rules' and that's what they stick to.'

Another participant said: 'I think there is something in here about bank rules. I think the language is interesting 'You can't do that'. Nothing to do with me – it's the organization.'

It is true, of course, that banks, just as other organizations, are worlds of formal rules and procedures, although in this case it turns out that this rule was incorrectly applied and outdated, if it had ever existed. It may be that the rule was an excuse and that the personal banker was relying on the rules as an excuse to justify her own actions, saving herself the trouble of having to defend an unfair decision.

Team dynamics

The following story is about a firefighter who wanted to further his career by training to use the unit which carries the heavy lifting and cutting gear. To do this he had to change stations and watch:

They moved the Fire Rescue Unit, which carried all the heavy lifting and cutting gear from Station 'A' up to Station 'B'. I'd put in to transfer to 'B' and do a course to drive the FRU. Nothing came of it and I was told that there weren't any vacancies. But then the person in charge of the FRU approached the training staff for some advice because he had a problem. And the problem was that there was a gay guy who wanted to transfer to train up on the Rescue Unit, and the guys on the watch weren't happy about it, so he wanted to know how he should handle it? I've spoken to my governor, but I want to work it out myself. The best thing to do is to work it all out, because either I won't get there, or I will get there and I'll have to work with them.

The problem here is that the watch had found out that this individual is gay, or has heard a rumour to that effect, and as a group they refuse to work with him. The implication is that all the firefighters currently working on the Fire Rescue Unit are heterosexual and they believe that heterosexuality should be a key qualification or recruitment criterion for being able to work there. What is more, the watch commander or team leader has taken their concerns seriously and has tried to get further advice on what he should do.

It seems as if either the commander shares their views, or sees some legitimacy in them, or the watch itself is in charge and that the commander does not really know how to manage them. It is presumably quite unusual to go to the training department for advice on issues such as these since it is not really a training issue as such. However, on hearing this story, other firefighters said: 'They're entitled to their views as well,' reflecting the much-vaunted view that as diversity gets an increasingly louder voice in the fire service white, male, heterosexual firefighters are not allowed to hold differing views. They expressed the view that on the one hand they were encouraged to be open and honest in their discussions with the fire service management. And yet, with this one issue they would not be able to be open and honest, because they would not be able to go to the chief fire officer and tell him that they did not want a gay man on the watch. Not all the views were negative, however; another watch identified this scenario as 'unacceptable' as follows: 'It's just unacceptable to discriminate against somebody just because he's gay.'

However, they went on to say that this sort of behaviour is not reserved for sexual minorities; people are always objecting to working with one another for one reason or another:

> People are always saying I don't want to work with him, or her, and it's a case of I'm sorry you'll do what you're told. That's the way that we've always dealt with it here. If you've got a problem it's your problem not anyone else's and you'll have to sort it out or leave.

The focus group also recognized that although that problems of this nature would be dealt with in their particular brigade by telling the watch that they would have to work with whom they were told to, it was not necessarily the same in every other Brigade and especially at junior management level there is inconsistency with the way that these sorts of problems are resolved. Tom recounted a very similar scenario from the Delta Department. I met him in a café in central London. An energetic, engaging storyteller, he admitted that, although in many ways he had had very positive reactions from people, there had, nonetheless, been negative experiences. He described the main one when he was promoted from his department's equivalent of executive officer (EO) to higher executive officer (HEO):

> I was given instructions to join one particular team, and then I was moved to another one without being consulted. I didn't think much about it at the time, but when I joined this other team, one of the people in my new team said that the team leader had made some comment that I was joining, and he said I hope that no one in this team has got a problem with that. I thought he was just paving the way a little bit. And then at Christmas time, my former Grade 7 (team leader) approached me, and he explained to me about the move. In the team I was originally posted to, three male members of the team said that they were not prepared to work with me. Their Grade 7 (team leader), instead of challenging them, went to the Grade 5 (head of division), and put forward the same case that these three guys had put forward. The Grade 5, who was a staunch Catholic, then facilitated my move to another team.
>
> I did think it was strange that at the time that not only did I move, but so did the work that I was doing. It was only when my manager came to see me at Christmas and explained that these were the machinations behind it all, that I realized what had gone on. And to cap it all, at that time I was the trade union rep! But the moment had passed, I had been promoted, and there was an element of goodwill on my part – I didn't want to make waves. When it settled in, I do regret not making a complaint – after all being the TU rep, if I can't make a complaint, who can? I was disappointed in myself for not following it through, but definitely disappointed in my senior officers for just accommodating this prejudice.

In this case, unlike the fire service example, the issue had gone up the hierarchy and the decision had passed through two different layers of senior management, neither of which questioned or challenged the view that this group did not want to work with a gay man. Of course, it could be argued that Tom had introduced prejudice of his own, by saying that the Grade 5 (or his department's equivalent of a Grade 5, a senior grade and a member of the Senior Civil Service) was a staunch Catholic. And although Tom perceived this to be discrimination against him, at least he received his promotion; the focus groups suggested that his story was probably more indicative of the department's inability to deal with management issues than any issue of institutionalized homophobia. One focus group participant said:

> If I was going to compile a book of department stories, then this one would be the first one in the book. This isn't just applicable to a gay person. This happens time and time again to anyone who happens to be in a minority, or

happens to be a victim. Unfortunately, we have a classic remedy. If there is a problem, and the problem is to do with prejudice – don't tackle the prejudice, move the victim. This is applicable to the whole of the Delta Department.

Indeed, so widespread is this phenomenon in the department that this particular story caused a cascade of other stories in a similar vein in the focus groups. One such true story, though a little risqué, is about an employee in the Delta Department who used to masturbate in an open plan office. Obviously, there were quite a few complaints and finally management were forced to act. Instead of sacking him, which everyone expected, they solved the problem by offering him an office on his own, which was normally reserved as a reward for promotion. Many of the comments in the other focus groups were in a similar vein:

> There is a general attitude of avoiding trouble and putting people on long term sick rather than dismissing people. The organization is terrified of going to an employment tribunal. People who are problems, we will just put up with them. It's the easiest way out.

This story created quite a negative reaction in one of Delta Department's focus groups, however. One woman became quite exercised and angry at the idea that Tom might have been upset at the way that he had been treated. The focus group was carried out in a town in the North of England and the woman was local, white and middle-aged. This is what she said:

> It seems to be that you can't upset *them.* I don't want to sound negative, but it all boils down to normal people ... Because the gay chap's upset, it then becomes a problem. It wasn't a problem before that ... It was alright till the gay person found out and then he was upset and it became a big thing. How about your normal person – how about if he'd been upset? It seems to be that everyone gets uptight when these minorities are upset. I was always brought up to think I'm a normal person. I've lived here all my life. I'm not anti-gay, I get on with anybody, me. But ever since I've grown up I feel I'm treading on eggshells and you can't say things and I think why should I tread on eggshells for everybody? Why should I have to change my life? We go on all these diversity courses – why should I have to change my way of thinking? If someone is anti-gay, so what? Why should they have to find out what these people are thinking and feeling? They've got things against us normal white folk and nobody says anything. That doesn't seem to matter. You can upset us and it doesn't matter, unless you're black or gay and you upset them and you've had it. There's a coloured person at work who can talk to me how she wants and it's not classed as racism and I retaliate and I've had it. They don't see themselves as racist. It's always the white ... I agree with what the department's doing, but the way they're doing it is alienating people and making the issue bigger. The only group that seems to be left out is the majority group.

The woman splits the world into 'normal' people and 'minorities'. Interestingly, she sees women as belonging to the 'normal' category, with black and gay people in the minority category, whereas in a focus group made up of men, women may well not have been seen as normal. She seeks to put the blame for upsetting the majority, white, heterosexual community on the minorities. The importance of identity construction comes out in this piece; she asks why she has to walk on eggshells, but of course identities are delicate things, and if you care about the identities of the people you are working with you have to treat them carefully. She objects to the idea that she might have to change her own identity or personality, in response to society changing around her. But her views do highlight the importance of recognizing that the identity of those in the majority are sensitive as well, and that heterosexuals may have difficulty in negotiating, not only the area of sexuality, but also the complex area of identity construction and reconstruction. Organizations have to think about how they include everyone in their diversity initiatives and about how not to exclude the majority. The woman's tirade actually has the effect of encouraging a gay man to come out during the actual focus group. He went on to talk extremely positively about the focus groups themselves and how they had been the first thing he had actually seen the department do for their gay employees:

> In the twelve years I have been in the Civil Service, this is the first time *ever* I've seen anything on sexual orientation, apart from the bland mission statement. This is the first positive move I have seen the organization make towards gay, bisexual and transgendered people. If you look at the statistics, we know how many women, how many part-timers and how many disabled people we have, and it's broken down by grade and their age group. The one thing we have never seen is how many gay people we have in this organization.

By this time, the focus group had broken down into chaos, as everyone started talking at once.

Promotion – or the lack of it

The next story is about the difficulties that some sexual minorities experience in getting promotion at work. But why should sexual minorities experience more problems in getting promoted than anyone else? Well, sexual information is used to make tacit judgements about people in the workplace, especially at more senior levels where technical qualifications become less important, and the way that the individual is viewed by their peers and superiors is the benchmark by which they gain promotion. Trust inevitably has a sexual dimension, as was described in the case study of the lesbian car-repair workshop, highlighting the importance of emotion in organizations. People want to build trust with others through, amongst other ways, finding common personal ground, for example talking about the wife, the kids, their schools and so on. Lesbians, gay men, bisexuals and transsexuals can be perceived as untrustworthy at worst and, at best, lacking the necessary fit to reach the senior levels of the organization. There is, of course, the phenomenon of 'homosocial reproduction', where managers promote (or reproduce themselves) in their own image. This concept has important implications for equality and diversity in general, and sexual minorities in particular, where those further up the organization tend to be openly heterosexual and surround themselves with people who exhibit the same sexual signs. Ben, a gay firefighter of officer rank, told me the following story about the difficulties that he had experienced in trying to get promoted:

> I was just coming up for a promotion, and I didn't get it. It sounds bitter and twisted, but I felt I didn't get the promotion because of one of the senior officers' attitude towards me. I didn't challenge it because it would have been a very difficult thing to prove. I decided instead to move on and to prove to myself and to him that I was capable. I put in for a promotion in another brigade. That was a lot harder to get because I was the outsider, against seven other people. I got it. It was nice to be able to say I'm leaving because you didn't give me the promotion I deserved, but I got it somewhere else. It was the best thing I ever did. I've got a whole new life now. The brigade's a lot bigger and a lot busier. It was hard because it was like going back to being a new boy again. Funnily enough, some time later, I spoke to one of the officers who was on the interview board who used to work for my brigade. I didn't know at the time, but he was aware that I was gay. Subsequently, I found out that when they offered me the job, this senior officer from my old brigade found out and rang him up and said, 'You do realize he's queer?'. And apparently this senior officer who'd just offered me the job, said, 'Yes I was aware of that, it's not a problem and he was the best one on the day.''

Although Ben succeeded, and there is a strong sense of achievement when he tells the story, he is nonetheless a victim of discrimination along the way. He refused to be cowed by this setback though and proceeded to be very successful in his new brigade. The views of the focus group participants ranged from suggesting that they would have a hard time proving that he had been discriminated against to suggesting that the senior officer should have kept his views to himself. For example: 'He's got a problem hasn't he and he likes telling people he's got a problem instead of keeping it to himself.'

The focus groups were clearly of the opinion that the discrimination that had gone on was unfair, but recognized that prejudice at quite a senior level was not uncommon: 'For him to ring up another senior officer – in any organization you're always going to get people like that.'

Inappropriate language and behaviour

In the police force, there are numerous examples of where inappropriate behaviour and language has been the response to someone's coming out in the workplace. Hugo, a bisexual civilian support officer in the police, told me the next story; we were sitting in his kitchen over a cup of coffee, and he explained that he had heard of two incidents where there were two separate examples of inappropriate language. One was from a civilian who was applying to join the police and the other from a police officer:

> There's a real culture of challenging inappropriate behaviour. There was a detention officer, who applied to join the regulars, but he failed the fitness test, and if you fail the fitness test you're out straightaway. It was alleged that he said, in the changing rooms to one of the other recruits:
>
> 'To get into this police force you've either got to be queer or a spade.'
>
> It wasn't reported back at the time, but this other recruit used it as evidence when he was interviewed for the police. He was asked when he had ever challenged inappropriate behaviour. He said:
>
> 'Funnily enough, in the gym the other day, one of your employees said "…" and I challenged it.'

Hugo explained that they followed it up and ended up sacking the detention officer, the internal candidate, for saying it. He continued:

> I thought was probably going too far the other way. There is a danger that they get too hypersensitive. On another occasion, a gay man had been given a beating by some squaddies, just because he was gay, or appeared to be gay, and the investigation was taken very seriously. There had been a gay murder in Plymouth shortly before that and it was dealt with very well. But one of the guys investigating this beating was in the canteen and someone was asking him about the incident, and a uniformed officer said:
>
> 'Serves him right for being a pouf.'
>
> That was dealt with by somebody saying to him:
>
> 'Don't be silly.'
>
> In the first example, the detention officer was sacked for a much less serious offence, but he was support staff. In the second example, he was a regular police officer, which just goes to show there is a real 'two-employee' culture.

Hugo's story is quite shocking, being an example of where a police officer thought that a gay man deserved to be beaten because he was gay. But the story here is also about the two-employee culture which exists in the police. In the focus groups where there were sworn staff present, people denied that there was a two-employee culture. Where there were focus groups exclusively made up of support staff, they were quite vociferous in their support of the idea that they were treated less well and they cited different examples: getting paid less; having fewer career opportunities given to them; and being treated differently in a disciplining situation as described in the story above. Indeed, since police officers are protected by police regulations, and support staff are not, it is in fact disingenuous of the police officers who took part in the focus groups to suggest that they are not treated differently. The main discussion that was generated by this story was that incidents like this had created a culture of fear of speaking out, and that this culture pervaded the police. One comment that was made in the focus group summed up the views of many: 'Bit severe that he was sacked and lost his job over a comment like that.'

Other views included that from a police inspector who explained that he thought the way that the two incidents had been dealt with had to do with the audience. He explained that if a more senior officer had heard the comment, or at least had heard of it from someone else, it would be more likely to be dealt with severely: 'The fact that he mentioned it to a high-ranking officer at his interview board meant that it was going to be dealt with severely. The guy in the canteen was probably spoken to by a sergeant who dealt with it at the time.'

Then, after someone had challenged the idea that the organization had sacked an individual for making a politically incorrect comment, there was a lull in the conversation; no one wanted to come forward and support his view. The silence went on for so long that I intervened and asked whether there were any comments, to which the answer from a uniformed police officer was a rather sulky 'no'. No one appeared as if they wanted to speak. Then, in an effort to explain the silence, a sergeant spoke up and explained about the fear of speaking out which now existed in the police:

> I think we're all hypersensitive about what we say these days, even in here, you're worried about what you're saying. In this day and age you just don't voice your opinions – it's as simple as that. In a way, he got what he deserved. It's a simple as that. You've got rules, you step outside them and you've got what's coming to you.

Even in a focus group, then, where the participants had been assured anonymity, they were still frightened of saying what things were really like in front of colleagues, for fear that someone would report them to a higher authority. I think that this situation rather interestingly demonstrates the Foucauldian view of power relations: power does not disappear, it merely reappears in another form of expression, or repression. This particular police force has demonstrated by its words and actions that bullying of sexual minorities is no longer acceptable, but has replaced one kind of oppression with another: that of not being able to speak freely.

In fact, silence has become an unwritten 'rule' of this organization. It is perhaps unsurprising that an organization, whose purpose is about following rules and ensuring that people are brought to book if they do not obey the rules, should have people within it who support such a harsh approach. It is an appalling comparison though that in Hugo's story, the man who lost his job was a support officer who was sacked for suggesting that you had to be black or gay to be successful in getting into the police. In the same story, a police officer who said that a gay man, who was beaten, deserved it just for being gay, did not get the sack.

Blake's story is interesting because he reports on the way that sexuality is dealt with at training school. He explained that the police have a special duty to ensure that their younger constables and those who are less experienced are appropriately trained to deal with the various different situations as well as the diversity that they will encounter during the course of their working lives. And yet, despite the significant amount of diversity training now carried out in the police in the United Kingdom, it is still focused on race, and remarkably little on sexuality. It is therefore interesting to note that, at the training school that Blake attended where, he assured me, there is no formal training input on minority sexualities, sexual minorities are set apart and divided through the carrying out of 'gay' scenarios, in order to be able to deal with gay members of the public. Blake explained that in his story a gay domestic argument was set up between two trainees in order, supposedly, to prepare the officers for having to deal with two gay men having an argument in reality:

> When I was at training school, I was walking past the place where police officers and trainers act out scenarios, for example an RTA or a domestic. There was an unsupervised scenario of two gay men having an argument. I couldn't believe what I was seeing and hearing. It was a case of (puts on very camp accent), 'Get out of my house you naughty boy, you've gone and slept with another man!'. It was pure Julian Clary, it was so camp. I challenged them on it, saying, 'Why are you acting so stereotypically?'. And they said, 'What's it to you?'. I replied, 'The reason I'm saying that is that I don't think most gay men act like that on the whole, though I'm sure some do.' They asked, 'How do you know?' so I replied, 'Well I'm gay! And I'm a bit offended by it.' One of them thought I was joking, and told me where I could put the banana I happened to have in my hand. I was prepared to leave it there, but they went and spoke to their trainer about it, the one who had sent them up to do this gay scenario. The staff trainer calls my staff trainer and I get called in to explain what had happened. He offered me all sorts of counselling. He asked if I would like to speak to a gay officer – he said that they had one in South Wales. I persisted and said that I was most dissatisfied that the trainer would send recruits to practise a gay scenario. I asked if they would do a black scenario? They said no, so I said, 'Well don't do a gay scenario, then.' You can't blame the boys who are doing it, because the diversity training at this particular training school, although very good quality and extensive, is all to do with ethnic minority issues. Not one minute is spent on lesbian and gay issues. In rural areas only a very small percentage of the population is from ethnic minorities.

If we imagine for a moment that a woman had told this story what becomes clear is that it is indeed ridiculous to do a gay scenario, just as it would be to do a female scenario or, as the storyteller pointed out, a black one. The trainer's response also becomes totally inadequate, to offer the complainant counselling, presumably for being too sensitive. The police has a habit of responding in a

medical way to homosexuality in the police. Clearly, Blake was offered counselling because the stereotypical view of gay men is that they are sensitive,
perhaps the trainer thought that he needed professional help in order to be able
to take a joke. The immediate reaction seems to have been that it was Blake's
fault and that he needed help. One focus group participant tried to explain why
gay scenarios are carried out at training school:

> 'I'll give you the party-line on it, if you like: the exercises where students
> are given gay role plays, are in relation to their attitudes and behaviour. In
> our training school we don't do black role plays because there are very few
> black officers and we wouldn't ask someone to portray somebody who is
> black. If we do have a black officer we do ask them if they wouldn't mind
> taking that role, although we are very much aware of the danger of making
> them a victim. So it's a balancing act. That should never have been an unsu-
> pervised role play. The lads that were sent to do it should have been given a
> firm briefing about what they were supposed to be doing.'

Role plays are therefore used is to test the attitudes of the majority of the students. And yet, the participant admits that they would not do black role plays for
fear of offending, nor would they automatically ask someone who was black to
take that role. Most focus group respondents thought that Blake should just have
ignored the role play and not said anything: 'I think he should just have ignored
it. Perhaps these trainees have not come across many gay people and they associate gay people with Julian Clary, and people in the public eye.'

This last comment provoked a conversation about how people do not generally know gay people and that when they get to know them you find out that
they are quite similar to you: 'Having said that we've got someone senior in the
force who's quite open and it's the first time I've had to confront it. When you
get to know them you find out they're quite similar to you.'

Inclusion in the workplace

These previous two stories have been about exclusion in the workplace. Now, let
us turn our attention to a more positive story about how sexual minorities can be
included in organizational events.

Rupert (if you remember, he's the guy who works for Alpha Bank) told me
about the recruitment event that they ran for lesbian and gay graduates:

> The lesbian and gay network recently organized a recruitment event for gay
> and lesbian graduates who were considering a career in investment banking
> but were scared that it may represent a step back into the closet having
> enjoyed a relatively liberal time at their college. There was a panel session
> and Angela Mason (the then Chairman of Stonewall, the London-based gay
> and lesbian lobby group) attended. It was well attended with over 100 stu-
> dents from all over the country, on a Friday night in the pouring rain. In the

end, though, it was a great success; a lot of graduates came, some of whom were out to shock, purple fingernails and outrageous dress and that kind of thing. It's quite interesting that there were a lot of senior guys who came along to support the initiative and I felt there was no tension. I was very impressed. I just thought the banking world can switch off. There were some negative comments too; some senior people asked 'what the fuck's going on?' Other people looked at our posters and said, 'what a waste of time!' I guess they were finally being honest about what they thought, which was a bit of a disappointment. They didn't have to do anything, they weren't asked to support it, make a stand or express their opinion, their reflex was to be negative. At a minimum, you should be able to expect people to say, not my issue, I'm not interested, but if that's what you're into, get on with it and all the best.

Even though a very positive story about how the bank encourages the inclusion of lesbian and gay employees in its official activities, the event still manages to attract an amount of criticism. It is interesting because it is about trying to attract sexual minorities into the organization, something which is very rare even in so-called gay-friendly organizations.

Dan, an employee in one of Beta Bank's call centres, told me another positive story about inclusion in the organization: it was about how well his boss reacted after a rather unpleasant homophobic attack. Dan picks up the story here in his own words:

One positive thing which came on the back of a very, very bad experience I had was when I went to a works' party, about two years ago. I was beaten up because I was gay. The guy who did it had been loud and aggressive to everyone all night, and I was with a girl about to go home; he was really mouthy to her and I turned round and said 'don't talk to her like that because she's a woman' and he said 'so are you', more or less. So I thought 'here we go'. I said 'I'm not getting into this right now.' Then he started, 'I've never liked you since you started, you shout your mouth off, you order me around,' and he started smacking me one. (I'd been promoted out of the help desk, but I was in charge of procedures and processes so indirectly still had an impact on their environment and had to ask them to do things for me.) The police were called and I phoned in the next day to explain what had happened to my boss. He was fantastic and told me to take a couple of days off, not to come in, and to wait until my face had calmed down, so that I didn't have to face people at work. The guy who did it was actually an agency guy. My boss spoke to the other girl and then phoned the agency and said that the guy wasn't welcome back if he was going to take that atti-tude at a works' party. Although it was outside work, it was a works' party and the same rules apply and he was asked to leave. They did everything they could to make sure I was OK – did I need more time off? Did I need a counsellor? That was a really positive experience.

Whilst the attack took place at a party, and therefore not in the workplace, it was a party which was almost exclusively for members of the bank and Dan's boss deemed it to be a work event. Although his attacker had accused him of being a 'woman', he never appeared to accuse him of being gay, and the accusations seemed to centre around his management style rather than his sexuality directly. It was almost as if the agency employee objected to being told what to do at work by a gay man. What is most interesting about this story from an organizational point of view is that the manager, presumably backed by the organization, asked the individual to leave and telephoned the agency to tell them that such behaviour was not going to be tolerated by Beta Bank. It was enough to help Dan see a very negative situation as an overall positive one in the way that he had been dealt with.

Every organization has its rites and rituals; amongst these are those occasions which are celebrations, such as birthdays, weddings or leaving-dos, where colleagues want to get together to show that they are pleased for the individual. Of course, the wedding has, until recently, been the epitome of heterosexual celebration. This is no longer the case, as in December 2005 Civil Partnerships were introduced in the United Kingdom. Civil Partnerships are, to all intents and purposes, identical to civil marriage for heterosexual partners. Pat, an employee in the Delta Department and the equivalent of a Civil service senior executive officer (SEO), was going to have a ceremony with her female partner; she told me the following short story about how they were treated by their colleagues:

> My partner and I had a ceremony; it was talked about quite a bit, you know. Someone did ask, 'Are you both going to be wearing dresses?' and, 'Are you both going to be wearing suits?'. It was talked about quite a lot, though. I had cards and presents. My senior manager came in and did a proper presentation in front of everybody. I don't think everybody knew I was marrying a woman, but a heck of a lot of them did. They had a collection and bought me a present and a lovely card. I don't know how comfortable people were with it, but they seemed comfortable, so that's fine.

A really heartwarming account of how Pat's colleagues made her feel welcome and included at work. Pat had been married to a man once upon a time, had had children, who were now grown up, and was now getting married again to someone of the same sex. She saw the two relationships and weddings as equal, thereby destabilizing the notion that marriage is purely between and man and a woman and is exclusively a heterosexual event. Pat's story is a joyful one of inclusion and positive interest in the individual's life outside work. Note the emphasis on 'It was talked about quite a bit', which is mentioned twice. Her ceremony is talked about a lot, but in a positive way, and the usual office ritual of passing round a card and collection takes place. This is a very positive story and is recognized as such by the focus groups: 'The organization didn't have to do that – that speaks volumes in terms of people moving forward.'

The groups did not necessarily see the question about whether they both wore dresses as a particularly negative question. For example:

> Heterosexuals don't always get married in a white wedding dress. All the weddings I've been to, the woman wears a nice suit and so does the man, so what does that mean? If you took the 'both' away it would totally change the question, but it's no different you'd ask anyone else.

This is one of the rare stories with a theme of celebration, and a good news story. This quality or ingredient may also exist in other stories, of course, but in this one it is a key element. The following story is not much more of an anecdote, but tells of the way in which Sam, a lesbian firefighter, was treated when she first joined the watch. One of the ways that new recruits become socialized within the watch is by going through some kind of initiation ceremony; in this case, Sam described what the socialization process was like for her, which involved the other firefighters betting on who from within the watch could sleep with her first, and in the process changing her sexual orientation:

> They actually ran a book, a betting book, to see who the first guy would be who could get off with me, and change me, or my orientation. I only found out about a year after it had been running, and they were like, 'we've given up now!'. And I was like, 'I wish you'd have told me if there was any money involved, it might just have done it. We could have shared, come on!.'

Rites, rituals, humour and banter

Sam's short scenario gives an insight into the rites and rituals that take place in the fire service. Firefighters relate that these are nothing compared to what they used to be, but often firefighters are still 'tested' by their colleagues when they first join the service, in what can be referred to as a rite of passage. In this case the initiation ceremony would have been for the new recruit to have sex with one of the male firefighters. This testing is, in fact, a second selection system, but one which is every bit as important in fire stations as the official one. There is an unspoken assumption amongst the male firefighters that sexual orientation is nothing more than an attitude of mind and that this can be changed almost at will. The story also shows how the individual can increase the likelihood of being accepted by the group by using humour and turning the tables on them. Once they realized that they would not be able to sleep with her, they began betting on when her period was due. Humour and banter play a special part in the fire service, and making fun of each other plays a large part in this. As one focus group participant said: 'You could get ribbed if you have an allotment.' Some of the personal attacks have a darker side, though, and it would be hard to describe the following anecdote as funny:

'When I joined as a whole-time firefighter, there was a character on my watch who was very outspoken. My name's O'Toole and the first thing he said to me was 'you IRA bastard', in a joking way. And basically he went on with this and then the whole watch started to say I was a member of the IRA, Gerry Adams' brother and then when they bombed Warrington it was like I WAS the IRA. This was a joke, and if I had objected he would have pushed it and it would have become oppressive intimidation.

It is hard to believe that the person who recounted this can have still thought that this was a joke. There were different explanations given as to why people indulge in this sort of banter. Some said it was because firefighters saw such terrible things that they had to indulge in humour and banter to deal with these situations. But by tolerating certain types of employee humour, the fire service runs the risk of reproducing an oppressive working environment. Others maintained that it was a way of testing new recruits:

It's just a bit of banter that every new person gets. It's not malicious. The old hands put people through it to see their strengths and weaknesses. At some point you're going to have to put your life in their hands. You want to know what limits you can go to.

Still other explanations were that the job was so boring that there had to be some light relief, illustrating the importance of the work context. Of course, much of the firefighter's job is spent 'hanging around' waiting for an emergency to happen; no one would want to ring the emergency services only to be told that they were busy and were on another call. Slack is therefore built into the system and hanging around is part of the job; it is during this down time that much of the banter and horseplay takes place. For example, as one firefighter said:

It makes it enjoyable to come to work, otherwise it would be boring; if you come to work and you're not allowed to speak to anyone for fear of offending them you'd be bored witless and the organization wouldn't get the best out of people. If you don't enjoy it … it's down to them, where the line's drawn.

It is interesting that, once again, the responsibility is given to the individual to indicate where people have gone too far. Occupying firefighters during this downtime can be a challenge, and fire stations are well equipped with pool tables, televisions and video recorders, kitchen facilities and, of course, the 'brew table' where the watch congregates, so called because the first thing they do at the beginning of the shift is to sit down around the table and drink tea. At nighttime, firefighters have rest areas, but because fires do not occur with the same frequency as during the day, most firefighters treat these areas as dormitories. There is a growing recognition within organization studies of the significance of joking in the workplace, and the idea that humour can actually be used to transmit serious messages. In the police it was suggested that joking around was a tool used to test whether people were to be relied upon in extreme situations. There were also many other examples in this research project in the fire service of humour, joking around and initiation ceremonies that had more sinister undertones; buckets of water above doors, bed-rigging and water fights. Name-calling was also prevalent; one respondent reported that one colleague's nickname was 'Noodles' because he collected the lids off Pot Noodles, and had actually appeared in the company magazine of the manufacturers.

Groups that are numerically scarce in organizations face a particular predicament; they find that they become tokens and are treated as representatives of their category, as symbols rather than individuals. They become community spokespeople, being asked to give the gay perspective on all sorts of issues. We return to Tom at the Delta Department; he told me the following story where a fellow tax worker approached him for his presumed specialist knowledge of male prostitutes. Apart from the issue of gay people as token, this story also demonstrates a situation in which humour might be used; in organizations, the funny stories that are told might just be unrelated humour, or they might be humour to do with specific aspects of the job:

> When I was a case worker, I worked in inheritance tax, and there was somebody who had a £50K debt for 'various entertainment'. So my colleague, the case worker, challenged this and asked what it was for. His sister explained that he had died of AIDS and, towards the end of his life, he had had lots of drugs and lots of male prostitutes. We had to decide whether that £50K was a reasonable sum or not; my colleague approached me and asked, 'What's the going rate for a male prostitute then?' There was just a lot of humour around the office. I probably was the obvious choice in the office for information about the gay scene. So I said, 'Well, it depends what service you're getting, what it is, how long it is and so on.' And then he went back to this chap's sister and said: 'In order to agree a figure for this, we need a few more bits of information.'

The temptation is to be righteously outraged on Tom's behalf, which was the reaction in all of the focus groups. Why should Tom know, as a gay man, information about the cost of prostitutes, and why should his colleagues have come to him? Even though he had told this as a funny story, it caused more offence amongst the focus groups: 'I think this story is nastier than the others and there is a nastiness in the way that it could be played out.'

They assumed that the case worker was making stereotypical assumptions about gay men: 'It also assumes that because that person was dealing with the case they know all about male prostitution and it's lumping all gays into one big box, therefore you must know about whatever.'

Another focus group participant asked whether heterosexuals would necessarily know the going rate for a prostitute, as follows: 'It's like all heterosexuals can tell you the going rate for a prostitute.'

Another person said,: 'I think if that had happened to me I would have said, excuse me, what are you implying?'

Of course, Tom takes the wind out of the sails of that particular line of interpretation by saying 'I probably was the obvious choice'. It was also an opportunity for him to throw the humour back at his colleague by saying 'It depends on what you're getting,' inviting his colleague to go into unwanted, perhaps embarrassing, details. The focus groups were surprised that Tom had not reacted in a different way:

> What sounds strange about this story is how passive the gay person sounded. He didn't sound offended, they went along with the jape in the office. He answered the question and cooperated. He was almost semi-conforming with the stereotype. Because even if you're out, you've still got to defend yourself.

Although perhaps Tom was doing what Erving Goffman had recommended: assuming that the 'normals' meant no harm and he was playing along with them in order to oil the wheels of social interaction of office communication.

For the next story of inclusion, we return to Rupert at Alpha Bank, who recounted the story of when the lesbian and gay network successfully persuaded the bank to provide sponsorship to Stonewall, the lobbying group for lesbian and gay equality:

> In 1999, the gay and lesbian network, approached the bank and asked if they would sponsor the Stonewall Equality Dinner. Stonewall is the lobby group for gay and lesbian equality. It was small fry compared to other corporate sponsorship that the Alpha Bank would have done for other corporate events. The bank agreed although initially nobody wanted to discuss the thing or have anything to do with this. There were other large companies who took part, and the bank had two main justifications for taking part; one was to make corporate business and private banking contacts and the other was to support the bank's gay and lesbian employees. Some eyebrows that were raised by some people, but private banking was told to come along and be supportive, which they did, with a certain amount of grace, as well, and a very good time was had.

Rupert then went on to recount the conflict that ensued between one of the bank's very wealthy private clients; someone who cannot be named here for legal reasons, but who was responsible in the 1980s for the successful running of a former public-sector organization, and making a lot of money in the process. As a very wealthy individual, he had a lot of influence with the bank; he was also notoriously homophobic, making no secret of his views, and it caused a lot of tension between him and the bank when he found out that they were to sponsor the Stonewall dinner. The dinner went ahead, with the bank's sponsorship, as it was considered more important to stand up for the minority employees of the bank rather than cave into the prejudiced views of a client, no matter how important. Rupert then went on to tell me how the evening went:

> Apparently it went very well. Although some of the businesses weren't that keen on going. There was a big article in the FT, a lot of press coverage at the time. I don't know what impact it did have on actual business coming in, but it was all good PR. Because this is all new territory, the fact that it happened at all, was noteworthy. Certainly, there were things that could have been improved upon, but it was a small but significant step.

Clients and customers

Visibility, particularly visibility of sexual minorities within organizations, means that you have to engage with different people in different ways, and not just the people you work with. You also have to deal with clients and customers, sometimes important customers who might disagree with your organization's positive stance towards sexual minorities. Visibility also means that dissenters in the organization may raise their voices; people are going to realize, perhaps for the first time, that there are lesbian and gay people working for their organization, and that there are activities within the organization specifically aimed at supporting the lesbian and gay cohort. The organization then takes a stance, perhaps a positive one, towards sexual minorities and co-workers might be very supportive, or they may react very badly. In one the stories we have heard so far, from Alpha Bank, not everyone was entirely positive when they heard about the sponsorship of the Stonewall dinner; Rupert told me about one of the reactions to it, where a senior manager in the bank, originally from Spain, apparently said when he heard about the dinner: 'In my country we burn these people.' He was, of course, referring to gay men and lesbians. Rupert also told me about the time one of his clients tried to find out whether he had a girlfriend or a boyfriend:

> I haven't been asked by a client whether I'm gay or not, but it is true to say that as a relationship becomes deeper with a client, there will be a certain amount of licence given. And, in fact, there's an interesting illustration of that when one of my clients, who I have a very good relationship with. I told them that I was going on holiday, and she always has been trying to find out whether I'm married or have a girlfriend or whatever, and, of course, I've been deliberately vague on the subject. So she says to me 'Ha! So you're going on holiday! So, you're going with your girlfriend are you?', and I said 'no, no, no', 'OK then,' she said, 'if you're not going with your girlfriend, you must be going with your *boyfriend.*'

Rupert managed to hide his shock and surprise, as this conversation was over the phone, but he was definitely taken aback:

My jaw just fell to the ground; because of course that was the last thing I expected her to say. And in fact, I said to her, 'no, no, no, it's just a friend', and she just gave a little chuckle down the phone. I genuinely was totally unprepared for that comment, plus the fact that a lot of gay men and women feel that they want to make their sexuality a known quantity when talking to clients. I'm a much more subtle person. I prefer, on a case by case basis, to see how things go. I don't think it's that relevant to be perfectly honest. Whilst I wouldn't deny it, I wouldn't be comfortable myself knowing that this is a very important client suddenly saying well yes actually I am going on holiday with my boyfriend. Although I told my boss about it – he chuckled and he thought it was absolutely hysterical. And, certainly there's been no harm done, so maybe it's my problem rather than theirs, but you know part of me wants to remain quite private so there's a limit to how much I do want to share. I had some clients come in last week, they came in last week, a husband and wife team, and they asked me if I was married, and I said I'm not married and we left it at that. So, it's certainly something that comes up.

Of course, the question of sexuality and sexual orientation sometimes goes beyond whether the client accepts it or not; sometimes it is a question of whether it actually helps you do business and strike deals. I met Miles, a business banker with a branch of Beta Bank in the City, for a coffee one lunchtime. He was quite camp and totally charming with it. He was very self-aware and, making reference to his mannerism, when he started telling me his story he said: 'Most of my customers know I'm gay; it must be the way I act!'. The angle that Miles was coming from was that being gay in central London was a positive advantage in the business world. He gave me the following example:

> I've got a couple of gay customers who are really glad that I'm gay. They say 'we don't *need* a gay bank manager, but it's quite nice to have one.' When I met them for the first time, I went down to meet them in their offices to talk about an empty building they were taking over for a new business. I obviously didn't know they were gay at the beginning, and I was having a really bad Monday. Then, when we started talking about the business and what they were going to do with the building they wanted, they told that me that they had a gay gym down in Vauxhall and that they wanted to expand and open another one in this new building. I was like 'Yes!'.

At this point, Miles punched the air to re-emphasize the point he was making. He continued:

> I was so pleased. It made my Monday, and the day didn't seem so bad after all. They hadn't realized I was gay and they had taken down all the pictures in their office that they thought might be offensive. I said that a) this is your business and your environment and b) you'd better have them up next time I come round because I might want to see them too!

Miles was firmly of the opinion that it helped to be gay in business, especially in central London, where quite a number of people he came across were gay, even if they weren't involved in specifically gay-oriented businesses, like the people he had referred to in the story. Other people in the Beta Bank focus groups thought it a good thing too, re-emphasizing the business case for diversity; one employee said: 'The view of this story is that it helps bring in more business – I certainly agree with that.' Another employee who came to the focus groups happened to be gay also, and made the following comment:

> I know the pink economy is huge and traditionally I don't think the bank has tapped into that. When I go round to the various gay prides around the country you always see XYZ (a competitor of Beta Bank), but you never see us. To me that is such a huge waste. One of our competitors has realized it and they are getting the business. We should never turn away business; as a shareholder as well I want to make as much money as possible. Also I want my profit sharing to be as big as possible. The problem is that people have a very staid image of us.

Another Beta Bank employee in the focus group was a woman who explained that this story, and her colleague's reaction to it, reminded her of what it had been like for women in the bank some years earlier. She admitted to going out to get business from women:

> We're still very conservative. When I was a relationship manager, I was one of very, very few female relationship managers at the time, and I think it helped. I had ten colleagues who were all male, and I deliberately went out to find female accountants and solicitors and things like this to try and get across the fact that there are female customers. And as for that comment in the story where he says: 'you don't need a gay bank manager', no it's quite true you don't, especially if people are open and honest, but it must be quite nice to sit down in front of somebody whom you feel can relate to you.

Another employee asked about the kind of business that the story was referring to, and I confirmed that it was a gym, but aimed at the gay market. He went on to say:

> I wish there was more customers like this. I know that when we recruited retail businesses in the past we wouldn't recruit anything in the sex trade, be it gay, straight or whatever; we are now recruiting some but we would use the same risk criteria as any other kind of business. We don't want a brothel, but so what if a shop is selling whatever?

But then the woman interjected and started to explain how difficult it had been for her working in the bank as a woman. She explained that when she was a bank manager in the branch network, she used to wheel a male messenger out to speak to certain customers (a messenger was a low-ranking employee who would take the post from one branch to another). 'Clients wouldn't talk to me, but they would talk to the messenger!'. But then she reiterated how important an understanding of diversity was to winning business for the bank, and that this was as important in the area of minority sexuality as any other. She explained:

> About seven years ago, I was a relationship manager and one other (male) relationship manager said to me 'he's a shirtlifter', referring to a customer, and I'm convinced we lost that business because that customer heard that comment. I felt very uncomfortable; I didn't know where to put myself. I knew it wasn't the right thing to do, but I was a junior manager and I found it difficult to challenge. I don't think the population has changed that much, actually.

What is interesting about these comments overall is that, perhaps axiomatically, when talking about customers and clients the argument for equal treatment is very definitely based on the business case, rather than it being the right thing to do. The first speaker talks about the power of the pink pound, and the fact that their competitors are being much more aggressive about going after this section of the market, for example having a presence at the gay pride events. Apart from the banks, the other organizations in this study were all public sector ones, and so it is perhaps no surprise that these organizations were the ones which referred to their customers most, and referred most to the business case and the profit imperative. The next story is also about dealing with customers, and was told to me by Leslie, a transsexual who joined the bank in one of their call centres. Initially, I didn't intend to include transgender individuals in the study, restricting my definition of sexual minorities to lesbians, gay men and bisexuals. The reason I set out this way was that I thought there were quite a few things which set the two communities apart: for example, it's about gender not sexuality; they may have been through physical changes that the gay community would not; and after all, they might not be gay. But then my definition changed after I was contacted by a number of transsexuals and transgender employees in the organizations I was working with who expressed an interest in taking part in the study. As Leslie explained to me, there were definitely reasons for taking part: one of them was that there were often issues of sexuality associated with gender change. For example, a previously straight man might, through a change in gender, become a lesbian; in other words, your sexual orientation is not necessarily going to change along with your gender. Transsexuals often experienced the same, or very similar, dynamics of discrimination in the workplace to lesbian and gay employees and, of course, there was the very simple reason that they were such a small community overall that joining together with the gay community was one way, and a legitimate one, of getting a voice. That said, Leslie's story was a heartrending one, starting as she did with the problems she had had at work as a pre-operative transsexual before she came to work for the bank:

> About three years ago, because of my gender change I lost my job through selective redundancy. When you're looking for another job, and when you're truthful about yourself, people find a way around employing you. And if you're not truthful they can dismiss you out of hand for not disclosing, so you're in a catch-22 situation between disclosure and non-disclosure.

And so, Leslie found herself living as a woman, but still pre-operative, without work for some considerable period of time. She described the period as 'very nerve-wracking and upsetting'. Nevertheless, she was a practical person and realized that she had to improve her chances at getting work by improving her academic qualifications, so she went on to study at university part-time (and was just finishing her third year when I interviewed her). She explained about how the poor treatment at work continued, still prior to her joining the bank:

> I had to subsidize my finances by getting myself a job and took a job as a dishwasher. There was no way any company would put me in the front line, so I was always put at the back. It was alright there for a bit, but after twelve months, a sixteen-year old lad came in. He was a trainee chef. He was very derogatory towards me, very lurid comments, calling me things like 'old slapper' and things like that, but in the end it got so bad that we had a head-to-head and he said something so foul that I hit him. I walked out of the job. Straight after that I went for a job at a hotel, I explained my position and I got a job in the kitchen washing dishes. But the female workers wouldn't let me use the female toilets. I was in the right to keep using them, but the management did approach me to ask if I would mind using a toilet that was separate. It was sort of segregating me. I moved out of the job.

Leslie realized that she had to get a job in a different work environment because the treatment she had received in the workplace was making her very unhappy indeed, to the point of having a serious impact on her health. She told me:

> I looked at Beta Bank. I took the interview test and passed it, but it was at the time of my operation, and I thought I'm going to lose the job. I told them that I had to go into hospital for an operation and that I would be in there for about three weeks, and they said you can start a month afterwards. I thought that was a great start. Most other places wouldn't have held the position open – that was the first time in forty-odd years that anyone has ever done that for me so it was special, very special. Before I'd even joined Beta Bank, they'd managed to make it special for me.

I shared Leslie's moving story with a focus group in a different call centre in the same bank, and the discussion which ensued is a fascinating insight into the way that call centre technology interacts with minority identities. One of the participants explained that, in her experience, the bank provided certain facilities which helped people in a similar situation:

When I worked in Manchester, I worked with a pre-op tran, and she had to live as a woman for two years before the operation; Beta Bank will provide you with a user card, so that you can have a female name on it and when you're going out as a woman you can use your female card.

She did admit, though, that the bank didn't do this especially for transsexuals; as long as you're the authorized user of that card you could have any name you wanted on it. Nevertheless, it was a useful support for people who were legally living with a different identity. In the focus group, there then followed an exchange about whether you would have a transsexual dealing with customers, either in a branch or call centre environment:

I don't know though – would they put a very obviously transgender person on the counter? They wouldn't. They still have an image and image still matters. They could be laughed at by the public, or they could say – what are you dressed up like that for, do you know what I mean? I think Beta Bank's doing a good to embrace transsexuals, but in terms of where they place them after employment, there's still an image issue, isn't there?

Another employee of the bank thought it might be easier to put a transsexual in a call centre:

I know a couple of people who have had a sex change and they sound alright, they don't sound any different – so if you're talking to somebody on the phone, you'll think 'that's a normal person', but if you see them face to face and you're thinking, she's had a sex change, she's a bit funny. If you're on the phone you can't see them.

But then other people identified potential issues. For example, 'If you sound like a man, the customer's just going to think they're talking to a man.' It also happens the other way around, of course. In a call centre, an operative may well question whether the caller is the right person if they have a very deep voice, but give a woman's name. As another employee of Beta Bank explained:

It's happened to me. People across the floor have said 'Sue, I need your help – I don't know if this is the right person.' It's happened to me twice, where the person on the other end of the phone has said I've had a sex change, and you're like (sharp intake of breath) what do I do now?

But, as the others agreed, you've got to challenge it. If someone says they're a woman, but they sound like a man, you can't assume that they're telling the truth because with the arrival of telephone banking getting the security right over the telephone is paramount. However, they insisted that when they hear the reason, there's no problem at all. Then there was a short exchange during which the employees discussed ways in which they could improve the experience for transsexual customers ringing up the bank's call centre. The most popular suggestion was for the bank to hold the information about the customer being transsexual on their computer system: 'You could put a note in (to the system). I'm sure that if there were a note on the system, they'd be so happy with that. You'd ask them – do you want me to make a note of it – I'm sure they'd be happy with it.'

Clearly, there would be a potential issue about keeping confidential and personal information in a computer file, but the focus group didn't think there would be a problem, likening the situation to the example of blind customers:

> We log things like Braille or partially sighted customers, but we don't log situations like that, on an account, which is probably the most obvious way of avoiding problems. 'People who have Braille statements, they don't mind the information being stored – it's the same thing essentially. Transsexuals have just got different needs, haven't they?

It seems to be quite a common occurrence to get a telephone call in a call centre from a transsexual, illustrating again the importance of the work context regarding the work experience of sexual minorities. This also demonstrates how technology can change the way that the bank interacts with its customers. In order to use the services of the bank before the use of call centres, a transsexual would have had to go into their local branch, and they would have been seen as a rarity, perhaps even as an oddity. Now, however, the use of call centres means that bank operatives cannot see their customers and have to rely on the voice that they hear as the only interaction with the customer. An additional security check is to ensure that a man is ringing about a man's account and a woman about a woman's, which is very difficult for transsexual customers as a low voice is very hard to disguise for male to female transsexuals. The bank's customer enquiries are centred on one call centre, and therefore people can be calling in from all over the country. This means that in the one organization the incidence of having transsexual customers can be much higher than it had been previously with the branch system. Nationally there might be quite a large number of transsexuals using Beta Bank's services, but when there was only a small branch in each local community, the employees of that branch might have gone for years without meeting a transgender customer.

Life at work is getting better

Times are changing for the better for gay people within the Civil Service. The final story in this chapter comes from the Micro Department discussing some of the very positive developments that have taken place within their department over the last few years, specifically aimed at sexual minorities:

> People now recognize that this department has gay issues which have to be addressed, we have a formal group set up, we've got a strong membership,

everyone on the group is out, we have our own website and you can now find the website just by looking under 'g' and 'l' instead of having to find it through some tortuous route of the equal opportunities unit website and then finding something subtly worded ... We've tackled some very serious issues, through the Equal Opportunities Unit, conferences that are run every year, attended by senior management. It got off to a good start two years ago; we put our witness statements down, our experiences in the department, and they were read out in focus groups sessions, and this was the first time that the impact of what it was like being gay in the department. I know for a fact that the majority of people I know have had a lot of negative experiences in the department, whether it's through not being promoted, unfair reports or blatant discrimination against them; especially the men, who have worked under the old-fashioned, homophobic, 'there's something wrong with you' managers. But things are different now; senior management has realized that a percentage of our staff are gay and they need to be catered for, their needs need to be taken on board as well as the ethnic minorities, as well as the disabled, as well as women. It used to be that we weren't allowed to advertise the meeting of the gay and lesbian group in case the journalists saw it and made a story of it. 'Gays are running Whitehall' or 'Are these people fit to set teacher policy', or whatever, that was the feeling. You could advertise the music group, or the chess society, but not the gay and lesbian group, but that must be five years ago. We advertise quite openly now. The group has a banner and went to Pride marching under the department's banner, had our photograph taken, with names and published in Feedback, things like that are a sign that things are changing. The gay agenda's taking off.

However, when I played this story back in a focus group in the Micro Department the reaction from other people wasn't totally in line with the view expressed in the story. One gay employee who had come along to the focus group explained:

'We had to get the permanent secretary's permission just to make the banner, and carry it. We did tone down the wording! Although we were very proud of this it didn't get any publicity. I come from the team which had the very famous story of the team leader who was moved, because of a political feeling that it wasn't right to have an out gay man in charge of the department's policy on issues of sexuality. The story was refreshed in my mind last Friday because there is a chance I will be given the job, and the person who is acting head of department said 'Do you have any fears about being an out gay man heading that team in the light of what happened last time there was a gay man'. I said that if there was any doubt in his mind that I didn't have the ability to lead that team, he should say what those doubts were. He said that he would have to clear it with the director, with this short-term succession plan. I was prepared to come to the focus group saying lots of positive things about the things that the department's done for me over the years, but it looks like I fell at the last hurdle.

Of course, this individual was referring to Raj's story that we heard earlier. Another participant in the focus groups explained that there was a political dimension to working as a gay Civil Servant. Many people had talked about the change in atmosphere when there was a change in administration, while others, such as the following participant talked about the power which the minister held with regard to these issues:

> There is a ministerial aspect to this which we have to be aware of. The problems in advertising the group is not what we think, but what this does to the ministerial profile. You have this kind of publicity and it puts ministers on the defensive, and they hate it. I was one of the authors of the tripartite statement and it took six months to persuade the minister for it to be released, even though we kept saying, sorry you don't have a choice. You are not in charge of this department – it's the permanent secretary and you don't make that sort of decision. Finally we got past him. We were quite clear that we were getting past a homophobic attitude.

Another member of the focus group backed up this point of view, describing the relationship with the minister as 'feudal':

> 'The relationship between the minister and the department is a sort of feudal situation, depending on their personality. When I first started my first manager was a gay man, and you couldn't be open, and it's changed a lot, but I've only worked in London and the HQ tends to be a different environment. You have a high-grade mix here as well. But when something is deemed to be against the minister's personal preference, the department won't stand up for itself or its employees.'

Clearly, there is a high degree of political influence and interference by the minister and the government in general in the internal workings of the Civil Service, even though it is an organization which is supposed to operate independently of its political masters. The way that gay people are treated in the department actually comes down to the personal preference of the minister or Secretary of State. The first person to speak is an out gay man, who referred to Raj's story as the 'Section 28' story. Despite repeated attempts to censor this story, it would not go away. This is just one example where a focus group participant brought it up, but there were many others. Interestingly he maintains that the department is in danger of repeating the situation again. His line manager was still going to have to go to the director to ask whether it was alright to put a gay man in charge of an area which dealt with policy on sexuality.

Summary

This chapter has highlighted the different ways that people in work organizations respond to difference which is important because, for gay people, a key part of managing their disclosed identity is dealing with the response that they see coming from other people in the organizations. When you are out at work, you tend to incorporate people's reaction to you as part of your self-narrative, and this forms part of the discursive formation of your own subjectivity.

I divided the responses to difference which the lesbian and gay respondents identified themselves into two main groupings: namely, the issue of inclusion and the issue of exclusion in the workplace. The ultimate exclusion for an employee is to be sacked but exclusion in organizations, although it can be quite serious and damaging, is often much more subtle. The stories in this chapter have ranged from Freddie's account of a witch-hunt against him in the police, a tale of institutionalized homophobia, to instances of exclusion of customers with rules, even if they didn't actually exist, such as in the example of the personal banker who said that you had to be related in order to have a joint bank account.

There were also more positive examples of inclusion, such as a recruitment event for sexual minorities in Alpha Bank, a presentation for the partnership ceremony of a same-sex couple, and inclusion through humour. There were also stories to do with the response through official policies and procedures, such as the treatment of sexual minorities at training school in the police, and discrimination through selection and promotion in the fire service.

This section also highlighted some of the different ways that the organizations which took part in this research project respond to difference, and the importance of the work context. For example, the banks involved had a response which was driven by the business case, making reference to the ways in which organizations had an imperative to treat sexual minority customers in the right way. They also had a response driven by technology as call centres affect the dynamics of dealing with sexual minority customers, in particular dealing with transsexual customers who no longer seem such a rarity as many more customers are dealt with in one location. In the fire service, inclusivity is affected by the physical arrangements, as well as having two radically different work environments which have an effect on the way that people are treated in both environments. The issue of banter and humour was highlighted as one of the ways that people act differently in one of those spaces. In the police some rather unusual responses were expressed, such as the idea that abuse from colleagues toughens you up for the outside world. Finally, in the Civil Service, the focus groups highlight the political context in which these government departments work.

Being out at work means having a different experience of working life. Sometimes this can be a very negative one as whole groups of people can join together to try and reject their gay colleague. Sometimes, reactions can be very positive, though, and even life-affirming.

7   Concluding stories

In the world of work in the early part of the twenty-first century, reported changes to the workplace experience of sexual minorities have been quite apparent: in 2000, the *Financial Times* featured an article about JP Morgan and their lesbian and gay network; in the same year, the *Pink Paper* featured an article about how Sainsbury's, the supermarket chain, was redefining the way in which it treated its gay staff; in 2006, there were over 130 large private sector companies and public sector organizations in Stonewall's Diversity Champions scheme, a scheme to help organizations address issues of sexual orientation in the workplace. The list includes some very well-known names indeed. Amongst others there were banks and financial institutions, including: American Express, Barclays Bank plc, Credit Suisse First Boston, Deutsche Bank, Goldman Sachs, HSBC Bank plc, Lehman Brothers and JP Morgan. Among the consultancy firms, there were: Accenture, IBM and McKinsey & Company. And among many other well-known names in various different sectors there were: the BBC, British Airways, BT, GlaxoSmith-Kline plc, the Metropolitan Police Service, Procter & Gamble United Kingdom, Sainsbury's, Shell and the Walt Disney Company Ltd.

And yet, despite all this change in the world of work, the world of organizational studies has been slow to respond. There is a relative dearth of data-rich discourse analytic studies pertaining to the experience of sexual minorities in the workplace. Critical researchers spend a lot of time theorizing about organizational discourse, but with a few notable exceptions, there has been little time spent analysing discursive processes in organizations close up, and certainly very little of that is to do with the real-life experience of lesbians, gay men, bisexuals and transsexuals in organizations.

And so, when it came to designing this research project, one half was relatively straightforward to design: research into the workplace experience of lesbians and gay men at work using storytelling was going to fill a gap in our knowledge about the workplace experience of sexual minorities. It would also provide access to narratives of sexual identity that allow for greater understanding of the processes at large in this area; it was also a method which is consistent with the theoretical basis of discourse theory, and responded to my own interest in stories and personal narratives. So, in summary, choosing to use stories wasn't difficult.

However, this method alone was not going to address the issue of finding out the nature of organizational discourse on the subject of sexual minorities; that is to say, I wasn't going to be able to describe what other people in organizations said about their lesbian and gay colleagues. Even hanging around the organization with a tape recorder (a frequently used technique for organizational researchers) would probably not have yielded this sort of information. You can imagine how people would have suddenly become very politically correct around the water-cooler once a microphone was thrust in front of them. I therefore devised a two-tier narrative technique, a novel approach but one that turned out to be very successful. I presented individual stories from sexual minorities to focus groups in the participating organizations and their reaction and subsequent discussions were captured as examples of micro-discourse on minority sexuality.

So, the project developed a different way of collecting organizational discourse, which should be of use to academic researchers, consultants and human resource managers alike. It is not, of course, unusual to be in a position of 'creating' discourse as a researcher, and this is done frequently in the form of interviews or focus groups. But with a particularly difficult and sensitive area of study such as this it was necessary to develop an approach which not only accessed self-narratives, which would give an insight into the subjectivity of sexual minorities in organizations, but also an approach which would allow the researcher to listen to ordinary members of the organization discussing sexuality, in both positive and negative ways. The results from using this research methodology have been rich in data, and this is therefore a potentially useful research method for data collection which can be replicated in other discourse studies, which can help balance the burgeoning literature on methods in discourse analysis.

From the data it has been interesting to educe the extent to which work context has impacted on the development of sexual subjectivity and subject positions. Intuitively, one would have expected different organizations to afford different environments and experiences for the sexual minorities who work for them, but there has only been very limited research in order to demonstrate this empirically, and therefore the findings of this project have developed our understanding in this area by demonstrating the ways in which the different organizational contexts have influenced the sexual minorities who worked within them. For example, the banks in the study used call centres, a technological development in the world of work, which was seen to have a real impact on identity construction. The fire service showed how the conflation of work and home could have a negative impact on sexual minorities, and the importance of identity performance was discussed in the police. Finally, the political aspect was particularly relevant in the Civil Service.

An insight into how identity is constructed in the workplace

We have seen how the organizational setting, as well as the discourse around certain incidents and the reactions of individuals, all impact social identity formation, as expressed through individual narrative. Crucial to the social identity of sexual minorities is the way that individuals choose to display sexual identity or keep it hidden, although in some circumstances coming out is forced upon those who are only partially out. For sexual minorities, their social identity is subject to change repeatedly, as coming out is a continuous process and is open to judgement and evaluation by others who either accept or castigate them. Sexual minorities often have to face identity incongruence, in other words a major difference between the way that they understand themselves and how other people see them. In organizations, this can be played out either through differences in how their identity is portrayed internally to their colleagues or externally to customers, or alternatively through the incongruence of their self and social identity, which can place stress on the individual.

Coming out is a process in terms of the different stages that lead up to coming out, it is a process in terms of the performative nature of the act of coming out itself and it is a process in terms of the performative aspect of living a minority sexual identity. Coming out is performative in the sense that it is reiterative, requiring sexual identity to be performed again and again.

Identity is not natural, but social, and our sense of self constantly changes through our discursive relations with others. Different elements of discourse include language, policies and procedures, physical arrangements, signs and symbols, and the way that the organization, and the people within it, responds to difference as expressed by the ways that dynamics around inclusion and exclusion operate within the organization. Whilst the idea that discourse constructs and develops identity is not new, nor that discourse is made up of a number of different elements, the stories we see here from lesbian, gay, bisexual and transsexual people in organizations give us a number of insights on the way that these elements interact with sexual minorities in the workplace. Reinforcing this theme, we return to a story told by Stefan, a gay officer in the police:

> I've worked at three or four different places now, within boroughs and I've had experiences of very, very good leaders and very bad ones. For example at Station C, in central London, we had a very homophobic chief superintendent there. Now the catalyst for my having problems at Station C was my being asked to do a TV programme. That's what started it all off. I was asked to appear on TV, as a gay police officer, as a sort of role model. So I decided that I would and that was the first step down that chance path, if you like. This was just after being beaten up (Stefan had been subjected to a vicious homophobic attack) and had spent six months recovering from my injuries, and three months later I was transferred.
>
> I saw appearing on TV as an opportunity to progress the issues and to raise the profile and to help other people in my position. I was flattered to be asked as well. And I thought I can do this. I'm a very black and white person; not a political thing, but I tend to look at things in very, very simple terms. And I say to myself is this the right thing to do, or is it the wrong thing to do? And a lot of the time my colleagues in LAGPA (Lesbian and

Gay Police Association) will say that it is to my personal detriment, because it will cost me dearly, personally, even though it is ethically or morally the right thing to do. When I was asked I thought, this is the right thing to do. No police force had ever allowed one of its officers to go on the television before to talk about being gay. This is an ideal opportunity to present it and the Met was going down this road of saying sexual orientation, support and opportunities, so let's test them.

So I went to my chief superintendent; it's a kind of protocol thing, when you're asked to do something, you go to your managers and you ask your managers whether you can do it. Effectively this is bigger than my division, so effectively I could have gone straight to New Scotland Yard and asked the senior officers there; this was going out through the entire country and was going to affect the police as a whole. I didn't know my chief superintendent very well at this point; I'd only just arrived there. I didn't know anyone. So I stuck in a report saying the benefits of what this initiative would be to the police, how it fitted in with our policies, how it fitted in with our five-year plan, diversity. So I was just laying out the business case of why I thought I ought to do it. Technically, what he should have done is to minute it, and because it's bigger than all of us, pass it up. What he did was immediately say no, you're not doing this, because this is not something that this division wants to get involved in. Those were his words. Bearing in mind, the area surrounding us was Soho, with its gay community, and this is the chief superintendent of Soho saying that this is not something we want to get involved in. That was the first alarm bells that started ringing, this can't be right. So I started doing a bit of research, and in the five years that he had been there he had got rid of all the community and liaison officers. So I just started to get the idea that this man did not like working with lesbians and gay men. Anyway I put in another report, saying this was an equality issue and the organization had to give me a good reason why I shouldn't take part in it. So he wrote back and said that it was Met policy that lesbian and gay officers may not appear on television in uniform and disclose their sexuality. This can't be right! There can't be a policy! And by this stage I had gone beyond what most people would have done in challenging the chief superintendent. Basically by entering into correspondence with him, he was old-school with thirty-five years service. He was used to saying no and that being no, he wasn't used to someone arguing with him. I was very tactful about it, very diplomatic and respectful about it; you know, further to your minute, please could you send me a copy of the policy which you refer to, because I've never heard of it, and I've phoned up this department and that department and they've never heard of it either, so maybe you know something I don't. By this time he's getting more and more furious at the need to cover himself, basically. He called me into his office and gave me a right dressing down, a right bollocking, he was a chief superintendent, I was only a sergeant, blah blah, and how dare I question his authority. And I said that's all very well and good, but where's the policy?

Then he said, it's not a written down policy, it's a verbal policy. Alright, so where's that come from then? Basically, he couldn't answer the question. The conversation ended with him saying that there was going to be no further discussion, I wasn't going to take part in the programme, and that was the end of it.

So I thought 'fuck it, I'm not happy with this at all.' I went above his head then, I went to see the commander, who at the time had the portfolio for liaising with the lesbian and gay communities in London. So I went to see him and explained that I had been turned down, and these are the issues, so he said 'right,' he was quite shocked by the whole thing, and I told him that I was feeling aggrieved by the whole thing, so he said 'send me all the paperwork, get the whole file and deliver to my office by Monday morning, and we'll go from there.' So then the chief superintendent was called into his office and given a dressing down for not authorizing or organizing it. And he was told that he will cooperate with the whole thing, that I would do the programme and his decision was overruled. The chief superintendent is absolutely furious now that he has been dragged in by the commander.

This is where the problems started. After that lots of other things started to happen. During the filming he totally ignored me; I find it absolutely bizarre that if I were chief superintendent, one of my officers appears on national television, regardless of whether he's out to his colleagues or not, he's now outed himself to the whole of the force and the whole of the public across the United Kingdom. There is a possible risk here; I knew the risk, but I was annoyed that he hadn't anticipated the risk and hadn't bother to sit down with me and talk to me about the implications of doing this and how to minimize that risk, and what he could do to support me. At the very least, I was working in Soho, so this was about the community in Soho, this programme might affect the community either positively or negatively, he wasn't interested in the effects on the local community, not interested in the publicity, nothing at all. At that point, I was doing some liaison with the local community, informally. At the request of colleagues who were having problems getting into the community, they knew I was gay, they knew I'd done the TV programme, so they'd asked me to assist them in the enquiries they were doing. One of them was a young gay bloke who had gone missing, believed to be in Soho, and the CID asked me to help them out a bit to try and help them find out where this young guy was, a young sixteen-year old in Soho. So I was helping them with that. He obviously got wind of that, so he told the divisional inspector that I was no longer entitled to do any more gay liaison work, and that he would decide who was going to do gay liaison work in this division, he did decide that no one was going to do it, he thought it was unnecessary. And all this was through the back door. He never spoke to me, but he would get other people to have a go at me. He stopped me doing that. I got loads of letters sent to me. Loads of letters of support, saying enjoyed the programme, very interesting, other people saying that they were going to come out at work. And they were all sent to the station because that was the only address they had. But when mail is received what normally happens is that the letter is logged and officially acknowledged and that the letter has been passed on the addressee. In this case, no one received an acknowledgement, in other words nothing that was sent to me went through the system. He'd decided that anything sent to me wasn't going to be acknowledged, wasn't going to be replied to. I got them, but they were just stuck in my personal tray. Another thing that should have happened was a representative sample of the letters should go on your personnel file as evidence of good work; none of them went on my file. This whole thing just spiralled downwards, really. And eventually my car got damaged in the police car park, scratched into the paintwork were the words 'faggot' all over it. Brand new car as well. £5,000 worth of damage to the MG that I drive. The investigation was mucked up – he wasn't interested in doing anything. In the end I took out a grievance against him as a chief superintendent who had failed to do ... and I listed all these complaints. And it ended up with him being disciplined, being served with discipline regulation notices for failing to undertake certain responsibilities as the divisional commander. He was removed from his post, and rather than being put on a discipline board, he agreed, or rather he was told it was this or this, and he was sent on a peacekeeping mission to East Timor for two years. He's only just come back; he'll be retiring now. He told one of his colleagues on the way out that there was a 'dark force of homosexuals operating in Soho', because they'd managed to overturn the decision of the chief superintendent and he said that in this day the chief superintendent's word would have been final and it was a sad day when the lower ranks can do this to you and all the rest of it. So clearly he didn't feel accountable to anybody for his decision; he thought that he could take decisions, exercise his homophobia, use his position and authority without question. That's where I saw things in black and white. Is there a moral question here? I felt it had to be challenged. As a consequence of that, the whole division has been investigated, the whole thing has changed, they have liaison officers, relations with the local community, everything. It took all of that grief for all of that to be achieved. But I think quite a lot of progress has been made there. It's just sad that it had to take that to achieve that level of progress.

In the run up to this story, Stefan explained to me that he had unfortunately been subject to a serious assault, a gay bashing, in other words. The papers had got hold of the story and instead of focusing on him as a victim, their objective was to out him as a gay police officer. Nevertheless, he was promoted from constable to sergeant and transferred to a new station, but was concerned because the story in the papers had obviously preceded him:

When I arrived at my new station in central London, there were other gay officers, but none of the others were out. I was the first out gay officer at my new station in the centre of London. I discovered that there was another guy there on my team who was gay, but he wasn't out. The trouble was I was joining a team, and I had a bit of a history, because there had been this assault and it had all been in the papers, and so they had preconceptions about me already. So I was concerned about that; I had to prove that I wasn't how the papers portrayed me to be. When I arrived on the team, this other gay officer was clearly very nervous about what I represented for him. Here's an out gay sergeant who's going to be my supervisor – what's he going to do? Is he going to out me? Is he going to be on a crusade, and all the rest of it?

Stefan then spent the next few months establishing his credibility, both with his immediate colleagues, but also with the other gay police officer on the shift. He picks up the story again:

So slowly, slowly, slowly over three months he worked out that, that wasn't they way I was at all. And eventually he came out to me. Unfortunately, there was a consequence to that, which was that he came out thinking everything was fine, and that it was safe to come out. Of course, after I became a target of homophobia by the management team, it spilled over to him, it was almost like a call to arms for the all the homophobes in the station. Then you've got this split; you've got the management team doing nothing about the homophobes, then you've got the victims on the other side trying to sort of throw back against that homophobia. He found himself suffering similar sorts of problems to me, just because I was out too. His mother got sent a letter, outing him, using the contact details that police officers have in the control room, next-of-kin details. The letter said that he was having a relationship with a sergeant, because you have a relationship with everybody that's gay, don't you? That he was having a relationship with me, that he was a dirty queer and that he should leave the Job, and all the rest of it.

Stefan explained that the knock-on effects of this abuse were quite severe, considering the emotional impact on the individual and his ability to carry out his duties effectively. Then, other things started to happen; Stefan explains:

His father died, whilst he was at work one day. It's quite a long story, but the long and short of it is that he was refused compassionate leave to attend his father's funeral. He was told that he would have to take annual leave in order to go to his father's funeral. That's just unheard of in the police – it just never ever happens!

Stefan explained that when it was pointed out to the superintendent in charge that he should not have forced that officer annual leave to go to his dad's funeral, he was quite adamant that he was quite entitled to refuse compassionate leave if he chose to. 'He said it was on business grounds and monetary grounds that he wouldn't allow this,' Stefan continued:

although of course it was all nonsense. And it all boils down to one thing: homophobia. This colleague of mine was the only officer that had ever been refused compassionate leave. And it took best part of year to get his annual leave reinstated and it took for this superintendent to be formally disciplined, reprimanded and transferred off the division before that leave was reinstated. It took me to have to put it in my grievance; he didn't want to take out a separate grievance, so I put it in my grievance with all the other things they had done wrong. They tried to take his issues out of my grievance, saying you can't be aggrieved at somebody else's treatment. If he wants to have a grievance against the superintendent for that issue, he's got to do his own grievance. So I said, let's stop looking at the process, let's look at the issue, and the issue is that that is wrong and that is homophobia. You know that that PC is not going to go to grievance because he just doesn't feel strong enough. So I had to get copies of the grievance procedure out and read the criteria to them to prove that I was entitled to feel aggrieved about the way that he was treated, on his behalf. They tried everything to not deal with this issue. And strangely enough, it was one of the few things that somebody actually got disciplined on. Because it was contrary to the personnel manual, that he was refused leave. It's frightening, and going back to what we said before, you actually have to drag it out of them. Not because it's the right thing to do. They even tried to stop him being witness at my grievance. Because of his mother being sent this letter, I cited that in my grievance as well. Basically I was trying to prove that there was a culture that existed at this station of homophobia, and I had to cite dozens of examples of where homophobia appeared to exist. They tried to minimize it by taking examples out, saying that's his, and that's his, so there was no case to answer, they tried to water it down. It was a real struggle to get them to acknowledge that there was an issue. It went on for about two and a half years; probably the longest running grievance in the police force!

The police is associated with men and masculinity; this was borne out from the stories which were told by individual officers, as well as in the extracts of discourse. Gay people are seen as unreliable, and as police work is seen as inextricably linked with the body and its performance, it is assumed that gay people cannot express outwardly the physical signs of being a police officer. Officers need to perform masculinity in order to be taken seriously, by both fellow police officers and the public and gay people are seen as unable to acquire the cultural markers associated with the attributes that are valued in the police. This homophobic attitude leads to frequent examples of poor treatment in the police and it is this treatment that has an enormous impact on the construction of gay officers' identity at work. Stefan's story illustrates the way in which many different elements of discourse at work can have an impact on your identity and your expression of it in the workplace. His story shows that language, policies and procedures, physical arrangements, signs and symbols can all have an impact on

LIVERPOOL JOHN MOORES UNIVERSITY
LEARNING SERVICES

the dynamics around inclusion and exclusion which operate within the organization. In turn, these dynamics have an enormous impact on the way that we express our identity in the workplace.

Power relations and minority sexual identity

It is often suggested that the exercise of power in organizations is driven by gender issues, but these suggest that power can also be a result of sexual orientation and sexuality. In the discussion on silence I suggested that silence can be used as an expression of power, in the different ways in which it impacts on sexual minorities: the absence of language; the blank response; suppression and censorship at work; as well as resistance and self-protection. Power relations have positive and negative aspects, and that power flows both ways in power relations, not just from the powerful to the less powerful.

When we talk about power and identity in organizations, as they relate to sexual minorities, one has to ask whether there are any advantages to being gay. Freddie, a gay senior officer in the police, definitely believes that there are. He told me:

> Most professional gay people have suffered at some stage, so gay people tend to be good at people issues. For example, we had a girl that drowned locally. After a particularly traumatic incident, you go through a process of counselling with the police officers involved, or ask them if they want to talk about it. Technically, we call it 'diffusing' the officers, although we would never refer to it as such, because there is a certain stigma attached to being seen as requiring counselling. Anyway, after this incident, one of the inspectors said, 'Better ask them if they want to be diffused!'. So, I said, 'Don't you dare – you don't say it like that! That immediately gives it a label.' So at the end of the day, I said to them, 'You've all had a tragic day, I've had training so if you want to speak about it, just give me a ring.' So, one of the lads went 'Boo, hoo, hoo', and pretended to cry, so I said, 'Right, in my office now!'. I don't normally do that sort of thing, but I said to him, 'You absolute bastard. There were about three people, young constables who were quite stressed about trying to save this girl and not being able to save her. You've instantly hit the stereotype of the twatty policeman.' Because of all the things that have happened to me, I could challenge him publicly and privately. I have the confidence to do that. I didn't embarrass him, but he knew he was going to get a bollocking. Being gay's given me additional strength. It's because of the process of realizing your orientation, it gives you skills to deal with it. People who don't belong to a minority wonder what all the fuss is about; I say – you want to try it sometime then you'll know what all the fuss is about.

Power relations can be expressed through the response to difference and the discourse that was created as a result of the focus groups demonstrates this. Sexual minorities can be included, or excluded, in organizations, and prejudice and exclusion can be allowed to thrive with very little in the way of sanction. But managers also have the choice to use their power in the organization as a positive way of making people included and accepted by the organization. Raj told me a very moving story, about how he came out in the organization, and was subsequently made to feel included, with 'hugely significant recognition'. He takes up the story:

> It was generally accepted that I had left my wife. There were rumours – the number of people I had supposedly shagged was very complimentary. There were rumours that I had left my wife for another woman, who also worked here. The rumour mill worked and did a lot of the work for me in covering up my sexuality. I just made no attempt to deny it. Shortly after coming to London, I met my partner, who was just a wonderful man, and he gave me such confidence to be myself. He was an extraordinary character, very strong. I found myself having a significant other to talk about, which I did to anybody I met. He was director of a charity so we had two or three glorious years, travelling to Berlin, New York, San Francisco, Paris, Toronto and various other places, and I travelled as his recognized partner. I didn't so much come out on the scene as explode on it!
>
> In terms of my work colleagues, I never had any negative reactions at all from anybody. One can never know what people say behind your back. But by then I was a Grade 7, I was in a good job, I was working with ministers – I'd written off any victim tattoo I'd previously had on my forehead. I didn't go around shouting from the rooftops, but it was clear that it was part of my identity and there wasn't going to be compromised, and if you didn't like it that was your call.
>
> Then, John died. He had had a heart complaint. For six months he had been a bit breathless, then he needed a heart transplant and it didn't happen quickly enough. We had been in Stockholm, and he was absolutely exhausted after a busy day. It was weird: we had been listening to a display of Chinese Opera from a Women's Collective in the middle of Stockholm. He died the following morning. It was difficult to cope with because he was also married.
>
> At work, my then director came to see me and express his regrets, and pointed out that there was the employee assistance service. He asked whether I had thought about keying into that service. I thought that this was an extremely positive reaction, because it wasn't only keying into the service, it was an indication that he had recognized my relationship as a valid one and mine was a valid loss. In fact, I had lots of expressions of sympathy and understanding. What showed how far we've moved on, the Secretary of State, she actually sent a letter, so … hugely significant recognition.

Other areas which demonstrated power relations around sexual minorities were, on the negative side, discrimination in promotion and on the positive side, humour and banter. The important thing here is that this is a way of understanding power dynamics in organizations, and that by studying the way that sexual minorities are treated, it is possible to have a window onto the organizational cultural issue of how power is expressed.

Implications for diversity management

I suggested at the beginning of the book that of all diversity categories, sexual orientation remains the one that continues to be under-researched by organizational researchers, and it struggles to be a recognized element of the diversity agenda within organizations. That is not to say that organizations do not refer to it; there are plenty of examples in organizations today where sexual orientation is referred to in the diversity statement or strategy, and as we have seen there are plenty of organizations which take part in Stonewall's Diversity Champions scheme. But in the world of research, it is just not taken as seriously. I believe that there are various reasons for this: one was the lack of a legal imperative in the past, which has meant that organizations and researchers of organizations have shown scant interest in minority sexuality; there is also the invisibility which has been a key feature of the experience of gay men, lesbians, bisexuals and transsexuals in organizations. Certainly, this book has lifted the shroud of invisibility and silence in those organizations that took part, demonstrating that even approaches which attempt to minimize the impact on the organization cannot help but have an effect on the organization being studied. In addition, this work adds to the growing interest in this area by academic researchers demonstrated by articles in management journals, for example in: *Personnel Review*; *Journal of Management Studies*; *Human Relations*; *Culture and Organization*; *Gender, Work & Organization*; and *Sociological Review*. A bibliography which researchers and human resource managers alike may find useful can be found at the end of the book. So what are the areas that researchers and human resource managers in organizations alike should look out for? Well, I believe that there are some key areas: language use in organizations; rules and the way that they are used or the way that employees work around them; physical arrangements – that is to say, the way that buildings, offices and facilities are designed and whether they bring people together or divide them; signs and symbols, like we have seen with the fire bell and the uniform in the fire service; and finally, dividing practices – whether there is anything about the ways of working in the organization which divide people from one another. I will briefly discuss each of these areas in turn.

Language

Discourse is not simply as a linguistic device, but is central to the 'social construction of reality'. As already discussed, it can be a vehicle for power, the means of domination of one group by another which coexist in an oppositional relationship. The dominated discourse is under pressure to be silenced, suppressed and eliminated and, as such, language can be to suppress the minority. Interestingly, though, what is actually allowed depends on the visibility of the minorities at the time.

One officer in the fire service, who was known to be gay, arrived at a Station and as soon as he arrived '(someone) grabbed something from the notice board, and screwed it up and threw it in the bin'. He was visible as an officer because of his uniform, and because of the previous knowledge his colleagues had about him. He retrieved the offending article from the bin, and it turned out to be a 'gay joke, taking the mickey out of someone, putting their picture on the cover of Gay Times'.

One of the ways in which power is expressed in organizations is the seen as the power to sustain particular discursive practices with particular ideological invest- ments in dominance over other alternative (including oppositional) practices; that is to say the power to use certain types of language and social practice. Many of the firefighters that took part in the focus groups were at pains to point out that sexuality and gay people in particular were not an issue, but the acknowledgement that they have a right to exist comes with strings attached. Having gay people around was OK, so long as they did not talk about it, effectively suppressing the discursive practices of the sexual minorities within the organization.

One aspect about language and sexual minorities is the extent to which sexual minorities can see what the culture of the workplace is before they come out. As previously mentioned, you can't tell someone's sexuality by just looking at them, even if sometimes you can have a pretty good guess. In the Micro Depart- ment, Raj told me they had a discussion forum on the organization's intranet called 'speaker's corner'. One day, he was looking at it and was shocked by what he saw. It was the day after a new television series called *Queer as Folk* had been screened on Channel 4, which had a significant gay theme to it, prob- ably bigger and more overt than any programme previously to be screened on British terrestrial television. He said:

> I remember going in to speaker's corner when *Queer as Folk* was on televi- sion. I went in out of curiosity; literally the volume of emails on the subject of that programme, it took up the majority of speaker's corner and reading through them, some of the comments – they were 'appalled that this was being screened on TV', 'Why did you have to have programmes which described people's experiences in such detail?' and 'Shouldn't have this sort of thing on our screens, there's a place for it' – you know. There were also comments like 'how disgusting', 'shouldn't be shown', 'God's good country'. I exchanged emails with a couple of guys, saying that I was offended by that because I was gay and as far as I was concerned that was the same as a programme about heterosexuals on TV, and I didn't know what their problem was. It wasn't just *Queer as Folk* – there was lots about Section 28. There's usually something about paedophiles. Whenever some- thing like that happens there's always something about relating that to being gay, because clearly that's what some people believe.

It has to be said that the Micro Department, through the personnel department, just pulled the discussion on the forum, as 'speaker's corner' is constantly monitored for any unacceptable remarks. On the one hand, it could be argued that at least people have their say; if people are censored, all that happens is that you think people are being OK on the surface, but underneath you've got the same views as you had before. On the other hand, of course, sexual minorities have an accurate insight into what people really think about them.

Rules

Rules in organizations can be both informal and formal, the latter often taking the form of policies and procedures. Much research has been carried out on policies and procedures in the area of gender in the workplace; less research has been carried out to look at the effect of rules on sexual minorities, both formal rules, like policies and procedures, and more informal, unwritten rules. Something that can have a very positive impact on individuals is merely being given permission to support their own minority group in the organization. Daniel, who worked for Alpha Bank, told me:

> Some of my straight friends are jealous of the sort of things I get involved in, like this is an interesting diversion for an hour today. Not long after the lesbian and gay network set up in London, we met up with three of the main board directors. And my colleagues were saying 'oh wow you've met these people!'. So, I get to meet important, interesting people. I got promoted from Associate to vice-president last year, and this was the result of a political campaign; you don't get promoted just on work, you need to let people know who you are. We have as part of our annual appraisal process, team reviews where people write what they think of you. You usually ask people to write these reviews on you. But you can also get what we call unsolicited team reviews. So some people just say I'm going to write about that person and send it to their manager because I've interacted with them either favourably or unfavourably during the year. Apparently when whatever the committee was choosing about me, and various managers were battling about their promotion prospects and somebody was trying to put me down, someone on the committee pulled out this team review about me about my input to the gay and lesbian activities in the bank. There are those people who would be cynical and would say it's favouritism for being gay, but I'm also very aware of the political aspect of an environment like this; you have to do your job well. And you have to put a little bit back in – you can't complain if the organization isn't good if you don't put a little bit back in.

Informal rules can also have a negative impact and can help, for example, to silence sexual harassment stories, keeping them part of the private domain. In the bureaucratization of sexual harassment, the rules, for good reason, are that it is not harassment unless you say no, keep a record and report it. Nevertheless, my research has shown that there may not be policies and procedures for guidance on recruitment, job moves and promotion, or decisions may be made in the absence of clear guidance or even if policies and procedures exist, sexual minorities themselves may feel unwilling, or unable to make a complaint.

A gay officer in the fire service recounted the time he went for promotion, and failed. That example demonstrated that being out at work also creates the possibility for discrimination as well as creating greater commitment to the organization as research suggests. Indeed, one might suggest that discrimination is given the oxygen of life when people come out; when they are in the closet, it is only possible to discriminate against the idea of their being gay. Stefan, the gay police officer, talked about there being more incidences of homophobia in areas where there were more gay people:

> You almost have to say 'Don't put up a diversity notice-board!', and they'll put one up to spite you. They have a diversity notice-board in *The Bill* (the television programme), but they don't have one in the police station in Soho! You know, it's the area that has the highest number of gay people in Europe! There are still battles to fight, but it's much improved on what it was fifteen years ago. But it is hard, there are still areas like Soho, and they're finding it hard to get their head around that they've got a problem there. It's the worst place for homophobic conduct anywhere that I've ever heard of! Anywhere! If you think about it, if you go to Kingston, for example, what is going to spark off homophobia in Kingston. Maybe an incident where somebody is gay, but it won't be an everyday thing. Most times you don't know what the sexuality of everybody is. But in Soho, it's happening all the time. So the chance of gay being an issue is huge, and not as huge anywhere else, so if someone is going to be homophobic in Soho, they've got ample opportunity to express it, and wouldn't have the opportunity at most other places. So, on the one hand, you'd think it was the most positive, because they've got the most experience, but they've also got the most opportunity to be homophobic. Even if it's only one or two people. It can be the worst place to be. On the other hand it's the best place to be because there are more gay people there than there are in most police forces. And some of these people think I'm a nutter, as battling against something that isn't there, because they personally haven't experienced it.

Another example of a blocked job move is the story from a gay firefighter who wanted to transfer to get additional training to develop and improve his job knowledge and responsibilities, but could not because he was gay. He was turned down for the transfer because the watch, to which he was to transfer, did not want to work with a gay man. Interestingly, instead of challenging the watch for their homophobic attitudes, the officer on the watch approached the training department to ask what he should do. Although they did not know the individual concerned, the fact that he was gay, was enough for the watch to express their unhappiness as a group to the officer-in-charge of the FRU. The difficulty in this situation may be created by the lack of policies. As a result the officer-in-charge has to ask for advice on how he should deal with the situation. This situation impacts on the way the individual firefighter experiences being gay at work; first he is put into a position because of his sexuality, and second he is left, at his own request, to resolve the situation himself.

Of course, it is not only in the fire service that policies and procedures have an impact on sexual minorities. Consider the story where a gay man was pro-moted and was going to go and manage a group of people; they found out and expressed their view that they did not want to have a gay man as a manager. Instead of challenging the views of the group, the organization decided to move the gay man instead. In this case the individual felt that he could not make an official complaint.

Policies and procedures, whilst they can protect minorities, can also be used as an excuse by those who wish to discriminate. There was an example from Beta Bank where the personal banker refused to open a join cheque account for same sex partners, blaming it on the 'rules'. Organizations are worlds of formal rules and procedures, after all, although in this case it turns out that this rule, even if had ever existed, had been incorrectly applied.

Physical arrangements

Previous research has highlighted the impact of the workplace environment on indi-viduals. Indeed, just because this is a discourse analytic study does not mean it is possible to ignore the physical environment. On the contrary, discourse analysis requires researchers to attend to aspects of bounded space, the landscape in which discourse is conducted. Clearly, the immediate physical locale in which a discursive episode is located can be very important; it is not simply a backdrop to language or discourse, the physical locale is actually embedded within it. Stories about physical location include the one by Gary, who planned a move because he worked in a small office; Gary actually changed his name and everything about himself. Here is another story in a similar vein. Seamus was a young gay man who worked for the Delta Department in a small office in Northern Ireland. This is his story:

> I joined because it was a job; and it was a permanent job, which in Belfast was a big thing – it was something that had a bit of prestige attached to it, and I had just turned nineteen. Initially, I never gave my sexuality a second thought. I was about twenty-three when I started thinking about it. I never wanted to come out at work; I was very defensive. Questions were asked and I hated going out with work colleagues drinking. Out of the blue they would fire this bolt at you. Most of the time it was said in a very humiliating way 'Are you a faggot or what?'. There wasn't any animosity – it was just their way of saying it. I would get up and leave, I've had enough of this and 'fuck you'. I felt I'd dug myself into a pit, by denying it so much. The

people who asked it weren't your friends – it was just gossip. I had to tell people eventually. There were a couple of females who were making passes. I thought who do I need to tell – I got pissed and told them – some were quite shocked. Some said 'Oh fuck' and then silence and then started laughing. I wished I'd done it when I was nineteen. I told my boss and she gave me a hug and said that this doesn't change anything. I was able to be open and honest with my friends. Then I met my partner in England; I went to welfare and asked for a transfer. The reaction of welfare was very good; I didn't want HR knowing all my business because Northern Ireland is so small. Everyone knows everyone. I didn't trust them because I knew some of them. So I said to them that I don't want HR knowing the reason for the transfer. She said that they'd had similar requests. The transfer requests are worded very anonymously. Here nobody batted an eyelid. The girl who sits next to me said 'oh my gawd you're not?' but then she was fine – people open up to you much more. People became more interested in you.

Scott, the firefighter, was someone else who had frequent job moves, which is unusual for the fire service, and had different experiences of coming out in each new location. He moved fire stations three times, and therefore had the experience of coming out three times. He also, like Stefan, had the experience of coming out to the whole shift, although there was considerably less bullying that prompted him to do it.

I left the forces. I had a couple of different options. I considered doing outward bound courses, but I decided on the fire service; I'd seen the literature and the claim to be an equal opportunities employer. I thought that I could have a good input into this. I wanted to serve the community and I thought I could be gay and be in the fire service. I thought if they find out I'm gay they can't kick me out. In July 1992 I entered the fire service in Essex. I finished my basic training. My first day was Christmas Day night. Strange day to start, not being able to drink and being worried about what the night was going to hold for you.

Scott then described that when he joined the fire service in Essex at the time, they did a home visit, specifically to meet your wife and family and talk to them. Even though he lived with his partner at that time, Scott described how he managed to erase any evidence of being gay:

I had this senior officer coming around to my flat, that had pictures of my partner, it wasn't chintzy or quaint, it wasn't obviously gay, but pictures, out you go, partner, out you go for this guy to spend half an hour. It was 'cleansed' of all gayness.

Scott's experience at training school was quite positive, and he described meeting people whom he assumed were also gay:

At training school I'm full of confidence and five or six of us worked together and helped each other clean their shoes and studying. We had a good regime going. The course went through sixteen weeks, and towards the end it was really strange. Just over halfway through I felt I was attracted to one of the guys on the course. I thought I had to put a bit of space between myself and this lad. You tend to know when someone else is gay. I thought there was something reciprocal. Then we got to the end of the course, and then there was somebody else. One of the guys couldn't do one of the exams, but he needed somebody else to go back with him to do the exam, because it was to do with breathing apparatus, and there was an exercise to do. He chose me. We had a conversation and I couldn't work out why he chose me. At the end of the course I told two people; one the first guy I was attracted to and I explained why I put a bit of space between us. The other guy turned round and said we should meet up another time for a drink. We never did meet up for this drink.

Scott then described the violent reaction from one of his colleagues, the first time he came out to his watch:

I still stay in contact with the guys of my first watch. We'd got a great boss. Really fair and I didn't envisage too many problems. Wide spread in age. I joined with someone else and whereas my approach was to be quiet, sit watch and learn and slowly integrate, the other lad was for ever stitching himself up. If there was any banter, he was getting it. A year down the line had elapsed and we were out celebrating Christmas, and I'd made the decision that I wouldn't come out until after my probation time, which was eighteen months. Anyway, after a few drinks, one of the guys made some comments and I came back to him, and I was really beginning to wind up, and I went, 'You wouldn't know a faggot if a faggot was stood beside you.' (He was using the term faggot.) He said, 'Yes I fucking would,' and so I told him that I was gay. He replied 'Right, outside let's sort it out.' For some reason he wanted to fight me, but I wouldn't fight with him because there was nothing to be gained. A few other guys jumped in and the night came to an abrupt end. It ruined the night a little bit. The next day this guy did the rounds of the watch, trying to get support for his views. He wanted me off the watch. Totally against anything gay. I'd slept in the same dorm as him for eighteen months, but from that night on he wouldn't sit in the same room as me. He had his own knife, fork, spoon and mug. A few months down the line, he moved watches and then he moved stations. The rest of the watch came out on my side. And he'd spent quite a few years on this watch.

Of course, coming out is not without its moments of humour:

One of the guys happened to be on leave and came in special and asked to have a word: he asked me if the rumour was true, that I was gay, which I confirmed. He shook my hand. We had a bit of banter because he was an ex-Marine and I was an ex-Matelot. Anyway, over the Christmas table we were going to give each other presents and he'd got a present lined up – a copy of *The Pink Pap*er and *Boyz* all wrapped up. He wanted to see my face when I opened it, but he'd done this before he knew. And of course me coming out to everybody had blown this out of the water. He was more upset about that than anything else. I told the gaffer and he said there's no problem, but you should have kept it quiet.

At this point, Scott described how he thought that he had been the only gay fire-fighter in the world. He described it as failure on his part not to do something about it and contact other people:

Fortunately, some people did do something about it and started the lesbian and gay group on a social basis to start with. Now we've progressed; we stretch the length and breadth of the country, and there is somebody to help you through those situations. I had planned on coming out to the watch, but of course I did so in the end because I was drunk. Anyway I've had three watches. The second watch was a different station within Essex. I was pro-moted. I was now going to be second in charge of a watch. I turned up on my first day and I could have put money on it happening. The watch boss was off. Automatically I had to take his place. The station was surrounded by motorways. I'd never had a motorway RTA in my career. We checked the wagons and went in for a cup of tea and I decided to tell them to allay any rumours or suspicions. We sat down took a sip of tea, and I started to tell them about myself. Then the bells went down – RTA on the M25. It killed the moment! We did discuss my sexuality after though, on the night shift, in a very relaxed way.

Scott then moved to the area where he is currently stationed because of this partner's job. He described the move to the new fire brigade:

It was weird because I had to have interviews there. I joined my watch. Great bunch. Three months passed and one of the guys was trying to set us up with his wife's best mate. Obviously they were asking why I moved up here. 'Always loved it up here. Used to come up here when I was in the Navy. Just decided to transfer.' In the end I went into the gaffer and said, 'There's something I've got to come clean about. I'm gay. I think I should tell the rest of the watch.' He said that he had had his suspicions. He thought that either I was gay or on the run from something. (He actually thought I'd done some misdemeanour.) So we then got them all in the lecture room. In the lecture room the chairs were all around with two chairs in the middle, where me and the gaffer sat. I said, 'Right, to the two I'd been drinking with last week, you know I said you were drinking like two poufs? Well you don't drink like this pouf.' I totally went over their head again. So then I just said, 'let's put it another way, I'm gay.' And I looked round the room and their chins just dropped. One of the lads asked, 'How do you want us to play it? Do you want us to keep it on the watch? Or now that you've told us, don't you mind if anyone knows?'. I said, knowing what the fire brigade is like, 'I don't give a damn who knows.' I didn't want to put them under the pressure of keeping a secret. We were then labelled the pink watch. The rest of the watch hadn't got a problem with it. When other people went to other watches there were comments made and these guys turned round and made a stand on my behalf. We had interesting and varied conversations. Some of the weirdest conversations are about gay sex. These are straight men, but they're intrigued about gay sex. They only see it as one thing, and that's anal sex. But when you tell them you've got other options, they want to know. We've spent hours sometimes, and then they'll revisit the subject. When I discuss it with any of them, they'll say, 'I don't know anyone gay,' and I'll say, 'Invariably you have met gay people before, you just don't know it.' That's because they haven't had the trust and the confidence and by changing their views they can give other people the confidence to come out. That's what the group's about, that we don't wear stilettos, we don't carry handbags.

Signs and symbols

This fire service is an organization, which has many signs and symbols. Even the public's view of this organization is full of symbols, as demonstrated by soap operas like *London's Burning*. Examples of symbols that have been discussed in the book so far include the uniform, representing the semi-disciplined service; the sirens and fire engines representing the emergency response aspect of the service; and the clearly visible fire stations represent the high public profile that the service enjoys.

All organizations have symbols, though, and the fire service in this respect is no way unique. I think that another key symbol, and one which is common to all the participating organizations in this project, is the extent to which the culture allows people to come out at work. We return now to Will, a banker with Beta Bank, who thought that being able to come out at work was very symbolic, almost a hygiene factor, which, when in place, allows you to do your job better:

Beta Bank sent me to work in Ashford, in Kent. But I lived in London with my partner and his daughter. I found it difficult to talk about the fact that I had childcare commitments. I was gone from the house for sixteen hours. It made the whole thing very difficult. It took me three years to tell Beta Bank that I had a child. To say that I have to work in London. They sent me to Swindon after Ashford because I still didn't feel as if I could say anything. I was on a graduate entrants' course, getting nine-month placements. I had a liaison officer to make sure I was getting what I needed. I'd already come out to close-ish friends but they weren't people I had daily contact with. I was called up fro a regular meeting and what I wanted to do for the next attachment – was there anything you want to do? I said I was gay, had a partner and a child and I have to work in London. She said that was cool, and I was surprised. I didn't know that it was safe to tell them. So it was a bit of a relief and I should have woken up a long time ago. They then gave me an attachment up the road.

Will was very grateful to be working in London, and in addition Beta Bank offered childcare facilities and so he could make use of that. But interestingly, he still didn't know whether it was acceptable to be gay at work:

The interesting thing about the organization was that it had never said that it would be OK. The only way I thought was OK was having AIDS because they wouldn't sack you with AIDS. At that point I was only out to the management development training people. I've only been fully out in this job which I've had since last year. The man that hired me flirted with me in the job interview. He guessed that I was gay. I'm very guarded around personal pronouns. I'll say 'my partner' and 'they' and my boss very quickly picked up and said, 'are you gay?' and I said yes and it was a huge release. He went around and told everyone. I felt fine about it because my only real concern was that it might affect how people judge me and if a senior manager goes around and says isn't marvellous then I wouldn't have too much to worry about.

Things then changed for Will, as he changed projects within the bank:

I then had to work for another project manager who was homophobic, my boss wasn't happy either; my boss went off and made a huge fuss. The manager who made the decision said if he doesn't want to do that he doesn't have to. They asked me to give it a go. The project manager came and gave me a hug and said that he wasn't homophobic and if anyone said anything against me he would have hit them. I'd got the idea because we'd gone to the pub and he'd sat down and made a throw away laddish comment. He left the bank shortly afterwards. It might have been an interesting learning point for him. Ever since I've come out at every step it's been more and more positive. I accept I've been working in e-commerce and people around me have been old-style; they are largely middle-aged northern white males, and very set in their ways. I work with marketers and e-commerce experts and make their money from being open-minded and quick-witted. My work environment is very open to the point where I feel able to talk about sexual exploits at the weekend and my colleagues feel able to tell me to shut up.

One of the most positive things working for Beta Bank was when the manager said that you don't have to work for a homophobe. But my high point as a gay man in the bank was delivering a presentation to a team of forty people who didn't realize I was queer at the start and did at the end. Involving everybody and making everybody laugh. The high point of my overall career at Beta Bank was delivering a big project about a year ago – but then I wouldn't have felt that good about doing that work if I hadn't had that original meeting where I came out to everyone. The most negative thing that the bank has done was not telling me up front that it was cool. For eighteen months it screwed up my personal life. It was an unusual situation, but it was a clear case of where the bank failed to say something it really impacted how I operated. My performance in Swindon was appalling. It's almost like a hygiene factor where your organization says – 'we don't hate you' – there's no clock ticking under your chair with them waiting to get rid of you.

Dividing practices

Sexual orientation, unlike other areas of diversity, is invisible; in organizations where few people feel able to come out, this means that the individual experiences an intense feeling of isolation. This might be the case in any organization, but in the fire service discussion of sexuality is still a real taboo, coupled with the prevalent assumption that gay and lesbian firefighters just do not exist. This story is not an isolated one, as other gay firefighters describe similar experiences: 'I always thought I was the only gay Firefighter in the United Kingdom, and I was told by many people or asked the question: would you be sacked if your employers found out?'. Socialization into an organization can take various forms, including wearing the same uniform, socializing or joining in with banter. One of the ways that new recruits become socialized within the watch is by going through some kind of initiation ceremony.

It should be re-emphasized, however, that reactions to people coming out are not always negative. Clearly, a book like this one is going to recount some horror stories, partly because human nature has a natural prurient interest in bad news, and partly because that really is the reality of being gay at work. In addition, it is in the nature of stories themselves for the storyteller to want to recount something unusual: dog bites man isn't newsworthy, whereas man bites dog is. But some experiences are nevertheless very positive, even life-affirming. Harry, a trader with the Alpha Bank, told me:

> I kept myself to myself and that was it. People did question whether I had a girlfriend and I lied quite a few times. I feel guilty about that now, but I didn't have the confidence to say that I was gay. Instead I said that I had girlfriends and stuff like that. There were only one or two people that the subject came up with, about the social life. It didn't come up that often. It was more to do with my own self-confidence and being gay; I wasn't 100 per cent comfortable with it. I wasn't out to very many people at all and I didn't want to come out to anybody else until I felt the confidence to tell. It was more to do with self-confidence and it wasn't anything specific to do

with the Alpha Bank. I knew if I did, with hindsight, that the vast majority of people wouldn't have given a toss really. One of the most memorable things about my career at Alpha Bank has been people's reactions when I told them about my sexuality. It was a big weight off my mind. I felt very happy that I told them. Their reactions have been very supportive and loving. It felt very good for me. I felt some relief, and I felt I could be completely comfortable with who I am and what I am. I've formed very close relationships with other gay guys in the bank as well. All in all it's been an extremely positive experience.

Cary, an American banker who had transferred with the Alpha Bank to London had also found his coming out an extraordinarily positive experience and had had quite an impact on the way in which he viewed work:

> I was a happier person. I really was and nothing really changed. I wasn't in the closet and then out of the closet. But meeting other people, that interaction, I just felt better about working in a place where I knew there were other people like me around. It sounds corny, even though I knew there were gay people was an irrelevance to what I was doing, to actually meet these people and see what they did and work across all sorts of departments in the bank was comforting in a way, and seeing the bank address these issues, it was so positive it just made me happier in my work. This is really one of the strong arguments: if you have a diverse atmosphere you'll have happier more productive people. I really do believe that. If you like what you're doing, where you're doing it and with whom you're doing it, you know all those positive things can't do anything but make you a more productive person. So it changed me in that sense.

Areas for further work

The project has also raised a number of questions and interesting areas for further work. This project was, quite deliberately, carried out in a United Kingdom context, even though some of the organizations involved had an international presence. Whilst some work in a non-Anglo-Saxon European context has been carried out, particularly in the area of union activism and sexual minorities, it would be useful from an organizational cultural perspective to consider whether the dynamics of minority sexuality in organizations are different in different national cultures.

The impact of silence on the construction of other identities and its interplay with power relations, may be a fruitful area for further research, as it is not just silence, but also the construction of identity itself which may have power over others. The idea of queer resistance as a concept in managers' identity construction is an interesting one and the idea of queering management has already been introduced in the literature by Martin Parker in 2001 and 2002. There is also further scope in organizational studies to bring in key concepts from Queer

Theorists such as: Judith Butler and her ideas about performativity; Stephen Seidman and his work looking at the fluid nature of identities; and Diana Fuss and Eve Kosofsky Sedgwick who have considered the contradictions of identity construction within the context of sexual minority identity. All of these well known researchers in the field of sociology and minority sexuality could add significantly to the body of knowledge in the area of organization studies.

Although gendered resistance at the level of identity construction has been explored, this could usefully be developed with more of a focus in the organizational studies literature on the queer dynamics of organizations and the identity construction of sexual minorities within them. Of course, organizations have different competing discourses, and different identities of which only minority sexuality is only one. The two-tier narrative method could be applied to the study of different types of identity, different performances and different types of identity work in the workplace.

Postscript
Researching sexual stories

This chapter is a reflexive note to end the book on. The research created a number of interesting stories about the research process itself, as well as creating and implementing a new research methodology based on storytelling, and this final note is an opportunity to share some lessons learned. In addition, it is hoped that an explanation of how access was obtained during this research, discussions about the ethical aspects of storytelling research and the difficulties encountered and how they were overcome will provide a useful resource for future students, academics, consultants and human resource managers.

Sampling

A key issue in the history of researching the workplace experience of sexual minorities over the last twenty-five years has been the recruitment of the sample. Some research in the past recruited sample populations from advertising in gay media, gay bars and gathering places, and 'homophile' organizations, such as gay interest groups or campaigning groups. Others used a process of snow-balling, or asking one interviewee to introduce the interviewer to others, and often began the process by asking personal friends. The issue of being able to locate respondents for study is one which social scientists immediately encounter when trying to study a population that is difficult to identify. It was still a significant one when Woods and Lucas began their seminal study in the spring of 1990, and they described encountering the problem and how they attempted to locate potential participants. They used snowballing, initiated through personal networks, and friends, just as other researchers did before, and continued to do for some years later. Interestingly, the sampling method did influence the choice of population and ultimately the overall study; Woods and Lucas focused on the experiences of gay men, as they found it difficult to recruit lesbians for their sample, whilst there have been examples since of lesbian researchers who have focused exclusively on the experience of lesbians, largely driven by access to participants.

Burke's study of the United Kingdom police, in 1993, was one of the first to focus on a specific organization, and his sample recruitment of both lesbians and gay men was made easier through the existence and engagement with the study of the Lesbian and Gay Police Association (LAGPA, now known as simply the GPA – the Gay Police Association), and the fact that Burke was a former Metropolitan police officer. It was not until six years later, in 1999, that another study was able to look at the experiences of lesbians and gay men in a specific organization, when Humphrey carried out her study in UNISON, one of the larger trades unions in the United Kingdom. She recruited her sample from male and female gay activists within the union, who worked together regularly on lesbian and gay issues, though they actually worked, for their principal areas of employment, in different public sector organizations and occupations. More recently in 2003, Miller, Forest and Jurik carried out a questionnaire study in a Midwestern police department, contacting seventeen gay police officers, again through their Lesbian and Gay Police Alliance. Apart from these two studies, however, the most common method of sample recruitment has been through advertising, networking and personal contacts. Even the most recent empirical study in this literature review has used this method.

It appears, then, that a key difficulty with this area of research has been the identification and recruitment of a sample of both lesbians and gay men within a specific organization. Neither networking, personal contacts, nor advertising in the gay media have been used in this project, and in that sense the study has been unusual, and even groundbreaking, in the level of access achieved at an organizational level. This perhaps signals a shift in the readiness of sexual minorities to speak out, although my being a gay man has probably facilitated access.

Data collection – the interviews

Collecting stories can be difficult, especially when the topic is particularly sensitive. Indeed, this sensitivity has been one of the reasons that relatively few stories have been collected from sexual minorities in specific organizations. In 1991, David Boje, a well known American academic working in the field of organization studies, and often using narrative as a research methodology, followed the participant-observer tradition of collecting stories, which occurred in various social scenes around an office-supply firm. He recorded everyday conversations and captured spontaneous storytelling episodes. I did not think it was going to be possible for me to follow this method, because of the specific aim of collecting stories which recounted the experience of sexual minorities within the organization, and whilst sexual minorities are often the topic of conversation it is unlikely that I would have been able to pick up these conversations whilst 'hanging around' with a tape recorder. I therefore decided to collect the stories through a series of interviews with lesbian, gay, bisexual and transsexual employees who were willing to take part in the study.

I recognized that gaining access to lesbian and gay interviewees would be a challenge. On the one hand, I was attempting to address a gap in the literature, which presumably was there for a good reason; it might have been because it was just too difficult. On the other hand, the population I was trying to access, that is to say lesbians, gay men, bisexuals and transsexuals in organizations, is a population which is often stigmatized, potentially invisible and silent and it would have been of little surprise if participants had been unwilling to come forward for fear that the research might identify them as a member of a disadvantaged group, thus putting them at risk within their organization. I guess that one of my key learning points from the research process was that anonymity is extremely hard to guarantee, and there is a very real risk of being identified after someone has talked to a researcher. If someone is very worried about being identified, it's probably better not to proceed with the interview; at the very least, I am now convinced of the importance of explaining the risks to the individual up front, no matter how much, as a researcher, you may want the interview.

The route of my initial contact with the organizations varied. I began by contacting Stonewall, the professional lobbying group for lesbians, gay men and bisexuals to ask whether they could recommend any organizations interested in taking part in this research. They put me in contact with the lesbian and gay group of Alpha Bank. Once I had been introduced to them, and recruited several volunteers from within the group, I then used the process of snowballing to recruit other volunteers, some of whom were not yet out at work. Alpha Bank formed my pilot study. Because I had accessed this organization through the lesbian and gay network, and not through more official channels in the organization, I found it difficult to carry out the focus groups, as well as collecting the individual stories. My learning point from this part of the field work was that I had to get access at the organizational level, and then access to the lesbian and gay employees, which is how I negotiated access with all the subsequent case study organizations (in the case of the police and fire service, the lesbian and gay networks are national, and the organizations regional, and so were not linked in the same way).

The Micro Department was unusual in that they, along with the Delta Department, contacted me. In 2001, I had presented a paper at an academic conference, which was reported in the news section of *People Management*, one of the professional human resources journals. As a result, the two government departments contacted me and expressed an interest in taking part in my study. In the Micro Department, there was a lesbian and gay network, which asked for volunteers amongst its own members. In the Delta Department, although there were two lesbian and gay networks, one based around the organization and the other based around the union, the organization recommended asking for volunteers on the organization's intranet. Everyone had access to it, and it was felt that the use of this tool would increase the response. In fact, from that one organization, there were over 140 volunteers to take part in the study.

Beta Bank was the next organization to be contacted. I had had some professional contact with them in the past and had become acquainted with the director of equality and diversity. I discussed my fieldwork with them, and suggested that, since they were interested in carrying out work in this area, the output of this research would give them valuable information on the experience of sexual minorities in their own organization. They readily agreed and put me in contact with the recently formed Sexual Orientation Task Force, whose members I interviewed.

With the police and fire service, I had to contact several regionally based organizations before I found the ones that would take part. In both cases I also contacted the lesbian and gay networks: LAGPA (the Lesbian and Gay Police Association, now known as the Gay Police Association) in the case of the police, and the Lesbian and Gay Section of the Fire Brigades Union (FBU) in the case of the fire service. Again, interviewees were also recruited from snowballing, as interviewees were able to introduce me to other employees, some of whom were not members of the network and some of whom were not out in the workplace, but who agreed to take part in the research nevertheless. The police and fire service were more difficult to access than other organizations, since the LAGPA and the FBU networks are national, and the organizations are organized on county or metropolitan boundaries.

Number of interviews

Storytelling as a form of data-collection is effective, but highly inefficient. Previous story researchers, such as David Boje and Yiannis Gabriel, found very few stories in their research, which would have been highly rated by folklorists. This is partly due to the content, but also due to the fact that some people are good storytellers and others are not. This aspect was certainly borne out by my research also, as some respondents not only saw their organizations as 'story-free spaces' but also saw their own sexual identity at work as being devoid of any story, which could inform, describe, or even entertain. Sometimes this was because they assumed the type of story I was looking for: surely a sexual story has to be a tragedy, with the interviewee taking the role of the victim? I assured the interviewees that I was not a tabloid journalist, I was certainly not looking for exposés, and I was just as happy with positive stories as negative ones. However, because the majority of the stories are negative, even shocking in some way, it raises the question whether interviewees tell the researcher what they think the researcher wants to hear, and select their stories accordingly.

It should come as no surprise therefore that I contacted as many as 110 people to be interviewed. The participation rate was extremely high; only eight of the people contacted were unwilling or unable to take part, giving a participation rate of nearly 93 per cent. I subsequently carried out interviews with 102 who described themselves as lesbian, gay, bisexual or transsexual. I did not use a further ten of these interviews as the organization in question did not wish to pursue the research. I therefore used a total of ninety-two interviews. Table 1 gives details of how many people were interviewed in each organization.

Ninety-two is a large number of interviewees, and compares favourably to previous qualitative research in this area. In the study by Woods and Lucas in 1993, the number of interviewees totalled seventy. In 2001, Shallenberger interviewed a total of twelve gay men, whilst Humphrey interviewed thirteen les-

Table 1 Number of interviewees in each organization

Organization	Number of interviewees
Alpha Bank	12
Beta Bank	16
Micro Department	17
Delta Department	22
Police	18
Fire Service	7
Total	92

bians and ten gay men. Clearly, quantitative studies have had much larger populations, and whilst the aim of qualitative studies is not necessarily to cover large sample populations or to be representative, the sample size in this project demonstrates that it is a significant study.

Profile of interviewees

I was interested in the communication of sexual identity rather than the actual sexual practices of individuals. In this sense, I followed the precedent of others such as Woods and Lucas, where they suggest that anyone who considers themselves gay must face the same identity issues that they wanted to study. I therefore asked each of the interviewees to describe their sexual identity in their own words. I used the phrase sexual identity rather than sexual orientation as the former is more inclusive of transsexuals and the latter less so. Most of the men described themselves as 'gay' or 'gay man', though some used the term 'homosexual'. Most of the women used the term 'lesbian', and a few used the term 'gay woman'. Two men and one woman in the study described themselves as bisexual, and two women were male-to-female transsexuals. Table 2 gives a breakdown of the interviewees by sexual identity in each organization.

The interviewees lived with more identities than just their sexual one. Of the usual diversity 'categories', three participants described themselves as Black,

Table 2 Number of interviewees by sexual identity and organization

Organization	Gay men	Lesbians	Bisexual men	Bisexual women	Transsexuals	Total
Alpha Bank	9	3	0	0	0	12
Beta Bank	13	1	0	0	2	16
Micro Department	11	6	0	0	0	17
Delta Department	12	8	1	1	0	22
Police	15	2	1	0	0	18
Fire Service	6	1	0	0	0	7
Total	66	21	2	1	2	92

and two described themselves as disabled. The ages of the interviewees ranged from twenty-one to fifty-three, with 38 per cent of interviewees in their thirties.

Structure of the interviews

The interviews were semi-structured; previous researchers have recommended less structure in interviews which aim to elicit narrative, thereby giving greater control to respondents. I had prepared a list of prompt questions to help the interviewee begin talking about their experiences, and to help them out if they faltered. Many of the interviewees needed some structure to help them identify and remember their own experiences. Beyond this loose structure, however, they decided on the content, the stories and how they would unfold. Please see the Appendixes for the list of prompt questions used in the interviews.

Data collection – the focus groups

One, if not the major, complication in carrying out research into sexual minorities in organizations is how to gather data when silence surrounds them. Silence because it is an under-researched area, but silence also because it is difficult to get people talking about the subject at all. A key challenge of this research was to create an approach and research method that could break and explore this silence. This approach aimed to resolve the tension between the individual and organizational level of analysis and to access not only what can be very private experiences of sexuality in organizations, but also to surface 'discourse' itself.

Individual stories were not enough. In order to explore the production of sexual identity with relation to discourse within the organization, the research needed to go beyond individual narrative to capturing group processes, and encouraging discussion on a topic which is often left unspoken, and where data would therefore take a long time to collect through observation or other methods. I therefore took the stories I had collected through individual interviews to focus groups in the same organization, to get people talking about the stories, and therefore the issues relating to sexual minorities, and how they, as members of the organization reacted to these stories told by their colleagues. Did they recognize the stories? How did they feel about the issues raised? Did they recognize the issues as valid?

The term focus group is a generic term referring to group discussions exploring a specific set of issues, using some kind of collective activity. They are invaluable in exploring how linguistic exchanges operate within given contexts. They offer great potential as a research method, especially when combined with another exploratory, qualitative approach such as the storytelling approach expounded thus far. However, they are open to careless or inappropriate use, I gave very careful consideration to a number of different factors: recruiting the groups and sampling methods; the size and make-up of each group; and ethical issues in focus group research.

Recruiting the groups and sampling methods

Researchers have described recruitment of the right people as the most underestimated aspect of organizing focus groups, and this study was no exception in presenting certain challenges. Statistical representation is not the aim of most focus group research, and often qualitative sampling is used. I made no effort to have any statistically valid breakdown of categories in the group, since it would not have been appropriate to the study; it was not my intention either to control for sexuality in the focus groups and, anyway, I felt that it would have been a fallacy to assume that any one individual can speak for their group, be it gender, race or sexuality.

I had almost complete control over the organization of the individual interviews with lesbian and gay employees but I recognized that focus group work often involved increased dependency on 'gatekeepers'. The risk in relying more heavily on managers in the organization to organize the focus groups was that the structure of the focus groups was out of my control, and particularly critical views may have been prevented from surfacing. However, I am confident that the selection of groups was not deliberately skewed in any particular way. For example, the fire service was keen to select different watches who were known to have different group characteristics, some more cooperative and others more negative towards the organization, to give a selection of different views. The police did not tell divisional commanders, or any recruit to the focus groups, the topic of discussion, precisely to avoid this problem.

The make up of the groups was structured differently in each organization, as in all cases the organization took a lead role in organizing the focus groups. There was a mix of volunteer and selected groups. The other organizations openly and honestly asked for volunteers, and to my knowledge there was no effort to control the membership of the groups. Where the organization selected groups, as in the case of the fire service, they did so precisely to get a mix of positive and negative views.

The focus groups in the government departments were recruited by the equality and diversity directorates, who advertised the groups, giving the dates and times when the groups would be carried out around the country. Only volunteers came to the groups. Clearly, the disadvantage with this approach is that only interested parties, or people who are already engaged with the topic, are likely to attend.

Beta Bank's focus groups were also organized by the equality and diversity department, there were three different types of group. The first of these was a 'Piggyback Focus Group', where the focus group was added to an already existing meeting; I attended a management meeting of sales managers and a two-hour slot in the agenda was devoted to the focus group discussion. Another was organized to be 'on location', and I carried it out in situ by visiting one of the bank's call centres; the manager released a number of people from their duties to attend the discussion. These two groups were therefore made up of selected people, not volunteers. Finally, two groups were carried out by asking for volunteers in the head office.

In the Shire Fire Service, the equalities officer arranged for me to travel around the county to different fire stations, and join different watches. These groups were unusual as they were neither selected nor volunteer groups; instead they were normal groupings of firefighters at work. In addition, two further groups were carried out at head office, which were made up of volunteers. All the groups were therefore carried out 'on location'.

In the Rural Police Constabulary, an order was sent out to divisional commanders by the assistant chief inspector to select and make available a number of people from their region. These were to be a mix of sworn staff (police officers), support staff and traffic wardens. None of the attendees in these focus groups were volunteers, and all but one of the groups took place 'on location'. One of the focus groups was a 'Piggyback Focus Group' with a shift of frontline police officers, taking place during the briefing session at the beginning of their shift.

No incentives, apart from the usual coffee and biscuits, were given. Groups took place during working hours and, where appropriate, participants were paid travelling expenses by the organization. It is perhaps worthy of note that these groups could not have taken place without the interviews first taking place with sexual minorities; these latter interviewees gave up their own time in lunch-breaks, evenings and weekends to speak to me, and paid for their own travelling expenses to do so.

The size and make-up of each group

I carried out a total of thirty-four focus groups, across five organizations, with a total number of 246 participants. One orthodoxy which has emerged from the market research literature on the running of focus groups is that the ideal size of groups is somewhere between eight and twelve people. In the Rural Police Constabulary, the groups were of this size. I had made this known when preparing for the groups, and the assistant chief constable had ordered for this number of people to be selected. However, it was quite difficult to control the size of the groups in this study for various different reasons. In the fire service, for instance, the size of the watch varied, and I felt that it was more conducive to effective group dynamics to work with the watch as a group, irrespective of their number. This was the case also for the managers' meeting in the bank where the advantage of going into a routine sales meeting to discuss issues of sexuality outweighed the disadvantage of having too many people in the group. Finally, the government departments tried to manage the number of volunteers in the groups by keeping a booking system, but this proved to be unreliable as people either did not turn up, or too many people came and I did not turn anyone away.

I did not control for sexuality; my aim was to recruit a number of different people across the organization, and not to create a 'straight' or heterosexual focus group. Neither was it the intention to create a 'gay' focus group as a large amount of data had already been collected on sexual minorities from the individual interviews. Greater detail on the focus group participants is given in the Appendix.

Ethical issues in focus group research

The discussion of ethical issues is very relevant to the discussion of focus group research. Issues include getting the informed consent of participants; this was not possible in some cases. For example, in the police, employees did not know in advance what they were coming to, and were therefore unable to give their informed consent. Another ethical issue was confidentiality. I warned all focus group participants that these groups were not confidential in the sense that I would be feeding back their views to the organization and then using their views in my research. However, they would be used anonymously and I would not, at any point, link any one particular view to a participant. That said, focus groups, by their very nature, involve different members of the organization who could have talked and gossiped outside the group about views expressed inside it. For that reason, I followed the advice of focus group researchers to set ground rules prior to the running the group which everyone agreed to. These focus groups were dealing with sensitive topics, and although they did not have the aim of encouraging personal disclosure from the participants in any way they did, nevertheless, involve the discussion of individuals' personal stories and the open discussion of taboo topics. Some researchers have even suggested that this can even introduce a certain thrill into the proceedings!

Silence in the research process

There is some discourse or banter that I could not pick up easily: it was impossible for me to record anything that was discussed outside the focus groups. When attendance is voluntary as it was in the two government departments, what of the talk or discourse of those people who chose not to attend? In the following extract, the reported banter is from a group of men who did not come to the focus group but worked with someone who did. They were a particularly jokey group, and their banter is reported by one focus group participant as follows:

> Take this (focus group) for example! Do you want to know why I came to this? Because I was getting fed up with the jokes about what kind of focus group this was going to be. If we get one more email asking us to go to this, and I have to listen to this any more, I'm going to go to this and put a stop to it, I'm going to volunteer. I can't remember specifics, just the general laughter, about sexuality, where the gays are breeding in Edinburgh, just nonsense. To me it's like cover up.

Clearly, it would have been very difficult for me to collect examples of homophobic banter, like this, and the focus group participant has provided a window into the world of her everyday office environment. Indeed, once people know the topic of the research, it actively silences this sort of conversation – which is an example of the research process having an effect on the organization. The focus group participant is a woman, who also takes the role of the bystander in the office. The men are the ones who are powerful in this group and are responsible for the banter. The role of the bystander is an interesting one, and there has been a significant amount of literature on the subject. The dictionary definition of bystander is as 'spectator', which indicates a passive, powerless role, but they are often in a position to do something to bring the situation to an end, as this woman had done by coming to the focus group. It could be considered to be an act of resistance, with the passive bystander deciding to do something to stop the banter, to move from the position of merely observing to doing. It is interesting to compare this with my role as researcher in the research process; the researcher is not merely a bystander. The fact that research has been carried out in the organization actually causes some change in the organization itself.

Silence also suggests the idea of a 'cover up'. Although the following extract is not from a focus group, it is an interesting text, nonetheless. I had submitted my report to the Delta Department, where there was a reference to a director saying that he would never promote gay men or Asian women. They requested me to take out the reference to a director. I received an email from the organization after I had submitted the report as follows:

> The item concerned is the quote from a member of staff as follows: 'Just recently I was speaking to a director who had the gall to say that he wasn't very keen on promoting Asian women or gay men'. (We) are extremely concerned about sharing the report with the Board or other senior officers whilst this comment specifically mentions a director. There is the potential for a conduct and discipline issue for the director concerned (not that we're going to ask who the quote was made by or about). (We) would feel a lot more comfortable however, if the word 'director' was taken out of this quote and the words 'senior manager' inserted. (We) wouldn't feel quite so reluctant to give the report a slightly wider circulation if this quote was amended. I realize this puts you in a very difficult position as it is someone else's words that I'm asking you to amend. How do you feel about this? I don't think using the term 'senior manager' lessens the impact of this particular quote or the report as a whole. If we don't change it, however I think some of the impact of the report may be lost as the degree of circulation will be limited.

This text demonstrates that it is not possible to admit that senior people may be in contravention of a policy that the department openly supports. It would have to be treated so seriously that there would have to be an investigation and possible disciplining of the individual concerned. Clearly, even equal opportunities staff have one eye on their own jobs, which would be at risk if they instigated an investigation of this sort. The other reason that it cannot be discussed openly is the idea of the organization having two faces; one, which it presents to the outside world, and the other with its quasi-private views which is inward-looking. The altering of this report is a clear example of the silencing as censoring which goes on in organizations which belies the idea that it is only those lower down the organization who engage in discriminatory behaviour or banter. The text also shows that no matter what organization you put in place (for example an equal opportunities organization in the case of this government department), there are other forces at play, which mitigate the ability to challenge. This supports Foucault's ideas of power relations; they do not go away, they just get redefined.

Identity of the researcher

My identity as researcher was important in a number of ways: first it influenced the selection of the research topic; and it affected data collection, especially the way that interviews were carried out, although I tried to mitigate against any serious influence on the outcome of the project. Clearly, my identity might have affected the way that questions were asked, as well as the answers that were given, and finally my identity might have affected the way that the data was interpreted and analysed.

Minority researchers are often more sensitive to the way in which their identity presented. I was certainly aware of my sexuality during this project, perhaps even more than I ever had been before. I decided that, as a member of a minority group, I had a unique opportunity to seek people's honest views about sexuality. Criticism might be levelled at my approach because although I told interviewees that I was gay, I did not do so with the focus groups. People might say that this approach is not ethical and is, in fact, dishonest. In actual fact, I believe that it merely reflects and mirrors day-to-day practice in organizations where employees and members of staff feel free to speak freely because of the invisibility of homosexuality.

Carrying out the focus groups

The groups of course are classified as 'sensitive' not only because of the topic under discussion, but also because of the potential for research in this area to raise strong feelings and opinions, or even to pose a threat to those involved, either to me as the researcher or the participants. To illustrate this point, I am going to relate a story of my own, demonstrating that focus groups dealing with sensitive topics, also have sensitive moments of their own.

This first focus group had not been the liveliest group I had facilitated during this research project (the police was the sixth and last out of six organizations to take part in the research). For this reason there was some time left over at the end of the session, and I decided to use one story which I had held in reserve. The story had been told to me by a lesbian personnel officer, who had interviewed two members of The Alpha Group, an evangelical Christian group, who wanted to use police premises for their meetings. This was the story she told to me:

I had a meeting with two members of the Alpha Group, an evangelical movement. There was an inspector and a member of the support staff. I asked whether they had experienced any discrimination. I also asked how inclusive they were of others. They said that lesbians and gay men would be welcomed into the group, but they would be left in no doubt that they were an abomination. He actually used that word. I don't know whether he knew that I was a lesbian. The member of the support staff was much less offensive in her language, but no less offensive in her overall view, which was that she wanted lesbians and gay men to come to the group but to realize that to be actively gay was incompatible with Christianity. I did challenge them about that and said that there are very different Christian views to sexuality; for example, I asked them if they would point out that there is a lesbian and gay Christian society they could join and get a very different experience. They were both immovable. Alpha is very visible in our headquarters. Just last week, I was in the training college waiting to go into someone's office, and there was an Alpha poster on the wall, and it's a bit like oh my God, there's the enemy here. There's a huge Alpha poster in the canteen, and for me the Alpha image is a very offensive one because all my experience with Alpha has been very homophobic. But the force dealt with that in a very positive way at a senior level.'

Shortly after I had handed out this story, a woman in the focus group said, *'It's me. The story is about me!'*, making reference to her being one of the Alpha Group members in the story, and she also said, *'What's more, it's not true.'* On hearing this I called the focus group to a close, saying that it would not be appropriate to discuss a story which made specific reference to an individual in the room. The group filed out, somewhat dejected, and I began to pack my things away. Minutes later, the door burst open and the woman's manager came in saying that she was in tears, very upset and I was to give an assurance that I would not use the story any more. I said that I could not give an immediate assurance, as I needed time to think. Within minutes, the incident had been escalated to the deputy chief constable, who delegated the matter to a chief superintendent. The latter was extremely sympathetic towards me, describing a similar incident which had occurred to him recently, but at the same time requesting me not to use the story any more, as the police had some issues with the Alpha Group and they did not want anything to exacerbate the situation. I agreed. However, the Alpha Group members wanted my contact details and my home address which were handed over to them. I felt under such pressure that, although I had been given a room in the headquarters to stay in, I felt that I could no longer stay on police premises, as I did not feel safe. I checked into a local B&B. Returning from the research trip, the fact that my home contact details had been handed over to people who were hostile to the research made me unsafe in my own home, and made me worry for the safety of my research output, tapes and transcripts, more to the point, and I imagined that I would return home from work one day and the front door would be swinging wide open on its hinges, with tapes and transcripts nowhere to be found. So, I took the precaution of backing up all my research material and hiding it in a safe environment away from home. As a postscript to this story, I can say, with some relief, that I received no harassment, and I may have overreacted, although at the time, it seemed very frightening and also richly ironic that life was imitating art: the story, which later proved to be true, was imitated in the research process as members of a religious minority set out to persecute a member of a sexual minority; in the story, a lesbian personnel officer working for the police, in the research process, a gay male researcher, researching minority sexual identity in the police.

This personal experience from the research process is particularly appropriate in illustrating the tension which can exist between two minorities in an organization and helps to describe how difficult it can be to reach a compromise which members of both minorities are happy with.

Data analysis

Recording and transcribing the output

Tape-recording provides richer data than just note-taking, and consequently all the interviews and focus groups were recorded. At the start of each interview or focus group, participants were asked whether anyone had any objections. No one did. They were also assured that their views would be reported anonymously, and no one from their organization would have access to the tapes.

Interestingly, the Delta Department, when negotiating the contract for access, asked for ownership and copyright of all the material used in and output from interviews and focus groups. I refused on ethical grounds, since the identities of the participants had to be protected and, even if the organization had never exercised their rights, they would technically have had the right to see transcripts and listen to the tapes. They relented and I maintained ownership and copyright of the research output.

I transcribed all the interviews and focus groups verbatim, involving between 756 and 1,008 hours (or between ninety-four and 126 days) of transcription. (On average, it took six to eight hours to transcribe each two-hour session whether interview or focus group. As previously mentioned ninety-two interviews and thirty-four focus groups were carried out.)

Classifying the data

Basic to the process of looking to see if there are trends in the data, is some kind of categorizing, often referred to as coding. For this project, a software package called QSR NVivo was used, to facilitate the process of sorting the data into categories. The package was used to analyse two types of data. First, stories were identified from the individual interviews, and then sorted into subject matter;

second, I used NVivo to codify the focus group data, and to identify common trends within it.

Voice – whose is it, the researcher's or the respondent's?

Silence was a theme which became apparent in the research process. There were two main issues; one was a question of voice, that is to say how much the researcher's own voice would silence those that had previously been silenced. The second was a question of discomfort around uncovering silence which had previously protected the sexual minorities.

A question of voice

I was very conscious of my own voice, agenda and viewpoint. I'm a gay man, with experience of working in a variety of corporate environments, and this was important in gaining access to respondents and building up the necessary trust with them to carry out the interviews. I believe that in carrying out this sort of research, having an agenda is essential, and therefore it is debatable whether the researcher's voice could, or should, be silenced. There are a number of metaphors that usefully illuminate the role of the researcher in articulating previously silenced voices. One is as a ventriloquist; as a researcher one can hope to be the spokesperson for others, but the goal of political representation jostles with the awareness that the researcher is 'performing an act of ventriloquism'. Another is the 'parrot' where one hopes to avoid a crude, loud parody of what can be an inexplicably complex array of experiences and emotions. Feminist researchers have discussed the problems of articulating silence, referring to a variety of ways of knowing; the power and lack of power in silence, the power to listen and to hear others' stories, and the use of others to advocate or articulate one's own narrative.

The final word: giving a voice to lesbians, gay men, bisexuals and transsexuals in the workplace

Potentially, most harm is done when interpretations are imposed on what the researcher claims to be authentic voices from the field. One of my aims here has been to render these voices to a wider audience and as such the stories that I have reproduced are faithful reproductions of the original stories, creating a platform through this book for those not previously heard. However, I have also attempted to analyse, using a critical perspective, the way in which multiple silences are articulated and the way that the identity of sexual minorities in organizations is constructed. In doing this, I have had to use my own voice both in analysing and in presenting the data. Giving a voice to those who were silent in the organization is not a comfortable process. Not all of the respondents were 'out' at work, and so I was involved in uncovering something, which had been covered over. My research brought private issues from the realm of the individual to the public arena for public scrutiny. At times, I felt like an intruder. However, I believe that by publishing these stories, as well as the process involved in researching them, will help other talk more about minority sexuality in organizations. It will also, I hope, act as a historical record of what life was like in work organizations for lesbians and gay men at the beginning of the twenty-first century in the United Kingdom.

Appendix A
Sexual orientation – glossary of terms

The following glossary of terms was developed during the research project with one of the client organizations to help managers with their reading of the final report. It is not intended to be an academic classification of terms, but it is included here to serve the same purpose in helping the reader with specialized terminology.

Biphobia	The irrational fear of people sexually orientated towards people of both sexes.
Bisexual	Men or women sexually orientated towards people of both sexes.
Closet	Disclosure of one's sexual and gender identity is a major issue for sexual minorities; the closet is a major metaphor (once a slang term, now in common parlance) representing non-disclosure.
Coming out	Makes reference to the 'closet' and means the disclosure either voluntarily or otherwise of one's sexual and gender identity.
Gay	Men or women sexually orientated towards people of the same sex.
Gender identity	Self-perception and identification as male or female.
Heterosexual	Sexually orientated towards people of the opposite gender.
Homophobia	The irrational fear of same-sex attraction.
Homosexual	Sexually orientated towards people of the same gender. This word is no longer acceptable as it is seen as being demeaning.
Lesbian	Women sexually orientated towards other women.
LGBT	Lesbian, gay, bisexual and transgender.
Out	The state of being open about one's sexuality and/or gender identity.
Post-operation	The stage after gender-reassignment surgery.
Real-life test	A period of up to two years, during which a transsexual man or woman lives in the new gender role on a full-time basis in every aspect of their life. It is usually a prerequisite of gender-reassignment surgery.
Sexual minorities	An umbrella term for the purposes of this report referring to people who self-identify as lesbian, gay, bisexual and transgender.
Sexual orientation	Refers to the sexual attraction to persons of the same or opposite gender.
Sexuality	For the purposes of this report, sexuality refers to sexual orientation and sexual identity; it includes homosexuality, bisexuality, heterosexuality and transsexuality.

Straight	A slang term for heterosexuality.
Transgender	People who have gender-identity disorder. However, this is an umbrella term including transsexuals and intersexuals. It has also been adopted to include transvestites.
Transitioning	The process of changing from one gender to another.
Transphobia	The irrational fear of transgender people and issues.
Transsexual	People who have gender-identity disorder and have a strong psychological desire or need to change their gender.

Appendix B

Question guide for semi-structured interviews

The following is a list of questions which were used as prompts in the individual, semi-structured interviews.

1 How did you come to join the organization?
2 Were you aware of how the organization treats its lesbian and gay employees before joining?
3 Were you out prior to joining the organization?
4 Are you out at work?
5 If so, what was the process of coming out like?
6 What were your colleagues like after this?
7 [If not out] Can you describe any incidents or experiences which demonstrate what it is like being a lesbian/gay man but not being out at work?
8 Were you ever in a situation where you felt excluded from banter?
9 Where is the barrier between work and home – for example, would you take your partner to a work's party?
10 Have you ever had any particularly positive experiences related to your sexuality?
11 Have you ever had any particularly negative experiences related to your sexuality?
12 Can you think of any incidents where being gay may have limited (or helped) your career in any way?
13 How has the organization influenced you as a lesbian/gay man?
14 Has being gay influenced the way that you have done your job, either positively or negatively?
15 How does the organization support your being open with customers/clients/the outside world?
16 What is it, do you believe, about the organization that makes it a positive/negative place to work?

Bibliography

Translations of quotations from French to English are by J.H. Ward, the author of this book, unless otherwise stated in the bibliography.

Ackroyd, S. and Thompson, P. 1999. *Organizational Misbehaviour*. London: Sage.

Adam, B.D. 2002. From liberation to transgression and beyond: gay, lesbian and queer studies at the turn of the twenty-first century. In D. Richardson and S. Seidman (eds), *Handbook of Lesbian and Gay Studies*: 15–26. London: Sage.

Adkins, L. 2002. *Revisions: gender and sexuality in late modernity*. Buckingham: Open University Press.

Ainsworth, S. and Hardy, C. 2004. Discourse and identities. In D. Grant, C. Hardy, C. Oswick and L. Putnam (eds), *The Sage Handbook of Organizational Discourse*: 153–173. London: Sage.

Albert, S., Ashforth, B.E. and Dutton, J.E. 2000. Organizational identity and identification: charting new waters and building new bridges. *Academy of Management Review*, 25(1): 13–17.

Alexander, C.J. 2002. When the researcher is gay or lesbian: issues of experimenter bias. *Journal of Gay and Lesbian Social Services*, 14(4): 105–108.

Althusser, L. 1971. *Lenin and Philosophy and Other Essays*. London: New Left Books.

Alvesson, M. and Deetz, S. 1996. Critical theory and postmodernism approaches to organizational studies. In S. Clegg, R.C. Hardy and W.R. Nord (eds), *Handbook of Organization Studies*: 191–217. London: Sage.

Alvesson, M. and Deetz, S. 2000. *Doing Critical Management Research*. London: Sage.

Alvesson, M. and Karreman, D. 2000. Varieties of discourse: on the study of organisations through discourse analysis. *Human Relations*, 53(19): 1125–1149.

Alvesson, M. and Willmott, H. 2002. Identity regulation as organizational control: producing the appropriate individual. *Journal of Management Studies*, 39(5): 619–644.

Austin, J.L. 1962. *How to do Things with Words*. Oxford: Oxford University Press.

Babuscio, J. 1999. The cinema of camp. In F. Cleto (ed.), *Camp: Queer Aesthetics and The Performing Subject*: 117–135. Edinburgh: Edinburgh University Press.

Badgett, M.V.L. 1995. The wage effects of sexual orientation discrimination. *Industrial and Labor Relations Review*, 48(4): 726–739.

Badgett, M.V.L. 2001. Lesbian and gay think tanks. In M. Blasius (ed.), *Sexual Identities, Queer Politics*: 359–376. Princeton: Princeton University Press.

Badgett, M.V.L. and King, M.C. 1997. Lesbian and gay occupational strategies. In A. Gluckman and B. Reed (eds), *Homo Economics: Capitalism, Community and Lesbian and Gay Life*. New York: Routledge.

Bailey, R.W. 2001. Sexual identity and urban space. In M. Blasius (ed.), *Sexual Identities, Queer Politics*: 231–255. Princeton: Princeton University Press.

Barthes, R. 1973. *Mythologies*. London: Paladin.

Beer, C., Jeffrey, R. and Munyard, T. 1983. *Gay workers, trade unions and the law*. London: NCCL.

Belenky, M.F., Clinchy, B.M., Goldberger, N.R. and Tarule, J.M. 1986. *Women's Ways of Knowing*. New York: Basic Books.

Berger, P.L. and Luckman, T. 1967. *The Social Construction of Reality*. London: The Penguin Press.

Binnie, J. and Skeggs, B. 2004. Cosmopolitan knowledge and the production and consumption of sexualized space: Manchester's gay village. *Sociological Review*, 52(1): 39–61.

Blasius, M. (ed.). 2001. *Sexual Identities, Queer Politics*. Princeton: Princeton University Press.

Boatwright, K.J., Gilbert, S., Forrest, L. and Ketzenberger, K. 1996. Impact of identity development upon career trajectory: listening to the voices of lesbian women. *Journal of Vocational Behavior*, 48: 210–228.

Boje, D.M. 1991a. Consulting and change in the storytelling organisation. *Journal of Organizational Change Management*, 4(3): 7–17.

Boje, D.M. 1991b. The storytelling organization: a study of story performance in an office-supply firm. *Administrative Science Quarterly*, 36: 106–126.

Boje, D.M. 1995. Stories of the storytelling organization: a postmodern analysis of Disney as 'Tamara-land'. *Academy of Management Journal*, 38(4): 997–1035.

Boje, D.M. 2001. *Narrative Methods for Organizational and Communication Research*. London: Sage.

Boon, J.A. 1982. *Other Tribes, Other Scribes: Symbolic Anthropology in the Comparative Study of Cultures, Histories Religions and Texts*. Cambridge: Cambridge University Press.

Bowen, F. and Blackmon, K. 2003. Spirals of silence: the dynamic effects of diversity on organizational voice. *Journal of Management Studies*, 40(6): 1393–1417.

Bowker, G.C. and Star, S.L. 1999. *Sorting Things Out: Classification and its Consequences*. Cambridge: The MIT Press.

Boyce, M.E. 1996. Organizational story and storytelling: a critical review. *Journal of Organizational Change Management*, 9(5): 5–26.

Brewis, J. and Grey, C. 1994. Re-eroticizing the organization: an exegesis and critique. *Gender, Work and Organization*, 1(2): 67–82.

Brocklehurst, M. and Ward, J.H. 2002. *Power, Discourse and Sexual Identity at Work*. Paper presented at the conference on Organizational discourse: from micro-utterances to macro-inferences, King's College, London, 24 July.

Brown, A.D. 2001. Organization studies and identity: towards a research agenda. *Human Relations*, 54(1): 113–121.

Brown, A.D. 2003. Authoritative sensemaking in a public inquiry report. *Organization Studies*, 25(1): 95–112.

Bruni, A. and Gherardi, S. 2001. Micro's story: the heterogeneous engineering of a gendered professional self. In M. Dent and S. Whitehead (eds), *Managing Professional Identities: Knowledge, Performativity and the New Professional*: 174–198. London: Routledge.

Bruni, A. and Gherardi, S. 2002. En-gendering differences, transgressing the boundaries, coping with the dual presence. In L. Aaltio-Marjosola and A.J. Mills (eds), *Gender, Identity and the Culture of Organization*: 174–200. London: Routledge.

Bruni, A., Gherardi, S. and Poggio, B. 2004. Doing gender, doing entrepreneurship: an ethnographic account of intertwined practices. *Gender, Work and Organization*, 11(4): 406–429.

Bruni, A., Gherardi, S. and Poggio, B. 2004, forthcoming. *Gender and Entrepreneurship: An Ethnographic Approach.* London: Routledge.

Burke, M.E. 1993. *Coming Out of the Blue: British Police OFFICERS TALK ABOUT THEIR LIVES in 'The Job' as Lesbians, Gays and Bisexuals.* London: Cassell.

Burke, M.E. 1994. Homosexuality as deviance: the case of the gay police officer. *British Journal of Criminology*, 34: 192–203.

Burkitt, I. 1998. Sexuality and gender identity: from a discursive to a relational analysis. *Sociological Review*, 46(3): 483–504.

Burkitt, I. 1999. *Bodies of Thought: Embodiment, Identity and Modernity.* London: Sage.

Burr, V. 1995. *An Introduction to Social Constructionism.* London: Routledge.

Burrell, G. 1984. Sex and organizational analysis. *Organization Studies*, 5(2): 97–118.

Burrell, G. 1992. The organization of pleasure. In M. Alvesson and H. Willmott (eds), *Critical Management Studies*: 65–89. London: Sage.

Burrell, G. and Hearn, J. 1989. The sexuality of organization. In J. Hearn, D.L. Sheppard, P. Tancred-Sheriff and G. Burrell (eds), *The Sexuality of Organization.* London: Sage.

Butler, J. 1990. *Gender trouble: feminism and the subversion of identity.* London: Routledge.

Butler, J. 1991. Imitation and gender insubordination. In D. Fuss (ed.), *Inside/Out: Lesbian Theories, Gay Theories*: 13–31. New York: Routledge.

Butler, J. 1993. *Bodies That Matter: On the Discursive Limits of Sex.* London: Routledge.

Butler, J. 1997. *Excitable Speech: A Politics of the Performative.* London: Routledge.

Butler, J. 1999. Preface. In J. Butler, *Gender Trouble: Feminism and the Subversion of Identity*, 2nd ed. London: Routledge.

Campaign for Homosexual Equality. 1981. What about the gay workers? London.

Carabine, J. 2001. Unmarried motherhood 1830–1990: a genealogical analysis. In M. Wetherell, S. Taylor and S. Yates (eds), *Discourse as Data*: 267–310. London: Sage.

Case, P. 2004. The blind people and the elephant. In Y. Gabriel (ed.), *Myths, Stories and Organizations: Postmodern Narratives for our Times*: 49–65. Oxford: Oxford University Press.

Casey, C. 2000. Sociology sensing the body: revitalizing a dissociative discourse. In J. Hassard, R. Holliday and H. Willmott (eds), *Body and Organization.* London: Sage.

Chung, Y.B. and Harman, L.W. 1994. The career interests and aspirations of gay men: how sex-role orientation is related. *Journal of Vocational Behavior*, 45: 223–239.

Clair, J.A., Beatty, J. and MacLean, T. 2002. Out of sight but not out of mind: how people manage invisible social identities in the workplace. *Academy of Management*, August.

Clair, R.P. 1998. *Organizing Silence: A World of Possibilities.* New York: University of New York Press.

Clandinin, D.J. and Connelly, F.M. 2000. *Narrative Inquiry: Experience and Story in Qualitative Research*, 1st edn. San Francisco: Jossey-Bass.

Clausen, J. 1997. *Beyond Gay or Straight: Understanding Sexual Orientation.* New York: Chelsea House Publishing.

Cleto, F. (ed.). 1999. *Camp: Queer Aesthetics and the Performing Subject.* Edinburgh: Edinburgh University Press.

Cockburn, C. 1989. Equal opportunities: the long and short agenda. *Industrial Relations Journal*, Autumn: 213–225.

Cohen, E. 1991. Who are 'we'? Gay identity as political emotion (a theoretical rumination). In D. Fuss (ed.), *Inside/Out: Lesbian Theories, Gay Theories*: 71–92. New York: Routledge.

Colgan, F. 1999a. Moving forward in Unison: lesbian and gay self-organization in action. In G. Hunt (ed.), *Laboring for Rights: Unions and Sexual Diversity across Nations*: 261–289. Philadelphia: Temple University Press.

Colgan, F. 1999b. Recognising the gay constituency in United Kingdom trade unions. *Industrial Relations Journal*, 30(5): 444–462.

Colgan, F., Creegan, C., McKearney, A. and Wright, T. 2006. *Lesbian, Gay and Bisexual Workers: Equality, Diversity and Inclusion in the Workplace*. European Social Fund and London Metropolitan University.

Collins, J. and Mayblin, B. 2000. *Introducing Derrida*. Cambridge: Icon Books.

Collinson, D.L. 2002. Managing humour. *Journal of Management Studies*, 39(3): 269–188.

Collinson, D.L. 2003. Identities and insecurities: selves at work. *Organization*, 10(3): 527–547.

Collinson, D.L., Knights, D. and Collinson, M. 1990. *Managing to discriminate*. London: Routledge.

Cornelius, N. 2001. *Human Resource Management*. 2nd edn. London: Thomson Learning.

Cornelius, N., Gleadle, P., Winstanley, D.C. and Ward, J.H. 2004. *Changing faces: sexuality, ethnicity and multiple identities in the workplace*. Paper presented at the British Academy of Management Conference 2004, University of St. Andrews: 30 August.

Coser, R.L. 1979. *Training in Ambiguity: Learning Through Doing in a Mental Hospital*. New York: Free Press.

Craib, I. 1998. *Experiencing Identity*. London: Sage.

Creed, D.W.E. 2003. Voice lessons: tempered radicalism and the use of voice and silence. *Journal of Management Studies*, 40(6): 1503–1536.

Croteau, J.M. 1996. Research on the work experiences of lesbian, gay and bisexual people; an integrative review of methodology and findings. *Journal of Vocational Behavior*, 48: 195–209.

Currah, P. 2001. Queer Theory, lesbian and gay rights and transsexual marriages. In M. Blasius (ed.), *Sexual Identities, Queer Politics*: 379. Princeton: Princeton University Press.

Czarniawska, B. 1997. *Narrating the Organization: Dramas of Institutional Identity*. Chicago: University of Chicago Press.

Czarniawska, B. 1998. *A Narrative Approach to Organization Studies*. Thousand Oaks: Sage.

Czarniawska, B. 1999. *Writing Management: Organization Theory as a Literary Genre*. Oxford: Oxford University Press.

Czarniawska, B. 2004. Foreword: a semiotic reading of strong plots. In Y. Gabriel (ed.), *Myths, Stories and Organizations: Postmodern Narratives for our Times*: vii–viii. Oxford: Oxford University Press.

Day, N.E. and Schoenrade, P. 1997. Staying in the closet versus coming out: relationships between communication about sexual orientation and work attitudes. *Personnel Psychology*, 50(1): 147–167.

Day, N.E. and Schoenrade, P. 2000. The relationship among reported disclosure of sexual orientation, anti-discrimination policies, top management support and work attitudes of gay and lesbian employees. *Personnel Review*, 29(3): 346–363.

de Levita, D.D. 1965. *The Concept of Identity*. Paris, France: Mouton & Co.

de Saussure, F. 1974. *Course in General Linguistics*. London: Fontana.

Deal, T. and Kennedy, A. 1982. *Corporate Culture: The Rites and Rituals of Corporate Life.* London: Penguin Business.

Derrida, J. 1976. *Of Grammatology* (trans. by G.C. Spivak). Baltimore: The Johns Hopkins University Press.

Derrida, J. 1978. *Writing and Difference* (trans. by A. Bass). London: Routledge.

Dickens, L. 1997. Gender, race and employment equality in Britain: inadequate strategies and the role of industrial relations actors. *Industrial Relations Journal*, 28(4): 282–291.

Dickens, L. 1999. Beyond the business case: a three-pronged approach to equality action. *Human Resource Management Journal*, 9(1): 9–19.

Dickens, L. 2000. Still wasting resources? Equality in employment. In S. Bach and K. Sisson (eds), *Personnel Management, a Comprehensive Guide to Theory and Practice*, 3rd edn.: 137–169. Oxford: Blackwell.

Dollimore, J. 1991. *Sexual Dissidence: Augustine to Wilde, Freud to Foucault.* Oxford: Clarendon Press.

Driscoll, J.M., Kelley, F.A. and Fassinger, R. 1996. Lesbian identity and disclosure in the workplace: relation to occupational stress and satisfaction. *Journal of Vocational Behavior*, 48: 229–242.

du Gay, P. 1996. *Consumption and Identity at Work.* London: Sage.

Eadie, A. 2000. J P Morgan sets a Gleaming example of workplace diversity. *Financial Times.* 5 November: A22.

Edwards, D., Ashmore, M. and Potter, J. 1995. Death and furniture: the rhetoric, politics and theology of bottom line arguments against relativism. *History of the Human Sciences*, 8(2): 25–49.

Epstein, S. 1996. A Queer encounter. In S. Seidman (ed.), *Queer Theory/Sociology*: 145–167. Oxford: Blackwell.

Esterberg, K.G. 2002. The bisexual menace: or, will the real bisexual please stand up? In D. Richardson and S. Seidman (eds), *Handbook of Lesbian and Gay Studies*: 215–227. London: Sage.

Fairclough, N. 1989. *Language and Power.* Harlow: Longman.

Fairclough, N. 1995. *Critical Discourse Analysis.* Harlow: Longman.

Fairclough, N. 2001a. Critical discourse analysis as a method in social scientific research. In R. Wodak and M. Meyer (eds), *Methods of Critical Discourse Analysis*: 121–138. London: Sage.

Fairclough, N. 2001b. The discourse of new labour: critical discourse analysis. In M. Wetherell, S. Taylor and S. Yates (eds), *Discourse as Data*: 229–266. London: Sage.

Farquhar, C. 1999. Are focus groups suitable for 'sensitive' topics? In R.S. Barbour and J. Kitzinger (eds), *Developing Focus Group Research: Politics, Theory and Practice*: 47–63. London: Sage.

Foucault, M. 1969. *L'archeologie du savoir.* Paris: Editions Gallimard.

Foucault, M. 1976. *Histoire de la sexualité; la volonté de savoir.* Paris: Editions Gallimard.

Foucault, M. 1984a. *Histoire de la sexualite II: L'usage des plaisirs.* Paris: Editions Gallimard.

Foucault, M. 1984b. *Histoire de la sexualite III: Le souci de soi.* Paris: Editions Gallimard.

Foucault, M. 1989. *Surveiller et punir.* Paris: Editions Gallimard.

Foucault, M. 1990. *Histoire de la folie a l'age classique.* Paris: Editions Gallimard.

Foucault, M. 1991. Politics and the study of discourse. In G. Burchell, C. Gordon and P. Miller (eds), *The Foucault Effect: Studies in Governmentality.* Chicago: University of Chicago Press.

Foucault, M. 2001. *Fearless Speech.* Los Angeles: Semiotext(e).

Freud, S. 1930. *Civilization and its Discontents*. London: Hogarth.

Fuss, D. (ed.). 1991. *Inside/Out: Lesbian Theories, Gay Theories*. New York: Routledge.

Gabriel, Y. 1991. On organizational stories and myths: why it is easier to slay a dragon than to kill a myth. *International Sociology*, 6(4): 427–442.

Gabriel, Y. 1998. Same old story or changing stories? Folkloric, modern and postmodern mutations. In D. Grant, T. Keenoy and C. Oswick (eds), *Discourse and Organisation*. London: Sage.

Gabriel, Y. 2000. *Storytelling in Organisations. Facts, Fictions and Fantasies*. Oxford: Oxford University Press.

Gabriel, Y. (ed.). 2004a. *Myths, Stories and Organizations: Postmodern Narratives for Our Times*. Oxford: Oxford University Press.

Gabriel, Y. 2004b. The narrative veil: truth and untruths in storytelling. In Y. Gabriel (ed.), *Myths, Stories And Organizations: Postmodern Narratives for Our Times*: 17–31. Oxford: Oxford University Press.

Gabriel, Y. 2004c. Narratives, stories and texts. In D. Grant, C. Hardy, C. Oswick and L. Putnam (eds), *The Sage Handbook of Organizational Discourse*: 61–77. London: Sage.

Gabriel, Y., Fineman, S. and Sims, D. 2000. *Organizing & organizations*. 2nd edn. London: Sage.

Galpin, S. and Sims, D. 1999. Narratives and identity in flexible working and teleworking organisations. In P. Jackson (ed.), *Virtual Working: Social and Organisational Dynamics*: 76–94. London: Routledge.

Gamson, J. 2000. Sexualities, queer theory and qualitative research. In N.K. Denzin and Y. Lincoln (eds), *Handbook of Qualitative Research*. 2nd vol.: 347–365. Thousand Oaks: Sage.

Gherardi, S. 1995. *Gender, Symbolism and Organizational Cultures*. London: Sage.

Giddens, A. 1976. *New Rules of Sociological Method: A Positive Critique of Interpretive Sociologies*. London: Hutchinson.

Giddens, A. 1979. *Central Problems in Social Theory: Action, Structure and Contradiction in Social Analysis*. London: Macmillan.

Giddens, A. 1984. *The Constitution of Society*. Oxford: Polity Press.

Giddens, A. 1991. *Modernity and Self-identity: Self and Society in the Late Modern Age*. Cambridge: Polity Press and Blackwell Publishers.

GLC. 1985. Danger! ... Heterosexism at work. London: Greater London Council.

Goffman, E. 1963a. *Behavior in Public Places: Notes on the Social Organization of Gatherings*. New York: The Free Press.

Goffman, E. 1963b. *Stigma: Notes on the Management of Spoiled Identity*. New York: Prentice Hall.

Goffman, E. 1969. *The Presentation of Self in Everyday Life*. London: Penguin Press.

Gramsci, A. 1971. *Prison Notebooks*. London: Lawrence and Wishart.

Grant, D. and Hardy, C. 2004. Introduction: struggles with organizational discourse. *Organization Studies*, 25(1): 5–13.

Grant, D., Hardy, C., Oswick, C. and Putnam, L. 2004a. Introduction: organizational discourse: exploring the field. In D. Grant, C. Hardy, C. Oswick and L. Putnam (eds), *The Sage Handbook of Organizational Discourse*: 1–36. London: Sage.

Grant, D., Keenoy, T. and Oswick, C. 1998. *Discourse and Organization*. London: Sage.

Grant, D., Hardy, C., Oswick, C. and Putnam, L. (eds). 2004b. *The Sage Handbook of Organizational Discourse*. London: Sage.

Greenberg, D.F. and Bystryn, M.H. 1996. Capitalism, bureaucracy, homosexuality. In S. Seidman (ed.), *Queer Theory/Sociology*: 83–110. Cambridge: Blackwell.

Grugulis, I. 2002. Nothing serious? Candidates' use of humour in management training. *Human Relations*, 55(4): 387–406.

Gutek, B.A. 1989. Sexuality in the workplace: key issues in social research and organisational practice. In J. Hearn, D.L. Sheppard, P. Tancred-Sheriff and G. Burrell (eds), *The Sexuality of Organisation*: 56–70. London: Sage.

Habermas, J. 1987. *The Philosophical Discourse of Modernity: Twelve Lectures*. Cambridge: Polity.

Hall, M. 1989. Private experiences in the public domain: lesbians in organisations. In J. Hearn, D.L. Sheppard, P. Tancred-Sheriff and G. Burrell (eds), *The Sexuality of Organisation*: 125–138. London: Sage.

Hall, S. 2001a. Foucault: power, knowledge and discourse. In M. Wetherell, S. Taylor and S. Yates (eds), *Discourse Theory and Practice: A Reader*: 72–81. London: Sage.

Hall, S. 2001b. The spectacle of the 'Other'. In M. Wetherell, S. Taylor and S. Yates (eds), *Discourse Theory and Practice: A Reader*: 324–344. London: Sage.

Halperin, D.M. 1995. *Saint Foucault: Towards a Gay Hagiography*. New York: Oxford University Press.

Hancock, P. and Tyler, M. 2000. The look of love: gender and the organization of aesthetics. In J. Hassard, R. Holliday and H. Willmott (eds), *Body and Organization*: 108–129. London: Sage.

Hancock, P. and Tyler, M. 2001. *Work, Postmodernism and Organization*. London: Sage.

Hardy, C. and Phillips, N. 1999. No joking matter: discursive struggle in the Canadian refugee system. *Organization Studies*, 20(1): 1–24.

Hardy, C. and Phillips, N. 2004. Discourse and power. In D. Grant, C. Hardy, C. Oswick and L. Putnam (eds), *The Sage Handbook of Organizational Discourse*: 299–316. London: Sage.

Hardy, C., Palmer, I. and Phillips, N. 2000. Discourse as a strategic resource. *Human Relations*, 53(9): 1227–1248.

Harris, L. 2001. Outing Alain L. Locke: empowering the silenced. In M. Blasius (ed.), *Sexual Identities, Queer Politics*: 321–341. Princeton: Princeton University Press.

Hassard, J., Holliday, R. and Willmott, H. (eds). 2000. *Body and Organization*. London: Sage.

Hawkes, T. 1977. *Structuralism and Semiotics*. London: Methuen & Co. Ltd.

Hearn, J., Sheppard, D.L., Tancred-Sheriff, P. and Burrell, G. (eds). 1989. *The Sexuality of Organization*. London: Sage.

Heracleous, L. 2004. Interpretivist approaches to organizational discourse. In D. Grant, C. Hardy, C. Oswick and L. Putnam (eds), *The Sage Handbook of Organizational Discourse*: 175–192. London: Sage.

Heracleous, L. and Hendry, J. 2000. Discourse and the study of organisation: towards a structurational perspective. *Human Relations*, 53(10): 1251–1286.

HM Fire Service Inspectorate. 1999. Equality and Fairness in the Fire Service – a thematic review. Home Office.

Hoddinott, B. 2003. *Drawing for Dummies*. New York: Wiley Publishing Inc.

Holland, J., Ramazanoglu, C., Sharpe, S. and Thomson, R. 2003. When bodies come together: power control and desire. In J. Weeks, J. Holland and M. Waites (eds), *Sexualities and Society: A Reader*: 84–94. Cambridge: Polity Press.

Holliday, R. 1999. The comfort of identity. *Sexualities*, 2(4): 475–491.

Holzhacker, R. 1999. Labor unions and sexual diversity in Germany. In G. Hunt (ed.), *Laboring for Rights: Unions and Sexual Diversity Across Nations*: 238–252. Philadelphia: Temple University Press.

Hood-Williams, J. and Harrison, W.C. 1998. Trouble with gender. *Sociological Review*, 46(1): 73–94.

Horrocks, C. and Jevtic, Z. 1997. *Foucault for Beginners*. Cambridge: Icon Books.

Howarth, D. 2000. *Discourse*. Buckingham: Open University Press.

Howarth, D. and Stavrakakis, Y. 2000. Introducing discourse theory and political analysis. In E. Laclau, D. Howarth, A.J. Norval and Y. Stavrakakis (eds), *Discourse Theory and Political Analysis: Identities, Hegemonies and Social Change*. Manchester: Manchester University Press.

Humphrey, J.C. 1999. Organizing sexualities, organized inequalities: lesbians and gay men in public service occupations. *Gender, Work and Organization*, 6(3): 134–151.

Humphreys, M. and Brown, A.D. 2002. Narratives of organizational identity and identification: a case study of hegemony and resistance. *Organization Studies*, 23(3): 421–447.

Irigaray, L. 1993. *An Ethics of Sexual Difference* (trans. by C. Burke and G.C. Gill). London: The Athlone Press.

Jackson, S. 2003. Heterosexuality, heteronormativity and gender hierarchy: some reflections on recent debates. In J. Weeks, J. Holland and M. Waites (eds), *Sexualities and Society: A Reader*: 69–83. Cambridge: Polity Press.

Jagose, A. 1996. *Queer Theory: An Introduction*. New York: New York University Press.

Jenkins, R. 1996. *Social Identity*. London: Routledge.

Jewson, N. and Mason, D. 1986. Modes of discrimination in the recruitment process; formalisation, fairness and efficiency. *Sociology*, 20(1): 43–63.

Johnson, C. 1997. *Derrida*. London: Phoenix.

Johnson, M. 2003. Anomalous bodies: transgenderings and cultural transformations. In J. Weeks, J. Holland and M. Waites (eds), *Sexualities and Society: A Reader*: 105–117. Cambridge: Polity Press.

Kanter, R.M. 1977. Men and women of the corporation. In H. Clark, J. Chandler and J. Barry (eds), *Organisation and Identities*. London: Chapman Hall.

Keen, S. 2003. *Narrative Form*. Basingstoke: Palgrave Macmillan.

Keenoy, T. and Oswick, C. 2003. Organizing textscapes. *Organization Studies*, 25(1): 135–142.

Kerfoot, D. 2000. Body work: estrangement, disembodiment and the organizational 'other'. In J. Hassard, R. Holliday and H. Willmott (eds), *Body and Organization*: 230–246. London: Sage.

Kilduff, M. and Keleman, M. 2004. Deconstructing discourse. In D. Grant, C. Hardy, C. Oswick and L. Putnam (eds), *The Sage Handbook of Organizational Discourse*: 259–272. London: Sage.

Kirsch, M. 2000. *Queer Theory and Social Change*. London: Routledge.

Kitzinger, C. 1987. *The Social Construction of Lesbianism*. London: Sage.

Kitzinger, J. and Barbour, R.S. 1999. Introduction: the challenge and promise of focus groups. In R.S. Barbour and J. Kitzinger (eds), *Developing Focus Group Research: Politics, Theory and Practice*: 1–20. London: Sage.

Klawitter, M.M. 1998. Why aren't economists doing research on sexual orientation? *Feminist Economics*, 4(2): 55–59.

Klawitter, M.M. 2002. Gays and lesbians as workers and consumers in the economy. In D. Richardson and S. Seidman (eds), *Handbook of Lesbian and Gay Studies*: 329–338. London: Sage.

Knights, D. 2002. Writing organizational analysis into Foucault. *Organization*, 9(4): 575–593.

Knights, D. and McCabe, D. 2003. Governing through teamwork: reconstituting subjectivity in a call centre. *Journal of Management Studies*, 40(7): 1587–1619.

Knights, D. and Willmott, H. 1989. Power and subjectivity: from degradation to subjugation in social relations. *Sociology*, 23(4): 535–558.

Knights, D. and Willmott, H. 1999. *Management Lives: Power and Identity in Work Organizations*. London: Sage.

Kossek, E.E. and Lobel, S.A. 1996. *Managing Diversity; Human Resource Strategies for Transforming the Workplace*. Cambridge: Blackwell.

Kress, G. 2001. From Saussure to critical sociolinguistics: the turn towards a social view of language. In M. Wetherell, S. Taylor and S. Yates (eds), *Discourse Theory and Practice: A Reader*: 29–38. London: Sage.

Krueger, R.A. 1994. *Focus Groups: A Practical Guide for Applied Research*. Thousand Oaks: Sage.

Lacan, J. 1977. *Ecrits: A Selection*. London: Tavistock Publications.

Laclau, E. and Mouffe, C. 1985. *Hegemony and Socialist Strategy: Towards a Radical Democratic Politics*. London: Verso.

Lee, R.M. 1993. *Doing Research on Sensitive Topics*. London: Sage.

Levine, M.P. 1979. Employment discrimination against gay men. *International Review of Modern Sociology*, 9(5/7): 151–163.

Levine, M.P. and Leonard, R. 1984. Discrimination against lesbians in the work force. *Signs*, 9(4): 700–709.

Levi-Strauss, C. 1994. *The Raw and the Cooked*. London: Pimlico.

Linstead, A. and Thomas, R. 2002. 'What do you want from me?' A poststructuralist feminist reading of middle managers' identities. *Culture and Organization*, 8(1): 1–20.

Lofstrom, J. 1997. The birth of the queen/the modern homosexual: historical explorations revisited. *The Sociological Review*, 25(1): 24–41.

Lucas, J.H. and Kaplan, M.G. 1994. Unlocking the corporate closet. *Training and Development USA*, 48(1): 34–38.

Lukes, S. 1974. *Power: A Radical View*. London: Macmillan.

McAdams, D.P. 1997. *The Stories We Live by: Personal Myths and the Making of the Self*. London: The Guilford Press.

McDowell, L. 1997. *Capital Culture: Gender at Work in the City*. Oxford: Blackwell Publishers Ltd.

MacIntyre, A. 1981. *After Virtue: A Study in Moral Theory*. Paris: University of Notre Dame Press.

McNay, L. 2003. Foucault: aesthetics as ethics. In J. Weeks, J. Holland and M. Waites (eds), *Sexualities and Society: A Reader*: 245–255. Cambridge: Polity Press.

McQuarrie, F.A.E. 1998. Expanding the concept of diversity: discussing sexual orientation in the management classroom. *Journal of Management Education*, 22(2): 162–172.

Martin, J. 1990. Deconstructing organizational taboos: the suppression of gender conflict in organizations. *Organization Science*, 1(4): 339–359.

Martin, J. 1992. *Cultures in Organizations: Three Perspectives*. Oxford: Oxford University Press.

Mead, G.H. 1934. *Mind, Self and Society*. Chicago: Chicago University Press.

Mead, G.H. 1994. The Self. In H. Clark, J. Chandler and J. Barry (eds), *Organisation and Identities*. London: Chapman & Hall.

Miller, S.L., Forest, K.B. and Jurik, N.C. 2003. Diversity in Blue: lesbian and gay police officers in a masculine occupation. *Men and Masculinities*, 5(4): 355–385.

Milliken, F.J. and Morrison, E.W. 2003. Shades of silence: emerging themes and future directions for research silence in organizations. *Journal of Management Studies*, 40(6): 1563–1568.

Mills, S. 1997. *Discourse*. London: Routledge.

Mintz, B. and Rothblum, E.D. 1997. Lesbians in academia: degrees of freedom. New York: Routledge.

Morrison, E.W. and Milliken, F.J. 2000. Organizational silence: a barrier to change and development in a pluralistic world. *Academy of Management Review*, 25(4): 706–725.

Mumby, D.K. 2004. Discourse, power and ideology. In D. Grant, C. Hardy, C. Oswick and L. Putnam (eds), *The Sage Handbook of Organizational Discourse*: 237–258. London: Sage.

Mumby, D.K. and Clair, R. 1997. Organizational discourse. In T.A. van Dijk (ed.), *Discourse as Structure and Process*. London: Sage.

Nardi, P.M. 2002. The mainstreaming of lesbian and gay studies? In D. Richardson and S. Seidman (eds), *Handbook of Lesbian and Gay Studies*: 45–54. London: Sage.

Newton, T. 1998. Theorizing subjectivity in organizations: the failure of Foucauldian studies. *Organization Studies*, 19(3): 415–447.

Noon, M. and Ogbonna, E. 2001. *Equality, Diversity and Disadvantage in Employment*. Basingstoke: Palgrave.

Norton, R. 1992. *Mother Clap's Molly House: The Gay Subculture in England 1700–1830*. London: Gay Men's Press.

Ochberg, R. 1993. Life stories and storied lives. In R. Josselson and A. Lieblich (eds), *The Narrative Study of Lives: Exploring Identity and Gender in the Narrative Study of Lives*. Vol. 2. London: Sage.

Oswick, C., Keenoy, T. and Grant, D. 2000. Discourse, organizations and organizing: concepts, objects and subjects. *Human Relations*, 53(9): 1115–1124.

Oswick, C., Keenoy, T. and Grant, D. 2002. Metaphor and analogical reasoning in organizational theory: beyond orthodoxy. *Academy of Management Review*, 27(2): 294–303.

Oswick, C., Putnam, L. and Keenoy, T. 2004. Tropes, discourse and organizing. In D. Grant, C. Hardy, C. Oswick and L. Putnam (eds), *The Sage Handbook of Organizational Discourse*: 105–127. London: Sage.

Parker, I. 1992. *Discourse Dynamics*. London: Routledge.

Parker, M. 2001. Fucking management: queer, theory and reflexivity. *Ephemera*, 1(1): 36–53.

Parker, M. 2002. Queering management and organization. *Gender, Work and Organization*, 9(2): 146–166.

Patton, P. 1998. Foucault's subject of power. In J. Moss (ed.), *The Later Foucault*: 64–77. London: Sage.

People Management. 2001. The gap between sexuality and equality. *People Management*, Vol. 7: 9.

Phillips, H. 2001. The gender police. *The New Scientist*, 2290: 38–41.

Phillips, L. and Jorgensen, M.W. 2002. *Discourse Analysis as Theory and Method*. London: Sage.

Phillips, N. and Hardy, C. 1997. Managing multiple identities: discourse, legitimacy and resources in the United Kingdom refugee system. *Organisation*, 4(2): 159–185.

Plummer, K. 1995. *Telling Sexual Stories: Power, Change and Social Worlds*. London: Routledge.

Plummer, K. 1996. Symbolic interactionism and the forms of homosexuality. In S. Seidman (ed.), *Queer Theory/Sociology*: 64–82. Cambridge: Blackwell.

Pratt, M.G. and Foreman, P.O. 2000a. The beauty of and barriers to organizational theories of identity. *Academy of Management Review*, 25(1): 141–143.

Pratt, M.G. and Foreman, P.O. 2000b. Classifying managerial responses to multiple organizational identities. *Academy of Management Review*, 25(1): 18–42.

Prichard, C., Jones, D. and Stablein, R. 2004. Doing research in organizational discourse: the importance of researcher context. In D. Grant, C. Hardy, C. Oswick and L. Putnam (eds), *The Sage Handbook of Organizational Discourse*: 213–236. London: Sage.

Rabinow, P. 1984. *The Foucault Reader*. London: Penguin.

Ragins, B.R. and Cornwell, J.M. 2001. *Walking the Line: Fear and Disclosure of Sexual Orientation in the Workplace*. Paper presented at the National Academy of Management Meeting, Washington, DC, 5–8 August.

Ravenhill, M. 2001. *Mother Clap's Molly House*. London: Methuen Publishing Ltd.

Rayside, D. 1999. On the fringes of the new Europe: sexual diversity activism and the labor movement. In G. Hunt (ed.), *Laboring for Rights: Unions And Sexual Diversity Across Nations*: 206–237. Philadelphia: Temple University Press.

Reed, M. 1998. Organizational analysis as discourse analysis: a critique. In D. Grant, T. Keenoy and C. Oswick (eds), *Discourse and Organization*: 193–213. London: Sage.

Ricoeur, P. 1991. Narrative identity. *Philosophy Today*, Spring: 73–81.

Riessman, C.K. 1993. *Narrative Analysis*. London: Sage.

Robinson, J.A. 1981. Personal narratives reconsidered. *Journal of American Folklore*, 94: 58–85.

Rodwell, J. 2002. *Drawing: A Complete Course*. London: Hamlyn.

Rorty, R. 1989. *Contingency, Irony, and Solidarity*. Cambridge: Cambridge University Press.

Roseneil, S. 2002. From liberation to transgression and beyond: gay, lesbian and queer studies at the turn of the twenty-first century. In D. Richardson and S. Seidman (eds), *Handbook of Lesbian and Gay Studies*: 27–43. London: Sage.

Sartre, J.-P. 1958. *Being and Nothingness*. London: Methuen.

Schope, R.D. 2002. The decision to tell: factors influencing the disclosure of sexual orientation by gay men. *Journal of Gay and Lesbian Social Services*, 14(1): 1–22.

Schuyf, J. 2000. Hidden from history? Homosexuality and historical sciences. In T. Sandfort, J. Schuyf, J. Duyvendak and J. Weeks (eds), *Lesbian and Gay Studies, An Introductory, Interdisciplinary Approach*: 61–80. London: Sage.

Sedgwick, E.K. 1991. *Epistemology of the Closet*. London: Penguin Books.

Seidman, S. 1994. *Contested Knowledge: Social Theory in the Postmodern Era*. Oxford: Blackwell.

Seidman, S. (ed.). 1996. *Queer Theory/Sociology*. Cambridge: Blackwell.

Seidman, S. 1997. *Difference Troubles*. Cambridge: Cambridge University Press.

Seidman, S. 2003. *The Social Construction of Sexuality*. London: W.W. Norton & Company.

Shallenberger, D. 1994. Professional and openly gay: a narrative study of the experience. *Journal of Management Inquiry*, 3(2): 119–142.

Simon, W. 2003. The postmodernization of sex. In J. Weeks, J. Holland and M. Waites (eds), *Sexualities and Society: A Reader*: 22–32. Cambridge: Polity Press.

Sims, D. 1999. Organizational learning as the development of stories. In M. Easterby-Smith, L. Araujo and J. Burgoyne (eds), *Organizational Learning and the Learning Organization*: 44–58. London: Sage.

Sims, D. 2003. Between the millstones: a narrative account of the vulnerability of middle managers' storying. *Human Relations*, 56(10): 1195–1212.

Sims, D. 2004. The velveteen rabbit and passionate feelings for organizations. In Y. Gabriel (ed.), *Myths, Stories and Organizations: Postmodern Narratives for our Times*: 209–222. Oxford: Oxford University Press.

Skidmore, P. 2004. A legal perspective on sexuality and organization: a lesbian and gay case study. *Gender, Work and Organization*, 11(3): 229–253.

Snape, D., Thomson, K. and Chetwynd, M. 1995. *Discrimination Against Gay Men and Lesbians, a Study of the Nature and Extent of Discrimination Against Homosexual Men and Women in Britain Today*. London: Social and Community Planning Research.

Sontag, S. 1999. Notes on 'camp'. In F. Cleto (ed.), *Camp: Queer Aesthetics and the Performing Subject*: 53–65. Edinburgh: Edinburgh University Press.

Spargo, T. 1999. *Foucault and Queer Theory*. Cambridge: Icon Books.

Stein, A. 2003. Becoming lesbian: identity work and the performance of sexuality. In J. Weeks, J. Holland and M. Waites (eds), *Sexualities and Society*: 132–142. Cambridge: Polity Press.

Stein, A. and Plummer, K. 1996. 'I can't even think straight': 'Queer' theory and the missing sexual revolution in sociology. In S. Seidman (ed.), *Queer Theory/Sociology*: 129–144. Oxford: Blackwell.

Stonewall, 2005. www.stonewall.org.uk.

Storr, M. 2003. Postmodern bisexuality. In J. Weeks, J. Holland and M. Waites (eds), *Sexualities and Society: A Reader*: 153–161. Cambridge: Polity Press.

Sullivan, A. 1995. *Virtually Normal: An Argument about Homosexuality*. London: Picador.

Sullivan, A. 2005. The end of gay culture and the future of gay life. *The New Republic*: November.

Sveningsson, S. and Alvesson, M. 2003. Managing managerial identities: organizational fragmentation, discourse and identity struggle. *Human Relations*, 56(10): 1163–1193.

Tajfel, H. 1972. La categorisation sociale. In S. Moscovici (ed.), *Introduction a la Psychologie sociale*: 272–302. Paris: Larousse.

Tangherlini, T.R. 1998. *Talking Trauma: Paramedics and Their Stories*. Jackson: University Press of Mississippi.

Taylor, N. 1986. All in a day's work: a report on anti-lesbian discrimination in employment and unemployment in London. London: Lesbian Employment Rights.

Taylor, S. 2001. Locating and conducting discourse analytic research. In M. Wetherell, S. Taylor and S. Yates (eds), *Discourse as Data*: 5–48. London: Sage.

Titscher, S., Meyer, M., Wodak, R. and Vetter, E. 2000. *Methods of Text and Discourse Analysis*. London: Sage.

Tyler, C.-A. 1991. Boys will be girls: the politics of gay drag. In D. Fuss (ed.), *Inside/Out: Lesbian Theories, Gay Theories*: 32–70. New York: Routledge.

van Dijk, T.A. 2001. Multidisciplinary CDA: a plea for diversity. In R. Wodak and M. Meyer (eds), *Methods of Critical Discourse Analysis*: 95–120. London: Sage.

Van Maanen, J. 1988. *Tales of the Field: On Writing Ethnography*. Chicago: University of Chicago Press.

Wallemacq, A. and Sims, D. 1998. The struggle with sense. In D. Grant, T. Keenoy and C. Oswick (eds), *Discourse and Organization*: 119–133. London: Sage.

Ward, J.H. 2001. *Setting the Diversity Issue Straight*. Paper presented at the 4th Conference on Ethical Issues in Contemporary Human Resource Management, Middlesex University, 19 April.

Ward, J.H. 2003. How to address sexual orientation. *People Management*, 9(21): 62–63.

Ward, J.H. and Winstanley, D.C. 2002. *The Absent Presence: Negative Space Within*

Discourse and the Construction of Homosexual Identity in the Workplace. Paper presented at the 18th EGOS Colloquium, Barcelona, 4 July.

Ward, J.H. and Winstanley, D.C. 2003. The absent presence: negative space within discourse and the construction of minority sexual identity in the workplace. *Human Relations*, 56(10): 1255–1280.

Ward, J.H. and Winstanley, D.C. 2004. Sexuality and the City: exploring the experience of minority sexual identity through storytelling. *Culture and Organization*, 10(3): 219–236.

Ward, J.H. and Winstanley, D.C. 2005. Coming out: the recognition and renegotiation of identity in work organizations. *Sociological Review* 53(3): 447–475.

Ward, J.H. and Winstanley, D.C. 2006. Watching the Watch: the UK Fire Service and its impact on sexual minorities in the workplace. *Gender, Work and Organization.* 13(2): 193–219.

Watson, M. 2001. Gays who want to go straight. *Evening Standard*, Friday 4 May: 10–11. London.

Webb, J. 1997. The politics of equal opportunity. *Gender, Work and Organization*, 4(3): 159–169.

Webb, J. 2000. Wild in the aisles. *The Pink Paper.* 8 September: 9.

Weeks, J. 1977. *Coming Out, Homosexual Politics in Britain, from the Nineteenth Century to the Present*. London: Quartet Books.

Weeks, J. 1989. *Sex, Politics and Society*. London: Longman Higher Education.

Weeks, J. 2003. Necessary fictions: sexual identities and the politics of diversity. In J. Weeks, J. Holland and M. Waites (eds), *Sexualities and Society*: 122–131. Cambridge: Polity.

Weeks, J., Holland, J. and Waites, M. (eds). 2003. *Sexualities and Society*. Cambridge: Polity.

Weick, K. 1995. *Sensemaking in Organizations*. Thousand Oaks: Sage.

Weinberg, M.S. 1970. Homosexual samples: differences and similarities. *The Journal of Sex Research*, 6: 312–325.

Welch, J. 1996. The invisible minority. *People Management*, 2(19): 24–31.

Weston, K. and Rofel, L.B. 1997. Sexuality, class and conflict in a lesbian workplace. In A. Gluckman and B. Reed (eds), *Homo Economics: Capitalism, Community and Lesbian and Gay Life*. New York: Routledge.

Wetherell, M. 2001. Debates in discourse research. In M. Wetherell, S. Taylor and S. Yates (eds), *Discourse Theory and Practice: A Reader*. London: Sage.

Wetherell, M., Taylor, S. and Yates, S. (eds). 2001. *Discourse as Data*. London: Sage.

Williamson, A.D. 1993. Is this the right time to come out? *Harvard Business Review*, July: 2–7.

Wilson, E. 2000. Inclusion, exclusion and ambiguity: the role of organisational culture. *Personnel Review*, 29(3): 274–303.

Winstanley, D.C. 2001. Existential stories on the myth and reality of motherhood. *Electronic Journal of Radical Organisation Theory* (August).

Winstanley, D.C. 2004. Phaethon: seizing the reins of power. In Y. Gabriel (ed.), *Myths, Stories and Organizations: Postmodern Narratives for Our Times*: 176–191. Oxford: Oxford University Press.

Woods, J.D. and Lucas, J.H. 1993. *The Corporate Closet: The Professional Lives of Gay Men in America*. New York: The Free Press.

Woodward, K. 1997. Concepts of identity and difference. In K. Woodward (ed.), *Identity and Difference*. London: Sage.

Woog, D. 2001. *Gay Men, Straight Jobs*. Los Angeles: Alyson Books.

Yin, R.K. 1994. *Case Study Research: Design and Methods*. Thousand Oaks: Sage.

Zanoni, P. and Janssens, M. 2003. Deconstructing difference: the rhetoric of human resource managers' diversity discourses. *Organization Studies*, 25(1): 55–74.

Zuckerman, A.J. and Simons, G.F. 1996. *Sexual Orientation in the Workplace*. Thousand Oaks: Sage.

Index

GEORGE
LUCAS

KT-161-719

GEORGE LUCAS

Chris Salewicz

ORION

First published in 1998 by Orion Media

An imprint of Orion Books Ltd

Orion House, 5 Upper St Martin's Lane, London WC2H 9EA

Copyright © Chris Salewicz 1998

The right of Chris Salewicz to be identified as the
Author of this Work has been asserted in accordance
with the Copyright, Designs and Patents Act 1988.

Project editor: Natasha Martyn-Johns

Designed by Leigh Jones

All rights reserved. No part of this publication may be reproduced,
stored in a retrieval system, or transmitted, in any form or by any
means, electronic, mechanical, photocopying, recording or otherwise,
without the prior permission of the copyright owner.

A CIP catalogue record for this book is available
from the British Library.

ISBN 0 75281 318 8

Printed and bound in Italy

CONTENTS

1 The Cruiser and the Force

In the late afternoon of Tuesday 12 June 1962, George Lucas drove towards his parents' home from the Modesto city library. The eighteen-year-old Californian was in his Fiat Bianchina, the tiny Italian car whose two-stroke engine he had stripped down and souped up until it was a fizzing, feisty lump of powerful metal. He had added an anti-roll bar and cut a sunroof into the top of the vehicle.

Like his biker friends at Modesto's Round Table hamburger joint, George Lucas affected greased-back hair and blue jeans, living the kind of Californian cruising lifestyle celebrated in the hotrodding songs just beginning to be recorded by the Beach Boys and Jan and Dean. That afternoon, however, he almost hit his own Dead Man's Curve. Swinging off the blacktop onto the dirt road that led to the Lucas family house, the setting sun obscuring his vision, he was sideswiped by a Chevrolet Impala. Flipping over, the tiny Fiat rolled like a tumbleweed towards a grove of walnut trees. The force of the impact tore apart his seat-belt – he was catapulted through the open sunroof and knocked unconscious as the car came to a halt by crumpling around a tree-trunk.

By the time an ambulance arrived, it seemed George Lucas was dead: he was not breathing and there was no sign of a heartbeat. When he eventually reached hospital, it was found that he had undergone huge internal bleeding. The four months he spent in bed recovering utterly altered his life. 'Before that,' said Lucas, 'I just went with what I enjoyed. I sat down that summer and did a lot of meditating on what I was here for.'

Would it be too fanciful to see a mortally injured Luke Skywalker lying in that hospital bed in the small northern Californian town of Modesto, grappling with notions of an energy field that binds the galaxy together? The idea that the Force may be with us is, after all, the most profound legacy of the *Star Wars* trilogy of films, the first of which George Lucas would unveil in 1977, that year of pivotal change that also brought us the earthquake of punk rock.

The George Lucas paradox could hardly be more marked: on one hand the *Star Wars* films sold over $3 billion worth of merchandising; on the other they offered in the Force, loosely interpreted as the power everyone has and seldom uses, a life philosophy that was sufficiently ambiguous and catch-all to make some considerable difference to the quality of thinking and existence in the last quarter of the twentieth century – and, we suspect, beyond that time as well. Darth Vader, meanwhile, entered the popular imagination as a synonym for all that was dark and diabolic. (So much so, indeed, that when James Earl Jones, the actor who played his voice, provided voice-overs on a series of American AT&T television advertisements, it was as though an extraordinary cultural confusion had been triggered off.)

At a lesser level, George Lucas, the architect of a profound way of thinking that is also populist as it could be, is the man who utterly altered cinema, the director-producer who introduced blockbuster event movies.

Yet this was from a director who believed his first talent to be editing. Lucas found himself to have an extraordinary sensibility for film that was literally at a frame-by-frame level, a gift with which Walt Disney also had been blessed, but, he feared, a weakness in character and narrative. To cover this perceived personal artistic flaw, he developed the use of unique soundtracks, skilled graphics and, above all, unprecedentedly fast cutting, becoming an innovator of a style taken up wholesale by video makers.

Deeply committed to what the musician Prince defined as positivity, Lucas equally has an almost Howard Hughes-like image, reminiscent of a grouchy Old Testament prophet, or, perhaps, Profit – if you're not careful, the P word can loom large in Lucas discussions: Largest Grossing This . . . Top Film of That . . . Billions Earned . . . Yet so much of this colossal amount of cash has been put into Skywalker ranch, to create even more billions – for this is the home of George Lucas and Lucasfilm, with its very lucrative Industrial Light and Magic (ILM) offshoot, another well of creativity.

Star Wars turned upside down Hollywood's attitudes towards science fiction; it was partly responsible for the notion of the Feelgood film; it changed the industry's definition of the spring and summer market; it re-established symphonic music in films and gave new importance to sound; it exploded the boundaries of special effects; it made merchandising the characters from a movie as important as the movie itself; it created a pop mythology, and

– as we have said – lodged the notion of the Force in the collective psyche.

And all that George Lucas had hoped when making it was that the first film would provide enough money to make a sequel.

2 Film School and THX 1138

George Walton Lucas Jr. was born on 14 May 1944, which was Mother's Day that year in the United States. He was the third of four children for Dorothy and George Lucas Sr., their only son and the apple of everyone's eye.

Modesto is in northern California, in the flat walnut-growing and wine-making region an hour's drive south of the state capital of Sacramento. The only times the Lucas family would leave the area would be for the annual family pilgrimages to Disneyland. George Lucas Sr. was the son of a Californian oilfield worker; a figure in the community, he had made good by running the local stationery store, which he had been rather hoping that his son would take over from him.

The young George Lucas, who would build soapbox derby racers and other feats of schoolboy engineering in the small shed at the back of the family house, was a thin, somewhat sickly child. This was perhaps because of a predisposition to frailty in the family blood (later George would discover that he was diabetic): his mother was often confined to bed, leaving her husband to care for the children. George, as the only son, experienced an awkward relationship with his well-meaning but martinet-like father (he would be made, for example, to have his head shaved every summer); this became the basis for the good/bad father figures of Obi-Wan Kenobi and Darth Vader.

The school grades of George Lucas Jr. were not impressive. For the most part, in fact, he was a D-student. It was in an effort to prepare himself for his final examinations, in three days' time, that on the day of his near-fatal car crash he had been attempting to study in the Modesto city library.

Like his near-contemporaries John Lennon and Keith Richards on the other side of the Atlantic, George Lucas was one of those children who was unsuited for academic life but could flourish in an artistic environment. Unlike those two examples, his desire to attend art school was not consummated: his strict father refused to cough up the money for any such course. George's interest in photography offered another route, however. Inspired by a friendship he had struck up with the celebrated cinematographer Haskell Wexler (whom he had met while attempting a photographic essay at the auto-shop where Wexler was having a sports car rebuilt), he had decided to go to film school at the University of Southern California in Los Angeles, thinking this was the closest he could come to a photography course.

In 1964 he signed up for classes in the history of film and animation, as well as the subsidiary subjects of English and astronomy. Unlike most of his young film-directing peers, Lucas up to that point had had little interest in pictures: his periodic excursions to Modesto's movie theatres largely had been a pretext for trying to pick up girls. But at USC he found himself: at the end of the first year, betraying the impetus that had made him sign up for the course by using a set of still photographs, he made a minute-long film that won awards at eighteen film festivals. 'Everything I did was involved with film and I couldn't think of anything else,' he said. *Freiheit*, which he made in the Malibu hills, was another short, about a man escaping from East to West Germany. This theme of a man breaking free of his past, which was to dominate the work of the student who had fled small-town Modesto, reappeared in *THX 1138: 4HB*, which he made in 1967 as a graduate student. Cannily linking up with navy cinema students, because they had access to colour film, Lucas constructed a short picture that used a wild mixture of Bach and indistinguishable air traffic control voices as the audio bed for the story of a man escaping a mechanized society. Shot in underground parking lots and other symbols of dehumanized society, the film had a sense of documentary about it: the framing was deliberately never perfect – in a sense that would prevail in Lucas's larger work. At the National Student Film Festival *THX 1138: 4HB* won the award for Best Drama.

In turn, it helped Lucas win a further award, from Columbia, to shoot a short film about the making of the western *McKenna's Gold*, which was being produced by Carl Foreman. More importantly, he also picked up the Samuel Warner scholarship offered by Warner Brothers: one student a year was allowed to work at the studio for six months. (Before he took this up, Lucas felt he should no longer delay the inevitable, and presented himself at his local draft board, expecting all along that he might be sent to Vietnam. It was then that to his amazement he found he was classified 4F at his medical – because he was diabetic.)

With suitable symbolism, George Lucas arrived at Warner Brothers on the day that Jack Warner cleared out his office and left, the venerable studio having been bought by a television packaging company. 'The whole place was shutting down, so I couldn't be assigned to the story department. They were only making one movie, *Finian's Rainbow*, so that's where I ended up.'

Finian's Rainbow, a musical about labour exploitation and race relations that had originally debuted on Broadway in 1947, was being directed by Francis Ford Coppola, already something of a legend amongst film school students.

Francis was the first film student to make it into the film business on a direct line, out of film school and into the industry. Other people had graduated, worked as writers for a couple of years and eventually broken in – some people did it through Roger Corman, but that didn't really count. They'd do exploitation films, and nobody ever knew what happened to them. They'd surface maybe ten years later on television, but that wasn't really 'making it'. You see, we were taught, it was the credo of the film school that we had drilled into us every day, that nobody would ever get a job in the industry. You'd graduate from film school and become a ticket-taker at Disneyland, or get a job with some industrial outfit in Kansas. But nobody had ever gotten a job in Hollywood making theatrical films. Then Francis did it, clearly and indisputably, and this happened just when we were in school. He was about five years ahead of me, and he was working on his second film already, his first big feature.

Coppola had not wanted to make *Finian's Rainbow*, but needed the work. The fact that the director and Lucas were about the only people under fifty on the set was not without significance. Without their being aware of it, both men were participants in a pivotal moment of Hollywood history. Not since the period immediately after the Second World War had Hollywood encouraged any new intake of talent into the movie-making business. 'A bit of history opened up like a seam,' said Lucas, 'and as many of us who could crammed in.' Virtually oblivious to the youth explosion triggered off by the 'Swinging' Sixties, the film industry was mired in a moribund conservatism that was deeply suspicious of any youthful newcomers. 'Grow a beard!' suggested the already hirsute Coppola to Lucas. 'It will make people respect you.' By so urging, he helped inspire a somewhat questionable facial fashion among young film-makers that was to linger for at least the next two decades.

At the time, however, Lucas had his own ambitions: 'What I wanted to do was get into the animation department: steal some footage or whatever and start making a film. About three weeks into the picture I told Francis I was bored, but he said, "Look, kid, stick with me, and I'll give you things to do." He did, and it turned out that we complemented each other very well. I was essentially an editor and a cameraman, while Francis is a writer and director – more into actors and acting.'

Coppola has gone on record as saying that Lucas was 'the only person I could talk to'. But wasn't there a more complex chemistry at work here? In *Take One* Lucas told Audie Bock what he perceived to be the essence of their relationship: 'I'm really conservative – he used to call me the seventy-year-old man – and Francis is always sixteen. He's always running off and being crazy. I'm Midwestern American and he's essentially New York Italian-American. It was a good

Francis Coppola (right) persuaded Lucas to write the screenplay for THX 1138. **Both are shown here on the set of the film.**

combination, and I started being his assistant.' (It is interesting that for Lucas, Modesto, only eighty miles from San Francisco, was as far mentally and intellectually from that free-thinking city as Iowa.)

In July 1968 they made *The Rain People* together. A fascinating road movie, made entirely on location with a constantly evolving script, the film fell by the wayside in comparison with *Easy Rider* – perhaps because it suggested that dropping out was escapism. For Lucas, who was employed to make a documentary about the making of the film, the movie held a larger purpose. On the set of *Finian's Rainbow*, Coppola had kept insisting that if he wanted to direct he must first learn to write. 'I can't write,' Lucas complained. 'Yes, you can: I'll help you,' was always Coppola's response.

Coppola then secured a deal with the new regime at Warner Brothers to deliver a package of 'youth' movies. There was a catch here, however: if Warners didn't go for Coppola's product, he would have to repay personally any money advanced. All the same, it was deemed that Lucas's last student project, *THX 1138: 4HB*, should have its title abbreviated to *THX 1138* and be worked up into a full-length feature, to become the first of these films out of the starting blocks. Accordingly, with Coppola goading him on, Lucas wrote *THX 1138* each morning from 4 to 6 a.m. during the production of *The Rain People*: he had been paid $3,000 as an advance for this script, which also served as his fee for working on the road movie. (On a second draft of *THX 1138* he brought in Walter Murch, an old friend from USC who later edited *Apocalypse Now*.)

Coppola and Lucas had already decided they would go for the big time, and would set up an independent studio outside

Hollywood. After finishing shooting *The Rain People*, Coppola visited a film company called Lanterna in Denmark that had been established in an old mansion. It was this that became the inspiration for the country-estate headquarters that he sought for what had now been named American Zoetrope. After then visiting the Fotokina exhibition in Germany, Coppola ordered the latest editing equipment from Kem and Steenbeck, and had it shipped to San Francisco.

But all the bids they made on houses in their favoured location, the old Marin County town of Ross, fell through. The new editing equipment was about to arrive, which they had to use for cutting *The Rain People*, and they had nowhere even to put it.

Then they found an old warehouse on Folsom Street in the middle of San Francisco. Moving in 'temporarily', they soon discovered that the costs of refurbishing the warehouse had eaten up all the money from the Warners development deal, and they couldn't move elsewhere. However, Coppola liked being there in the city's 'bohemian atmosphere'. Later he bought property in Mill Valley, where Lucas could live and work in the heat of which he was so fond.

('As soon as we got set up,' said Lucas to Audie Bock. 'I started pulling in all of my school friends – Bill Huyck and Gloria Katz, John Milius, Matt Robbins [*Corvette Summer*], Hal Barwood [producer of *Corvette Summer* and co-scenarist with Robbins on Spielberg's *Sugarland Express*]. We were all outsiders banding together again, and the group came to include Marty Scorsese and Brian de Palma, who were in the same situation in New York.')

THX 1138 was shot in San Francisco's just-completed Bay Area subway system – the concrete wastelands are turned

With Robert Duvall on the set of THX 1138.

into an endless white set, against which are juxtaposed the entirely white-clad characters. Lucas improvised the explosions in the plot, on a miniature set that he built himself, with ten dollars' worth of fireworks. The film starred Robert Duvall as an outlaw hounded by robot police after he and Maggie McOmie have fallen in love, sex being banned in this test-tube world. A bleak but believable picture that also starred Donald Pleasence, it is often visually extraordinary as images are played out from different perspectives. Warners loathed it.

Ted Ashley was now in charge of Warners, which had been taken over by the Kinney Parking Corporation. Ashley considered Lucas's cut of *THX 1138* to be disturbingly uncommercial. So, for the first time in Warners' history – though perhaps setting a precedent for what was to become a standard film-making practice – a film was taken away from its director and producer; *THX 1138* was passed over to Rudi Fehr, a Warners in-house editor.

Not predicting such a response – convinced, moreover, that the *THX 1138* cut would be considered a success by the studio – Coppola had brought with him to the screening seven more scripts for films Zoetrope wanted to make; these included those for *Apocalypse Now* and *The Conversation*. Yet Ted Ashley was so disturbed by *THX 1138* that he scrapped the Zoetrope deal – which meant that all the money invested, including that for making *THX 1138*, had to be paid back. George Lucas took upon his own shoulders the personal responsibility for the sunken Zoetrope dream; and as a counterpoint to this, a deep anger at Warners welled within him: the fact that ultimately only four minutes were cut from his film would do nothing to appease this huge internal rage at Hollywood's power-brokers. 'They were all interesting, adventurous scripts,' Lucas told journalist Stephen Farber. 'But then Warners decided not to finance any more youth-oriented, adventurous, crazy movies. They went back to hard-core entertainment films. For them it was a good decision, because they made a lot of money on that decision. But they sold us completely down the river.'

Eleven years later, as studios feverishly pitched for the release of *Raiders of the Lost Ark*, Ted Ashley would apologize to Lucas for having taken his picture away from him. Not that it helped him, for it was Paramount who put out *Raiders*, not Warners.

In fact, *THX 1138* was not a disaster: it brought Warner Brothers $945,000 in rentals. After the success of *Star Wars*, the film was re-released, with the cut footage restored. The film also earned Lucas a cult following in France, where it was a hit.

Struggling against the studios in the late 1960s to put their personal visions on screen were various alumni of American film schools. One of these was a man called Gary Kurtz, another product of USC's film-making course, who was endeavouring to push ahead as a producer. Born in July 1940, as a child Kurtz would religiously attend Saturday morning picture shows: he would be fascinated by *Flash Gordon* and other cliff-hanger serials.

Later, Kurtz had gone to Vietnam as a marine film-maker. The horror he saw there forced a spiritual awakening. Introduced one day in Mill Valley to George Lucas, Kurtz felt he had met someone he understood to be a fellow traveller.

Not long after, Lucas called him up to see if he was interested
in working on a movie about Vietnam and the media circus
that he was trying to get off the ground, to be called
Apocalypse Now.

Since he had been at USC, Lucas had wanted to make a
movie about the Vietnam War. He and John Milius, the gung-
ho writer and later director, talked about it a lot: 'Surfing and
bombs', they decided, was to be the main theme. Although
Milius thought the film should be based on a helicopter journey, Lucas decided it should be a boat ride upriver. But this
was long before any reference was made to Joseph Conrad's
Heart of Darkness.

Investigating relevant source material, Lucas and Kurtz
were taken with Kurosawa's 1958 classic *Hidden Fortress*.
This is the story of a samurai leading a stroppy princess
across wild enemy territory. The eventual central story of the
first *Star Wars* draft bore a considerable resemblance to it.

The conflict in Vietnam was still raging, however, and
Hollywood was unhappy about using an unconcluded war as
subject-matter; among the studios there was no enthusiasm
whatsoever for the project.

3 American Graffiti

Needing a paying gig, George Lucas filmed the 1969 Rolling Stones show at the Altamont Speedway for the Maysles brothers: they were making the documentary that became *Gimme Shelter*, the title being that of a song that was part of the group's repertoire. It could even have been Lucas who shot the footage of a fan being stabbed to death by a Hell's Angel, a recurring sequence in the film. The concert was considered a cultural watershed, the anti-Woodstock, as much a signifier of the end of the Sixties as the break-up of the Beatles the next year. Surely it must have had an immense impact on Lucas? Hardly at all – and as to whether or not he shot the footage of the killing, he simply doesn't know.

Besides, a different era of rock 'n' roll was starting to seep out from where it had logged itself away in his soul. What he wanted to do was make a film that was far from the futuristic world of his first feature. He would go back in time, rather than forward: specifically, he would make a movie about the world of cruising that had nearly ended his life. In doing so, Lucas continued the precedent begun with *THX 1138*: none of his films has ever been placed in the present-day.

Concerned with what he considered to be his personal weakness at story-telling, Lucas decided to let the narrative of his next film be driven by rock 'n' roll music of the late 1950s and early 1960s. And he would call the movie *American Graffiti*. The picture would be set during one hot summer's night in 1962 (the year Lucas graduated from college), when the lives of a group of young men interlaced and their futures became set in stone. The date was significant: this was the year prior to the assassination of President John F. Kennedy, marking the end of innocence in the United States.

But wouldn't he need more than one idea to attract studios? Feeling he needed a second carrot to dangle, George Lucas went forward in time again: always having loved the swashbuckling cliff-hanger *Flash Gordon* and *Buck Rogers* space serials he would watch on television as a child, he made an abortive attempt to purchase the rights to Alex Raymond's *Flash Gordon* books – but these already had been optioned by Federico Fellini.

> I loved the *Flash Gordon* comic books [Lucas told *American Film*]. I loved the Universal serials with Buster Crabbe. After *THX 1138* I wanted to do *Flash Gordon* and tried to buy the rights to it from King Features, but they wanted a lot of money for it, more than I could afford then. They didn't really want to part with the rights – they wanted Fellini to do *Flash Gordon*.
>
> I realized that I could make up a character as easily as Alex Raymond, who took his character from Edgar Rice Burroughs. It's your basic super-hero in outer space. I realized that what I really wanted to do was a contemporary action fantasy.

Knowing he needed to take another tack, Lucas decided instead to immerse himself in deep research into mythology.

The script for *American Graffiti* was initially developed for United Artists: they thought the project was too risky and dropped it. A year later, with the help of his recently acquired agent, Jeff Berg at Creative Management, Lucas pinned Universal down to a deal on the film. Lucas had refused to abandon the project.

> We were in dire financial straits, but I spent a year of my life trying to get that film off the ground. I was offered about three other pictures during that time. They all turned out to be duds. One of them was released at the same time as *Graffiti* – it's called *Lady Ice*. I turned that down at the bleakest point, when I was in debt to my parents, in debt to Francis Coppola, in debt to my agent; I was so far in debt I thought I'd never get out. Everybody in Hollywood had turned down *American Graffiti*. Universal had already turned it down once. And they offered me $75,000 to do *Lady Ice*, which is more money than I'd made in my entire life. And I said no. I said, 'By God, I've got a movie here, and I'm going to get it made somehow.' And I did.

Lucas had worked on the treatment and on the screenplay with Willard Huyck, whom he had met at USC, and Huyck's wife Gloria Katz, a graduate of the UCLA film course. 'I'm really quite lazy and I hate to write,' Lucas told Stephen Farber. 'Bill and Gloria added a lot of very witty dialogue and wrote all the scenes that I couldn't find my way to write. In my script, the characters of Steve and Laurie didn't work at all, and I couldn't make them work. The Huycks saved that. And they brought a lot of character to the hoods. My screenplay was much more realistic, and they added a lot more humour and fantasy to it, and improved it a great deal.'

The Universal contract partially hinged on the big guns that Lucas could bring to the table: specifically, Francis Ford Coppola, whose *The Godfather* had recently opened, immediately becoming an enormous hit that was also considered a deeply credible piece of art. For Universal, Coppola's name was an added fillip – they could already see the poster strapline: 'Produced by the director of *The Godfather*. . .' 'Francis was giving me a hard time too, and kept telling me to make something "warm and human" to prove I wasn't a cold guy. "You want warm and human?" I said, "All right, I'll give it to you." And I wrote *American Graffiti*.'

With his Zoetrope partner as part of the package, Lucas sold Universal on the idea. The studio agreed to finance and distribute *American Graffiti* – though they hated the title, suggesting instead that the film be called *Another Slow Night in Modesto* – an aberration that was defiantly resisted. The film was budgeted, however, at only $600,000, peanuts even by the standards of the time; later Jeff Berg managed to up the figure to $750,000.

Universal insisted, moreover, that this figure include all the music rights, which Columbia, who had passed on the film, had estimated could alone cost $500,000. In the end, the music cost only $90,000 for forty-five songs, thanks to a 'favoured nation' precedent-setting deal that Gary Kurtz managed to strike through his friend Dennis Wilson of the Beach Boys for the group's songs 'All Summer Long' and 'Surfin' Safari'. ('The Beach Boys were the only rock group who actually chronicled an era,' said Lucas. 'The blonde in the T-bird is from "Fun, Fun, Fun". "I Get Around" is about cruising . . . "Little Deuce Coupe" could be about John and his deuce coupe. "All Summer Long" – which is sort of the

theme song of the film – talks about T-shirts and spilling
Coke on your blouse . . . I always loved the Beach Boys
because when we'd cruise, we'd listen to their songs, and it
was as if the song was about us and what we were doing.')

Spurred on by the Universal deal, Lucas decided to rewrite
the *American Graffiti* script himself. As he did so,
he had his old records playing constantly, and this soundtrack to his writing shows: the film has the rhythm
and energy of great early rock 'n' roll 45s. When George
and Marcia Lucas cut the film together, each scene was set
over the soundtrack of yet another rock 'n' roll classic. 'All
good rock 'n' roll is classic teenage stuff, and all the scenes
were such classic teenage scenes that they just sort of
meshed, no matter how you threw them together. Sometimes
even the words were identical. The most incredible example
– and it was completely accidental – is in the scene where
Steve and Laurie are dancing to "Smoke Gets in Your Eyes"
at the sock hop, and at the exact moment where the song is
saying "Tears I cannot hide", she backs off, and he sees that
she's crying.'

The songs were tied together with the introductions and
back-announcements of Wolfman Jack, the legendary disc
jockey who broadcast rock 'n' roll to the entire United States
from XERB, a radio station based in Mexico. ('When I was
at USC, I made a documentary about a disc jockey. The idea
behind it was radio as fantasy. For teenagers the person closest to them is a fantasy character. That's the disc jockey.')

Lucas himself had listened to Wolfman Jack when he was
growing up in Modesto in the late Fifties and early Sixties.
'When we were cruising we could get Wolfman Jack from
Tijuana. He was a really mystical character, I'll tell you. He was

wild, he had these crazy phone calls, and he drifted out of nowhere. And it was such an outlaw station. He was an outlaw, which of course made him extremely attractive to kids.'

American Graffiti had a depth of feeling entirely missing in *THX 1138*; what is ostensibly a lightweight film has an extremely serious heart. Lucas was aware of this: he had become warm and positive, and it was as though his success came as some karmic consequence of that.

'After I finished *THX*,' he admitted to Stephen Farber, 'I was considered a cold, weird director, a science-fiction sort of guy who carried a calculator. And I'm not like that at all. So I thought, maybe I'll do something exactly the opposite. If they want warm human comedy, I'll give them one, just to show that I can do it. *THX* is very much the way that I am as a film-maker. *American Graffiti* is very much the way I am as a person – two different worlds really.'

The simplicity of *American Graffiti* was its strength. And the fact that it dealt with an Everyman reality: young people dangling on the cusp between teenagerdom and adulthood. The plot had four simple, cross-cutting storylines. Curt and Steve are to fly east to college in the morning. Steve, the super-straight class president, dates Laurie, the head cheer-leader. Curt, sensitive and introspective, is having second thoughts about leaving a town that means more to him than he had realized. Thinking over his future, Curt searches for a mysterious woman in a Ford Thunderbird who has mouthed an enticement to him. Meanwhile, he is harassed by a duck-tailed gang called the Pharoahs. His indecision about leaving town cloaks the decision they must all meet: how to leave their world of childhood dreams.

Two other local teenagers get into further predicaments that are close to tragi-comic and deeply revealing. John, who rules the local drag strip, models himself on James Dean and drives the meanest deuce coupe in the valley, finds himself tricked into chaperoning twelve-year-old Carol. Terry the Toad is a nerd-like kid who rides only a Vespa scooter but finally gets a chance to play the stud: enticing a blonde bimbo called Debbie into the car that Steve has lent him, he then becomes anxious to hang on to her.

Only Curt and Steve have the option of leaving town and going to college. But after a car crash from which she emerges miraculously unscathed, Laurie throws herself into Steve's arms and begs him not to leave her. A decision made in the heat of emotion and insecurity seals his fate – Steve abandons his plan to leave town and go to college so that he can stay at home with his girl. Curt is the only one to climb aboard a plane out of the town in the morning – the only one to break free. Steve sees him off.

Although *THX 1138* had been impressive technically, the movie felt dry, even laboured, and it was clearly an effort to feel sympathy for its characters. Yet *THX* and *American Graffiti* have similar themes: *THX*, which is essentially a rewrite of George Orwell's 1984, describes how an individual breaks out of a spiritually deracinated, controlled world; *American Graffiti* also ends with one of the teenage boys breaking out of his background and escaping its cocoon.

'I've always been interested in that theme of leaving an environment or facing change, and how kids do it,' admitted Lucas. 'When I was eighteen or nineteen, I didn't know what I was going to do with my life. Where was I going to go, now that I was more or less free? What was I going to become? You can do anything you want at that age. And the kids who don't believe that are wrong. Both *THX* and *American Graffiti* are saying the same thing, that you don't have to do anything; it still is a free country.'

Beyond *American Graffiti*'s clearly autobiographical impulses, the film reflects Lucas's interest in sociology and anthropology: 'When I was in junior college, my primary major was in social sciences. I'm very interested in America and why it is what it is. I was always fascinated by the cultural phenomenon of cruising, that whole teenage mating ritual. It's really more interesting than primitive Africa or ancient New Guinea – and much, much weirder.'

Many of the events that take place in the film, said Lucas, 'are things that I actually experienced one way or another. They've also been fantasized, as they should be in a movie. They aren't really the way they were but the way they should have been.'

The film is filled with vignettes so familiar they are almost embarrassing.

> I started out when I was young as Terry the Toad, and I think everybody starts out as Terry the Toad [Lucas told Stephen Farber]. And I went from that to being John; I had a hot car, and I raced around a lot. Finally I got into a very bad accident and almost got myself killed, and I spent a lot of time in the hospital. While I was in the hospital, I became much more academic-minded. I had been working as a mechanic, and I decided to give up cars and go to junior college, to try to get my grades back. So for the next two years, while I was at junior college, I more or less was Curt. I was thinking about leaving town, and I had a lot more perspective on things.'

But who was going to play these sharply drawn characters?
At Haskell Wexler's commercials studio in Hollywood Lucas
videotaped a shortlist of actors. In retrospect, the final line-
up can be seen as a cast of extraordinary prescience. Among
the actors *American Graffiti* introduced were Harrison Ford,
Richard Dreyfuss (who played Curt), Ron Howard (Steve),
twelve-year-old Mackenzie Phillips (the daughter of John
and Michelle Phillips of The Mamas and The Papas group,
who took the part of Carol), Cindy Williams (Laurie),
Kathleen Quinlan, Kay Lenz, Suzanne Somers, Charles
Martin Smith (Terry the Toad), Bo Hopkins, Candy Clark,
and Paul LeMat (John the Cruising King).

As became an established part of his own mythology,
Harrison Ford was largely making a living as a carpenter in
the Hollywood area. New Yorker Dreyfuss, who had yet to
appear in a movie, was initially offered the choice of playing
either Curt or Toad. Paul LeMat, who plays the iconic John, a
cigarette pack stuffed up the rolled sleeve of his T-shirt, had
been a professional boxer. As for Ron Howard, although he
was by now eighteen, he still carried his 'child actor' mantle
– for years he had played Opie on *The Andy Griffith Show*.

What these soon-to-be stars were as yet unaware of, of
course, was that each of the main actors was playing a part
of George Lucas.

Filming on *American Graffiti* started on 26 June 1972. Lucas
had just twenty-eight days to complete production, all of
which would be a night shoot, on home ground in Marin
County. 'We'd start at nine at night and end at five in the
morning. In a regular movie, if you don't get what you're
supposed to shoot one day, you can just throw up a few arc

Gary Kurtz, co-producer with Francis Coppola of
American Graffiti**, confers with Lucas on the set.**

lights and shoot for another hour. On *Graffiti*, when the sun
came up, that was the end of the ballgame. We couldn't get
one more shot. It was very hard on the crew. Nobody gets any
sleep, so everybody's cranky. And it was very cold – like
forty degrees. We had to shoot it in twenty-eight days, and
sometimes we'd do as many as thirty set-ups in one night. So
we had a horrendous problem.'

Things did not begin very auspiciously: the day before
shooting began, a crew member was busted for possession of
marijuana – although, as *Graffiti* was a 'youth' movie, this
might well have been considered a positive omen.

But there were to be more difficulties. Night one was to be
shot in San Rafael, a small town near where Lucas lived in
Mill Valley. But the director could not get the cameras up on
to the cars – his first shot was not filmed until 2 a.m.

Most of the scenes were set to be shot in San Rafael. On the
second night, however, the cast and crew turned up only to be
told that their filming permit had been revoked after a local
bar claimed to have lost business the previous evening. A
temporary truce was struck under which filming could
continue in San Rafael for a further three nights. Then the
production would shift to Petaluma, twenty miles to the north.

But the hassles of the second night had not yet ended: first
the streets were blocked by traffic after fire ravaged a restau-
rant; then Barney Coangelo, the assistant cameraman,
slipped and was run over by the car he was filming.

George Lucas began to be worried. And there was more to
come: the cameramen he had hired had minimal feature-film
experience and he quickly learned that they couldn't come
up with what he wanted. Accordingly, Lucas turned to his old
friend Haskell Wexler for help. There was no money left in

the budget, so instead Lucas offered Wexler a point of the
film's profits to take over as cinematographer – a deal that
turned out to be extremely lucrative.

Each night Wexler would arrive in Petaluma from
Los Angeles, where he would spend the days shooting
advertisements. Then he would film *American Graffiti*
all night. Wexler demonstrated that he thoroughly deserved
his title of lighting cameraman: to create the neon Wurlitzer
jukebox look that Lucas sought for the movie, for example,
he taped soft glowing lights all over the inside of the
car roofs.

'He's really, in my estimation, the best cameraman in this
country,' said Lucas. 'Essentially he was working in a
medium he hated – widescreen. He hated Technoscope
because it's very grainy and doesn't look very good. I wanted
the film to look sort of like a Sam Kartzman beach-party
movie, all yellow and red and orange. And Haskell figured
out how to do it. He devised what he calls jukebox lighting
. . . The movie looked exactly the way I wanted it to look –
very much like a carnival.'

In *American Graffiti* there were plenty of knowing in-jokes:
the local movie theatre, for example, is showing *Dementia
13*, Coppola's first feature; and Milner's deuce coupe carries
the licence plate *THX 1138*. In scene one a girl parks an
Edsel at Mel's Drive-in.

Although Lucas wanted his wife Marcia to cut *American
Graffiti*, Universal insisted on someone with more experience. The studio was pleased with the work of Lucas's former
employer Verna Fields on *Sugarland Express*, a film by
Steven Spielberg, another young director. The prospect of

working with her again stimulated Lucas, and in ten weeks
Fields took the film to rough-cut stage.

At 10 a.m. on Sunday 28 January 1973 at San Francisco's
Northpoint Theater, *American Graffiti* was previewed for the
first time. What followed was extraordinary: Ned Tanen,
representing Universal, was in a bad mood: on the flight from
Los Angeles he had refused to sit with others on their way to
the preview. After the film ended, to an ecstatic response
from the eight hundred-strong audience, Tanen immediately
left the venue, stepping out into the street with Gary Kurtz.
He was apoplectic with anger. 'This is in no shape to show to
an audience. It's unreleasable,' he raged.

Then he returned to the theatre, almost immediately
running into Francis Coppola. The team making the film had
let him down, he snapped. George Lucas heard what the
studio executive said and immediately went into deep shock,
fearing a repeat of his *THX 1138* experiences.

Coppola fought back on the spot, not mincing words. In
front of the departing audience, he let Tanen know precisely
what he thought: 'You should get down on your knees and
thank George for saving your job. This kid has killed himself
to make this movie for you.' Then he delivered a long lecture
to Tanen, berating him for his insensitivity towards Lucas,
and ending with an offer to buy the film from Universal. 'This
movie's going to be a hit! The audience loved this movie! I
saw it with my own eyes!' he told Tanen.

At a further meeting in San Francisco the next day Tanen
was mollified. He still insisted, however, on several changes.
Lucas was infuriated by this: again, a movie he had made
was being taken away from him. But a compromise was

arrived at, and Lucas set out to make the changes himself. After the director had spent a month recutting and remixing the film, Tanen was still dissatisfied. Lucas, Coppola and Kurtz came to the conclusion that they should ask Verna Fields to rejoin the film, operating as a buffer between themselves and Universal. Ultimately, the cuts only amounted to four and a half minutes of footage.

Yet again Lucas considered himself to have been mortally betrayed by the studio. Like the characters in his subsequent films, he only saw life as good and bad, light and dark; rightly or wrongly, there were no shades of grey in George Lucas's life.

Tanen scheduled another screening for 15 May 1973, at the Writers' Guild Theater in Beverly Hills.

Operating as what would be known nowadays as a spin-doctor, Gary Kurtz worked to ensure that *Graffiti* would only be shown to Universal executives when they were counterbalanced by the company of an appropriately youthful audience. At Kurtz's request Wolfman Jack packed the place with kids; most of the film's stars also attended. The film was a huge hit; Steven Spielberg considered it the most powerful screening he had ever attended.

American Graffiti opened on 1 August 1973. That evening, Cindy Williams happened to drive past the Avco Cinema in the Westwood section of Los Angeles, an area with a large student population. She was astonished at what she saw. 'I never thought I'd be in a movie with lines around the block,' she told friends in amazement.

The film was an enormous hit, the most profitable film investment that its Hollywood studio had ever made. It cost

$775,000 and sold $117 million in tickets, making it the highest cost-to-profit ratio film Fox had ever had. It simply ran for ever.

With the success of *American Graffiti*, Lucas had shown he was adept at tapping into and understanding the cutting edge of the *zeitgeist*. Despite its skilful 'Where Were You In '62?' poster, *American Graffiti* was a film that was resolutely about the 1950s and rock 'n' roll, even if from time to time it commented on them ironically. In fact, it helped spur the first flood of nostalgia for the era. *Happy Days*, which appeared shortly afterwards, was a television version of *American Graffiti*, with Ron Howard re-working his film role. *Grease*, *That'll Be the Day*, *Hot Wax* and biopics of Elvis Presley (by John Carpenter) and Buddy Holly (starring Gary Busey) would soon follow.

'In a way the film was made so my father won't think those were wasted years,' Lucas confided to Stephen Farber, referring to his teenage cruising lifestyle. 'I can say I was doing research, though I didn't know it at the time.'

But what was George Lucas going to do next? The director was in debt to the tune of $15,000: the money from *Graffiti* had not yet come in. He knew he had to start repaying his debts.

And so, sufficiently inspired, he set about the research for *Star Wars*.

4 Star Wars

When the *American Graffiti* money was freed up, it poured into Lucas's bank account as though from an open tap – his promise to his father that he would be a millionaire by the time he was thirty had been easily achieved. This did not make Francis Ford Coppola happy, however: had he financed *American Graffiti* himself, he would have made $30 million on the deal. But wasn't the perspective of George Lucas more sound? 'I had never been interested in making money, just in making movies. I became rich and successful by accident. The only thing I worried about was that the studio might lose money. As long as the film broke even, I felt I had done my job. Believe me, I did not set out to make a blockbuster movie with *Graffiti*.' The success unleashed a subtext between the two film-makers, in which each suspected the other of wanting to dominate him.

When the 1973 Academy Awards were announced, *American Graffiti* had been nominated for several Oscars: those for Best Picture, Best Direction, Best Original Screenplay (the Huycks and Lucas), Best Supporting Actress and Best Film Editing. In the end, it did not win any of these, the Paul Newman and Robert Redford vehicle *The*

Sting sweeping the awards that year. *American Graffiti* ended up with the consolation prize of a Golden Globe for Best Comedy Picture of the Year.

What was George Lucas to do with his new-found wealth? In an unprecedented gesture, he gave quite a lot of it away to people who had worked on the film. Several individuals who had been given points on the film became millionaires. The principal cast members had one point split ten ways between them. Richard Dreyfuss, for example, had been paid $5,000 to make the film, but received an additional $70,000. Haskell Wexler got his one point – then Coppola gave him two more: Wexler made almost a million dollars from a job that had literally been moonlighting.

As well as *Star Wars*, George Lucas had other eggs in the basket. *Apocalypse Now* had been one of the Zoetrope projects dumped by Warner Brothers. But Coppola had paid back the development money out of his *Godfather* profits, which meant he owned the screenplays.

Yet Lucas still wanted to make *Apocalypse Now* himself. After finishing *American Graffiti*, he struck a development deal for the Vietnam film with Columbia. He wanted the film to be cheap, with a budget of under $2 million, using 16mm cameras. Lucas and John Milius worked on a screenplay that they soon completed. Gary Kurtz went location-scouting in the Philippines.

George Lucas was partly hedging his bets, because he had become doubtful about his ability to get *Star Wars* into shape, having identified the colossal weight of research and writing that was going to be involved. *Apocalypse Now* seemed to be the next logical film to make. But the subject-matter of

Apocalypse Now was beginning to cause an internal conflict: *American Graffiti* had provided a powerful lesson: 'I discovered that making positive films is exhilarating.' And Coppola was insisting that because of the previous Zoetrope deal, he would take twenty-five per cent of the profits as producer if Lucas did make the Vietnam picture; while Lucas would have to split his twenty-five per cent with Milius. Lucas smarted at this – and went back to work on *Star Wars*.

A man of personal integrity, Lucas was disturbed that the studios had cut a few minutes from both *THX 1138* and *American Graffiti*. But he anticipated more battles with studios:

> Every time you have a successful film, you do get a few more things in your contract. The film I'm writing now,*The Star Wars*, has been turned down by a couple of studios already, but now we're finally getting a deal because they say, 'Oh, he's had a hit movie. We don't really know about the idea, but he's a hot director, so let's do it.' They don't do it on the basis of the material: they do it on the kind of deal they can make, because most of the people at the studios are former agents, and all they know are deals. They're like used-car dealers.

He also sensed that audiences were tiring of the grittier, bloody new cinema. 'You can learn from cynicism, but you can't build on it,' Lucas said to the *Los Angeles Times* in 1973.

In 1974 Coppola tried again with Lucas: he told him he thought they could do even better with *Apocalypse Now* than they had with *American Graffiti*. Lucas told Coppola he was ploughing ahead with *Star Wars*. All the same, he admitted that he still did really want to make the Vietnam picture and asked Coppola to wait until *Star Wars* was finished. By now, however, Coppola was insisting that *Apocalypse Now* should come out in 1976, the US bi-centennial year.

In the end, the making of *Apocalypse Now*, with Coppola as director, took more than two years – it came nowhere near that 1976 release date. And it nearly finished Coppola, who did all the same give Lucas two production points. For his own part, Lucas had been shocked that Coppola would not wait for him to direct the film, in which he had invested six years of his life. When Coppola finally completed *Apocalypse Now*, it contained a brief scene in which Harrison Ford appeared. As Coppola zooms in on his shirt, the name tag can be clearly read: Col. G. Lucas.

Then matters took a further twist: Lucas had closed a deal for *Star Wars* with Fox. Alan Ladd Jr., a Fox production executive and son of the film star, had talent-spotted him at the time of *THX 1138*, admiring his directing and vision. Meeting him, he had also been impressed by Lucas's honesty and professionalism – and he was extremely taken with *American Graffiti*.

Ladd had a reputation for creating a warm, congenial work atmosphere, conducive to the flow of creativity. One of the filmmakers he supported was Mel Brooks: Warners had refused to release *Blazing Saddles* until Ladd scooped it up for Fox.

At a further meeting Ladd failed to grasp Lucas's concept of *Star Wars*.

As a kid I read a lot of science fiction [Lucas told Stephen Zito in *American Film*]. But instead of reading technical, hard-science writers like Isaac Asimov, I was interested in Harry

Harrison and fantastic, surreal approaches to the genre. I grew up on it. *Star Wars* is a sort of compilation of this stuff, but it's never been put in one story before, never put down on film. There is a lot taken from western, mythology, and samurai movies. It's all the things that are great put together. It's not like one kind of ice-cream but rather a very big sundae . . . It's very surreal and bizarre and has nothing to do with science. I wanted it to be an adventure in space, like *John Carter on Mars*. That was before science took over, and everything got very serious and science oriented.

Star Wars has more to do with disclaiming science than anything else. There are very elaborate, Rube Goldberg explanations for things. It's a totally different galaxy with a totally different way of thinking. It's not based on science, which bogs you down. I don't want the movie to be about anything that would happen or be real. I wanted to tell a fantasy story.

Lucas sold *Star Wars* to Ladd as being a blend of *Buck Rogers*, *Captain Blood* and *The Sea Hawk*: the director said that the idea of the film was 'a subtle suggestion that opening the door and going out there, no matter what the risk, is sometimes worth the effort'. Though Ladd didn't quite get what Lucas meant, he expressed his desire to link up with him on the project.

His chance soon came. Although Universal had released *American Graffiti*, they passed on giving Lucas the $25,000 he asked for to turn his *Star Wars* treatment into a script. Had they done so, the studio would have made $250 million.

The day after Universal turned Lucas down on *Star Wars*, Ladd said he'd give Lucas $50,000 to write the film and $250,000 to direct it. Furthermore, forty per cent of the net profits would go to the Star Wars Corporation, a company Lucas had created. Lucas, meanwhile, would retain rights of control over *Star Wars*; especially over its merchandising (Lucas was to receive fifty per cent of every merchandising deal that Fox struck for *Star Wars*), soundtrack and – most importantly – sequel rights. Extraordinarily, Fox signed a deal with Lucas without demanding sequel rights.

Although the initial budget was set at $2.5 million, Lucas knew that the film would cost much more: he was trying to keep Ladd locked into the deal. This in turn took time to put together. By November 1975, Lucas had spent most of his first $1 million chunk of *American Graffiti* profits on *Star Wars* pre-production.

The Making of *Star Wars*
The birth of cinema coincided approximately with that of flight. Since George Melies made *A Trip to the Moon* in 1902, science fiction had proved an enduringly appealing theme, one to which Hollywood periodically applied itself. In the 1950s there had been a burst of films – *Invasion of the Body Snatchers*, *It Came from Outer Space*, *Forbidden Planet*, *The Day the Earth Stood Still* amongst others – that were seen as metaphors for the Cold War. The last significant cinematic piece of science fiction had been Kubrick's *2001: A Space Odyssey*, in 1968 – despite huge critical acclaim, the revered film had been tardy in earning back its budget.

In post-war children's fantasies, spacemen had always run a distinct second to cowboys, the stars of Hollywood's far more successful genre, the western. However, westerns had fallen out of favour with the studios after television had turned out an enormous number of cowboy series; they had

also gone through considerable revision in order to accommodate the era's shifting cultural positions, especially
towards native Americans.

So there had been a switch: new kinds of cowboys were
needed, ones who could exist in the expanded consciousness
of inner and outer space. And to find them, why not go back
to the traditional Hollywood values of humour and adventure
films?

> I wanted to do a modern fairy-tale, a myth [George Lucas told
> Stephen Zito in *American Film*]. One of the criteria of the myth-
> ical fairy-tale situation is an exotic, faraway land, but we've
> lost all the fairy-tale lands on this planet. Every one has disap-
> peared. We no longer have the Mysterious East or treasure
> islands or going on strange adventures.
>
>   But there is a bigger, mysterious world in space that is more
> interesting than anything around here. We've just begun to take
> the first step and can say, 'Look! It goes on for a zillion miles out
> there.' You can go anywhere and land on any planet.

Since finishing *American Graffiti*, Lucas had worked assiduously. That film, he told David Sheff in *Rolling Stone* in
1987, had been about

> the fact that you can't hang on to the past. The future may be
> completely strange and different and scary, but that's the way it
> should be. I thought that was one of the biggest challenges
> facing teenagers. I got to do what I wanted to do by not being
> frightened by the future and the unknown, and I figured that was
> a good message to get across. *Star Wars* says the same thing in
> terms of technology, space flight and opening up the world.

. . . The idea is not to be afraid of change. There are bad robots, good robots, aliens and monsters in all forms. *Star Wars* shows progression. You may be frightened – and it's sad because you are leaving something behind – but go forward. That's what life is about. You can either have a good attitude about change or a bad attitude about it. You can't fight tidal waves, you can only ride them. So the best thing to do is get your surfboard and make the best of it.

Now for his next movie he researched mythology and social psychology, 'studying the pure form to see how and why it worked. When I did *Star Wars*, I consciously tried to find age-old themes. I think of mythology as archaeology of the mind,' he said later.

Lucas hated writing. Every sentence was dragged out of him. 'Three hours writing and five hours thinking' was how he defined his work method. Scissors were kept on his desk: in a haze of neurotic frustration, he would snip away at his hair and beard.

But he took notes constantly, which paid off all the time. Once, while out with a disc jockey friend, Terry McGovern, the DJ's car bumped over a hole in the road. 'Must have run over a wookie back there,' ad-libbed McGovern, inventing a generic name. Meanwhile, Indiana, George and Marcia Lucas's black-and-white malamute, evolved into Chewbacca, Solo's partner. In his turn, the character of Han Solo was based on John Milius.

In the first treatment of the film George Lucas set the story in the twenty-third century: the Jedi-Templar warriors swore allegiance to the Alliance of Independent Systems. Jungle and desert planets, and a city suspended in the clouds were the three settings. Individuals, animals and areas were described in the most minute detail, becoming living entities.

The film's title mutated. *The Story of Mace Windu* became *Adventures of the Starkiller, Episode One of the Star Wars*, which evolved into simply *The Star Wars*. The script was now something like five hundred pages long, almost five times as long as was necessary. Then George Lucas divided the story up into three parts. After putting away two of these sections, to be later wrestled to the ground, he worked at honing the remainder into what finally became the first *Star Wars* film.

The central character, Luke Starkiller, worked on his uncle Owen Lars's farm on the desert planet of Tatooine. At this stage Lars was a clear character who had taken his nephew's money to set up his farm. Owen Lars knew the true identity of Luke's father, Anakin Starkiller.

Leia was a sixteen-year-old hostage of the Empire: Lucas resisted the entreaties of Coppola who wanted him to have a pre-pubescent young girl star as what evolved into the Princess Leia character. Obi-Wan Kenobi guarded the more arcane knowledge and wisdom of the Jedi knights and the Force, the notion of which came from the story in Carlos Castaneda's *Tales of Power* in which the Native American shaman, Don Juan, talked of a 'life force'.

Both Lucas and Gary Kurtz were extremely taken with the works of Carl Jung and the concept of archetypes. They were heavily influenced by Joseph Campbell's *Hero with a Thousand Faces*, his enlightening survey of world mythology: when, years later, Campbell filmed a series of television interviews, the shoot took place at Lucas's premises.

In fact, many of the stories and themes in *Star Wars* already had been selected by Joseph Campbell in *Hero with a Thousand Faces*. The Arthurian quest of the knight, for example, as well as the biblical renewal of faith, the struggle of man versus machine, and the notion of the Good and Bad father which became separated into the characters of Darth Vader and Obi-Wan Kenobi. Even the Jonah and the whale story becomes incorporated into the plot: in *The Empire Strikes Back*, the *Millennium Falcon* is swallowed whole by a monster.

The trilogy of films, in fact, is stitched together with so much cosmic symbolism that it becomes taken as a given: for example, both Yoda's swampland of the bog planet Dagobah and the barren wastelands of Tatooine symbolize aspects of the soul and the unconscious.

'All I was trying to say in a very simple and straightforward way is that there is a God and there is a good and bad side,' was how George Lucas explained away *Star Wars* later.

To do so, he created characters who were archetypes. Luke Skywalker, for example, is a traditional adolescent hero who undergoes a mythological-like rite of passage to manhood. His aunt and uncle having been tragically killed, he undertakes a mission against superhuman and supernatural odds, overcoming the threat of destruction and death.

The psychological and philosophical underpinning of the *Star Wars* trilogy was expressed through assorted gurus and the constant of the Force, as though Lucas had defined the deity as consisting of pure energy – again, a cutting-edge belief. The Force was an energy field created by all living things in the universe: after death, their energy was collected like a force in the sky into which the magician-warriors who comprised the Jedi knights were able to tap. The Force had both a dark and a light side, and with subtlety embodied the tenets of Christianity, Buddhism, Judaism and Islam, as well as more personal philosophies. 'The laws really are in yourself,' Lucas was fond of saying, and he later defined this intangible spirit: 'The Force is what happens in spite of us that we can either use or not use. We can fight these changes, or we can use them, incorporate them into our lives, take full advantage of them.'

The origins of some of the *Star Wars* characters, however, were mundane rather than arcane. The robots R2-D2 and C-3PO had the function of providing comic relief, like science-fiction versions of Laurel and Hardy. During the cutting of *American Graffiti*, Walter Murch had once asked George Lucas for R2, D2 (Reel 2, Dialogue 2) of the film. Lucas had liked the abbreviated sound, thinking it matched perfectly his notion of a 'cute' robot – the original inspiration for which had come from the robot in Douglas Trumbull's *Silent Running*.

As well as studying mythology, George Lucas made sure he understood his potential audience. Each weekend he would go out and buy up all the science-fiction magazines and comics he could find, telling Marcia he was trying to understand the minds of ten-year-old boys.

Lucas was plugged into a different culture from that of the studio executives. He knew how important it was, in helping create a word-of-mouth buzz, that he had done a deal with Marvel for a *Star Wars* comic.

Also, that he had cut a deal to have a *Star Wars* novelization published, as well as a book about the making of the film.

That *Star Wars* should not be sold as science fiction he also knew to be crucial: such a marketing campaign had damaged *THX 1138*. The paradox here is that the main influence on *Star Wars* is *THX 1138*: the robot police became stormtroopers; OMM is a benevolent version of the Emperor; the hunchbacked shell dwellers became Jawas; THX, the hero who escapes and faces the responsibilities of his new existence, became Luke Skywalker.

From the *Flash Gordon* serials he had loved, George Lucas took art deco sets, blaster guns, medieval costumes and video screens. And he took their constant action. Ming, the evil ruler of Mongo in the *Flash Gordon* books, became a model for Lucas' emperor. From *John Carter on Mars*, he took *Star Wars'* beasts of burden, the banthas. The library of old movies he devoured covered the spectrum from *Forbidden Planet* to *The Day the World Ended*.

Lucas found all this research, even all the meetings, quite palatable. But writing the script remained a nightmare. Writing in pencil in tiny cramped handwriting, using a number two hard lead pencil, Lucas had stomach and chest pains and constant headaches until the screenplay was finished.

As he wrote, the plot of *Star Wars* mutated. Originally the *Star Wars* hero had been a Jedi knight general. Lucas saw there could be more character change if Luke Skywalker was a young man who became a Jedi. The resulting character, moreover, was rooted in the dualism within Lucas: half innocent and idealistic naïf, half cynical pessimist. Eventually, the second aspect of this psychological make-up was removed to become Han Solo.

But as Luke's character grew, that of Princess Leia receded from her previously dominant stance: to maintain the inter-

est of the audience she was given a love interest with Han
Solo.

The first screenplay took a year to develop and was
finished in May 1974. Screenplay two was finished on 28
January 1975. It had been given a title: *Adventures of the
Starkiller, Episode One of the Star Wars*.

Version two was set in the Republica Galactica, a land
torn by civil strife and banditry. Part of the plot involved a
search for the Kiber Crystal, whose energy field was in
charge of the destiny of all life.

Only Lucas understood the world he was creating, which had
a total span of fifty-five years. For the time being he was
to concentrate on the middle trilogy. The first trilogy would be
set twenty years before *Star Wars*: its story was that of young
Ben Kenobi and Luke's father. The final trilogy would tell the
story of the adult Luke's final war between the Empire and the
rebels. C-3PO and R2-D2 were the only constants common to
all nine films.

This new version of *The Star Wars* continued to have two
elements: a rescue mission to save a hostage taken by Darth
Vader and the ensuing struggle to destroy the Death Star. The
final air battle had been in the script from the onset of the writing, and Lucas felt obliged to contain it within the final script.
But despite its technological bravura, in the finished film it
can almost feel like an add-on. (By choosing the *Millennium
Falcon* as the name of Han Solo's spaceship, Lucas had
touched on the unconscious resonance of the present time as
it shifts into the next thousand years, at the same time giving
a timeless quality to the vessel.)

Version three of the screenplay was handed in on 1 August
1975. In it the Force was still symbolized by the Kiber

Crystal. But it was no longer there in version four, completed by the end of March 1976. This script still included Luke's older brother Biggs, who survived right through to the final shoot, only to be edited out of the final cut.

To help him secure his deal with Fox, Lucas initially had called on the work of Ralph McQuarrie, who had sketched the Apollo missions for CBS News and created the Boeing parts catalogue. He wanted the look of *Star Wars* to be, he told him, 'used space'.

McQuarrie was given the third version of the screenplay, as well as illustrations from *Flash Gordon* books and comic book examples. McQuarrie was commissioned to paint five scenes: these included a group portrait of the major characters and the final attack on the Death Star. As much as the paintings had sold the film to the studio, so they clarified Lucas's vision for him. McQuarrie, for example, thought that Darth Vader was insufficiently sinister when wearing black robes: he introduced the idea of the Lord of Darkness as a figure armoured in black. The colour was right, but the texture was still wrong: to the armour he added a black cloak.

Lucas took on board McQuarrie's suggestions of Chewbacca's look, but softened it – though leaving the trademark looping cartridge belts.

With the script and the look of the film in place, all that was needed was someone to play the characters.

A large cast had to be found. To reduce the stress of this task, Lucas made a pact with Brian de Palma, who was about to cast for *Carrie*, a Hitchcock pastiche. Together they looked

Harrison Ford's good looks as well as his fractious mood during the audition made him perfect for the part of Han Solo.

at the legions of prospective talent. Lucas kept firmly in the background: at Mark Hamill's audition he was sufficiently low-key for Hamill to imagine he must be de Palma's gofer.

Following his habitual financially astute path, Harrison Ford had gone back to his craft of carpentry after *American Graffiti* – this was partly because his *Graffiti* earnings had allowed him to buy such an expensive tool-set that he felt he ought to be employing it on tasks other than doing up his ramshackle home in the Hollywood hills. While the *Star Wars* auditions were taking place Ford was putting in a new door at Francis Coppola's offices. Although he knew of the casting, Ford had heard that Lucas had said he wouldn't be using any actors from *American Graffiti*. All the same, Lucas asked Ford if he wouldn't mind reading the male parts as he tried out actors for the role of Princess Leia. Ford complied, but grew testy as he began to realize he was reading parts which would not be his. Lucas, however, picked up that his fractious mood was ideal for the similarly argumentative Han Solo: physically rugged, Ford also projected a sly intelligence.

Finally Lucas had it narrowed it down to two groups of possibles: the first consisted of the New York stage actor Christopher Walken as Han Solo, television actor Will Selzer as Luke, former Penthouse Pet, Terri Nunn as Leia; and the second of Harrison Ford, Mark Hamill and Carrie Fisher, the eighteen-year-old daughter of Eddie Fisher and Debbie Reynolds. It may have been her showbiz aristocratic background that gave Fisher the sufficiently regal and imperious manner she brought to the part; she also seemed slightly asexual. Soon Lucas plumped for the second set of actors.

Harrison Ford was awkward about money. He was only being offered $1,000 a week to play Han Solo: he could make more than that in his carpentry business, he insisted. But Lucas wouldn't move. Accordingly, Ford refused to commit himself to a deal to appear in any sequels – as Hamill and Fisher already had agreed to do.

Lucas had always seen Obi-Wan 'Ben' Kenobi acted by someone of the stature of Sir Alec Guinness; and in 1975 he found Guinness in Los Angeles, filming the Neil Simon-scripted spoof thriller *Murder by Death*. Not only did Guinness go for the part – he had found the script compulsive reading – but he brought his own thoughts to it, assisting Lucas to understand the essential conflict between Obi-Wan Kenobi and Darth Vader.

Eventually George Lucas decided that if no one in Hollywood could offer him the special effects he wanted, he would build them from scratch. In Los Angeles he hired John Dykstra, a special effects assistant on *2001*, *The Andromeda Strain* and *Silent Running*, who had some experience of computer-controlled cameras.

Computer-controlled cameras were already changing television but so far had hardly been used in feature films. Dykstra was given the task of altering this. In July 1975 Lucasfilm Ltd created a subsidiary called Industrial Light and Magic, to be run by the special-effects wizard. Dykstra set about creating the computer system for the over 350 special effects in the film. The method he devised hinged around a giant camera mounted on tracks, powered by high-torque motors controlled by a computer. Each shot was programmed into a computer and played back a number of times to accommodate the model elements in the shots, creating the effect of live-action shots.

It was not until December 1975 that *Star Wars* was given the final green light by Fox. By then Lucas had poured a million of his own dollars into development. Since Lucas had first linked up with Alan Ladd, the budget had spiralled seemingly out of control.

When Lucas had first gone to Ladd, the director had said that the film would cost $3.5 million. Then Lucas and Gary Kurtz worked out what they considered to be the real budget – and found that it came to almost four times that much: $12 million. When that budget was shown to Ladd, he had pared it down to a figure of $8.5 million. Somewhere down the line Lucas put in a budget of $7.887 million – it became a running joke at Fox that the *Star Wars* budget was the same backwards or forwards.

Whatever, Lucas already knew he didn't have enough money. Moreover, until the budget was crisply finalized, Fox had wanted to stop all pre-production work. Armed with his *American Graffiti* cash cow, however, Lucas declared he would push on – even if it meant financing the movie himself. Which forced Fox to quicken its decision-making process.

The Shooting of *Star Wars*

Despite Fox having approved a final budget, it was imperative to keep costs down. Accordingly, Gary Kurtz made the economical choice to shoot the film in England, at Elstree, an hour's drive from central London: if *Star Wars* had been shot in the US and not Elstree it would have cost $13 million.

With shooting about to begin, much was still not quite ready. For example, Lucas asked Bill Huyck and Gloria Katz at the last minute to take the dialogue up another level, especially the smart-ass raps between Han Solo and Princess Leia. The pair were given percentage points on the film.

Industrial Light and Magic (ILM) were supposed to have come up with shots against which the action could be back-projected. But nothing was ready. Just before filming began, Lucas decided that instead he would blue-screen the action – they would film against a blank blue background and add the optical special effects in post-production.

And George Lucas had something else on his mind. He was endlessly undecided: should the hero of *Star Wars* be called Luke Starkiller or Luke Skywalker? It was not until the day before filming began that he came to a final decision.

Casting had continued when the production moved to London. Chewbacca was to be played by Peter Mayhew, a seven foot two inches tall London hospital porter, the possessor of one of the biggest pairs of feet in England.

In London Anthony Daniels had been chosen to play C-3PO, the robot that had all manner of resonations with the character of The Tin Man in *The Wizard of Oz*. For the making of C-3PO's mould, Daniels was stripped naked, his private parts protected with plastic film. Then he was covered in Vaseline and coated from head to toe in plaster.

Sir Alec Guinness had needs of a different sort. Specifically, this grand old man of the English stage and cinema required a five-figure cheque. And he also took two and a quarter per cent of the gross profits of *Star Wars*. Guinness would make more money from *Star Wars* than from any other film that he had appeared in.

Shooting was not to begin in Elstree, but in the hospitable North African country of Tunisia. On the edge of the Sahara desert they had found ideal territory to represent the arid wastelands of Tatooine.

Day one of the *Star Wars* shoot, 26 March 1976, was reminiscent of the disaster-strewn first night of filming on *American Graffiti*. The day after the production crew and cast had set up in the tiny desert town of Chott el-Djerid it rained for the first time in fifty years. The parched landscape was transformed into an ocean of mud.

When filming finally got under way, the crew were struck by the beauty of C-3PO, this golden man illuminated by the glare of the desert sun. But being trapped inside the robot's body for twelve hours a day in the desert heat was torture for Anthony Daniels.

Fortunately for the future of the film, an instant empathy sparked between Mark Hamill and Sir Alec Guinness; they struck up a friendship that showed on the screen. Guinness already had been through a not inconsiderable crisis. For Lucas had made a significant script change: Obi-Wan Kenobi, he had decided, would die in a duel with Darth Vader. Then he would reappear as a spirit guide, thereby becaming the personification of the Force. Disturbed by this script-change, Guinness had threatened to withdraw from the production before Lucas won him over.

While in Tunisia, Hamill tried a pass at a scene by playing it precisely as he imagined Lucas himself would respond in similar circumstances. 'Perfect,' assessed the director. Ah, thought Mark Hamill, so Luke Skywalker *is* George Lucas. But he also noticed that at no point did Lucas come and talk to him about his character. Although this was characteristic of Lucas, he was all the same taken with Hamill's innocence.

In retrospect, the desert conditions of Tunisia were clearly a pointer to future climatic conditions on the production: 1976 was to be Britain's then hottest summer of the twentieth century. Even inside the normally cool sound stages, Elstree was sweltering.

And George Lucas himself was to become particularly hot under the collar when he learned that, in the British film business, nothing comes without its price. Never having previously worked in Britain, the director was enraged to discover that the solidly unionized British film crews refused to work past 5.30 in the afternoon. When Lucas proposed that they stay for an extra two hours' shooting each night, the suggestion was resoundingly defeated in a union ballot.

'George wasn't happy there – he doesn't like to be away from home,' admitted Gary Kurtz. 'There are a lot of little things that are bothersome – light switches go up instead of down. Everything is different enough to throw you off. . . All film crews are a matter of chemistry. George is not a particularly social person. He doesn't go out of his way to socialize. It takes him a while to know somebody, to get intimate enough to share his problems with them. It's easier for him to work with people he knows.'

Notwithstanding the weather, Lucas was sickly throughout the shoot, with assorted stress-related colds and flus. And only he really knew what he wanted the film to be, which immediately put him at odds with his cinematographer, Gilbert 'Gil' Taylor, an E-type Jaguar-driving, gentleman

During the filming of Star Wars, **Fisher became the target of Lucas' sometimes hectoring manner –** 'Stand up, be a princess!' she would be told.

farmer who had filmed Richard Lester's *A Hard Day's Night*, Stanley Kubrick's *Dr Strangelove*, and Alfred Hitchcock's *Frenzy*. Taylor had few problems with Lucas's work method, however: quickly he learned that Lucas likes to shoot fast – going for it, getting the adrenalin racing. With a clear view of how his story-boarded scene would look in the cutting-room, he would rarely film more than four or five takes; he showed an instinctive understanding of how to move and pace a film, notably when integrating the three big set-piece situations in each of the *Star Wars* films.

Alfed Hitchcock had directed his first films at Elstree in Borehamwood – 'Boring Wood', as Harrison Ford renamed it. Often it seemed as though Lucas was going along with Hitchcock's apocryphal opinion that actors were no better than cattle: from time to time Carrie Fisher would become the target of Lucas' sometimes hectoring manner – 'Stand up, be a Princess!' she would be told.

Up until then Carrie Fisher had only had one day's acting work on a film set, seducing Warren Beatty in *Shampoo*. The script's description of her character as 'beautiful' unnerved her; she had been ordered to lose ten pounds but had only managed half that: 'I didn't think I was pretty. I was a Pilsbury doughgirl.'

Her part was always wooden. Princess Leia never quite lives. But this is partly because of schisms in the character. Her feminity is always under threat: she had a ram's-horn hairdo; she was covered from neck to foot in a long white gown; her breasts were held down with gaffer tape because, she said facetiously, 'there was no sex in outer space'; we first see her when she's firing her weapon.

Fisher had a British drama background and consequent accent. During the shooting of the film she was reading Colette 'just to be pretentious. I was very quiet. Whatever they asked me to do, I said, "Fantastic", because I didn't want to lose the job. I was also described as bovine and was told I'd inherited the worst qualities of both my parents.'

Arriving at Elstree from Tunisia, Lucas had ordered the sparkling sets created by John Barry, the production designer on *A Clockwork Orange*, to be dirtied up. A gleaming R2-D2 was rolled on the ground until it was scuffed and chipped. The director was similarly anxious that none of his cast should look other than lived-in and of their time: Luke's shirt was made from curtain-lining material, while Princess Leia's clothes looked as if they came from a Renaissance court.

And as George Lucas was Luke Skywalker, so Harrison Ford was Han Solo. The character had a deep background personal story: Solo had been raised by Wookies, expelled from the Space Academy, had a past as a spice smuggler and was an enemy of the Empire.

The pace of filming accelerated. By the final week's filming at Elstree, Lucas was operating three crews, one led by himself, another by Gary Kurtz, and a third by Robert Watts. In Los Angeles, meanwhile, where John Dykstra continued in his efforts to build a computer-controlled camera, Industrial Light and Magic had turned into a problem. ILM's two-storey warehouse in Van Nuys in the San Fernando Valley, the other side of the hills from Hollywood, was staffed largely by hippies: accordingly, it proceeded along a lateral, somewhat anarchic course that had the added fillip of generally being rather good fun for its employees. One hot summer's day, with the temperature soaring over the hundred-degree mark, the ILM employees rigged up an inflatable swimming-pool, running a chute to it from the building's roof. Just as the staff began plunging down into the water, a limousine's-worth of suitably startled Fox executives arrived.

Perhaps that kind of incident was a logical consequence of having the *Star Wars* special effects factory manned by young and relatively inexperienced people. Lucas had chosen young people not because of any abiding belief on his part in the creative zeal of youth, but so that he could have more control over them.

> I wanted to be able to say, 'It must look like this, not that.' I don't want to be handed an effect at the end of five months and be told, 'Here's your special effect, sir.' I want to be able to have more say about what's going on . . . either you do it yourself, or you don't get a say.
>
> Technically [Lucas told Stephen Zito] you always compare things against *2001*. If you took one of our shots and ran it on the light box and set it next to one of Kubrick's shots, you would say, 'Well, his are better.' But there is no way, given the time and money we've had, that Kubrick could do any better. He was striving for perfection and had a shot ratio thirty times what we have. When you spend that kind of time and money you can get things perfect. We went into this trying to make a cheap children's movie for $8 million. We didn't go in and say that we were going to make the perfect science fiction film, but we are gonna make the most spectacular thing you've ever seen!

All the same, there were communication problems between Dykstra and Lucas, as the special-effects expert explained to the same writer in 1997:

The major problem we encountered on this show was being able to apply what George started out with conceptually. From the day we met we talked about World War II dogfight footage which involved lots of action, continuous motion, moving camera, streak, loops and rolls, and all of the things aerial photography allows you to do in live action. This has been difficult to do in special effects with multiple ships, planet backgrounds and stars, because of the problem of angular displacement, matching shots and depth of field.

It's hard to explain that a concept won't work because of some technological thing, and this becomes a bone of contention. When a director shoots an exterior, he can see the lighting and the set-up and the action and hear the dialogue, but when he comes in here, all there is is a camera running down a track about three inches a second photographing a model . . .

The neat thing about George is that he has a sensibility. He is really involved in his movie, he is really attached. He's hard-headed about stuff, but, if he's wrong, he'll change his mind rather than say, 'I'm the director, I've made a decision and that's it.' He's got taste. He's got that gift for popular narrative. People like what he does: it's active; it's fast; there's humour in it. *Star Wars* is gonna be exciting all the way. The aerial battle that takes up the last reel of the film is going to be as exciting as the car chase in *The French Connection*.

But things were not always as amicable between them. When Lucas returned from England, ready to enter the cutting-room with his 340,000 feet of footage, he flew down to Los Angeles from San Francisco and went to see Dykstra. He could hardly believe what the ILM head honcho told him: that after a year's work ILM had spent a million dollars and come up with only three usable shots. Lucas lost it: furious, he screamed at Dykstra, who gave as good back.

During the flight back to San Francisco that evening, Lucas experienced severe chest pains. Hospitalized until the next day at Marin General Hospital, where he was diagnosed as suffering from extreme exhaustion, he spent a dark night of the soul in which he came to one overwhelming conclusion: that never again would he direct a film.

Making a motion picture on the scale of *Star Wars* carries continual potential for problems, especially those of a human kind. There were still some scenes Lucas needed to complete in California, notably the Mos Eisley Cantina sequence, which Lucas had intended as Dante's Inferno-in-Space. When Alan Ladd had to go to the Fox board to ask for an additional $20,000 to shoot the cantina scene, he played his ultimate card: *Star Wars*, he told the money-men, was the greatest picture ever made.

The cantina sequence, which is like a surreal vision of a classic western saloon-bar scene, was to be shot in the Californian desert; at the same time, Lucas would film the scenes featuring Luke's landspeeder in the Tatooine wilderness. On the morning of the shoot, however, Lucas learned that Mark Hamill had been in a serious car smash on the Pacific Coast Highway the previous evening: he was in Los Angeles County General Hospital

with facial injuries. Accordingly a body double was employed
and close-ups were avoided.

The ILM experience notwithstanding, science and technology generally could be more predictable than human frailty.
Adversity had been turned to advantage through the need for
blue-screening, which had turned out to be pure benedic-
tion. The final battle, in which the Death Star is destroyed,
was based on a ten-minute montage of filmed aerial battles
that Lucas assembled from such First and Second World War
flying movies as *The Big Max*, *633 Squadron*, *Tora! Tora!
Tora!*, *The Bridges of Toko-Ri* and *The Battle of Britain*. 'We
cut them all together into a battle sequence to get an idea of
the movement,' Gary Kurtz told *American Film*. 'It was a very
bizarre-looking film – all black-and-white, a dirty 16mm
dupe. There would be a shot of the pilot saying something,
then you cut back to a long shot of the plane, explosions,
crashes. It gave a reasonably accurate idea of what the battle
sequence would look like, the feeling of it.'

These battle sequences were shown to special-effects
experts and to artists who transferred this compilation to
storyboards. 'It's very easy to take your hand and fly,' said
Gary Kurtz. 'But it's very hard to convert that movement to
what John Dykstra and the other special effects people had
to do with the models.'

Perhaps most crucial of all was that the Star Destroyer at
the beginning of the film should look credible: if the audience laughed, as they had been seen doing at R2-D2 during
a Westwood cinema screening of forthcoming attractions,
they were in trouble.

Where members of the production crew had simpler tasks, the results came more easily. Ben Burtt, for example, was a sound engineer extraordinaire.

Burtt's task, among others, was to seek out the exact sound that the *Millennium Falcon* and other craft would have. Accordingly, he went to Los Angeles International Airport, to military bases and to airshows recording the noise of screaming jet engines. The tone of the Imperial Cruisers engines, meanwhile, came from a slowing down of the sound of the advertising blimp used by Goodyear Tyres. He created the noise of the lasers by wacking a cable attached to a radio tower.

Burtt wasn't only a technohead. Intergalactic languages needed to be devised for the non-human characters. For Greedo, the bounty-hunting alien in the cantina, he came up with the idea of having him speak in Quechua, an extinct Incan language.

It was George Lucas who came to the conclusion that the voice of Dave Prowse, who played Darth Vader, was simply neither sufficiently evil nor aristocratic. What would be perfect would be the deep baritone of James Earl Jones, who had been nominated for an Academy Award for his lead role in *The Great White Hope*, the story of the first black boxer to become world champion. The fact that Jones was black was possibly not without intention: inadvertently, *Star Wars* had been cast without a single black actor.

George Lucas had applied to *Star Wars* the economies he had learned during the making of *American Graffiti*: fast-and-loose, hit-them-on-the-run film-making, but with a project that had taken a quantum leap in scope.

Towards the end of the production he admitted to Stephen
Zito in *American Film* that many of his problems on the film
had been a consequence of his chronic inability to delegate
authority and responsibility:

> I come up from the film-makers' school of doing movies, which
> means I do everything myself. If you are a writer-director, you
> must get involved with everything. It's very hard for me to get
> into another system where everybody does things for me, and
> I say, 'Fine.' If I ever continue to do these kinds of movies, I've
> got to learn to do that. I have a lot of friends who can, and I
> admire them. Francis Coppola is going through that now, and
> he's finally learning, finally getting to the point where he real-
> izes he can't do it all. He's getting into the traditional system:
> 'Call me when it's ready and it better be right, and if it's not,
> do it again and spend whatever it costs to get it right.' But you
> have to be willing to make very expensive movies that way. You
> can't make cheap movies.
>
>   If I left anything for a day, it would fall apart, and it's purely
> because I set it up that way and there is nothing I can do
> about it. It wasn't set up so I could walk away from it.
> Whenever there is a leak in the dam, I have to stick my finger
> in it. I should learn to say, 'Somebody else go plug that up.'

For those film-makers who were close to him, George Lucas
held a screening of a rough cut of *Star Wars* that had as yet
had no music added: John Milius, Steven Spielberg, Matthew
Robbins, Hal Barwood, Bill Huyck and Gloria Katz, Jay
Cocks of *Time* magazine and Brian de Palma were all there.

None of them seemed colossally taken with the film –
de Palma was especially disparaging, making jokes about

the 'almighty Force' – except for Spielberg and Cocks who took him on one side and gave positive advice. Then de Palma redeemed himself by saying that he and Jay Cocks would rewrite the opening crawl that gave the story's background.

But the film took a quantum leap when John Williams' music was added soon after. Williams' soundtrack took the classic form of an expanded cliff-hanger serial, brimming with dramatic counterpoints and changes: the composer based much of this work on the musical influence of Erich Korngold, who had scored such great Errol Flynn swash-bucklers as *Robin Hood*, *The Sea Hawk* and *Captain Blood*. In some scenes the excitement, which seemed to stem from the magic of special effects, was simply an emotional response to the power of Williams' epic score. His music immeasurably expanded the movie, swamping nearly every frame and commenting alertly on the action. Lucas thought that working with John Williams was 'wonderful: just the way life should be.'

'It's the underpinning, a grease that each movie slides along on and a glue that holds it together so that you can follow it,' Lucas told Paul Scanlon in *Rolling Stone* in 1983. 'There's always been a scene or a moment in which the music connects so strongly with the visual that it sends shivers up my spine every time I see it.'

Deals had been struck with Marvel comics and Del Rey books – although initially the toy industry was harder to bust through. Lucas' experience on *THX 1138*, however, had shown him precisely who was his base market – science fiction fans.

And so this was who was targeted: such visible aspects of the Star Wars Corporation as Ralph McQuarrie's sketches and assorted story-boards were taken on a tour of science fiction conventions across the United States throughout the winter before the film was due to open; at the World Science Fiction Convention in Kansas City not only was there a sparkling C-3PO and a full-size model of Darth Vader, but Mark 'Luke Skywalker' Hamill was there to enlighten onlookers about the models of the *Millennium Falcon*, droids and other hardware.

When his film opened, George Lucas wanted to make sure that at least some people would come to it. After all, gloomy prognostications continued to dribble forth from Fox: now the studio's research was arguing that the word 'war' in a title was a no-no – women simply would not go to see such a film, insisted the marketing men. At first the film seemed a hard sell: after the negative responses to the preview trailers, they were pulled from cinemas. At the urging of Lucas to Ladd, *Star Wars* was pitched through teenage media, even through advertisements on cable television in college dormitories.

The studio, in fact, believed that its only sure-fire hit for 1977 would be *The Other Side of Midnight*: a Second World War story – subject-matter that its bland, catch-all title steered safely away from – by Sidney Sheldon, starring Marie-France Pisier, John Beck and Susan Sarandon. Fox even gave some cinema owners a choice: book *Star Wars*, or they would not get *The Other Side of Midnight*. Later the studio was fined $25,000 for this.

To be economically viable, *Star Wars* needed to be under two hours long. When final cutting-room sacrifices were

required, Lucas completely removed all scenes and references to Biggs Darklighter (played by Garrick Hagon),
Luke's fellow rebel pilot and boyhood friend. Not wanting
the film to be saddled with the slur of 'kid's-movie', Lucas
and Kurtz pushed for a 'PG' rating – and got it.

On 25 May 1977, *Star Wars* opened in the United States in
thirty-two cinemas. In New York and Los Angeles shows
began at 10 a.m. In each case there were long queues two
hours before.

Some were drawn by science fiction freaks' word-of-
mouth. Most came, however, because the picture had drawn
superlative reviews. 'I loved *Star Wars*,' wrote Jack Kroll in
Newsweek, 'and so will you . . .' And in the rival *Time* Lucas
got six pages of coverage, with the banner headline '*Star
Wars*: The Year's Best Movie', and adulation in the prose that
described it as 'a grand and glorious film that may well be
the smash hit of 1977 . . . a subliminal history of movies,
wrapped in a riveting tale of suspense and adventure, orna-
mented with some of the most ingenious special effects ever
contrived for film.' In *Variety*, meanwhile, Harrison Ford was
selected as 'outstanding'.

By titling it *Star Wars IV: A New Hope*, the makers of the film
established a sense that everything we were about to see we
somehow were already familiar with: which we were, of course,
as Lucas had dredged most of its characters and themes from
the collective unconscious of mythology.

Star Wars stomped all over the other contenders – *The
Deep*, *Sorcerer*, *Exorcist: The Heretic* – in that summer of
1977; *Smokey and the Bandit* was the only other substantial
box-office success. More than one in twenty filmgoers in

1977 saw *Star Wars* more than once. When the film was released, Fox's stock was $12 a share. Four years later it went for $70 a share.

From now on, the movie business was to be changed for ever.

For the Academy Awards to be held in April of the next year, *Star Wars* received ten nominations: these included Best Direction, Best Screenplay and Best Picture. Along with Richard Chew and Paul Hirsch, Marcia Lucas was nominated for the Best Editing award. Other contenders were John Barry for art direction, John Mollo for costume design, John Williams for musical score, and John Dykstra, Richard Edlund, Grant McCune, John Stears, and Robert Blalack for special effects.

The special-effects team, who had literally sent Lucas sick to hospital, won their nomination, as did sound man Ben Burtt. But the only award the Lucas family received went to Marcia for her editing, along with Chew and Hirsch: as he had been with *American Graffiti*, George Lucas was kept completely out of the awards loop, overshadowed by Woody Allen's more 'sophisticated' *Annie Hall*, which took the awards for Best Picture, Best Direction and Best Screenplay. Whether it was because of the slickness with which he tied up Hollywood in deals that suited him, rather than vice versa, or simply because of jealousy at a colossal success that seemed to come out of left-field, George Lucas - like his friend Steven Spielberg at the time – never won a major Academy Award. Clearly, he was to be kept soundly in his place.

Buoyed by the Oscar night publicity, Fox re-released the film that summer: it quickly took in another $46 million in tickets. It was not until November 1978 that *Star Wars* finally ended its run in US cinemas: by then it was the number one grossing film of all time, having taken $273 million gross. With overseas markets added on, *Star Wars* grossed $430 million by the end of 1979, and for the first time Hollywood studios had come to understand the significance of foreign sales.

5 Sand, Plans and More Graffiti

How did George Lucas survive *Star Wars*-mania? By the surest known method of not being overcome by one's success: he simply didn't take it very seriously.

As soon as the film was released, George and Marcia Lucas went on holiday, to Maui, their first vacation since 1969. Soon Lucas was joined there by Steven Spielberg. Mythic reverberations, cod 'inner child' psychology and comic absurdity: each jockeyed for position as Lucas celebrated the success of *Star Wars* by constructing a sand-castle with his fellow director. As they played on the beach, the two men opened up about their filmic dreams.

What did Spielberg tell Lucas he wanted to do? To make a picture like a James Bond film. Why not, asked Lucas, drawing on a favoured source of inspiration, structure it in the style of the Thirties and Forties movie serials? What's more, he said, he already had had some thoughts along these lines. 'I said, "I've got a great idea. And I can't get anybody interested in it." So I told him the idea, and he said, "That's fantastic! I'd love to do that." And that's really how it got started.'

Lucas outlined to Spielberg an idea he had come up with a couple of years previously about a playboy adventurer: in

1975 he and film-maker Phil Kaufman had spent three weeks dreaming up a film idea about such a character that was based on Adolf Hitler's obsession with acquiring ancient religious artefacts, specifically, the Ark of the Covenant – a notion given full flight in the then popular book *Spear of Destiny*. Spielberg loved the idea and they agreed to make the film.

'*Raiders* was an old project that I had even before *Star Wars*, and I was trying to get people to do it. At one point Phil Kaufman was having a difficult time with his career,' Lucas told *Film Comment*, 'so I said, "I've got this great movie. C'mon, let's do this picture, and we'll get Francis, or somebody, to get us a deal somewhere." So I told him the story, and he told me about the ark and all that stuff, and we had about half a dozen story conferences over the period of about three weeks . . .' At the end of that period, however, Kaufman was offered the job of directing *The Outlaw Josey Wales* – he was subsequently fired from the film, its star Clint Eastwood taking over the director's chair.

With the project revived, Lucas and Spielberg agreed to work on it, and to seek out a writer. For now, however, there was further work on the schedule.

Star Wars had made George Lucas $20 million wealthier. But he put all this money into safe investments: he would be needing it soon, he knew, as he intended to finance the sequel to *Star Wars* himself. In the end the director – or producer, as he was now to be – lent this $20 million to Lucasfilm as collateral to finance *The Empire Strikes Back*, as *Star Wars 2* came to be called. The only addition to the lifestyle of George Lucas seemed to be the used Ferrari the former cruiser now drove around in. By this time, the cash was coming in from the assorted *Star Wars* merchandising deals: Lucasfilm would shortly be ringing up around $10 million a year from toys alone.

Others around him who had been in the film benefited fabulously. With his 0.25 per cent of the net, Harrison Ford did not do badly. Yet he was nowhere near the financial league of the far more experienced Sir Alec Guinness, whose deal gave him 2.5 per cent of gross royalties – he earned more from playing Obi-Wan Kenobi than from all his other film roles put together. On a creative level, moreover, Guinness considered Lucas to be the apotheosis of directors, and delivered the ultimate compliment: George Lucas, said Sir Alec, had a similar 'eye' to Sir David Lean.

More American Graffiti

Before he was free to move on to his next space adventure, George Lucas was committed to completing a sequel to *American Graffiti* for Universal. To make the first film he had agreed to a three-picture deal – the third film, *Radioland Murders*, would not appear until 1994.

In 1971 Lucas had been taken with an impressive film called *Cisco Pike*, a Los Angeles-set counter-culture story about the world of drug-dealing which starred Gene Hackman and Kris Kristofferson. *Cisco Pike* developed a cult reputation that has stood the test of time. Yet its subject-matter had proved a poisoned chalice for Bill Norton, its young writer-director, another USC alumnus whom Lucas had known when he was studying there. As had been the experience of the Zoetrope partners, the kind of 'alternative' cinema that once would have got you on to the cover of

Rolling Stone no longer impressed Hollywood moguls; Norton had not directed any more movies. Subsequently he had made his living by script-writing, which seemed a good enough reason for George Lucas to contact him: 'He said that if he liked the script, I could direct it.'

Norton discovered that Lucas already had the four main stories of the film, to be called *More American Graffiti*, which was set on four New Year's Eves from 1964 to 1967. The gang from the first film have finished high school two years previously. Paul Le Mat is still racing cars; Cindy Williams is pregnant with Ron Howard's child; Wolfman Jack is back, hectoring the USA with his street wisdom, spinning songs from the mid-Sixties.

What Lucas decided was that he personally would executive produce *More American Graffiti*, and that his former USC classmate Howard Kazanjian would be the actual producer. Bill Norton, as he had hoped, was given the directing job.

The multiple stories, however, proved a problem and the film did not seem to hang together. 'In *More American Graffiti* we were asking a lot of the audience, because things were happening at different times, as well as in different places,' said Norton.

The job of editor was given to Tina Hirsch, a relative of *Star Wars* editor Paul Hirsch. But Lucas took over as soon as she handed in her first cut. This became his practice: he would let a hired director deliver his first cut, but step in personally if he felt it necessary.

In Lucas's canon of work, *More American Graffiti* is something of a footnote: it only broke even two years after its 1979 release, following sales to pay television.

6 The Empire Strikes Back

After such a success as *Star Wars*, only the best would do for its sequel. To write the film George Lucas accordingly hired Leigh Brackett, the author of science-fiction novels and the co-writer of such cinema classics as *The Big Sleep* and *Rio Bravo*. Lucas admired the terseness of the speech, the straight narrative drive of her films. In March 1978 she handed in her first draft: for Lucas her hard-boiled dialogue was just what he needed – the script was going in the direction he wanted. But two weeks later Leigh Brackett died of cancer.

It seemed like a curious twist of fate. For the third time in a row this man who loathed writing – yet had proved colossally successful when doing it – was obliged to write the script himself: there is something funny and endearing about the image of this magician-like figure tucked away in his room, extracting the essence of a film drop by drop.

Right through the summer of 1978 he laboured, all the while looking for a writer to take over from him. Then he realized this figure was right in front of him. Steven Spielberg had held Lucas to his sandy handshake and gone ahead with *Raiders of the Lost Ark*, as their 1930s playboy-adventurer movie had come to be titled. At Spielberg's suggestion,

Lawrence Kasdan had been hired to write the film; Kasdan was a former advertising copywriter who had written *Continental Divide*, a comedy that Spielberg had almost directed. When Kasdan flew up to San Francisco to deliver the first *Raiders of the Lost Ark* draft, Lucas asked him to take over the *Empire* writing job before he'd even looked at it. 'I said, "Don't you want to read this first?" George said, "Well, if I hate it tonight, I'll call you up and take back the offer. But I just get a feeling about people." '

With a writer finally on board, Lucas made his announcement that he personally would finance *The Empire Strikes Back*. And Fox would distribute it.

The Empire Strikes Back had three acts, each around thirty-five minutes long. Just as Lucas had wanted, the structure of the 105-page screenplay that Lawrence Kasdan turned in was a precise reflection of this. Lucas had told him that he needed to establish rapidly who were the main characters and then quickly set these up in the first experiences they were to undergo. For the sake of visual continuity, Lucas once again employed Norman Reynolds as production designer and Ralph McQuarrie as illustrator.

So that audiences could see this was a new film, however, Lucas made sure that new creatures and settings were introduced at the beginning of the movie. And an important new plot possibility was brought out as early as possible: Lucas wanted to implant in the minds of the audience the idea that Luke might kill Vader, with all its implications of patricide.

The basic plot, as sketched out by Lucas first to Leigh Brackett and then to Lawrence Kasdan was revenge drama of the almost classically Elizabethan formula: Luke tries to save his friends from Darth Vader; Vader in turn uses Han, Princess Leia and Chewbacca as his bait to trap Luke, whom he is trying to switch to the dark side of the Force. Key elements from *Star Wars* were reintroduced almost immediately: the rebellion against the Empire; the love/hate relationship between Princess Leia and Han Solo; the rivalry/loyalty between Han and Luke; the platonic affection between Luke and Leia.

And the notion of the Force was expanded even further. Obi-Wan Kenobi, killed by Vader in the previous film, was now only a shadowy apparition. For the first time the Emperor was given a physical presence – a hooded figure with an aura of infinite evil of whom even Darth Vader was scared.

As a counter-balance, the character of Yoda was introduced. Twenty-six inches tall, Yoda was the guru-like Jedi master and sage, an 800-year-old shaman. The model of Yoda was worked on for over a year: Stuart Freeborn, the designer, based Yoda's image on a picture of Albert Einstein set against his own reflection. Yoda's voice and operating were performed by Frank Oz, the Muppet master who had fulfilled the same functions for Miss Piggy.

In the scene on Dagobah, the bog planet, in which Yoda attempts to initiate Luke Skywalker into the way of the Jedi warrior, many of the essential precepts are those of Buddhism. (To create the visual realism, an Elstree sound stage was filled with ankle-deep water, which was then sprayed with mineral oils.)

There were other new locations: the ice planet Hoth, which was the rebels' army base until they were attacked by imperial troops. And Bespin's Cloud City, ostensibly reigned over by Han Solo's old friend, the new character of Lando

Calrissian, played by Billy Dee Williams, a black actor who had first come to Lucas's attention when he saw him playing opposite Diana Ross in the Billie Holiday biopic, *Lady Sings the Blues*: given the subliminal history of how James Earl Jones came to be hired for the voice of Darth Vader, you might feel that here a certain amount of political correctness was being exercised.

Although both Lawrence Kasdan and Gary Kurtz had been concerned that the script suffered from a lack of scene-by-scene emotional resolution, Lucas's response was simple: give 'em enough action, and no one will notice. He wasn't being glib here: simply covering up his recurrent fear of delivering work that was too slow. 'The trick is to know what you can leave to the audience's imagination,' Lucas told Dale Pollock, his official biographer. 'If they start getting lost, you're in trouble. Sometimes you have to be crude and just say what's going on, because if you don't, people get puzzled.' Besides, the action-enhancing special effects in *The Empire Strikes Back* – as in both the other *Star Wars* films – were always driven by the story and never existed simply for their own ends.

Wanting to expand his career, Harrison Ford had been reluctant to return to the part of Han Solo. He would only do so, he said, if the script showed his Solo character undergoing considerable development. What he especially felt was needed was a real love triangle between himself, Luke and Leia. As this was precisely what had been developed in the screenplay, he agreed to climb aboard the project.

Who would direct the film? Gary Kurtz again was to be the film's line producer. And he knew a man who seemed perfect for the job. He had first met Irvin Kershner, another former USC graduate who had also taught on the film course, while he was directing *Stakeout on Dope Street*, an anti-drugs documentary, back in 1958. More recently he had made *The Eyes of Laura Mars*, a thriller with a troubled production history originally written by John Carpenter; more crucially for Lucas, in 1976 Kershner had directed *The Return of a Man Called Horse*, a sequel that eclipsed the original in almost every way.

Now in his late forties, Kershner was a man of many parts; he was also, for example, a classical musician. And he had a reputation for working fast. A vegetarian and Buddhist (the character of Yoda was to appeal to him), Kershner was very taken with the notion of the Force: having assiduously researched fairy-tales and mythology himself, he had seen how effectively one could thereby reach the subconscious of audiences.

Even though he was also a student of Zen, Kershner was worried about the danger of losing control through working with Lucas. He was, however, hardly likely to turn down an opportunity to join the dream team that had made *Star Wars*. So, in order to circumvent potential problems, Kershner sketched out every shot in the film: eventually he had a book of drawings nine inches thick. He made two copies of this, and gave one to Lucas; then he departed to the winter of Norway, where the scenes on the ice planet Hoth were to be filmed before sound-stage work commenced, again at Elstree. Irvin Kershner proved the opposite of Lucas when it came to handling actors: he was more than open to improvisation and debate. The director and Harrison Ford empathized well.

In the first week in March 1979, almost one hundred foreigners descended on the tiny Norwegian hamlet of Finse, more than doubling its population. The hinterland of Finse had been chosen as the location for the surface of the ice planet Hoth. Finse had been the training camp for Captain Scott before he set out on his fatal expedition to the South Pole. So it seemed hardly inappropriate that, as soon as all the equipment was in place in Norway and Carrie Fisher and Mark Hamill had installed themselves in the Finse ski lodge, a furious snow blizzard raged and avalanches cut them off from the rest of the world.

The winter of 1978–9 was the worst in Europe for many years. So filming on *The Empire Strikes Back*, which began on 5 March, was following the familiar pattern of the beginning of shoots on George Lucas movies. This dreadful, dangerous weather forced Plan B to be enacted. Shooting was re-scheduled and Harrison Ford flew in from London, only just managing to make it through the blizzards to the location. Kershner had opted to shoot the scene in which Han prevents Luke from freezing to death by wrapping him in his dead Tauntaun – he is saved by the last remaining body heat from this fantastical beast, a creature devised by Lucas as appropriate for the emerging mythology of a new time.

The weather conditions were the coldest in which anyone involved with the film had ever worked. Harrison and Hamill both wore two pairs of thermal pants and four pairs of socks. The camera equipment had to have lightweight oil put into it to prevent it from freezing up. If you touched a camera without wearing gloves your skin would freeze to the metal: the only way to free yourself was by slicing it away with a razor blade. In this extreme cold the film would become brittle and crack.

For seven weeks they worked in conditions in which ten degrees below zero was considered warm. For days at a time the crew would be snowed into their motel. By the time they headed for England, only 33,000 of the required 75,000 feet of film had been shot.

At least it had been warm at Elstree: on 24 January, much of the studio had gone up in flames. Stanley Kubrick, who was there making *The Shining*, had been delayed in his filming and was unable to vacate the sound stages he was using. In his turn Kubrick now slowed down Gary Kurtz in his set building, which had to be ready for when the crew arrived from Norway at the end of April.

Once filming began at Elstree there were further problems, exemplified by the fact that many of the electronic gadgets simply didn't work. Although the involvement of Muppet co-creator Frank Oz had filled senior members of the team with great confidence, no one knew if Yoda was actually going to respond in the manner in which it was intended.

As director of photography, Peter Schuzitsky, who had shot the Ken Russell extravaganza *Lisztomania*, replaced Gil Taylor, the *Star Wars* cinematographer. But *Empire* was not without its measure of tragedy: on 6 June art director John Barry collapsed, complaining of a headache. He died within hours in hospital, of infectious meningitis.

The involvement of Sir Alec Guinness had also initially been in jeopardy: eight months before production began he had developed a serious, sight-threatening eye infection. Luckily, he recovered.

Over two years had passed since Mark Hamill's car crash. Despite having undergone plastic surgery, he still bore some facial scars from the accident: seeing this, George Lucas wrote in a scene in which Luke had been mauled by a Wampa, then healed.

What was the hardest thing to do in the shooting of *Empire*? To freeze Han Solo in the large block of carbonite that ends the film. Irvin Kershner's concept was that this sequence would resemble a mad-scientist film of the 1930s: central to it would be a forty-foot cylinder of spiralling metals and gushing steam, melting plastic objects and emitting fumes; the sequence had a German Expressionist graphic quality, especially the Shroud-like woodcut of Han Solo in carbon freeze.

It was apparent that this was a more physically exacting film than *Star Wars*. 'This one would have laid George out,' said Gary Kurtz. All the same, although Irvin Kershner directed it, people still think of *The Empire Strikes Back* as a George Lucas film and are largely unaware that another director was at the helm. As had been the case with Bill Norton and *More American Graffiti*, Lucas gave Kershner his first cut . . . and then re-edited the film himself with Marcia.

Although the original budget for *The Empire Strikes Back* had been $15 million, it had gone up to $18.5 million, almost twice the cost of *Star Wars*, before shooting even began. In the intervening three years, the cost of making films had risen dramatically. This was partly because *Star Wars* had established a new set of ground rules: in *The Empire Strikes Back*, there were over 600 'opticals', or special effects shots – twice the number used in *Star Wars*.

Once production started, making the film was costing Lucas nearly $100,000 a day. And he was almost excessively conscious that it was his own money that was being spent, often referring to this. Moreoever, this was a time when the value of the pound against the dollar suddenly soared: when *Star Wars* had been made, one English pound would buy around 1.55 dollars; just before shooting began on *Empire*, after all costs had been locked in place, the pound soared to around the 2.40 dollar mark, a huge difference when it came to paying costs and wages in the UK.

A few weeks into filming, Gary Kurtz had to tell Lucas that the film would cost $22 million. Although Lucas had been given his first production loan from the established movie money supply line, the Bank of America in Los Angeles, it refused to give him the extra $6 million he suddenly found he needed.

In the end Lucas had to go with his hat out to Fox to ask the studio to guarantee a loan of $3 million from First National Bank of Boston. Fox agreed – in exchange for fifteen per cent of the *Empire* profits. Currency fluctuations notwithstanding, Lucas was deeply unhappy that the team of Kurtz and Kershner eventually went $10 million over budget. After all, always hanging over him was the grim spectre of Francis Coppola's huge financial overage on *Apocalypse Now*.

The Empire Strikes Back was scheduled for release by Twentieth Century Fox on 21 May 1980. The studio, however, was not happy: its feeling was that the deal Lucas had struck for himself was so advantageous that it would become the laughing-stock of Hollywood. Yet Fox had begun to be some-what mollified by the $26 million it took from cinema owners in advance bookings.

Fans began lining up outside the Egyptian Theater in Hollywood three days before the film opened. After six days the box office was through the $9 million mark. Three months on from 21 May, Lucas had his investment back. *Empire* easily eclipsed its nearest box-office rival that summer, the counter-culture extravaganza *The Blues Brothers*, starring John Belushi and Dan Ackroyd. (That summer's other hits? *Fame*, *Brubaker*, *Rough Cut*, *Can't Stop the Music*.) *The Empire Strikes Back* sold more than 300 million tickets around the world. And Fox earned $40 million in distribution fees. At the beginning of the 1990s it was the third most successful film of all time, behind *E.T.* and *Star Wars*.

As a result, perhaps, of the same small thinking that had Fox worried they would be laughed at in Hollywood, and that was possibly also responsible for Lucas never receiving a major Academy Award, he then ran into an egregious piece of pettiness on the part of the Directors Guild of America.

In accordance with the film's visual style, Irvin Kershner's credit was not shown at the beginning of the film: the template had been set on *Star Wars*, where the opening crawl of text gave the story's background, and Lucas had not credited himself until the end of the film. Because of this, Lucas received a communication from the Directors Guild of America, fining him $250,000. Finally, Lucas settled out of court for $25,000 after having been threatened by the DGA that all copies of the film would have to be removed from cinemas if the issue went to arbitration.

7 Raiders of the Lost Ark

Before plunging into the hell of writing *The Empire Strikes Back*, George Lucas had met Steven Spielberg and Lawrence Kasdan in Los Angeles for a brainstorming session on *Raiders of the Lost Ark*. The location was Lucas's small office on Lankershim Boulevard in north Hollywood, across the way from Universal.

Spielberg was somewhat bemused by Lucas's suggestion that the lead character be named Indiana: he was only too aware that this was the name of George Lucas's dog. All the same, they seemed to be a potentially strong team: Spielberg shoots on the hoof, filming the action as it enfolds; for his part, Lucas can already see what this will look like in the cutting-room; Kasdan's writing, moreover, had an immediacy and wit that heightened its powerful narrative drive.

'Larry Kasdan, Steve and I worked together on it, but basically when I laid out the story, it was fairly articulate,' Lucas told *Film Comment*. 'Every scene was described. They changed and personalized it a lot the way they wanted, but essentially the concept remained the same.'

Spielberg wanted *Raiders* to be like a Disneyland ride; Lucas wanted it to be true to the serials of the 1930s.

Together they watched fifteen episodes of *Don Winslow of the Navy* . . . and came to the conclusion that it was actually not very good at all, in writing, acting or direction – it simply didn't stand the test of time.

The cinema matinee serials, they realized, could be no more than a starting-point: they needed to create something entirely original. Lucas sketched out his vision: *Raiders of the Lost Ark*, as the film was to be called, was to be a seven-act film divided into sixty scenes, each two pages long. There would be six cliff-hanger moments – every twenty pages there would be a new piece of excitement. 'The advantage that *Raiders* had was that there was no previous film. He was sort of establishing certain criteria that wouldn't be in conflict with anything else. When I wrote *Raiders*, I actually wrote four stories, four different stories. One of them was a very action-oriented kind of thing, which was what Steve wanted to do. I would watch that he didn't go against what the character was supposed to be throughout the series. The character has to be consistent. Some of his traits Steve wasn't enamoured with and wanted to avoid.'

The model for Indiana Jones was to be Humphrey Bogart in *Treasure of the Sierra Madre*. Although he would be an unscrupulous academic playboy, who financed his work by selling dubiously obtained antiquities, he was still a highly moral figure, with a developed sense of right and wrong, insisted Lucas: 'Steve wanted to make him a lot sleazier at home. He was for a while very anxious to have him be an alcoholic, and I said no.'

They came to an impasse. Then Spielberg suggested the Jones character was 'just like Harrison Ford'. Lucas was completely against hiring anyone who wasn't a new film face:

On the set of The Empire Strikes Back**. From left: director Irvin Kershner, producer Gary Kurtz, executive producer George Lucas and screenwriter Lawrence Kasdan.**

he had already been trying to get Tom Selleck for the part, but had found he couldn't get him out of the contract he had for *Magnum, P.I.* – Selleck had only made a pilot for the programme, but as soon as CBS learned of this high level interest in him, they put the series into their upcoming schedule.

Spielberg eventually talked Lucas into using Ford: there was a phrase he loved to use about the actor that he felt summed up the man and why he fitted the part so perfectly – 'grizzled irrepressibility'. Finally, Lucas went for the idea. (Ford, however, did not immediately understand why he had been especially selected for the role: 'George, the man's a grave-robber!' he told Lucas.)

'Indiana Jones is a college professor – on the one hand, a professor of archaeology, anthropology, and on the other hand, he's sort of a soldier of fortune,' Lucas told *Film Comment* shortly before the picture was released.

He's a sleazy kind of character, who is right on the edge of legality in terms of the ways he acquires things and deals a great deal with the occult. He's really an expert on the occult. Those are the two sides of him that are shown in *Raiders*. They're essential to the story. But Indiana is also a 1930s playboy. He has nights on the town and spends a lot of money.

He doesn't get that from teaching college. The original irony was: here's this college professor. How can he get enough money to live this other life that he's living with all these girls and these fancy cars and furs and stuff? Well, the secret of it is – how he acquires it – is by buying antiquities, which he sells for a great deal of money to museums, and that's to finance his habit.

At this LA story conference, Lucas talked Spielberg and
Kasdan out of their big ideas. The logic was always crucial:
would the audience be able to follow it? 'Films grow compli-
cated and film-makers forget why they're making them,' he
kept insisting to them.

Indiana Jones, it was established, would have two enemies:
a rival French archaeologist and a slimy Nazi. Marion
Ravenwood, the heroine, to be played by Karen Allen (Debra
Winger had been first choice, but was unavailable), was not
far removed from Princess Leia in spirit: self-assured, arro-
gant, and capable of pulling the trigger one last time. It was
Marcia Lucas, however, who spotted that because Marion
disappears from the plot there was no emotional resolution to
the film: this was accordingly corrected.

Apart from that glitch, the plot was exceedingly strong,
again dealing in the same archetypal areas that Lucas had so
effectively mined in *Star Wars*. It was clear who were the
good and who were the bad guys: and in Christian-Judaic
culture there could hardly be a more profoundly resonant
quest than the archaeologist adventurer's search for the Ark
of the Covenant.

The creative package had been put together. Now a financial
deal had to be struck. Hardly a problem, surely? These two
men had, after all, made *American Graffiti*, *Star Wars*, *Jaws*,
and *Close Encounters of the Third Kind*, the most successful
films of all time.

'Let's make a creative deal. Let's go for a deal that will
make history,' George Lucas urged Spielberg. The result was
that every studio except one turned them down. The deal
they were trying to strike was virtually prohibitive. The

studio would put down the $20 million needed to make the
film – originally it had been costed at $7 million, and it
ended up as $22 million. After the money was recouped, it
would be split sixty-forty between Lucas and the studio.
After rentals had reached $50 million, the split would be
fifty-fifty. After $100 million it would be forty-sixty.

Only Michael Eisner at Paramount, spurred on by his
second-in-command Jeffrey Katzenberg, was prepared to go
for Lucas's 'killer deal'. In the end the studio made $49
million in rentals from *Raiders*; Spielberg personally made
$22 million; and Lucasfilm made $21. Its success allowed
Paramount to make a dozen other films.

Having put the movie into motion, Lucas worked on *Raiders*
until it started shooting. He also kept a sharp eye on the
budget, reducing some of Spielberg's more extravagant
requirements: two thousand extras were cut to just six
hundred; a four-engined flying boat became a two-engined
flying boat.

Deciding that he would see the initial shooting was
running smoothly, George Lucas went to Tunisia. But on the
very first day he was so badly sunburned that his skin was
permanently damaged: his face now turns bright red if
exposed to the sun.

Apart from that personal tragedy, filming went smoothly:
Lucas had wanted *Raiders* shot in eighty-five days – speedy
Spielberg had the job done in seventy-three. Perhaps in
the hands of even the hammiest of directors, its subject-
matter alone – essentially, *The Quest for the Holy Grail* –
could have helped to give *Raiders of the Lost Ark* its high
philosophical dimensions. But at his finest, as in *Schindler's*

List, the great populist that is Steven Spielberg can connect with the purest essence of a theme. In *Raiders* every intellectual muscle and intuitive brain cell are at peak tone, honed to perfection by his working partnership with George Lucas. Simple effects are used for simple ideas so effectively that by the end of the film, your belief is utterly suspended and you are carried breathtakingly away by the profundity of the sight of the melting villains choking on their own precious bodily fluids.

'When it was finished, I took over the editing. Spielberg did a first cut, and said, "This is as good as I can make it." I had the film for about a month after that, and I recut it,' said Lucas. All the same, he considered *Raiders of the Lost Ark* ('I think it will be a hit,' he suggested modestly to *Film Comment*) to be a Steven Spielberg film when it is just as much a George Lucas one.

There was an irony here. While Spielberg had hoped to found a Disney-like empire, Lucas had wanted to make his career as a director. But after *Raiders* he described Spielberg as 'the most naturally talented director I've ever met. Whatever talent I have is . . . being in tune with mass sensibility. My talent is not particularly in making films.' In turn, Spielberg described Lucas thus: 'If he wasn't a movie-maker, he'd run a newspaper; he'd be Charles Foster Kane.'

With the success of *The Empire Strikes Back* and *Raiders of the Lost Ark*, which was released in 1981, George Lucas had become the most successful film-maker in the history of motion pictures. The fact that Spielberg's *E.T.*, released the next year, replaced *Star Wars* as the biggest box-office success of all time did little to tarnish this glory.

Furthermore, the gamble of personally financing *The Empire Strikes Back* had paid off. Although it had come close to bankrupting him, it had made George Lucas rich beyond his dreams. And now he started using this money for the purpose for which it had been intended all along.

In Marin County, some thirty miles north of San Francisco's Golden Gate Bridge, George Lucas chose and bought five thousand acres of land. Here, at the end of a mile-long narrow valley with its own creek, he would build Skywalker Ranch, intending it to be his base of operations.

The word 'ranch', with its frontier connotations, was something of a romantic, film world misnomer: it was really a re-created Victorian hamlet of vaguely New England-style cottages and sheds around a multi-turreted mansion. This main house was furnished with extraordinary opulence: expensive antiques, Victorian trimmings, lamps and stained glass were all chosen by Marcia Lucas. With carefully rusted antique farm machinery in its pastures, the premises also had their own old red-brick winery. The winery was built in 1870, Lucas would claim, and the cottages later. Here, however, he was simply creating an elaborate back story for the property, as befitted a man who had contrived an entire new mythology for *Star Wars*: the truth was that, like a Disney frontier ride, the place had been built from scratch. (Not that Lucas always noticed his surroundings or even other individuals: like many creative people, living deep inside his thoughts, he would pass people in corridors and hardly seem to see them.)

On Skywalker Ranch, in fact, there are fourteen fantasy structures concealing a secret movie factory with all the most up-to-date, computerized film-editing and sound equipment that modern film-making has to offer: there is a sound stage, for example, big enough to hold the Los Angeles Philharmonic orchestra. Down the valley are administrative offices, sufficient for 450 staff, an archive building, a games complex with pools, stables, tennis courts, gyms and a child-care room. The creek spills over man-made waterfalls into an artificial lake. In the end, George Lucas was to spend over $60 million on building a property that might be considered to rival Citizen Kane's *Xanadu*.

'I love it,' the producer-director explained to Audie Bock of *Take One* magazine as they sat in the heat of the new Lucasfilm offices in the rambling Victorian house that houses them. 'It reminds me of the Central Valley around Modesto where I grew up – hot, dry heat and nothing but walnut groves. I thrive on it. In fact when we first came to this area to set up American Zoetrope, I wanted to settle in Marin. Francis is more of a city person, so we ended up in San Francisco, but now I'm doing what I always wanted to do.'

Like one of those children who have been brought up by a father who is terrible with money, Lucas had vowed that he would never follow the heartstoppingly catastrophic finan-cial example of Francis Ford Coppola, his mentor. In addi-tion, Lucas had not forgotten that *THX 1138* and *American Graffiti* were taken away from him, and that Fox dogged his heels throughout the making of *Star Wars*. He simply did not trust Hollywood, and wanted to be far from it. Fair and amicable with everyone until wronged, Lucas then would never forgive or forget: sometimes he seemed to think his ability to hold a grudge was some kind of virtue.

Among the many ambitious facilities at his new headquar-ters, such as state-of-the-art film projection equipment, was its library: this contains sounds and clips catalogued according to subject. And the genesis of Skywalker Ranch, Lucas told Bock, went back as far as his first film.

> I cut *THX* in the attic of that house in Mill Valley. One downstairs bedroom had been turned into a sound studio. I would cut during the day and Walter Murch would come in and cut sound effects during the night. Then, when I started to do *Graffiti*, I finally convinced Francis that what he really needed was to buy a house out here we could work at, because I wasn't going to work in the city. So we bought a house, and I cut *Graffiti* there in an apartment over the garage.
>
> After *Graffiti* became a hit, I bought my own big Victorian house, built a screening room in the back, and used it for my base of operations. I made *Star Wars* there and *More American Graffiti*.
>
> Then I decided I would build a new version of it out at the house. Essentially all the ranch is is a big Victorian house that's used as offices. It's got a library and it's got a screening room. It's for writers and for post-production, and eventually the sound-mixing facility will be moved out there.

Anxious to build permanent financial security that didn't depend on the whims of cinema, Lucas had made a decision to use merchandising as a financial foundation from which to diversify into areas separate from film. And he put together a $5 million computer company to pursue the possibilities of what would become digital editing. Taken with video games ever since he had first encountered an onscreen ping-pong tournament, Lucas – years before most other people were alerted to such an idea – was also interested in the possibilities of more sophisticated electronic developments such as multi-media.

But what was all this colossal expense and ingenuity really about? It was so that Lucas's film headquarters at Skywalker Ranch should recreate the atmosphere of his film school days and the consequent creative hothouse of USC: 'Room 108, where we had screenings going on all the time, and then we'd go out in the grassy courtyard and talk about films, share our ideas and help each other with our problems . . . The studio people never go to the movies. Sometimes they're forced to sit through the films they're producing, but basically they don't care about movies. We do. We all went to film school because we love movies, and we know what we need to make them.'

Charles Weber, who was brought in to run the business, persuaded Lucas that the Egg Company, as ILM was facetiously nicknamed, should stay in Los Angeles. But the entire scheme began to be a huge financial strain: in the 1980s, Lucasfilm cost $9 million a year to run. One day Weber suggested that Skywalker Ranch was too great a drain on the company. Lucas saw straightaway that Weber was missing the point. He closed down the LA office and brought some of the employees north. Lucas had regained control of Lucasfilm, whose only constant profit came from merchandising.

8 Return of the Jedi

In his own individual way George Lucas remained true to his first love of film. In 1980, for example, he had persuaded Francis Coppola to join him in executive producing Akira Kurosawa's next picture, *Kagemusha*, and had chivvied Fox to put up half the money to finish the film. *Kagemusha* subsequently won the Palme d'Or at the Cannes Film Festival.

The next year he oversaw Lawrence Kasdan make the steamy film noir thriller *Body Heat*, having first convinced Alan Ladd of the first-time director's talents. Although he was paid $250,000 and given five per cent of its profits, Lucas kept his name off the film – ever the political pragmatist, he was concerned that the decidedly adult content of *Body Heat* could interfere with the more family-orientated mood that surrounded the image and brand name of Lucasfilm.

After all, there was a larger work to be completed: the final film in the *Star Wars* trilogy. Following the success of *Raiders of the Lost Ark*, George Lucas wanted Steven Spielberg to direct the third *Star Wars* film. His friend, however, was unavailable. Irvin Kershner, he had learned early on in the *Empire* shoot, was too intellectual a director, endlessly open to debate about

Remaining true to his love of film throughout his career, Lucas persuaded Francis Coppola to join him in producing Akira Kurosawa's Kagemusha.

the course of the plot and characterization. What Lucas really needed was someone he felt he could control. 'He wanted to hire a director who would be creative,' said Gary Kurtz – who was not entirely unbiased as he had been dumped from the Lucasfilm camp as a sacrificial victim after *Empire* had raced over budget – 'but did everything exactly the way he wanted it.'

Checking out available possibilities, Lucas came across Richard Marquand, a Welshman in his early forties who had been educated at Cambridge university. Marquand had directed a popular television series, *The Search for the Nile*. He had followed it up with *The Legacy*, a loony English-country-house horror film starring Katherine Ross, and *The Eye of the Needle*, a much better Second World War spy thriller starring Donald Sutherland. (In 1985 Marquand was to make a successful modern thriller, the Joe Eszterhas-scripted *Jagged Edge*.) Marquand agreed not only to move his family to California but to give Lucas all access during post-production and during filming. He got the job.

We spent the day together [Lucas told Paul Scanlon in *Rolling Stone* in August 1983]. It's a matter of getting to know the person: his opinions on politics, life, philosophy and religion. All these things will meld in the movie, so his sensibilities have to be consistent with the sensibilities of the *Star Wars* movies . . . I've got to find a director who's willing to give up some of his domain to me and is willing to work with me and accept the fact that he's essentially doing a movie that's been established, that ultimately I'll have the final say . . .

I think, one, he has a great deal of enthusiasm for the project: he liked *Star Wars*. Two, I think he wanted to work with me, which helps. Finally, it's a very good career move for him. Obviously he's going to make an enormous amount of money, and he will be catapulted into the top directors thing and his salary will skyrocket. Then there's that practical side to it, too. It's a good job. It's a two-year job, but it's a good job. It's more than you can say about most movies.

Things had changed: George Lucas wrote the first draft for *Return of the Jedi* in four weeks, but then he asked Lawrence Kasdan to take over on the script. In this third film in the *Star Wars* trilogy would be the resolution of the problems created in the darker second film – the three films in the trilogy may be seen as the three acts that make up a classic Aristotelian drama. Soon Kasdan was locked away in long sessions with Richard Marquand. During a *Jedi* script conference, Lucas told Kasdan: 'The whole emotion I am trying to get at the end of this film is for you to be emotionally and spiritually uplifted and to feel absolutely good about life. That is the greatest thing that we could ever possibly do.'

And the plot emerged: Han Solo is freed by Princess Leia and Luke Skywalker, assisted by Lando Calrissian, from Jabba the Hutt and the carbonite in which he had been frozen; then the three hero figures head for the imperial bunker on the moon of Endor, from where the new Death Star is being controlled. On the way they encounter a new race of creatures, the Ewoks, tree-dwelling teddy bears (Lucas had thought up the idea of cut-down Chewbaccas) who become their allies.

Lucas's quality control never lapsed: only sixty of the hundreds of creatures manufactured at the Monster Factory made it as far as the film. The idea for the Ewoks, Lucas told

With Carrie Fisher on the set of The Return of the Jedi. **'It's as fast as you can make it and still tell a comprehensible story,' said Lucas.**

Scanlon, was 'just a short Wookie . . . they evolved and started getting cute. Dare to be cute. The worst we could do is get criticized for it . . . A lot of people are going to be offended by Ewoks. A lot of people say the films are just an excuse for merchandising: "Lucas just decided to cash in on the teddy bear." Well, it's not a great thing to cash in on, because there are lots of teddy bears marketed, so you don't have anything that's unique. If I were designing something original as a market item, I could probably do a lot better.'

But he made no bones about how essential marketing and merchandising were to Lucasfilm and its subsidiaries: 'We market everything in the movie. That's what keeps funding the other things we do – the computer research and all the other things. Again, people tend to look at merchandising as an evil thing. But ultimately, a lot of fun things come out of it, and at the same time, it pays for the overhead of the company and everybody's salary.'

The three principal characters were all six years older: Harrison Ford argued strongly that Han Solo should die at the end of the film. Lucas would not agree: he felt that it would ruin the ending of what was intended to be a positive film. Wasn't Ford's suggestion an indication that he had outgrown the *Star Wars* films? *Raiders of the Lost Ark* and *Blade Runner*, in which he also starred, had been superior pictures cinematically.

Carrie Fisher, meanwhile, was going through troubled times: she had been in a relationship with the singer-song-writer Paul Simon for seven years before marrying him. Then, after eleven months, the marriage had broken up.

Mark Hamill, meanwhile, had tried in vain to escape

Lucasfilm, discovering that he was so typecast as Luke Skywalker that he was virtually unemployable elsewhere.

Elstree aside, further locations were sought out for the January 1982 beginning of shooting. Buttercup Valley, near Yuma, Arizona, had the right sand dunes for another world. And the giant redwood forest at Crescent City, on the California/Oregon border, became Endor. At the time it was the largest film set ever built on location.

> You look at the Jabba the Hutt scene in *Return of the Jedi* [Lucas told Paul Scanlon] and say, 'Oh, that's what he wanted the cantina in *Star Wars* to be.' Or you look at the end battle, and you say, 'Oh, that's what the end battle was supposed to be in the first one.' But we couldn't have done this movie then. I mean, it just was not humanly possible or even financially possible. So a lot of these things I have finally worked out. I finally got the end battle the way I wanted it, I got the ground battle that I wanted, I got the monsters the way I wanted them.

During the making of *Star Wars*, Lucas's constant refrain on the film's aesthetics had been 'Faster – more intense.' On *Return of the Jedi* – known for some time as *Revenge of the Jedi* – this philosophy would seem to have reached fulfilment: the pace of *Return of the Jedi* is far closer to that of *Raiders of the Lost Ark* than to that of *Star Wars* or *The Empire Strikes Back*. In the *Star Wars* space battle the ships move slowly, continuity is virtually non-existent, and there are never more than two or three ships in a shot: in *Return of the Jedi* the storm of fighter aircraft is constructed from sixty-seven layers of film. 'It's as fast as

you can make it and still tell a comprehensible story,' said
Lucas to Scanlon. '*Jedi* is almost incomprehensible in
certain areas. It's designed more for kids. It's sort of natural
to the way I feel about things. I think it's the most emotional
of the three films; at least it is for me. The end of a story,
where everything comes together, is always the most
emotional part.' And of that final battle in *Return of the Jedi*,
he said to Scanlon:

> It was designed for all the stories to come together.
> Stylistically, all the films are designed to have a big climax,
> and this one's sort of got everything in it. When we started,
> we said, 'Okay, now we're gonna do it the way we always
> wanted to do it. We've got the money, we've got the knowl-
> edge – this is it.'. . .
>
> Whatever little event in history that *Star Wars* is going to
> be, at least it's done. If people want to look at it, they can
> look at the whole piece. That dumb screenplay I first wrote
> ten years ago is at least finished. It's all in a movie now. I was
> always contemplating rewriting the story, making it into more,
> because it was originally written as just a simple thing. It
> wasn't meant to be the giant phenomenon it turned out to
> be. You say, 'Well, now is this gonna live up to the phenom-
> enon?' But I ultimately decided to stick with it and say, 'Look,
> that was the way it was written ten years ago, and this is
> where I was coming from. If it's not good enough, then tough
> luck.' You have to sort of have that attitude. For better or
> worse, I like it.

Released 25 May 1983, six years to the day after *Star Wars*,
Return of the Jedi showed that the phenomenon indicated no

signs of waning. Queues began forming eight days before *Jedi* opened. It proved to be even more successful than *The Empire Strikes Back*, becoming the third most successful film of all time, behind *Star Wars* and *E.T.*

But the film did not have unanimously favourable reviews. The New York critics were split: ten in favour, seven against, with those against, such as Pauline Kael, branding it a merchandising vehicle; or insisting that the human actors were overwhelmed by special effects. All the same, there was the usual rush of figures that accompanied the release of a *Star Wars* movie: on 25 May the film set an opening-day record of $6.2 million; the following Sunday it established a single-day record of $8.4 million; in week one *Return of the Jedi* pulled in $45.3 million; by mid-June it had grossed $70 million.

In that August 1983 interview with Paul Scanlon in *Rolling Stone*, Lucas had spoken in glowing terms of his relationship with Marcia Lucas: 'Being married to somebody in the film business helps. She worked on this film, and she worked on a number of the other films. There's a collaboration; we'd never have been able to survive otherwise. I don't know that many people in the film business who have managed to make it work. It's been very hard on Marcia, living with somebody who is constantly in agony, uptight and worried, off in never-never land.'

As is so often the case with event-pegged publicity, the interview had been conducted in advance of the premiere of *Return of the Jedi*. In the film Luke Skywalker works out what may loosely be termed as his 'father problem' – in other words, George Lucas' 'father problem'. But there was a sad irony to this: for in so doing had Lucas been neglecting any similar difficulties he had experienced with his female archetype?

A week after *Return of the Jedi* was released, Lucas held a staff meeting at Skywalker Ranch. With tears in his eyes, he announced that he and Marcia were to divorce.

9 Doom, Crusade and Star Wars to Come

His divorce sent George Lucas into 'a seven-year tailspin', as he later admitted to the *New York Times*. Although Lucasfilm and its associated companies were not affected by the resulting settlement with Marcia, he lost much of his personal fortune. *Star Wars*, however, had given him one of the definitive American movie empires, by now seemingly unstoppable in its snowballing course.

Although he had intended to take a two-year sabbatical after the completion of the *Star Wars* trilogy ('Suddenly my life is going to be mine. It's not going to be owned by Luke Skywalker and his friends,' he had declared to Paul Scanlon), the crisis in his personal life pushed him back into work. Even before *Return of the Jedi* hit the screens, he had been location scouting in Sri Lanka with Steven Spielberg, preparatory to setting up the shoot for the film that would become known as *Indiana Jones and the Temple of Doom*. For this movie the script had been written by Lucas' old friends Willard Huyck and Gloria Katz, who had put a final spin on the *Star Wars* dialogue and turned in a final draft of *American Graffiti*. Fearful that Spielberg might back out of his commitment to direct the movie, Lucas had impressed upon them the need to get a script to him as fast as possible.

Like the second *Star Wars* film, this second of what had become a planned *Indiana Jones* trilogy was – at Lucas's urging – by far the darkest of the three movies. Released in 1984, it was another enormous hit. Perhaps, as the critic David Thomson has suggested, Lucas's work was becoming a testament to the principle that American pictures are produced, not directed.

Like Woody Allen, the man who kicked *Star Wars* into touch with *Annie Hall* during the Academy Awards in 1978, George Lucas is never satisfied with a film that he has finished, and for the same reasons: he has always thought that it could have been so much more, that there was always a significant gap between the original idea and what finally appeared. But in this expression of discontent, Lucas is uttering a mythical tale of his own: the artist's quest for perfection, for the matching of the idea and its expression. 'Each film has accomplishments that I like. It's not that I didn't like the movies, but that if I look at them now, each one falls a bit short of what I had hoped it to be – because I guess I either set my sights a little bit lower, or we actually do get a little bit better.'

Whatever he may have thought of the films (and television series) he was about to release, Lucas' beliefs were about to be tested. Lucasfilm was now as financially secure as it could hope to be – although, allowing for the exigencies of box-office fate, this might mean very little. But none of the films it would produce for the next five years would come anywhere close to the epic box-office standards established by the *Star Wars* and *Indiana Jones* series.

Much of the time, however, it seemed Lucas would hardly expect them to, and that he was simply paying respect to other fine film artists, as with Paul Schrader's *Mishima: A Life in Four Chapters* in 1985 and his mentor Haskell Wexler's *Latino* the same year. The next year brought *Howard the Duck*, directed by Willard Huyck and a financial flop. But 1988 saw Lucasfilm sponsoring Godfrey Reggio's wonderful, innovative, determinedly uncommercial *Powaqqatsi*; and Francis Coppola's inspired but fiscally doomed *Tucker: The Man and His Dream*, the story of the man who took on the might of the Motown automobile manufacturers. 'I've dealt with things like *Tucker*, which, in terms of connecting with an audience, don't work, but I've never made a movie I'm not happy with,' Lucas stated in a biographical television programme in the BBC's *Omnibus* series.

'George', Coppola informed the same programme, 'was one of the most talented American film directors of that time and somehow, because of *Star Wars*, we were deprived of those movies he was going to make. Instead, we have an enormous industrial marketing complex.'

Faring far better at the box office that year for Lucasfilm was Ron Howard's *Willow*, which re-worked many of the mythological themes of the *Star Wars* trilogy. 'There were definitely some parallels between some of the characters and situations of *Star Wars* and *Willow*,' said Howard, 'and I was working against that. But it wasn't a problem, because the *Star Wars* characters weren't really original either – they were an acknowledgement and all he had done was put them in this sci-fi world. And all we were doing was creating this world of magic and sword and sorcery.'

On *American Graffiti*, Lucas remembered, Ron Howard was never without an 8mm camera: 'He was always running around taking movies of us making the movie and saying how he was going to film school and become a director . . . These films, I think, deal with some very important issues of today – Good versus Evil, how to conduct yourself in society . . . It's just that they're not talking about them directly. *Willow* is about people and ideas. The underlying issues, the psychological motives are the same as in all my movies: personal responsibility and friendship, the importance of living a compassionate life as opposed to a passionate or selfish life. These issues are, I think, very relevant to what you can be today.'

It was down to *Indiana Jones and the Last Crusade*, the third film in the series, to return Lucasfilm to the world of box-office smashes. In this film, in which Jones is joined by his father, played by Sean Connery, the quest continues for the Holy Grail, with evil Nazis again the enemy. Superior to the second movie, the film was arguably a match for *Raiders of the Lost Ark*.

Spielberg defined his mission perfectly, interlocking his personal skills with those of ILM's special-effects department. Visually, the film was extraordinary: the apparently impossible shot of a German gunner flying in locked focus towards the camera; the extraordinary scene, stripped down to symbolic essentials, in which our resourceful hero battles a tank from horseback; the Leap of Faith in which the ledge across an immense ravine is hidden by spatial distortion.

What is remarkable about the completion of the first *Star Wars* trilogy is that George Lucas could have had the ambition, the steely determination and the nerve to conceive and carry it out.

'The three movies were originally one idea, one big story, one screenplay – a 300-page script, a six-hour-and-fifteen-minute movie,' he said. 'The first one is a very elaborate introduction of the characters. The second obviously sets everything up, and the third is the one that pays it off.'

Despite the colossal scale of his ambition, Lucas had played it all along one step at a time.

You know, *Star Wars* was a success, but I didn't have any idea then what was going on. I didn't know whether I was even going to be able to make the next two films. I had taken two-thirds of the original script and thrown it away. In my mind, I was saying, 'Gee, if this is really a big hit, then I can make a movie out of all the early material that I developed.' *Empire* and *Jedi* were what that first film was supposed to be. And after that, I can tell another story about what happens to Luke after this trilogy ends. All the prequel stories exist: where Darth Vader came from, the whole story about Darth and Ben Kenobi, and it all takes place before Luke was born. The other one – what happens to Luke afterwards – is much more ethereal. I have a tiny notebook full of notes on that. If I'm really ambitious, I could proceed to figure out what would have happened to Luke.

But, George Lucas said, he would only make the prequel films if they could be made more cheaply and simply. 'I couldn't afford to make another like *Jedi*. I wouldn't take the risk. Inflation in films is astronomical . . . I think if we started the next series, we would probably try to do all three of them at once.'

And then . . . *Nothing!*

Or so it seemed. In fact, Lucas was quietly active all the time, through ILM his influence on contemporary cinema larger than when he was making and releasing the *Star Wars* and *Indiana Jones* trilogy: *Jurassic Park*, for example, being dependent on Industrial Light and Magic. And it was only after ILM showed they could render a credible tornado that a studio backed *Twister*.

In fact, at first directly through his own work and then via the unparalleled efficiency and influence of ILM, George Lucas has dictated for two decades the essential broad notion of what is cinema. The list of hits – films that could not have otherwise existed – with which ILM is associated is staggering and shows the full influence of George Lucas on modern cinema. It includes *Ghost*, *Terminator 2: Judgement Day*, *E.T.*, *Poltergeist*, the *Star Trek* series, *Out of Africa*, *The Money Pit*, *Labyrinth*, *The Golden Child*, *The Witches of Eastwick*, *Empire of the Sun*, *Who Framed Roger Rabbit?*, *The Last Temptation of Christ*, *Field of Dreams*, *Ghostbusters II*, *The Abyss*, *Back to the Future II* and *III*, *Always*, Akira Kurosawa's *Dreams*, *The Hunt for Red October*, *Die Hard 2*, *The Godfather III*, *The Doors*, *Backdraft*, *The Rocketeer* and *Hook*.

Special effects and narrative had become inextricably interwoven, the effects becoming part of the content. And ILM had become an intriguing blend of aesthetic impact and business success. George Lucas himself said, 'Special effects are just a tool . . . without a story, it's a pretty boring thing.

In 1996 an announcement came forth from Lucasfilm headquarters: the next year production would begin, at the new Millennium Studios in Leavesden, Hertfordshire, on the

The 'restored' version of The Return of the Jedi**, released as a special edition with** Star Wars **and** The Empire Strikes Back**, in 1997. All three films had digitally cut footage and scenes added.**

three *Star Wars* prequel films. From 1999 onwards these
would appear at two-yearly intervals. Tellingly, we were
told that Pepsi-Cola would finance them to the tune of
roughly $2 billion.

What was more, the original *Star Wars* trilogy would be re-
released from January 1997 onwards; this 'special edition'
would have had cut footage digitally restored and, in certain
(albeit minor) cases, scenes added.

By the time this re-cut version began to appear, the *Star
Wars* trilogy already had earned $1.3 billion (mind you, this
was less than half the $3 billion it had brought in from
merchandising). The whims and fancies of succeeding years,
however, meant that it was now a long while since *Star Wars*
had been the top-earning picture of all time. On that opening weekend at the end of January 1997, however, Luke
Skywalker and his friends once again turned everything on
their head: the first weekend's box-office take was over $36
million (Lucas had predicted something in the $10 million
range), and by the time it ended its run, *Star Wars* was once
again the biggest earning film of all time – twenty years after
its first release. (Although even in the market-led 1990s we
always had to bear in mind that commercial success was not
an *ipso facto* guarantee of quality. 'No matter how many
billions of dollars *Star Wars* can earn, and no matter how
valuable that franchise, it isn't worth a tenth of what he's
worth and capable of doing as an artist,' said Francis Ford
Coppola, the controversial artist to the last, commenting on
the course of his friend's career.)

'The prequels will be a much darker and more complex set
of films,' announced Rick McCallum, their producer. 'They
hinge around the story of Anakim Skywalker, who is Darth

Vader. And we meet Anakim as a young boy, and we watch him become a Jedi knight, and watch him meet Obi-Wan, who becomes his mentor. But much more importantly, all of these films lead up to that crisis point in his life when he chooses the dark side.'

'You actually get the full story,' said Lucas to *Omnibus* about the prequel, 'and you're able to see them in context and you understand Vader's side of the story, which you haven't heard yet. Ultimately, with *Star Wars* the big chance I'm taking is I'm working on something I started on twenty years ago, and whether it will fit into the modern world marketing-wise I don't know. Fortunately I'm in the position where I don't have to worry too much.'

THE

REVIEWS

THX 1138

March 17, 1971

Abstract, handsomely stylistic but sluggish sci-fi drama about future enslavement by computer. Nixed b.o. at present, but could become a future buff class. Hollywood, March 9. (COLOR)

Warner Bros. release of an American Zoetrope production; executive producer, Francis Ford Coppola; produced by Lawrence Sturhahn. Directed by George Lucas. Screenplay, Lucas, Walter Murch, from a Lucas story; camera (Technicolor), Dave Meyers, Albert Kihn; editor, Lucas; music, Lalo Schifrin; art direction, Michael Haller; sound, Murch, Lou Yates, Jim Manson. Reviewed at Loews Hollywood, L.A., March 8, '71. (MPAA Rating: PG.) Running Time, 88 MINS.)

THX 1138	Robert Duvall
SEN	Donald Pleasence
SRT	Don Pedro Colley
LUH	Maggie McOmie
PTO	Ian Wolfe
NCH	Sid Haig
TWA	Marshall Efron
DWY	John Pearce
Police Robots	Johnny Weismuller, Jr.,
	Robert Feero
IMM	Irene Forrest
ELC	Claudette Bessing

"THX 1138" is a psychedelic science fiction horror story about some future civilization regimented into computer-programmed slavery. Likely not to be an artistic or commercial success in its own time, the American Zoetrope (Francis Ford Coppola) group production just might in time become a classic of stylistic, abstract cinema. Story has some disturbingly plausible overtones, but only a portion of the esoteric audience may turn onto the Warner Bros. release at this time. Heavy exploitation may yield mixed results.

Film is a feature-length expansion of George Lucas' student film which won kudos some three years ago. In that brief form, the story of one man's determination to crash out of his wordly prison was exciting; the expansion by director-editor Lucas with Walter Murch succeeds in fleshing out the environment, but falls behind in constructing a plot line to sustain interest. Robert Duvall heads cast as the defector after his mate Maggie McOmie is programmed into the cell of Donald Pleasence, a corrupt computer technician. Don Pedro Colley is another fugitive, who helps Duvall reach his freedom. Dave Meyers and Albert Kihn photographed superbly the extremely handsome futuristic physical values designed by Michael Haller. Lalo Schifrin's score is outstanding. Murch is credited with the excellent sound montages which blend some familiar recorded-announcement cliches with the low-key terror of an Orwellian "Alice In Wonderland", where drug use and sexual suppression are mandatory, and the major crimes are drug evasion and sex relations. With political paternalism rampant at both extremes of the spectrum, Lucas is onto something. In any case, we'll know for sure in about a generation.

Murf.

AMERICAN GRAFFITI

June 20, 1973

Outstanding evocation of '50s teenagers, told with humor and heart. Strong outlook. Hollywood, June 16. (COLOR)

Universal Pictures release, produced by Francis Ford Coppola; co-producer, Gary Kurtz. Directed by George Lucas. Screenplay, Lucas, Gloria Katz, Willard Huyck; camera (Technicolor), Haskell Wexler; editors, Verna Fields, Marcia Lucas; music supervision, Karin Green; art direction, Dennis Clark; set decoration, Douglas Freeman; sound, Walter Murch, Arthur Rochester; asst. director, Ned Kopp. Reviewed at Directors' Guild of America, L.A., June 15, '73. (MPAA Rating: PG.) Running Time: 109 MINS.

Curt	Richard Dreyfuss
Steve	Ronny Howard
John	Paul Le Mat
Terry	Charlie Martin Smith
Laurie	Cindy Williams
Debbie	Candy Clark
Carol	Mackenzie Phillips
Disc Jockey	Wolfman Jack
Bob Falfa	Harrison Ford
Gang Members	Bo Hopkins, Manuel Padilla Jr., Beau Gentry
Rock Band	Flash Cadillac and the Continental Kids
Teacher	Terry McGovern
Policeman	Jim Bohan
Wendy	Debbie Celiz
Blonde in Car	Suzanne Somers
Vagrant	George Meyer
Thief	James Cranna
Liquor Store Clerk	William Niven

Of all the youth-themed nostalgia films in the past couple of years, George Lucas' "American Graffiti" is among the very best to date. Set in 1962 but reflecting the culmination of the '50s, the film is a most vivid recall of teenage attitudes and mores, told with outstanding empathy and compassion through an exceptionally talented cast of relatively new players. The Universal release, filmed in small towns north of San Francisco, is first-rate Americana which should strike its most responsive chord among audiences of 40 years of age and under, though older filmgoers certainly should enjoy it also.

Francis Ford Coppola was the nominal producer, and Gary Kurtz was co-producer. The superior original screenplay, in which the predominant comedy values are deftly supported by underlying serious elements of adolescent maturation, was written by director Lucas in collaboration with Gloria Katz and Willard Huyck. This is Lucas' second feature; his first, "THX 1138," was a futuristic socio-political drama, not quite the total fantasy many might have thought it to be.

"American Graffiti" occupies that very lonely ground between the uptight misunderstood teenage mellers of its era, and the beach-party fluff on which American International held the only successful patents. Its milieu is the accumulated junk and materialism of the Eisenhower years, an endowment of tin theology and synthetic values which, in younger generations, sowed the seeds of an incoherent unrest that would mature violently a decade later.

Design consultant Al Locatelli, art director Dennis Clark and set director

Douglas Freeman have brilliantly reconstructed the fabric and texture of the time, while Walter Murch's outstanding sound collage – an unending stream of early rock platter hits – complements in the aural department. "Visual consultant" (read: cameraman) Haskell Wexler has done an excellent job in capturing the mood, refreshingly devoid of showoff lensing gimmicks. Even the limitations of the now-rarely used Techniscope anamorphic process contribute an artful touch of grainy, sweaty reality.

Against this chrome and neon backdrop is told the story of one long summer night in the lives of four school chums: Richard Dreyfuss, on his last night before leaving for an eastern college; Ronny Howard, less willing to depart the presence of Cindy Williams; Charlie Martin Smith, a bespectacled fumbler whose misadventures with pubescent swinger Candy Clark are as touching as they are hilarious; and Paul Le Mat, 22 years old on a birth certificate but still strutting as he did four years earlier.

Mackenzie Phillips, in real life the 12-year-old daughter of composer John Phillips, is sensational in film debut as a likeable brat whom Le Mat cannot shake from his car. Harrison Ford is a hot-rodder whose drag-race challenge to Le Mat provides a discreetly violent climax to the story's restless night. Bo Hopkins leads a gang of toughs, and longtime deejay Wolfman Jack is heard regularly on the sound collage, and appears briefly in a scene with Dreyfuss.

There is brilliant interplaying, and underplaying, of script, performers and direction which will raise howls of laughter from audiences, yet never descends

on the screen to overdone mugging, pratfall and other heavy-handed devices normally employed. Some petting scenes get their point across without the patronizing voyeurisms so often found in nostalgia pix. The filmmakers' hearts obviously were with their characters all the way. Lucas has done a truly masterful job.

Murch's sound track uses about 40 platter hits, not all of which were precisely contemporaneous but no harm done. Film opens with Bill Hayley's "Rock Around The Clock," which serves Lucas as well now as it did Richard Brooks in 1955 in that never-to-be-forgotten whammo main title of "The Blackboard Jungle." Karin Green was music coordinator. Kim Fowley produced the two original recordings for the film, done by Flash Cadillac and The Continental Kids, playing a local rock band engaged for a freshman hop.

In such a meritorious filmmaking ensemble, lots more people contributed: hair stylists Gerry Leetch and Betty Iverson; editors (to 109 minutes) Verna Fields and Marcia Lucas; operating cameramen Ron Eveslage and Jan D'Alquen; costume designer Aggie Guerard Rodgers; choreographer Tony Basil; production sound recorder Arthur Rochester; sound editor James Nelson; and casting supervisors Fred Roos and Mike Fenton.

Without exception, all players fit perfectly into the concept and execution, and all the young principals and featured players have a bright and lengthy future. And so does Lucas. "American Graffiti" is one of those rare films which can be advanced in any discussion of the superiority of films over live perfor-mances; the latter can vary from show to show, but if you get it right on film, you've got it forever.

Murf.

STAR WARS

May 25, 1977

Outstanding adventure-fantasy. All-age appeal. Huge outlook. Hollywood, May 19. (COLOR)

Twentieth Century-Fox release, produced by Gary Kurtz. Written and directed by George Lucas, Camera (Technicolor; prints by Deluxe), Gilbert Taylor; second unit camera, Carroll Ballard, Rick Clemente, Robert Dalva, Tak Fujimoto; editors, Paul Hirsch, Marcia Lucas, Richard Chew; music, John Williams; production design, John Barry; art direc-tion, Norman Reynolds, Leslie Dilley; set decoration, Roger Christian; sound (Dolby), Don McDougal, Bob Minkler, Ray West, Mike Minkler, Les Fresholtz, Richard Portman, Derek Ball, Stephen Katz; costumes-wardrobe, John Mollo, Ron Beck; stunt coordinator, Peter Diamond. Reviewed at 20th-Fox Studios, L.A., May 19, 1977 (MPAA rating: PG.) Running time: 121 MINS.
Additional Production Credits

Special photographic effects supervisor, John Dykstra; special production and mechanical effects supervisor, John Stears; production supervisor, Robert Watts; production illustration, Ralph McQuarrie; special dialogue and sound effects, Ben Burtt; sound editors, Sam Shaw, Robert R. Rutledge, Gordon Davidson, Gene Corso.

Miniature And Optical Effects Credits

First camera, Richard Edlund; composite optical photography, Robert Blalack (Praxis); optical photography, Paul Roth; animation and rotoscope design, Adam Beckett; stop-motion animation, Jon Berg, Philip Tippet.

Luke Skywalker...................Mark Hamill

Han Solo...........................Harrison Ford

Princess Organa [sic]..........Carrie Fisher

Grand Moff Tarkin.............Peter Cushing

Ben Kenobi......................Alec Guinness

C3PO............................Anthony Daniels

R2D2..................................Kenny Baker

Chewbacca.......................Peter Mayhew

Lord Darth Vader..............David Prowse

Uncle Owen Lars...................Phil Brown

Aunt Beru Lars................Shelagh Fraser

Chief Jawa..............................Jack Purvis

Rebel Generals..............Alex McCrindle,

....Eddie Byrne

Imperial Military Chiefs .Don Henderson,

...Richard LeParmentier, Leslie Schofield

Rebels ....Drewe Henley, Dennis

Lawson, Garrick Hagon, Jack Klaff,

William Hootkins, Angus McInnis, Jeremy

Sinden, Graham Ashley

"Star Wars" is a magnificent film. George Lucas set out to make the biggest possible adventure-fantasy out of his memories of serials and older action epics, and he has succeeded brilliantly. Lucas and producer Gary Kurtz assembled an enormous technical crew, drawn from the entire Hollywood production pool of talent, and the results equal the genius of Walt Disney, Willis O'Brien and other justifiably famous practitioners of what Irwin Allen calls "movie magic." The 20th-Fox release is also loaded with boxoffice magic, with potent appeal across the entire audience spectrum.

The story is an engaging space adventure which takes itself seriously while occasionally admitting an affectionate poke at the genre. The most immediate frame of reference is a Flash Gordon film, but it's more than that; it's an Errol Flynn escapist adventure, and befitting that, composer John Williams and orchestrator Herbert W. Spencer have supplied a rousing score worthy of Korngold and Steiner.

Like a breath of fresh air, "Star Wars" sweeps away the cynicism that has in recent years obscured the concepts of valor, dedication and honor. Make no mistake – this is by no means a "children's film" with all the derogatory overtones that go with that description. This is instead a superior example of what only the screen can achieve, and closer to home, it is another affirmation of what only Hollywood can put on a screen.

In casting his principals, Lucas chose three not-so-familiar faces, all young, talented and designed to make the story one of people, not of garish gadgetry. The superb balance of technology and human drama is one of the many achievements; one identifies with the characters and accepts, as do they, the intriguing intergalactic world in which they live.

Carrie Fisher, previously in a small role in "Shampoo," is delightful as the regal, but spunky princess on a rebel planet who has been kidnapped by Peter Cushing, would-be ruler of the universe. Mark Hamill, previously a tv player, is excellent as a farm boy who sets out to rescue Fisher in league with Alec Guinness, last survivor of a band of noble knights. Harrison Ford, previously in Lucas' "American Graffiti" and Francis Coppola's "The Conversation," is outstanding as a likeable mercenary pilot who joins our friends with his pal Peter Mayhew, a quasi-monkey creature with blue eyes whom Fisher calls "a walking rug."

Both Guinness and Cushing bring the right measure of majesty to their opposite characters. One of Cushing's key aides is David Prowse, destined to a fatal duel with Guinness, with whom he shares mystical powers. Prowse's face is never seen, concealed as it is behind frightening black armor. James Earl Jones, unbilled, provides a note of sonorous menace as Prowse's voice, Anthony Daniels and Kenny Baker play a Mutt-and-Jeff team of kooky robots.

The heroes and the heavies joust through an exciting series of confrontations, replete with laser guns and other futuristic equipment, building suspense towards the climactic destruction of Cushing's war-mongering planet. Several chase and escape sequences are likely to stimulate spontaneous audience applause.

Lucas is no credit hog, and all contributions are acknowledged on the end titles, bearing all the names listed above as well as assistants in various categories. The film opens after the 20th logo, with the type of receding crawl that Flash Gordon fans will recognize. Locations in Tunisia, Death Valley, Guatemala and Africa were utilized, and interiors were shot at EMI's British studios where the terrific score was also recorded. But the technical effects work was all done here. Technicolor did the production color work, and DeLuxe the prints. Use of Dolby sound enhances the overall impact.

Lucas' first feature, "THX-1138," was also futuristic in tone, but there the story emphasis was on machines controlling man. But in "Star Wars" the people remain the masters of the hardware, thereby strik-

ing a more resonant note of empathy and hope. This is the kind of film in which an audience, first entertained, can later walk out feeling good all over.

Murf.

MORE AMERICAN GRAFFITI

July 25, 1979

Ambitious sequel over-reaches itself, to boxoffice detriment. Hollywood, July 19. (COLOR)

A Universal Pictures release of a Lucasfilm Ltd. production. Produced by Howard Kazanjian. Exec producer, George Lucas. Directed by B.W.L. Norton. Features entire cast. Screenplay, Norton, based on characters created by Lucas, Gloria Katz, Willard Huyck; camera (Technicolor), Caleb Deschanel; editor, Tina Hirsch; art direction, Ray Storey; sound (Dolby Stereo), David McMillan; costume design, Agnes Rodgers; set decoration, Doug Van Koss: assistant director, Thomas Lofaro. Reviewed at Goldwyn Theatre, BevHills. July 19. '79. (MPAA Rating: PG) Running time: 111 MINS.

Debbie Dunham	Candy Clark
Little Joe	Bo Hopkins
Steve Bolander	Ron Howard
John Milner	Paul Le Mat
Carol/Rainbow	Mackenzie Phillips
Terry The Toad	Charles Martin Smith
Laurie Bolander	Cindy Williams
Eva	Anna Bjorn
Major Creech	Richard Bradford
Ralph	John Brent
Newt	Scott Glenn
Sinclair	James Houghton
Lance	John Lansing
Beckwith	Ken Place
Teensa	Mary Kay Place
Andy Henderson	Will Seltzer
Felix	Ralph Wilcox

"More American Graffiti" may be one of the most innovative and ambitious films of the last five years, but by no means is it one of the most successful. In trying to follow the success of George Lucas' immensely popular 1973 hit, writer-director B.W.L. Norton overloads the sequel with four wholly different cinematic styles to carry forward the lives of "American Graffiti's" original cast. Initial returns should be very strong, on title lure alone, but repeat biz looks to be shallow.

While dazzling to the eye, the flirtation with split-screen, anamorphic, 16m and 1:85 screen sizes does not justify itself in terms of the film's content. What Norton and producer Howard Kazanjian are attempting, and what a variety of technicians pull off flawlessly, is daring, but ultimately pointless.

There's a lot going on in "More American Graffiti", as Norton takes the characters (minus a few exceptions) created by Lucas, Gloria Katz and Willard Huyck, and advances them two, three, four and five years into their future.

Paul Le Mat's still rooted in the early '60s, drag-racing and pursuing an Icelandic beauty (Anna Bjorn) with whom he's no more successful in communicating than he was in the original with Mackenzie Phillips. Charles Martin Smith and Bo Hopkins are assigned to a helicopter unit in Vietnam, while Candy Clark and Phillips have gone the flower power route in San Francisco. As expected, Ron Howard and Cindy Williams have married.

Part of Norton's presumed goal, of course, is to show how the 1960s fractured and split apart, and that the cohesiveness that marked Lucas' (and the participants' lives) film is now dissipated, as characters branch out, and in some instances, are snuffed out.

But without a dramatic glue to hold the disparate story elements together, "Graffiti" is too disorganized for its own good, and the cross-cutting between different film styles only accentuates the problem.

Otherwise, Lucasfilm Ltd. has amassed an extraordinary cast and crew that succeeds in almost snatching victory from the jaws of defeat. The aural counterpoint via period recordings that virtually changed the conception of film soundtracks is again employed to excellent, if more downbeat, effect by music editor Gene Finley, supervising sound editor Ben Burtt and re-recordist Bill Varney, Steve Maslow and Greg Landaker.

Work of cinematographer Caleb Deschanel, and optical coordinators Peter Donen, and Bill Lindemann, is extraordinary in meshing the four film sizes, which are beautifully handled in effortless segues. Especially noteworthy are the Vietnam sequences, filmed in Central California, and almost as impressive as some of the "Apocalypse Now" footage.

Smith tops the performers as the likeable klutz, unable to get himself wounded and sent home even in the midst of the Vietnam War. Clark carries off her psychedelic scenes with panache, and Howard and Williams sparkle as the young marrieds force to confront a changing society.

Bjorn is terrif as Le Mat's uncomprehending Venus, and Le Mat himself shows remarkable continuity in characterization, especially after a six-year layoff. Supporting players are uniformly well-chosen, with Scott Glenn and Ralph Wilcox very good as rock band members.

Mary Kay Place as Bjorn's girlfriend, and Ralph Place as Le Mat's competitive buddy. Richard Dreyfuss, only cast principal not to return, is sorely missed, but Harrison Ford shows up in an unbilled cameo as a motorcycle cop. Phillips, one of the first film's most delightful characters, gets short shrift in this version.

Rest of thesping and tech work is all more than acceptable, but doesn't help. "More American Graffiti" offers conclusive proof that in the case of sequels, less can be more.

Poll.

THE EMPIRE STRIKES BACK

May 14, 1980

The Force Is Still With It. Hollywood, May 7. (COLOR)

A 20th Century-Fox release, produced by Gary Kurtz. Exec producer, George Lucas. Directed by Irvin Kershner. Screenplay, Leigh Brackett and Lawrence Kasdan, based on story by Lucas; camera (Rank Film Color/DeLuxe prints), Peter Suschitzky; editor, Paul Hirsch; sound (Dolby Stereo), Peter Sutton; special visual effects, Brian Johnson, Richard Edlund; associate producers, Robert Watts, James Bloom; art direction, Leslie Dilley, Harry Lange, Alan Tomkins; set decoration, Michael Ford; make-up and special creature design, Stuart Freeborn; costumes, John Mollo; design consultant, Ralph McQuarrie; music, John Williams. Reviewed at 20th Century-Fox, May 7, 1980. (MPAA rating: PG) Running time: 124 MINS.

Luke Skywalker	Mark Hamill
Hans Solo	Harrison Ford
Princess Leia	Carrie Fisher
Darth Vader	David Prowse
C3PO	Anthony Daniels
Chewbacca	Peter Mayhew
R2-D2	Kenny Baker
Yoda	Frank Oz
Lando Calrissian	Billy Dee Williams
Ben Kenobi	Alec Guinness

Other cast: Jeremy Bulloch, John Hollis, Jack Purvis, Des Webb, Kathryn Mullen, Clive Revill, Kenneth Colley, Julian Glover, Michael Sheard, Michael Culver, John Dicks, Milton Johns, Mark Jones, Oliver Maguire, Robin Scobey, Bruce Boa, Christopher Malcolm, Dennis Lawson, Richard Oldfield, John Morton, Ian Liston, John Ratzenberger, Jack McKenzie, Jerry Harte, Norman Chancer, Norwich Duff, Ray Hassett, Brigitte Kahn, Burnell Tucker.

Additional Production Credits

Production supervisor, Bruce Sharman; studio second-unit direction, Harley Cokliss, John Barry; studio second-unit camera, Chris Menges; location second-unit direction, Peter MacDonald; location second-unit camera, Geoff Glover; assistant directors, David Tomblin, Dominic Fulford, Bill Westley, Ola Solum; mechanical effects supervision, Nick Allder; sound design, Ben Burtt.

Miniature and Optical Effects Unit Credits

Effects photography, Dennis Muren; optical photography, Bruce Nicholson; art direction-visual effects, Joe Johnston; stop motion animation, Jon Berg, Phil Tippet; matte painting, Harrison Ellenshaw; model maker, Lorne Peterson; animation and rotoscope, Peter Kuran; visual effects editing. Conrad Buff.

"The Empire Strikes Back" is a worthy sequel to "Star Wars," equal in both technical mastery and characterization, suffering only from the familiarity with the effects generated in the original and imitated too much by others. Only boxoffice question is how many earthly trucks it will take to carry the cash to the bank.

From the first burst of John Williams' powerful score and the receding opening title crawl, we are back in pleasant surroundings and anxious for a good time – like walking through the front gate of Disneyland, where good and evil are never confused and the righteous will always win.

This is exec producer George Lucas' world. Though he has turned the director's chair over to the capable Irvin Kershner and his typewriter to Leigh Brackett and Lawrence Kasdan, there are no recognizable deviations from the path marked by Lucas and producer Gary Kurtz.

Having already introduced their principal players, the filmmakers now have a chance to round them out, assisted again by good performances from Mark Hamill, Harrison Ford and Carrie Fisher. And even the ominous Darth Vader (David Prowse) is fleshed with new – and surprising – motivations. Killed in the original, Alec Guinness is limited to ghostly cameo.

Responding, too, to the audience's obvious affection for the non-human sidekicks, "Empire" makes full use of Chewbacca (Peter Mayhew), C3PO (Anthony Daniels) and R2D2 (Kenny Baker). Among the new characters, Billy Dee Williams gets a good turn as a duplicitous but likeable villain-ally and Frank Oz is fascinating as sort of a guru for the Force. How this dwarfish character was created and made to seem so real is a wonder, but it's only one of many visual marvels.

There are new creatures like the Tautaun on the ice planet Hoth and dreadful new mechanical menaces such as the giant four-legged, walking juggernauts, plus the usual array of motherships and fighter craft, odd space stations and asteroids.

But it's all believable given the premise, made the more enjoyable by Lucas' heavy borrowing – with a splashing new coat of sci-fi paint – from many basic film frameworks. The juggernaut attack on infantry in the trenches with fighter planes counterattacking overhead is straight out of every war film ever made.

Even more than before, Lucas and Kershner seem to be making the comparisons obvious. Vader's admirals look now even more dressed like Japanese admirals of the fleet intercut with Hammill's scrambling fighter pilots who wouldn't look too out of place on any Marine base today.

Oz's eerie jungle home would not confuse Tarzan and the carbon-freezing chamber that threatens Ford could be substituted for any alligator pit in a Lost Temple. Naturally, too, the laser saber battles of the first are back again even more, along with the wild-west shootouts and aerial dogfights.

At 124 minutes, "Empire" is only three minutes longer than its predecessor, but seems to be longer than that, probably because of the overfamiliarity with some of the space sequences and excessive saber duels between Vader and Hamill.

Reaching its finish, "Empire" blatantly sets up the third in the "Star Wars" trilogy, presuming the marketplace will signify its interest. It's a pretty safe presumption.

Har.

RAIDERS OF THE LOST ARK

Wednesday, June 10, 1981

Smashing adventure-fantasy that brings back the good old days. Major b.o. prospects. (COLOR)

A Paramount Pictures release of a Lucasfilm Ltd. Production. Produced by Frank Marshall. Executive producers, George Lucas, Howard Kazanjian. Directed by Steven Spielberg. Features entire cast. Screenplay, Lawrence Kasdan; story, Lucas, Philip Kaufman; associate producer, Robert Watts; camera (Metrocolor), Douglas Slocombe; music, John Williams; editor, Michael Kahn; production designer, Norman Reynolds; art direction, Leslie Dilley; visual effects supervisor, Richard Edlund. Reviewed at Paramount screening room, N.Y., June 2, 1981. (MPAA Rating: PG) Running time: 115 MINS.

Indy	Harrison Ford
Marion	Karen Allen
Dietrich	Wolf Kahler
Belloq	Paul Freeman
Toht	Ronald Lacey
Sallah	John Rhys-Davies
Brody	Denholm Elliott
Gobler	Anthony Higgins
Satipo	Alfred Molina
Barranca	Vic Tablian

"Raiders of the Lost Ark" is the stuff that raucous Saturday matinees at the local Bijou once were made of, a crackerjack fantasy-adventure that shapes its pulp sensibilities arid cliff-hanging serial origins into an exhilarating escapist entertainment that will have broad-based summer audiences in the palm of its hand. Even within this summer's hot competitive environment, boxoffice prospects are in the top rank.

Steeped in an exotic atmosphere of lost civilizations, mystical talismans, gritty mercenary adventurers, Nazi arch-villains and ingenious death at every turn, the film is largely patterned on the serials of the 1930s, with a large dollop of Edgar Rice Burroughs.

Story begins in 1936 as Indiana Jones (Harrison Ford), an archaeologist and university professor who's not above a little mercenary activity on the side, plunders a South American jungle tomb. Fending off an awesome array of deadly primitive booby-traps – ranging from light-sensitive poison darts and impaling spikes to legions of tarantulas – he secures a priceless golden Godhead, only to have it snatched away by longtime archaeological rival Paul Freeman, now employed by the Nazis.

Back in the States, Ford is approached by U.S. intelligence agents who tell him the Nazis are rumored to have discovered the location of the Lost Ark of the Covenant (where the broken 10 Commandments were sealed). The ark is assumed to contain an awesome destructive power which Hitler ("he's a nut on the occult," we learn) is intent on using to guarantee his global conquest.

Ford's mission is to beat the Germans to the ark, a trek that takes him first to the mountains of Nepal to retrieve a hieroglyphic medallion that will pinpoint the ark's location, from his onetime flame Karen Allen. Latter, a feisty, hard-drinking spitfire, operates a Nepalese gin-mill; after a massive shootout with medallion-seeking Nazis, the pair wing it to Cairo, where Ford finally makes it to the digging ground.

The action unfolds as a continuing series of exuberantly violent and deadly confrontations – with the Nazis, hired Arab assassins, thousands of venomous snakes that guard the ark, etc., in which Ford miraculously outwits the elements in approved comic strip fashion before fending off the next round of dangers.

As such, the film has some surprisingly explicit violent action and bloodletting for a PG-rated entry and at least one scene (when the Nazis open the ark, liberating Divine fury in the form of spectral beings that melt the defilers' faces and explode their heads into smithereens) that would be attention-getting in an R-rated pic.

Still, for all but the most squeamish that won't detract an iota from the film's overall effect and the virtual start to finish grip of the off-beat tale on its viewers. Lawrence Kasdan's script (exec producer George Lucas and Philip Kaufman penned the original story) spins along the storyline, reveling in all the dialog clichés of the genre without really tipping into self-mockery. Film, cheerfully wearing its improbabilities on its sleeve, is constantly leavened by humor. The kids should love it.

Spielberg has harnessed a perfect balance between escapist fun and hard-edged action, and the film is among the best-crafted ventures of its kind. Suspense components kick in virtually from the first frame onwards, and are maintained throughout the pic.

More important, Spielberg has deftly veiled the entire proceedings in a pervading sense of mystical wonder that makes it all the more easy for viewers to willingly suspend disbelief and settle back for the fun.

Conforming to the traditions of the genre, characterizations are hardly three-dimensional. Still, Ford marks a major turning point in his career as the occasionally frail but ever invincible mercenary-archaeologist, projecting a riveting strength of character throughout. Allen's pugnacious personality provides bristling romantic counterpoint and supporting roles (including Ronald Lacey in the most outrageously offensive Nazi stereotype seen on screen since World War II, John Rhys-Davies as Ford's loyal Egyptian helpmate and Denholm Elliott as his university colleague) are all delightfully etched.

Technically, the film is another standard-setter from the Lucas-Spielberg camps (this is their first collaboration), with Douglas Slocombe's lush lensing and John Williams' dramatic score underscoring both the action and the globe-hopping epic scope.

Recruited from the "Star Wars" ranks, production designer Norman Reynolds and art director Leslie Dilley have created a vibrant and period-perfect world of wonders. Michael Kahn's crisp editing keeps the pace and energy unflagging, and Richard Edlund's photographic effects – highlighted by the apocalyptic unveiling of the ark – are intelligently spectacular.

Film's ending leaves the field wide open for a sequel (Lucas already has two more chapters up his sleeve). Hopefully the film's broad commercial promise going in will translate to a large enough bottom-line to keep his Raiders coming for a long time.

Step.

RETURN OF THE JEDI

May 18, 1983

Great creatures and effects equals smash b.o. [box office] for trilogy's finale, but weak on the human side. Hollywood, May 9. (COLOR)

A 20th Century-Fox release of a Lucasfilm Ltd. production, produced by Howard Kazanjian. Exec producer, George Lucas. Directed by Richard Marquand. Features entire cast. Screenplay, Lawrence Kasdan, George Lucas; camera (Rank Color; prints by Deluxe), Alan Hume; editors, Sean Barton, Marcia Lucas, Duwayne Dunham; sound (Dolby Stereo), Tony Dawe, Randy Thom; sound design, Ben Burtt; production design, Norman Reynolds; visual effects supervisors at Industrial Light & Magic, Richard Edlund, Dennis Muren, Ken Ralston; costumes, Aggie Guerard Rodgers, Nilo Rodis-Jamero; assistant director, David Tomblin; makeup and creature design, Phil Tippett, Stuart Freeborn; music, John Williams. Reviewed at the Academy of Motion Picture Arts & Sciences, Beverly Hills, May 9, 1983. (MPAA Rating: PG). Running time: 133 MINS.

Luke Skywalker	Mark Hamill
Han Solo	Harrison Ford
Princess Leia	Carrie Fisher
Lando Calrissian	Billy Dee Williams
C-3PO	Anthony Daniels
Chewbacca	Peter Mayhew
Emperor	Ian McDiarmid
Darth Vader.	David Prowse
Vader voice	James Earl Jones
Ben Kenobi	Alec Guinness
Yoda	Frank Oz
Anakin Skywalker	Sebastian Shaw
R2-D2	Kenny Baker

Other cast: Michael Pennington, Kenneth Colley, Michael Carter, Denis Lawson, Tim Rose, Dermot Crowley, Caroline Blakiston

Additional Production Credits

Production supervisor, Douglas Twiddy; location camera, Jim Glennon; assistant directors, Roy Button, Michael Steele; art direction, Fred Hole, James Schoppe: special effects supervisor, Roy Arbogast, Kit West; stunts, Glenn Randall, Peter Diamond; choreography, Gillian Gregory; conceptual artist, Ralph McQuarrie; co-producers, Robert Watts. Jim Bloom.

Miniature & Optical Effects Unit Credits

Visual effects art direction, Joe Johnston; optical photography supervisor, Bruce Nicholson; matte-painting supervisor, Michael Pangrazio; modelshop supervisors, Lorne Peterson, Steve Gawley; visual effects editor, Arthur Repola; animation supervisor, James Keefer; stop motion animation, Tom St. Amand.

There is good news, bad news and no news about "Return Of The Jedi." The good news is that George Lucas & Co. have perfected the technical magic to a point where almost anything and everything – no matter how bizarre – is believable. The bad news is that the human dramatic dimensions have been sorely sacrificed. The no news is the picture will take in millions regardless of the pluses and minuses.

As heralded, "Jedi" is the conclusion of the middle trilogy of Lucas' planned nine-parter and suffers a lot in comparison to the initial "Star Wars," when all was fresh. One of the apparent problems is

neither the writers nor the principal performers are putting in the same effort.

Telegraphed in the preceding "Empire Strikes Back," the basic dramatic hook this time is Mark Hamill's quest to discover – and do something about – the true identity of menacing Darth Vader, while resisting the evil intents of the Emperor (Ian McDiarmid). Unfortunately, this sets up a number of dramatic confrontations that fall flat.

Though perfectly fine until now as daringly decent Luke Skywalker, Hamill is not enough of a dramatic actor to carry the plot load here, especially when his partner in so many scenes is really little more than an oversized gas pump, even if splendidly voiced by James Earl Jones.

Even worse, Harrison Ford, who was such an essential element of the first two outings, is present more in body than in spirit this time, given little to do but react to special effects. And it can't be said that either Carrie Fisher or Billy Dee Williams rise to previous efforts.

But Lucas and director Richard Marquand have overwhelmed these performer flaws with a truly amazing array of creatures, old and new, plus the familiar space hardware. The first half-hour, in fact, has enough menacing monsters to populate a dozen other horror pics on their own.

The good guys this time are allied with a new group, the Ewoks, a tribe of fuzzy, sweet little creatures that continually cause ahhs among the audience (and will doubtlessly sell thousands of dolls). Carrying their spears and practising primitive rites, they also allow Lucas to carry on the "Star Wars" tradition of borrowing heavily from familiar serial scenes.

Though slow to pick up the pace and

saddled with an anticlimactic sequence at the finish, "Jedi" is nonetheless reasonably fast paced for its 133-minute length, a visual treat throughout. But let's hope for some new and more involving characters in the next chapters or more effort and work for the old.

Har.

INDIANA JONES AND THE TEMPLE OF DOOM

May 16, 1984

Noisy, overkill prequel headed for smash b.o. Hollywood, May 7. (COLOR)

A Paramount Pictures release of a Lucas-film Ltd. production. Executive producers, George Lucas, Frank Marshall. Produced by Robert Watts. Directed by Steven Spielberg. Stars Harrison Ford. Screenplay, Willard Huyck, Gloria Katz, from a story by Lucas. Camera (Rank color; prints by Deluxe), Douglas Slocombe; editor, Michael Kahn; music, John Williams; sound design (Dolby), Ben Burtt; production design, Elliot Scott; chief art director, Alan Cassie; set deco-ration, Peter Howitt; special visual effects supervisor, Dennis Muren at Industrial Light & Magic; costume design, Anthony Powell; mechanical effects supervisor, George Gibbs; second unit director, Michael Moore; choreography, Danny Daniels; associate producer Kathleen Kennedy. Reviewed at MGM Studios, Culver City, Calif., May 7, 1984. (MPAA Rating: PG). Running time: 118 MINS.

Indiana Jones....................Harrison Ford
Willie Scott ....Kate Capshaw
Short Round......................Ke Huy Quan
Mola Ram ....Amrish Puri
Chattar Lal ....Roshan Seth
Capt. Blumburtt ....Philip Stone
Also with: Roy Chiao, David Yip, Ric Young, Chua Kah Joo, Rex Ngui, Philip Tann, Dan Aykroyd, Pat Roach.

Special Visual Effects Unit Credits

Industrial Light & Magic; visual effects supervisor, Dennis Muren; chief camera-man, Mike McAlister; optical photography supervisor, Bruce Nicholson; ILM general manager, Tom Smith; production supervi-sor, Warren Franklin; matte painting supervisor, Michael Pangrazio; modelship supervisor, Lorne Peterson; stop-motion animation, Tom St. Amand; supervising stage technician, Patrick Fitzsimmons; animation supervisor, Charles Mullen; supervising editor, Howard Stein; produc-tion coordinator, Arthur Repola; creative consultant, Phil Tippett. Additional optical effects, Modern Film Effects.

Additional Technical Credits

U.K.crew: assistant director, David Tomblin; production supervisor, John Davis; production manager, Patricia Carr. U.S. crew: production manager, Robert Latham Brown; assistant director, Louis Race. First unit: stunt arrangers, Vic Armstrong (studio), Glenn Randall (location); addi-tional photography, Paul Beeson; sound mixer, Simon Kaye, chief modeller, Derek Howarth; chief special effects technician, Richard Conway; floor effects supervisor, David Watkins; research, Deborah Fine; post-production services, Sprocket Systems.

London second unit: second unit director, Frank Marshall; assistant direc-tors, David Bracknell, Michael Hook; cameraman, Wally Byatt; floor effects supervisor, David Harris.

California Unit: Second unit director, Glenn Randall; director of photography, Allen Daviau; art direction, Joe Johnston; stunt coordinator, Dean Raphael Ferrandini; special effects supervisor, Kevin Pike; sound mixer, David McMillan; production

coordinator, Lata Ryan.

Asian unit: assistant director, Carlos Gil. Macau: production supervisor, Vincent Winter; production manager, Pay Ling Wang; assistant director, Patty Chan. Sri Lanka: production supervisor, Chandran Rutnam; production manager, Willie de Silva; assistant director, Ranjit H. Peiris; steadicam photography, Garrett Brown; art direction, Errol Kelly; sound mixer, Colin Charles.

Aerial unit: second unit director, Kevin Donnelly; director of photography, Jack Cooperman.

Just as "Return Of The Jedi" seemed disap-pointing after the first two "Star Wars" entries, so does "Indiana Jones And The Temple Of Doom" come as a letdown after "Raiders Of The Lost Ark." This is ironic, because director Steven Spielberg has packed even more thrills and chills into this followup than he did into the earlier pic, but to exhausting and numbing effect.

End result is like the proverbial Chinese meal, where heaps of food can still leave one hungry shortly thereafter. Will any of this make any difference at the boxoffice? Not a chance, as a sequel to "Raiders," which racked up $112,000,000 in domestic film rentals, has more built-in want-see than any imaginable film aside from "E.T. II."

Spielberg, scenarists Willard Huyck and Gloria Katz, and George Lucas, who penned the story as well as exec produc-ing with Frank Marshall, have not tampered with the formula which made "Raiders" so popular. To the contrary, they have noticeably stepped up the pace, amount of incidents, noise level, budget, close calls, violence and everything else, to the point where more is decidedly less.

Prequel finds dapper Harrison Ford as Indiana Jones in a Shanghai night-club in 1935, and title sequence, which features Kate Capshaw chirping Cole Porter's "Anything Goes," looks like something out of Spielberg's "1941".

Ford escapes from an enormous mêlée with the chanteuse in tow and, joined by Oriental moppet Ke Huy Quan, they head by plane to the mountains of Asia, where they are forced to jump out in an inflatable raft, skid down huge slopes, vault over a cliff and navigate some rapids before coming to rest in an impoverished Indian village.

Community's leader implores the ace archaeologist to retrieve a sacred, magical stone which has been stolen by malevolent neighbors, so the trio makes its way by elephant to the domain of a prepubescent Maharajah, who lords it over an empire reeking of evil.

Remainder of the yarn is set in this labyrinth of horrors, where untold dangers await the heroes. Much of the action unfolds in a stupendous cavern, where dozens of natives chant wildly as a sacrificial victim has his heart removed before being lowered into a pit of fire.

Ford is temporarily converted to the nefarious cause, Ke Huy Quan is sent to join child slaves in an underground quarry, and Capshaw is lowered time and again into the pit until the day is saved.

What with John Williams' incessant score and the library full of sound effects, there isn't a quiet moment in the entire picture, and the filmmakers have piled one giant setpiece on top of another to the point where one never knows where it will end.

Film's one genuinely amazing action sequence, not unlike the airborne sleigh chase in "Jedi" (the best scene in that film), has the three leads in a chase on board an underground railway car on tracks resembling those of a roller-coaster.

Sequence represents a stunning display of design, lensing and editing, and will have viewers gaping. A "Raidersland" amusement park could be opened profitably on the basis of this ride alone.

Overall, however, pic comes on like a sledgehammer, and there's even a taste of vulgarity and senseless excess not apparent in "Raiders."

Kids 10-12 upwards will eat it all up, of course, but many of the images, particularly those involving a gruesome feast of live snakes, fried beetles, eyeball soup and monkey brains, and those in the sacrificial ceremony, might prove extraordinarily frightening to younger children who, indeed, are being catered to in this film by the presence of the adorable 12-year-old Ke Huy Quan.

Compared to the open-air breeziness of "Raiders", "Indiana Jones," after the first reel or so, possesses a heavily studio-bound look, with garish reds often illuminating the dark backgrounds.

As could be expected, however, huge production crew at Thorn EMI-Elstree Studios, as well as those on locations in Sri Lanka, Macao and California and in visual effects phase at Industrial Light & Magic, have done a tremendous job in rendering this land of high adventure and fantasy.

Ford seems effortlessly to have picked

up where he left off when Indiana Jones was last heard from (though tale is set in an earlier period), although Capshaw, who looks fetching in native attire, has unfortunately been asked to react hysterically to everything that happens to her, resulting in a manic, frenzied performance which never locates a center of gravity. Villains are all larger-than-life nasties.

Critical opinion is undoubtedly irrelevant for such a surefire commercial attraction as "Indiana Jones," except that Spielberg is such a talented director it's a shame to see him lose all sense of subtlety and nuance.

In one quick step, the "Raiders" films have gone the way the James Bond opuses went at certain points, away from nifty stories in favor of one big effect after another. But that won't prevent Spielberg and Lucas from notching another mark high on the list of alltime b.o. winners.

Cart.

INDIANA JONES AND THE LAST CRUSADE

May 24–30, 1989

Hollywood. A Paramount Pictures release of a Lucasfilm Ltd. production. Executive producers, George Lucas, Frank Marshall. Produced by Robert Watts. Production executive (U.S.), Kathleen Kennedy. Directed by Steven Spielberg. Screenplay, Jeffrey Boam, from a story by Lucas, Menno Meyjes, based on characters created by Lucas and Philip Kaufman; camera (Rank color), Douglas Slocombe; additional photography, Paul Beeson, Robert Stevens; editor, Michael Kahn; music, John Williams; sound (Dolby), Ben Burtt; production design, Elliot Scott; art direction, Stephen Scott, Richard Berger (U.S.), Benjamin Fernandez (Spain), Guido Salsilli (Italy); set design, Alan Kaye (U.S.); set decorators, Peter Howitt, Ed McDonald (U.S.), Julian Mateos (Spain); visual effects supervisor, Michael J. McAlister, Industrial Light & Magic; mechanical effects supervisor, George Gibbs; costume design, Anthony Powell, Joanna Johnston; makeup supervisor, Peter Robb-King; stunt coordinator, Vic Armstrong; associate producer, Arthur Repola; assistant directors, David Tomblin (U.K.), Dennis Maguire (U.S.), Carlos Gil, Jose Luis Escolar (Spain), Gianni Cozzo (Italy); second-unit directors, Michael Moore, Frank Marshall; second-unit camera, Rex Metz (U.S.); second-unit assistant director, Gareth Tandy (U.K.); production supervisor, Patricia Carr (U.K.); unit production managers, Roy Button (U.K.), Joan Bradshaw, Ian Bryce (U.S.), Denise O'Dell (Spain); location managers, Bruce Rush

(U.S.), Christopher Hamilton (Italy); casting, Maggie Cartier, Mike Fenton, Judy Taylor, Valerie Massalas. Reviewed at Mann National theater, L.A., May 16, 1989. (MPAA Rating: PG-13.) Running time: 127 MINS.

Indiana Jones	Harrison Ford
Professor Henry Jones	Sean Connery
Marcus Brody	Denholm Elliott
Elsa	Alison Doody
Sallah	John Rhys-Davies
Walter Donovan	Julian Glover
Young Indy	River Phoenix
Vogel	Michael Byrne
Kazim	Kevork Malikyan
Grail Knight	Robert Eddison
Fedora	Richard Young
Sultan	Alexei Sayle
Young Henry	Alex Hyde-White
Panama Hat	Paul Maxwell

To say that Paramount's "Indiana Jones And The Last Crusade" may be the best film ever made for 12-year-olds is not a backhanded compliment. What was conceived as a child's dream of a Saturday matinee serial has evolved into a moving excursion into religious myth.

More cerebral than the first two Indiana Jones films, and less schmaltzy than the second, this literate adventure should make big bucks by entertaining and enlightening kids and adults.

The Harrison Ford-Sean Connery father-and-son team gives "Last Crusade" unexpected emotional depth, reminding us that real film magic is not in special effects.

For Lucas and Spielberg, who are now entering middle age, the fact that this is more a character film than f/x extravaganza could signal a welcome new level of ambition.

Jeffrey Boam's witty and laconic screenplay, based on a story by Lucas and Menno Meyjes, takes Ford and Connery on a quest for a prize bigger than the Lost Ark of the covenant — The Holy Grail.

Connery is a medieval lit prof with strong religious convictions who has spent his life assembling clues to the Grail's whereabouts. Father and more intrepid archaeologist son piece them together in an around-the-world adventure, leading to a touching and mystical finale that echoes "Star Wars" and "Lost Horizon." The love between father and son transcends even the quest for the Grail, which is guarded by a special 700-year-old knight beautifully played by Robert Eddison.

This film minimizes the formulaic love interest, giving newcomer Alison Doody an effectively sinuous but decidedly secondary role. The principal love story is between father and son, making Ford's casually sadistic personality more sympathetic than in the previous pics.

The relationship between the men is full of tension, manifesting itself in Connery's amusing sexual one-upmanship and his string of patronizing putdowns.

There's also a warmth and growing respect between them that makes this one of the most pleasing screen pairings since Newman met Redford.

Connery confidently plays his aging character as slightly daft and fuzzy-minded, without blunting his forcefulness and without sacrificing his sexual charisma.

The cartoonlike Nazi villains of

"Raiders" have been replaced by more genuinely frightening Nazis led by Julian Glover and Michael Byrne. Most of the film takes place in 1938, and Spielberg stages a chilling scene at a Nazi book-burning rally in Berlin, where Ford has a brief encounter with Adolf Hitler.

But exec producers Lucas and Frank Marshall, producer Robert Watts and Spielberg do not neglect the action set-pieces that give these films their commercial cachet.

There's the opening chase on top of a train in the Utah desert, involving a youthful Indy (River Phoenix) in 1912; a ferocious tank battle in the desert; a ghastly scene with hundreds of rats in a Venice catacomb; some aerial hijinks with a zeppelin and small planes, and many more outlandish scenes.

Perhaps the film's most impressive technical aspect is the soundtrack, designed by Ben Burtt. While the noise level sometimes becomes painful, the artistry is stunning.

Douglas Slocombe's lensing has a subtly burnished look, and Elliott Scott's production design is always spectacular.

The Industrial Light & Magic visual effects — supervised by Michael J. McAlister with Patricia Blau producing for the aerial unit — are artful and seamless.

John Williams' score again is a major factor in the appeal and pacing, and editor Michael Kahn makes the film move like a bullet. Other tech contributions are impeccable.

This is a film of which Lucas and Spielberg and their collaborators long will be proud.

Mac.

Bibliography

The following books and articles were used, among others, as background material.

Bock, Audie, 'George Lucas, an interview', *Take One*, May 1976

Brackett, Leigh and Kasdan, Lawrence, *Star Wars: The Empire Strikes Back* (Faber & Faber, 1997)

Champlin, Charles, *George Lucas: The Creative Impulse* (Virgin, 1997)

Fairchild, Jr., B. H., *Songs of Innocence and Experience: The Blakean Vision of George Lucas*, Texas Woman's University Press

Jenkins, Garry, *Empire Building: The Remarkable Real Life Story of Star Wars* (Simon & Schuster, 1998)

Kasdan, Lawrence and Lucas, George, *Star Wars, Return of the Jedi* (Faber & Faber, 1997)

Klemesrud, Judy, 'Graffiti is the story of his life', *New York Times*, 7 October 1973

Lucas, George, *Star Wars: A New Hope* (Faber & Faber, 1997)

Pollock, Dale, 'George Lucas', *Sunday Express*, 22 May 1983

Pollock, Dale, Skywalking: *The Life and Times of George Lucas* (Samuel French, 1990)

Scanlon, Paul, 'George Lucas who plays guitar', *Rolling Stone*, 4 August 1983

Strick, Philip, 'Indiana Jones and the Temple of Doom', *Films and Filming*, July 1984

Sweeney, Louise, 'The movie business is alive and well and living in San Francisco', *SHOW*, April 1970

Thomson, David, *A Biographical Dictionary of Film* (Andre Deutsch, 3rd edn, 1994)

Tuckman, Mark and Anne Thompson, 'I'm the boss', *Film Comment*, March 1983

Vallely, Jean, 'Motion Pictures', *Rolling Stone*, 12 June 1980

Yule, Andrew, *Steven Spielberg: Father to the Man* (Little, Brown, 1996)

Zito, Stephen, 'Far Out', *American Film*, March 1977

'George Lucas' Galactic Empire', *Time*, 6 March 1978

Acknowledgements

The author would like to express his deepest thanks to all involved with this project, who gave generously of themselves at various times. Most specifically, sincerest gratitude is owed to Suzanne Fenn, Martha Jones, Dickie Jobson, Perry Henzell, Rick Elgood, Don Letts, Adrian Boot, Suzette Newman, Mark Booth, Juliet Hohnen, Trevor Dolby, Natasha Martyn-Johns, Alex and Cole (who really understand these things), the staff of London's BFI Library, Julian Alexander, Kirsten Romano and Peter Katz. May the Force be with you.

The publishers would like to thank the following for providing the pictures in this book: Capital Pictures for page 143, Katz for pages 2 and 119, Photofest for pages 6, 16, 32, 52, 59, 89 and endpapers and The Kobal Collection for pages 19, 99, 102, 114-15, 123, 125, 129, 132 and 134.